D1715214

British
Buckeyes

BRITISH
Buckeyes

THE ENGLISH, SCOTS, AND WELSH IN OHIO, 1700–1900

William E. Van Vugt

THE KENT STATE UNIVERSITY PRESS

Kent, Ohio

Library of Congress Catalog Card Number 2005008615

ISBN-10: 0-87338-843-7

ISBN-13: 978-0-87338-843-6

Manufactured in the United States of America

10 09 08 07 06   5 4 3 2 1

Library of Congress Cataloging-in-Publication Data

Van Vugt, William E., 1957–

British Buckeyes: the English, Scots, and Welsh in Ohio, 1700–1900 / William E. Van Vugt.

p. cm.

Includes bibliographical references and index.

ISBN-13: 978–0–87338–843–6 (alk. paper) ∞

1. British Americans—Ohio—History. 2. Scottish Americans—Ohio—History. 3. Welsh Americans—Ohio—History. 4. Immigrants—Ohio—History. 5. Ohio—Social conditions. 6. Ohio—Emigration and immigration—History. 7. Great Britain—Emigration and immigration—History. 8. England—Emigration and immigration—History. 9. Scotland—Emigration and immigration—History. 10. Wales—Emigration and immigration—History. I. Title.

F500.B7V36 2005

977.1'00413—dc22   2005008615

British Library Cataloging-in-Publication data are available.

For Phyllis and Harvey

Contents

Acknowledgments

This book began when I was asked to write a short piece on the history of the British in Ohio. As I dug into the sources it immediately became clear that this was a significant, largely unexplored story, waiting to be told in depth. Old and new histories of Ohio pay little if any attention to the British explorers, travelers, and especially the immigrants, who were essential to the state's development. And when the literature does mention that early important Ohioans— including the first territorial governor, the first governor, and many pioneers and economic and cultural leaders—were British, it does not address what their Britishness had to do with anything. My early research into the primary sources uncovered a host of lesser-known Britons who were also at the center of Ohio's development but are not mentioned in any books or articles. It was then that I decided to write this history of Ohio, as it was shaped and lived by British people.

I am much indebted to Professor Robert P. Swierenga, Albertus C. Van Raalte Research Professor at the A. C. Van Raalte Institute, Hope College, and professor emeritus of history at Kent State University. His pioneering work on economic history and migration, and his knighthood from Queen Beatrix of the Netherlands for his contributions to Dutch-American studies, testify to his distinguished career. Professor Swierenga encouraged me to write this book, read an early manuscript version, and made suggestions for deeper analysis and better presentation. Any remaining errors or shortcomings are mine alone. I also owe so much to my mentor, Charlotte Erickson, professor emeritus of history at Cambridge University. She also saw the need for a book on the British in Ohio and kindly allowed me to use her voluminous files and birth- and marriage-certificate collection. Professor Erickson also arranged for Corpus Christi College to provide me wonderful accommodations during my research forays in Cambridge.

Also in England I was assisted by the staffs of the British Newspaper Library at Colindale, the British Library of Political and Economic Science, the London Metropolitan Archives, and the Institute of Historical Research. At the Institute for United States Studies (now the Institute for the Study of the Americas), Deborah Hart-Stock was helpful with her assistance. Jane Ferenzi-Sheppard, of the Somerset and Dorset Family History Society, was especially helpful through her own expertise on migration and for arranging conferences in Dorset and Exeter University, where I first presented some of this work. At Oxford University I met Steven Brumwell, who alerted me to the memoirs of Robert Kirk. Researching on the island of Guernsey was an adventure, and I thank Jean Videmour and the staff of the Privaulx Library in St. Peter Port for their kind assistance. The staff at the Guernsey Archives was also helpful and gracious. And as always, my dear friends Patricia Orme and David Ash offered their hospitality and their own insights into English history and culture.

In North America, Greg Rose of Ohio State University generously provided his maps of British settlement in Ohio, and Bruce Elliott of Carleton University in Canada gave advice on sources. The staff of the Ohio Historical Society in Columbus was very helpful, as were the people at the Western Reserve Historical Society in Cleveland, and the Athens County Library Services. I would also like to thank the East Liverpool Historical Society for their permission to use a photograph. Philip Rickerd and Sarah W. Vodrey of the Museum of Ceramics, in East Liverpool, provided help and useful information about that photograph, and about the Staffordshire potters who settled there. And I thank Joanna Hildebrand Craig of the Kent State University Press and Mike Busam for their expert work in editing the manuscript and preparing it for publication.

I am especially grateful to Calvin College for granting me a sabbatical leave and for funding research assistants, John Vander Meer and Ryan Noppen. I also thank the college for its McGregor Summer Research Fellowship Program, which funded the assistance of Paul Christians. Paul helped research the county histories, formed the database, and provided valuable help in editing and producing the endnotes and bibliography. The Calvin College Alumni Association also provided a generous grant for research in London and Guernsey. Lorrie Menninga, the administrative assistant in Calvin College's history department, proofread the manuscript for technical errors. The Calvin College Heckman Library was extremely helpful in obtaining rare volumes through interlibrary loan, and I would like to thank librarians Conrad Bult, Kathy Struck, and Greg Sennema for their assistance.

Finally, I owe more than I can say to Lynn Heemstra-Van Vugt, who was always supportive and encouraging and was the perfect traveling companion for my research in England and on the enchanting Channel Islands of Guernsey and Sark.

Introduction

So little has been written about Ohio's most influential European immigrants—
the British: the English, Scots, and Welsh.[1] Long before statehood, Britons
arrived in Ohio as soldiers, traders, travelers, and immigrants, and they continued to arrive quite steadily for many years to come. Furthermore, they were
essential to the political, cultural, agricultural, and industrial development of
the state. "British Buckeyes" were at the center of Ohio history.*

This legacy was rooted in a special cultural and economic relationship
shared by Great Britain and the United States. In their language, religion, political heritage of elected governments, and trade, Britain and the United States
were more closely intertwined than any other sovereign states. Together they
built an "Atlantic economy" based on the free flow of people, capital, goods,
technology, ideas, and attitudes. They were each other's largest trading partners, and most British emigrants chose the United States as their destination.
The United States gained much from this relationship—and no state more so
than Ohio. Ohio's history, particularly its development to 1900, shows an
astonishing prominence of British immigrants. In reality, Ohio's long and rich
history cannot be fully understood and appreciated without knowing the
British Buckeyes.

Not that the British were the most numerous immigrants in Ohio. In 1850,
nearly half of Ohio's foreign-born people were Germans while only one in five
were English, Scottish, or Welsh. The Irish were a little more numerous. By 1880
there were over 64,000 British-born people in Ohio (comprising over 16 percent
of the foreign-born population), compared to nearly 80,000 Irish and over
190,000 Germans.[2] The British numbers are substantial; but they do not capture
the historic importance of these fascinating people. The British were the first
Europeans to penetrate the Ohio Territory and settle in large numbers, and for
over a generation Ohio was part of the British Empire. After independence and
statehood in 1803 the British presence grew, and helped the young state to flourish and her economy and society to evolve.

Ohio attracted a wide variety of British immigrants. It offered opportunities

*The first known use of the nickname "Buckeye" for Ohioans dates back to 1788. The term
Buckeye comes from the indigenous nut, which resembles the eye of a buck.

in growing towns and cities and emerging industries, openings for professionals, and of course, land—everything from virgin frontier to improved farms. It was a beautiful and healthy land, not dissimilar to many parts of Britain, and reasonably accessible. As William Amphlett, an English settler in Ohio who published a popular emigrant guide in 1819, said, "The [English] emigrant who chooses to fix himself in the State of Ohio, will find himself much more at home in many respects than if he went farther on. The lands are more cleared, the country has more hill and dale, the climate is more temperate, than the States to the west of him, and the air is esteemed more pure than any-where south of the Ohio. Access to this State is easy at all points, either by land or water: good improved land may be bought with requisite buildings upon them, in very favourable situations . . . as the value of lands varies so much, according to their situation, any man can purchase according to his ability."[3]

It is no wonder that after the Napoleonic Wars, the completion of the Erie Canal in 1825, and the subsequent canal-building boom, British immigration to Ohio surged. Ohio was a gateway between East and West and geographically defined by two major water routes—the Great Lakes and the Ohio River. For half a century Ohio was the Midwest's fastest growing, most rapidly developing state, and British immigrants were highly involved in that development.

A number of qualities distinguish the British among Ohio's other immigrants and made them especially important and noteworthy. First, they came from a remarkably broad spectrum of economic and occupational backgrounds, like no other immigrant group before or since. This was a result of the fact that Great Britain was the world's first industrial nation, with the most advanced and diversified economy and a labor force with the greatest variety of backgrounds and skills. Accordingly, British immigrants brought valuable skills and much of the industrial revolution to Ohio. Secondly, the English especially were unique for being "invisible."[4] They found it relatively easy to "blend in" because they shared the same language and cultural heritage with the majority of Ohio's white population, most of whom were themselves of British extraction, or "Anglo Americans," as they are often and tellingly called. With the exception of some Scots, many Welsh, those from the Isle of Man, and a few others, the British generally did not form separate communities or enclaves, but integrated more quickly and fully into society. As we shall see, these two defining characteristics—industrial skills and cultural similarities that allowed rapid assimilation—were central to the story of British immigrants in Ohio.

The special nature of British immigrants in Ohio is rooted in the seventeenth and early eighteenth centuries, when people from specific parts of Britain settled in specific parts of America and established distinct regional cultures. In the 1630s, during Charles I's "personal" autocratic rule and the attempt to purge the Anglican Church of Puritans, a wave of Puritans mainly from East Anglia and Cambridgeshire settled in Massachusetts and brought their distinctive culture. Then in the 1650s, during the interregnum and the rule by Oliver Cromwell and the Puritan oligarchy, Royalist cavaliers mainly from the south of England settled in Virginia and brought their aristocratic sensibilities and hierarchical social culture. During the Restoration of the monarchy, especially the 1670s and 1680s, a third wave composed mainly of Quakers from England's North Midlands settled in the Delaware Valley in search of greater religious freedom. And after the Glorious Revolution and the rise of the landed oligarchy in the English government, a fourth migration wave occurred during 1717 to 1775, composed mainly of people from northern England and the Scottish lowlands. They settled in the mountainous "backcountry" of America's Appalachians and brought a fierce sense of natural liberty they had developed while living so far from London.[5]

These waves of British immigrants brought "folkways"—language and speech patterns, religion, foods, customs of marriage, dress, work, sport, architecture, and attitudes toward freedom—all of which shaped the American colonies and made them regionally distinct. And in spite of the arrival of immigrants from other places and the passage of time, these folkways by and large persisted and the descendents of these colonial immigrants came to new places like Ohio and brought these folkways and British heritage with them. Settlers from Massachusetts and Connecticut carried their Puritan-based English culture to northern Ohio; people of the Delaware Valley brought English culture to central Ohio; and some of the Virginian tidewater culture made its way to southern Ohio via Maryland and Kentucky. Then, in the late eighteenth and nineteenth centuries, British immigrants to Ohio met Americans with whom they had much in common. In many ways British immigration to Ohio was a continuation of the planting of "Albion's Seed."[6]

Of course, this Anglo American world had changed between the arrival of the "Old British" who established the colonies and the "New British" who settled in Ohio. Seventeenth- and early-eighteenth-century English women and men and their descendents became Americans. The impact of the Revolution was certainly great: a republic replaced a monarchy, and a more egalitarian society emerged. But still, the basic patterns of society, economy, and culture were based on America's British inheritance. For many years after the Revolution foreign travelers in the United States often noted the Englishness of American culture. As one wrote in 1818, "Whoever has well observed America cannot doubt that she still remains *essentially English*, in language, habits, laws, customs, manners, morals, and religion. . . . The great many of our people is of English origin."[7] There was no chasm between British immigrants and their Ohio-born neighbors, as was the case with other European immigrants.[8]

One particularly significant English importation to America was the concept of land as property, something to be privately owned, bought, and sold. This concept grew under the influence of John Locke, the English philosopher who persuaded most Englishmen and American colonists that one of government's main purposes was to protect property rights. This profound historic development set the stage for the rapid acquisition of American land. It is no accident that in the nineteenth century both Britain and America expanded into empires out of a sense of divine mission and greed for territory. There was more in common between hierarchical Britain and the republican United States than most people realized.[9]

The story of British migration to Ohio, then, has special significance and relevance beyond the state's borders. Ohio was where Britons from the widest variety of backgrounds—agricultural, industrial, and professional—settled during American expansion, urbanization, and industrialization. In that history we have much of America's history. Moreover, looking at Ohio's British people is an insightful way of studying Ohio's history. No other immigrant group came in such steady numbers for such a long time and got so involved with building the economic, social, and political foundations of the state. We will take a broad sweep of Ohio's history from their perspective and experience and see how they intersected with Ohio's development and shaped it in profound ways.

With a focus on the British influence on Ohio, this book has a thematic rather than a purely chronological organization. Chapter 1 introduces the first British Buckeyes, those who arrived during the early part of the eighteenth century, the French and Indian War, the era of the Revolutionary War, early statehood, and the second war with Britain in 1812. During this century the English, Scots, and Welsh helped lead the exploration of Ohio, its integration into the British Empire, and its development into statehood in 1803. We will see that during and after the Revolution the immigrants, soldiers, traders, and explorers were on both sides of the political divide and were intimately connected with native culture. Between statehood and the War of 1812 they came in greater numbers and continued to shape the young state.

Chapter 2 offers an overview of British migration to Ohio during the nineteenth century. It sets the context of British-American relations and describes the journey from Britain to Ohio. It also presents the migrants' general occupational characteristics and migration patterns, including their precise origins, places of settlement, and their broad cultural traits that affected assimilation.

Chapter 3 presents four discreet settlements—the failed English Courtauld family settlement in Athens County, the Welsh in various parts of Ohio, the Manx (from the Isle of Man) in the Cleveland area, and the Channel Islanders of Guernsey in Guernsey County. These ethnic settlements show that some British immigrants did not fit in so easily and assimilated more gradually. Their stories also tell us much about the drama and aspirations behind these settlements.

Chapter 4 is devoted to one of the central themes in Ohio history—agriculture. The British played important roles in Ohio's agricultural history. As some of the first pioneers they brought their farming methods and attitudes to the Buckeye State. Perhaps most remarkable is the fact that many Britons from nonagricultural backgrounds set out to farm in Ohio, and many succeeded against all odds. They made an impact on Ohio agriculture that has not been examined until now.

Chapter 5 explores another central theme—craftwork and industrialization. The English, Scots, and Welsh were vital to Ohio's crafts and especially industries, and we will see how the immigrants filled key positions and accelerated their development with their invaluable skills and experience. Chapter 6 examines religion and its relationship to reform movements. Britons made important religious and cultural contributions as preachers, teachers, university professors, reformers, abolitionists, and soldiers in the Civil War. Chapter 7 continues with the theme of ideas by looking at British professionals, newspaper editors, and publishers who shaped public opinion, those in theater and the arts, and those in political office and civil service. We then have our conclusions, which might be summarized here in a nutshell: Ohio's history cannot be told without the British Buckeyes.

1

The First British Buckeyes

Ohio: Iroquoian word for "Great River"

SINCE the early eighteenth century, Ohio has had an intimate relationship with the people of Great Britain. Traders, adventurers, and soldiers from England, Scotland, and Wales followed the river systems into much of Ohio and made it a strategic part of the western fringe of the British Empire. And many returned home with tantalizing tales of a beautiful virgin land with exotic native peoples. One of the first persons to travel through the region and write about it was the famous Welsh cartographer and geologist, Lewis Evans. By 1743 Evans completed an expedition that traversed the southern shores of the Great Lakes, and in 1755 he published "A General Map of the Middle British Colonies in America." This included the first printed description of the Ohio territory. Evans called Ohio the "Flower of the whole Globe" and "the finest Country on Earth." The timing of such glowing accounts was perfect. After the Ohio Company was established in 1748, land beyond the Alleghenies was granted to British subjects and formal explorations of Ohio began in earnest. Then came the influx of early settlers, many from Great Britain, who heartily agreed with Evans's assessment. Ohio was indeed "the Flower of the whole Globe."[1]

Most British immigrants and travelers entered Ohio from Pittsburgh and took the water route down the Ohio River. These adventurers did not necessarily intend to stay in Ohio, but some did. Their influence was often profound and indelible, and their relationship with the natives was more complex than one

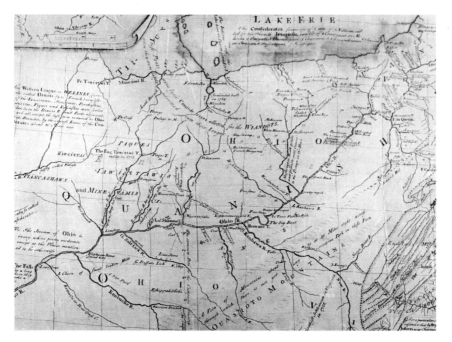

Thomas Pownall's edition of Lewis Evans's map of Ohio, 1776. This map might have informed early British traders like Thomas Ridout, who arrived after the Revolution.

might expect. Along with imperialism and dispossession came acculturation and interethnic cooperation. On the vast Ohio frontier, the very edge of the British Empire, there was in fact a great deal of cultural exchange, mediation, and interpenetration between the British and the American Indians. Something new resulted—a "middle ground" between cultures, peoples, and empires, a distinctly frontier American culture that had not been seen before, and that thrived until the young United States government stepped in.[2]

The natural river highways—the Ohio, Scioto, Great and Little Miamis, Muskingum, and Maumee—allowed British traders, soldiers, and immigrants to penetrate Western Ohio at remarkably early dates. By 1710 Pennsylvania traders of British origin or ancestry were using the Ohio River to channel British goods to Ohio's natives. Most of their contact was with the Miami and Shawnee Indians. Although the French were already in Ohio, the British arrived in greater numbers and eventually, after 1750, superseded the French by offering better goods to natives at lower prices. Already in 1749 the Marquis de la Galissoniére, governor-general of New France, remarked: "Behold, then, the

English already far within our territory; and, what is worse, they are under the protection of a crowd of savages whom they entice to themselves, and whose number increases every day." And when Captain Pierre-Joseph de Celoron de Blainville set out to punish natives for trading with the English, he was told that "to separate them from the English would be like cutting a man into halves, and expecting him to live."[3]

The English enjoyed a trading advantage because some of the goods were made in the colonies and did not require shipment across the ocean, unlike many French wares. But more importantly, they were able to entice the natives through their modernized textiles industry, which produced a variety of colorful cloths the Miami and other Indians found attractive.[4] They were capitalizing on their leadership in manufacturing and trade and using the marketplace to their geopolitical advantage in the remote corners of Ohio. As a "nation of shopkeepers" on the cusp of launching the world's first industrial revolution, the English were becoming the economic powerhouse of Europe, with financial resources that could determine the outcome of wars and strip the French of their North American empire. Altogether, Britain's commercial enterprise, their professed sense of individual liberty, and their growing demographic might in America enabled them to prevail over the French in Ohio, but not without conflict and temporary setbacks.

The Indians' preference for British goods and traders, and the shift of their alliance from France to Britain, was noticeable in some parts of Ohio by the mid–eighteenth century. The most remarkable episode involved a Piankashaw chief named Memeskia (Dragonfly), whom the French called La Demoiselle. His village was in northeastern Indiana but he also traveled extensively in Ohio where he frequently met and befriended British traders. Already by 1736 he had developed a pro-British stance and the British affectionately nicknamed him "Old Briton." Becoming disenchanted with the French because their policy was confining and their goods were exploitatively priced, Old Briton relocated his village near Kekionga (Fort Wayne) by 1745. Here he urged the Miamis of Indiana and Ohio to join him in allying with the British, whose political control over western tribes was minimal in comparison with that of the French and whose goods were of better quality and price.[5]

Old Briton was not the only chief in Ohio who was turning away from the French. The Huron chief Nicolas, based at Sandusky and influenced by Senecas and British traders, encouraged attacks on French forts. Old Briton joined a plan in which Nicolas would lead an attack against Detroit, the Chippewas would take Michilimackinac, and Old Briton would attack the French post at

Fort Miami, near the headwaters of the Maumee River. Unfortunately for the Indians, the French learned of the plot, foiled Nicolas's plans, and prevented the others from being fully executed.

After the failure to drive the French out of the area, Old Briton led some Miamis from Kekionga to a new British fort called Pickawillany, at the confluence of the Great Miami River and Loramie Creek, just north of Piqua in what is now Shelby County, Ohio. Pickawillany quickly grew to include some fourteen hundred Indians from several tribes, though mostly Miami, and Old Briton's influence grew with the support of the British traders and military personnel. Here the British embraced Old Briton and his people with an agreement of "Friendship and Alliance" and assured them that the Miami were "our own Flesh and Blood, and what hurts them will equally hurt us." On July 23, 1748, the British commissioners and Miami delegates signed a formal treaty in Philadelphia. This elated Old Briton, who felt assured that the British would ensure prosperity and protection from French reprisals.[6]

These developments concerned the French, of course, who saw Old Briton's community and the British at Pickawillany as a threat to their control over the Ohio Valley. Accordingly, the Marquis de la Galissonière made plans to drive the British out and destroy Old Briton and his people. He ordered Captain de Celoron to find Old Briton and negotiate his return to Kekionga, if necessary by force. In September of 1749 Celoron and 265 men met with Old Briton, but the negotiations came to nothing. Old Briton had no intention of leaving Pickawillany, which was looking better to him all the time. In late 1749 the Scotch Irish trader George Croghan arrived from Pennsylvania with a large group of British traders, and they and their plentiful goods pleased Old Briton greatly. After a failed attempt to bribe Old Briton into returning, the French launched a raid in 1750, which convinced the chief to take up arms. To show his anger he ordered three captured French soldiers killed and a fourth to have his ears cut off before sending him back to the governor as a warning.

In 1752 the French organized another raid led by the influential French Ottawa officer Charles-Michel Mouet de Langlade. He assembled a force of about 180 Chippewas, 30 Ottawas, and 30 French soldiers from Detroit and headed for Pickawillany. On the morning of June 21 the raiders—composed mainly of Indians and a few Frenchmen—attacked and overwhelmed Old Briton's people and a handful of British traders. Most of the Indian men had gone hunting and many of the British traders and soldiers were also absent. The Indian force, led by the French, struck so suddenly that many Miami women were captured while working in their cornfields. The violence and aftermath were ghastly. The raiders seized one English trader, cut his heart out, and ate it in the presence of horrified British and Indian captives. Old Briton was killed, butchered and boiled, and eaten. For the Chippewas and Ottawas who ate the unlucky Englishman and Indian, cannibalism was a ritual that transferred their enemies' power literally into themselves. But for the English, such a hideous and ignominious death was proof of the Indians' savagery. Such were the experiences of some of the first British Buckeyes.[7]

In effect, the destruction of Pickawillany was but a prelude to the French and Indian War, part of the Seven Years' War which affected the world so deeply. Even while the slaughter at Pickawillany was taking place, the Ohio Company of Virginia was planning a settlement at the Forks of the Ohio River to challenge French hegemony in that region. The French were equally determined to exclude the British from the Ohio Country in order to ensure their access to the vital Ohio River system and preserve the links between their settlements in Canada and those in the Mississippi Valley. The British, on the other hand, viewed Ohio as a vast area for future settlement, and more arrived after war broke out in 1756.

The prosperity and viability of the British Empire in the Great Lakes region depended on the fur trade, which required good relations with the Indians. In the summer of 1758 an important turning point in favor of the British occurred when Ohio Indians broke their alliance with the French and made peace with the British. The peace treaty to which the Indians signed their marks called the native peoples "children" and "subjects" of George III, and it proclaimed the King's "Sovereignty Over all and every part" of the Ohio Country. It is doubtful the chiefs fully comprehended the extent of the subordination. But the new alliance did require the British to offer favorable terms of trade and to hold back the encroaching white Americans, who were still British subjects.

During the period of British control over the Ohio Country, from the start of the French and Indian War through the American Revolution, many British soldiers and traders interacted extensively with Ohio's natives. They made a lasting impression on native culture, and were themselves changed.[8] As for the soldiers, recent scholarship has challenged the simplistic American stereotype of the British redcoats as the dregs of society—rough, uncouth, and stupid, and held in order only by coercion and brutal military discipline. Though that type of redcoat could certainly be found—especially among the foot soldiers—the officer corps and even some of the rank and file came from a variety of social and economic backgrounds. Many regulated their behavior according to incentives and a sense of honor and duty as much as the threat of the lash. Redcoats of all varieties found themselves in Ohio during the French and Indian War, sometimes against their will and that of the British military. For the Scotsman

Robert Kirk, a cooper from Ayrshire and a member of Colonel Archibald Montgomery's 1st Highland Battalion, his ten months in Ohio was a mixture of horror and adventure but also an opportunity to gain an appreciation of Ohio's native peoples. Wounded and captured by Shawnees after a failed British attack on Fort Duquesne in September 1758, Kirk was taken west into Ohio. Here he was tortured and nearly scalped, until the brave who captured him intervened, treated him kindly, and reassured him in broken English that he would not be harmed further. Fortunately for Kirk, his captor had lost his own brother to the Cherokee several months earlier and saw the redcoat as a replacement sent by the gods. Unfortunately, the eight other redcoats taken prisoner were not so treated: Kirk witnessed five of them burned to death "in the most cruel manner."[9]

As the "brother" of a Shawnee warrior, Robert Kirk was taken west down the Ohio River into Ohio Country, was dressed in Indian clothing, had his hair cut "after the Indian form," and was painted and greased like his brother. He was given a gun, ammunition, a tomahawk, and a scalping knife, and he even inherited the wife and son and cornfield of the dead warrior he had replaced. Kirk spent the next ten months in Ohio with Shawnee hunting parties, and he showed his worth as a successful trapper and skillful trader of furs and skins with the French. With his proceeds he even obtained a blanket that he gave "as a present to my adopted spouse, which was received as a great mark of my love and affection." Through May 1759 Robert Kirk lived the life of an Ohio Shawnee, and he even volunteered to join a party of forty warriors to attack their Cherokee rivals. He took part in a dance, with his face "black'd, in token of the destruction and immediate death which we meant to give our enemies." But as the war party dispersed to forage for food, Kirk saw his chance to escape. He abandoned his Indian life and three weeks later stumbled into Fort Cumberland.[10]

Robert Kirk rejoined his regiment and resumed fighting the French. The British took Fort Duquesne in 1759 and rebuilt it as Fort Pitt, in honor of the great prime minister whose military strategy and financial genius allowed victory and the taking of France's North American empire. Then at Bushy Run, in 1763, Kirk fought Ohio Indians to save Fort Pitt. He saw his duty and destiny with the British Army; nevertheless, he was deeply affected by his life as a Shawnee brother and warrior. While serving in the Royal Highland Regiment under Colonel Henry Bouquet during the Muskingum campaign, Kirk was actually reunited with his "brother" and Shawnee friend at a peace conference. The Shawnees were overjoyed to see Kirk again—assuming that he had been killed by the Cherokee on the day of his escape—and they begged him to return to his "family." Kirk, though he eventually returned to Britain, likewise felt deep devotion and affection for his brother and recalled, "I believe I shall always have a high regard for him, as his friendship was the most sincere I ever met in all my life and if it is ever in my power I will requite his kindness."[11] Thus in the remarkable story of Robert Kirk we have a glimpse of how some Britons left deep impressions and memories on Ohio natives, and how the natives also transformed the spirit and understanding of some Britons.

One part of Ohio where the British and Indian cultures intermingled in complex and interesting ways was the Maumee River Basin, which embraces northeastern Indiana, parts of Michigan, and northwestern Ohio. During the French and Indian War and the Revolution, the center of activity in this region was in Ohio, at a place known as the Glaize, at the center of the basin, where the Auglaize and Maumee rivers join (near present-day Defiance). Here the buffalo had long wallowed in the mud, before their extinction from the area. The Glaize was also the birthplace of Pontiac, born to an Ottawa father and Miami mother, who at the urging and support of the French after their defeat in the French and Indian War led his "rebellion" against the British in May 1763. The revolt occurred after Lord Jeffrey Amherst—Britain's military commander of North America—eliminated ritual gift giving in 1762 and slashed the budget of the Indian Department.

Just before the rebellion, English captain Thomas Morris of the 17th Regiment was sent to negotiate with Pontiac to prevent hostilities. Morris might have been killed by warriors except for the intervention of Pontiac, who treated him roughly but respected his ambassadorial office. Pontiac allowed Morris to proceed up the Maumee to negotiate for peace with other Indians as well, and here he met a mixture of harassment and indignation. But Morris also reaped the rewards from the interactions between English and Indian culture. When he met a leader named "Little Chief," Morris traded some of his gunpowder for a volume of Shakespeare that the Indians had somehow obtained. Later one day Morris was observed relaxing in a canoe, totally absorbed in his reading of *Antony and Cleopatra*.[12]

Unfortunately these negotiations came to naught, and the "conspiracy" of the warrior tribes to do what the French could not—expel the British—was launched. They managed to destroy the British outpost of Sandusky and inflict heavy losses, including the capture of two hundred English soldiers at the Battle of Bloody Run in July of 1763. But the following year, after Bouquet's expedition into the Muskingum and Scioto River Valleys to subdue Mingo, Delaware, and Shawnee resistance, the tide turned and the British maintained their hold on Ohio.

After the French and Indian War, relations between the British and many of Ohio's Indians improved. With the Proclamation Line of 1763 Britain showed some resolve to limit further white expansion, preserve the Indians' lands, and keep the peace. Among its main intentions was that "the several Nations or Tribes of Indians with whom We are connected, and who live under our Protection, should not be molested or disturbed."[13] Though these noble intentions were never perfectly implemented as policy, it is not surprising that during the American Revolution most Indians in Ohio sided with the British, keenly aware that a patriot victory would unleash an unstoppable tide of white settlement.

While the colonists in Boston began resisting British authority, Britons continued to enter Ohio and experience their own drama with Indians in ways more voluntary than those of captives like Robert Kirk. The amazing life of Nicholas Cresswell provides a vivid picture of how some Britons interacted with Ohio Indians and helped transform their culture. Born in the beautiful hills of Edale in Derbyshire to the family of a prosperous sheep farmer, Cresswell was twenty-four when he sailed from Liverpool and entered Ohio in 1774. For four years he engaged in the fur trade with the Shawnee, Delaware, and other Indians. Cresswell meandered in and out of eastern Ohio and western Pennsylvania, and even crossed the Ohio River into Kentucky and Virginia, but much of his adventure with the Indians occurred in what became Coshocton and Tuscarawas Counties, and the area around Cincinnati. He started out traveling with a party of fourteen that included two other Englishmen, a Welshman, and two Irishmen, as well as some other Europeans, Americans, an African, and a person of mixed race. Their clothing was essentially Indian: "breech-clouts, leggings and hunting shirts, which have never been washed only by the rain since they were made." This was not a costume, but a highly functional and practical form of dress that took them a step toward being Indians themselves.

Cresswell faithfully recorded his experiences and observations in Ohio prior to the time of extensive white settlement. He admired Indian paintings on the trees. Along the Ohio River he and his men occasionally killed buffalo for food. One they shot eight times but the enormous animal still got away. At a place called "Elephant Bone Lick" Cresswell saw huge bones and ivory tusks (one "six foot long, very sound but yellow") that he assumed to be from elephants, but were apparently the remains of ancient mastodons. A piece of tusk that he took for a souvenir was later broken by the "Damned Irish rascal" who accompanied him, which "put me in a violent passion [that I] can write no more."

Traveling through a remote and forested wilderness seen by few if any whites, was a challenge for a young man from a modern and comfortable part of England. At times Cresswell and his men survived on poorly jerked meat that had become infested with maggots. The party also proved overly fearful of natives who lived near the junction of the Little Miami and Ohio rivers. Floating down the Ohio one day in June of 1775, they suddenly found themselves surrounded by Indians. Cresswell's group panicked and grabbed their guns, only to find most of them too wet to fire. While the terrified men braced themselves for the attack, Cresswell took charge to rally them. The Irishmen grabbed their rosary beads and "prayed and howled in Irish" and "lay crying in the bottom of the Canoes and refused to stir." So Cresswell "set the muzzle of my Gun to O'Brien's head, threatening to blow his brains out if he did not immediately take his paddle. It had the desired effect, he begged for his life, invoked St. Patrick, took his paddle and howled most horribly." Throughout this nightmarish panic the Indians sat, highly amused, and then "laughed at us for our fears." The natives turned out to be a group of friendly Delaware Indians whom they had met upriver a few days before. After doing some trading, the Indians "proceeded up the River very merry at the expense of our cowardly companions."[14]

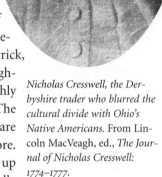

Nicholas Cresswell, the Derbyshire trader who blurred the cultural divide with Ohio's Native Americans. From Lincoln MacVeagh, ed., The Journal of Nicholas Cresswell: 1774–1777.

As the summer of 1775 progressed, Cresswell traveled alone to meet Indians and other whites in the region and became more fully absorbed in the native culture. He hired an Indian woman to make him "a pair of Mockeysons and Leggings," and after another English trader warned him that his Indian customers would be offended if he wore a hunting shirt in their presence, he "got a Calico shirt made in the Indian fashion, trimmed up with Silver Brooches and Armplates so that I scarcely know myself."

One night, losing his way in the dark, the Englishman made his way into an Indian camp, where he found two Indian women who knew no English, so through sign language he "made them understand what I wanted and they put me right." The nature and frequency of sexual relations with Indian women is hinted at in Cresswell's writings. Another night, Cresswell recorded, "one of the Indian Squaws invited me to sleep with her, but I pretended to be sick. She was very kind and brought me some plums she got in the woods." Apparently he did not find her attractive, but four nights later he told a different story. Arriving at another camp an Indian girl tended to his horse and with other women fed him around the fire that evening. While two older women and a boy lay down opposite him, the girl "came and placed herself very near me. I began to think," he continued, "she had some amorous design upon me. In about half an hour she began to creep nearer me and pulled my Blanket. I found what she wanted and lifted it up. She was young, handsome, and healthy. Fine regular features and fine eyes, had she not painted them with Red before she came to bed." Thereafter, Cresswell refers to her only as "My Bedfellow." The girl accompanied the young Englishman and served as his guide as he traveled through the deep woods of Ohio to other Indian camps. He "attempted to speak Indian, which diverted her exceedingly."[15]

Several days later Nicholas Cresswell arrived at Coshocton, which he called "Co-a-shoking," at the forks of the Muskingum River. He lodged at a Mohawk Indian's house, where he traded "to good advantage." But here he also traded bed partners, as his host offered Cresswell his sister to sleep with, which Cresswell was "obliged to accept." Two days later he was on his way but found that his new "bedfellow" was "very fond of me . . . and wants to go with me." Although female companionship and physical intimacy were no doubt enjoyable for Cresswell, today one can fault him for his opportunism and exploitation. But he recorded that he found such companionship necessary, if nothing else than to fend off other such offers: "I must often meet with such encounters as these if I do not take a Squaw to myself," he explained. "She is young and sprightly, tolerably handsome, and can speak a little English. Agreed to take her."[16] Indians also found such unions advantageous. The bride's father, a prominent man in the community and perhaps a chief, gained more influence and respect because his family now had a greater role in getting and distributing the European goods that his people wanted. And the wife herself gained prestige as a link between the European and Indian cultures, as would any children they produced.[17]

On the last day of August 1775, Cresswell visited other Indians in and around Coshocton, where he sold all of his goods for furs and did his best to befriend the Indians and socialize with them. One afternoon he "rambled about the Town, smoking Tobacco with the Indians and did everything in my power to make myself agreeable to them." He went to see the "king" of the tribe, whose lack of English-style majesty disappointed Cresswell, though his kindness did not. The king "lives in a poor house," he observed, "and he is poor in dress as any of them, no emblem of Royalty or Majesty about him. He is an old man, treated me very kindly, called me his good friend, and hoped I would be kind to my Squaw. Gave me a small string of Wampum as a token of friendship."

The next evening was a highlight for the young man from Derbyshire, who more and more understood and appreciated Indian culture. "Saw an Indian Dance in which I bore a part," Cresswell recorded proudly. "Painted by my Squaw in the most elegant manner. Divested of all my clothes, except my Calico short breech-clout, leggings, and Mockesons. A fire was made which we danced round with little order, whooping and hallooing in a most frightful manner. I was but a novice at the diversion," Cresswell admitted, "and by endeavouring to act as they did made them a great deal of sport and ingratiated me much in their esteem. This is the most violent exercise to the adepts in the art I ever saw. No regular figure, but violent distortion of features, writhing and twisting the body in the most uncouth and antic postures imaginable."

Cresswell skillfully used words to paint a most vivid picture of the Indian music and dance in which he was participating, though as an Englishman he could not fully understand what he recorded. The images he conjured up with his pen are a wonderful record of a local Ohio Indian ceremony that has long passed:

> Their music is an old Keg with one head knocked out and covered with a skin and beat with sticks which regulates their times. The men have strings of Deer's hoofs tied round their ankles and knees, and gourds with shot or pebblestones in them in their hands which they continually rattle. The women have Morris bells or Thimbles with holes in the bottom and strung upon a leather thong tired round their ankles, knees and waists. The jingling of these Bells and Thimbles, the rattling of the Deer's hoofs and gourds, beating of the drum and kettle, with the horrid yells of the Indians, render it the most unharmonious concert, that human idea can possibly conceive. . . . Saw an Indian Conjuror dressed in a Coat of Bearskin with a Visor mask made of wood, frightful enough to scare the Devil.[18]

The only element of the dance that Cresswell recognized were the bells around the dancers' feet, which he likened to the ancient traditional Morris dancing that he observed in his native Derbyshire and that exists in England to this day. But he did join the dance. He and other early British traders and travelers in Ohio lost to history were in effect reinventing themselves on the frontier by adopting cultural motifs of the Indians. This occurred through their use of native dress, their attitudes toward nature, and their participation in other rituals. To an extent Cresswell's self-identity had changed. In Ohio the Englishman was at the center of mutual transculturation as he joined the dance around the fire, "whooping and hallooing" and making the most "uncouth and antic postures imaginable."

But acculturation flowed the other way as well. Three days after his dance Cresswell traveled to Newcomerstown, about twenty miles east of Coshocton, where he visited Delaware Indians who had been converted to Christianity by Moravian missionaries. Cresswell listened to an Indian playing an old violin made of tin and making "tolerable good music." Here he was also shown an Indian scalp. And the next day he enjoyed listening to an Indian play the piano at a Moravian church service. It was seven years later, during the Revolution, that these same Delaware Indians were massacred by American militiamen at Gnadenhutten. They had assimilated even to the extent of adopting white dress and hair styles, and the Christian religion. They were pacifists and had been friendly to the white Americans. But they were still Indians, on good land, and were senselessly punished for the resistance of nearby Shawnees. On March 9, 1782, about ninety of the Christian Delaware Indians—men, women, and children—were clubbed to death; some were scalped.[19]

As whites headed west, violence against natives became more common; so too did changes in the natives' economy and society—often with mixed results. British traders like Cresswell certainly brought a higher level of affluence to Ohio's natives. They transformed indigenous culture by bringing items like handkerchiefs and silver ornaments, which opened up more natives to wealth and the status that came with it. In the process they pulled the Indians into the marketplace and introduced a greater acquisitiveness to their culture.

Hunting in order to acquire European goods, which Britons like Cresswell encouraged in eighteenth-century Ohio, certainly brought the Indians material benefits and raised their level of prosperity to unprecedented levels. But in the process, traditional lines of authority were undermined, as was the restraint that previously prevailed when hunting was for sustenance and had a sacred dimension. Overhunting of fur-bearing species became epidemic. Tribal cohesion also eroded as the Indians tried to cope with growing numbers of Europeans. Undoubtedly the increasing contact and trade with the British resulted in much cultural dislocation and reinvention. But the reinvention of both Indian and British culture was voluntary. As the story of Nicholas Cresswell illustrates, some early British Buckeyes were willing to adopt Indian elements and become nearly as Indian as they were British. For the Indians too, acculturation was often highly pragmatic and noncoercive; but at the same time it was corrosive to their traditional culture.

Thus early British Buckeyes like Nicholas Cresswell were active and important players in some of the most culturally formative episodes of Ohio's frontier history. They were mediators who blurred the lines of cultural difference and stimulated Ohio's development. And though Nicholas Cresswell returned to England after several more years in America, he was never the same. Nor were his native "bedfellows," his "temporary wife," or the others with whom he traded, danced, and lived.[20]

The Revolutionary War presented unique challenges to the British in Ohio at the time. Many had to confront the issue of changing loyalties. For some the shift of loyalty to the American cause came naturally. But others found the idea of rebellion against the British government and its constitution—the most advanced and admired in Europe—abhorrent. Nicholas Cresswell was one such person. In late June of 1775, after traveling throughout Ohio and trading with Indians for about a year, he met some whites who told him about an early battle, presumably Bunker Hill; they passed on the exaggerated claims that the Americans had killed seven thousand Englishmen. "I hope it will prove that the English have killed several thousand of the Yankees," Cresswell recorded, shocked by the news of such a violent rebellion. Two weeks later he came across Americans attempting to organize "the best riflemen that can be got to go to Boston . . . for the humane purpose of killing the English Officers. Confusion to the Scoundrels," he exclaimed in his journal.

When in contact with white Americans the Englishman frequently found himself peppered with annoying questions and accusations by those who suspected him of being a spy, which made him feel "very much fatigued." He also complained that "the people here are Liberty mad, nothing but War is thought of." And after spending more time with colonials while preparing to make another trading expedition deep into the forests of Ohio, he described some of the bellicose people as "a set of vile brutes." Upon hearing that "the Congress have discarded all the Governors on the Continent and taken all affairs Civil and Military into their management," Nicholas Cresswell again muttered to his journal, "Independence is what these Scoundrels aim at. Confusion to their schemes."[21]

Cresswell was not the only Englishman in Ohio during the Revolution to face the ugly hostility of overzealous patriots. As the tensions of war escalated, British immigrants were commonly harassed and accused of disloyalty, regardless of their views. Those who expressed any affection for the land of their birth—even those who supported independence—were sometimes assumed to be Loyalists and treated with suspicion. But others whose service to the new nation was known were more readily accepted. Some Britons who actually fought in support of the American Revolution settled in Ohio. Stephen Price, born in Wales in 1757 and trained in London for the ministry, had a radical change of mind one day. At age nineteen he ran off to America in search of adventure greater than the pulpit could provide and immediately found it in the patriot cause. After the war Price settled in Mifflin Township, Franklin County. His war record left no room to doubt his loyalty to his adopted country and he was readily accepted as an American.[22]

Interestingly, British soldiers who fought for the Crown also made their way to Ohio after the war ended, and some were welcomed as neighbors. One such group settled in Williamsburg, Clermont County, in the late 1790s. Because they fought for the Crown during the Revolution, they were regarded as "peculiar" and "formed a special group." Even so, their Ohio neighbors treated them with kindness. Perhaps the story of one of their members, Robert Christie, explains their toleration. The second son of a Scottish laird, Christie ran away from his father at age seventeen and joined the British Army. He became a sergeant under Cornwallis at Yorktown, but after the surrender he quit the army and refused to return to England. As a deserter, he sacrificed the estate that he would have inherited when his older brother died. Instead he chose Ohio, which endeared him to the Americans, who tended to be hypersensitive about how the foreign-born viewed the young republic.[23]

Englishmen like Christie made an interesting and committed addition to Ohio's growing population during the Revolutionary War era. So did Englishwomen like Ann Bailey. She was born Anne Hennis in Liverpool in 1742. After her parents died, at age nineteen she sailed for America to join relatives in Virginia. There she married Richard Trotter, a frontiersman and Indian fighter who was killed by Indians near Gallipolis in 1774. This event transformed Ann, and made her obsessed with revenge. During the Revolution she served as a frontier scout and spy for the patriots and became famous as a crack shot and expert horsewoman. All the while she longed to fight Indians. Ann was certainly up to the task. She was described as "short and stout, and of coarse masculine appearance," and endowed with "masculine habits" that included drinking hard liquor and flaunting "her skill in boxing." She always carried a tomahawk and butcher's knife, and she intimidated men greatly. Yet, she could read and write and was considered highly intelligent.

Like Nicholas Cresswell, Ann adopted frontier and Indian dress while retaining much of her Englishness. She was a curious blend of Liverpool lass and frontier American. Unlike Cresswell, she retained no loyalty to the British crown. This was probably a lingering effect of her upbringing in Liverpool, where many people had a fierce sense of independence and did not readily bend to royal authority. "Clad in buckskin pants, with petticoat, heavy brogan shoes, a man's coat and hat," armed with tomahawk and knife and a "long rifle on her shoulder," Ann Bailey was a remarkable person on the frontier. She rode a black horse, which she named "Liverpool," shot her gun and paddled her canoe—

both of which she also named "Liverpool"—as she carried messages between the frontier posts along the Ohio River and Kanawha Valley. She effectively recruited locals to join the patriot militia and quickly became legendary throughout the region.

Ann Bailey's most famous exploit occurred in 1791, when she single-handedly saved Fort Lee (now Charleston, West Virginia), where she was fighting Indians. When Indians surrounded the fort and the frontiersmen ran out of gunpowder, the captain of the garrison called for a volunteer to get more. Ann stepped forward. She stormed out of the fort on old "Liverpool," ran the gauntlet, rode one hundred miles through the wilderness to the nearest fort for more powder, rode back, and again stormed through the Indian lines to resupply the fort. Her heroic deed earned the respect and awe of both whites and Indians. The Shawnees thought her insane and therefore protected by the "Great Spirit." Out of respect they called her "The Great White Squaw of the Kanawha."

After hostilities with the Indians ended, Ann married John Bailey and continued the frontier life on the banks of the Ohio River in Gallia County. She built her own cabin out of old fence rails, mud, and straw, and packed old rags between the gaps; the cabin had one door, one window, a dirt floor, and no furniture. At age fifty she still hunted bears in the forest and established her own mail service among Ohio's southern settlements. At the age of nearly eighty she frequently walked nine miles each way to visit friends in Gallipolis. She also took it upon herself to enforce the Sabbath by rounding up unruly boys and forcing them to sit in her cabin where she taught them good manners and lessons, threatening them with a good thrashing if they refused. By this time the aging Liverpudlian had a coarse low voice "like the growl of a lion," and she "chewed tobacco like a pig," with the juice drooling down the corners of her mouth. She always carried a gun and shot-pouch on her shoulder, and yet the legendary woman was a welcome guest at any home. Her Ohioan neighbors referred to her affectionately as "Mad Ann Bailey" and the "Heroine of the Great Kanawha Valley" because she was utterly fearless and had saved Fort Lee from annihilation. She remained a heroic figure for

"Mad Ann Bailey." A nineteenth-century sketch of the Liverpool woman who became the "Great White Squaw of the Kanawha" and a legend on the Ohio frontier. From Henry Howe, *Historical Collections of Ohio,* vol. 1.

the rest of her days. Ann Bailey was a legendary Buckeye whose remarkable character and role in Ohio's early history was rooted in her upbringing and early adulthood in Liverpool. She died in Gallipolis in 1825.[24]

The American Revolution altered the course of Ohio history. The change had much to do with the new political relationship with Great Britain, which had intended to create a stable North American empire and maintain it through close centralized control from London. Generally, as illustrated by the ill-fated Proclamation Line of 1763, the British attempted to restrain and regulate rapid western settlement, which some frontiersmen interpreted as an infringement on their liberty. Furthermore, Britain usually took complaints from Indians about her aggressive subjects seriously. British officials often served as mediators between Ohio's Indians and whites in hopes of ensuring order. After the Revolution the British empire of constraint was supplanted by the American empire of liberty—a liberty restricted to individual white males but liberty nonetheless. This new form of liberty was inherited partly from Britain, but was also modified by the American environment and the ideals of the Enlightenment. American liberty was sacrosanct. And whereas British empire in the Ohio River Valley proved elusive, the American empire of liberty became a reality as land-hungry individuals headed west beyond government control and exercised their own authority. The new American government had neither the intention nor the ability to regulate settlement according to the British model.[25]

As the constraints that the British had imposed on white settlement evaporated, people rushed to fill the vacuum of authority. The Proclamation Line was erased and forgotten. Settlers, especially squatters, who were steeped in the antiauthoritarian, liberty-drenched ideology that flourished during the Revolution, poured west and took Indian lands. But for British-born residents of Ohio, change did not necessarily occur until Jay's Treaty (1794) and the Treaty of Greenville (1795) effectively ended both Britain's continued presence in the northwest area and freedom for the natives. In the roughly twenty years between the American Revolution and the Treaty of Greenville, the British military and government still exerted a powerful influence in the history and culture of Ohio. And this was especially true at the Glaize, in the heart of the Maumee River Basin.

After 1783 the Glaize became a truly multicultural community composed of Indians, British, and French traders, and some Americans still loyal to the British Crown. It also included a number of whites who had been captured by Indians and held for ransom. Others were adopted as children and raised as Indian family members, and there were even some Africans who were captured during raids on settlements. Altogether they formed a population of about two thousand people. Some of the British traders at the Glaize married Indian women, produced families of mixed race, and helped create a culture that was a curious blend of British and Indian.

Standing astride the cultural divide was the Shawnee chief Blue Jacket, a tall and dignified person who wore a large medallion of King George III around his neck. The symbol conferred considerable power upon him because others saw him as a link with the king of the great Empire whose goods and culture were becoming more and more prevalent. Blue Jacket was clearly favorably impressed with the British in Ohio, as the British were of him. He was said to have held a commission as brigadier general in the British Army and he had his two highly intelligent sons educated by British teachers. He also had frequent contact with British government officials in Detroit, where he traveled from time to time to represent his people.[26]

A Mohawk woman named Coo-coo-chee also lived at the Glaize. She was a refugee from the Montreal region who was welcomed by the Shawnees in Ohio and revered for her spiritual power and skills with medicines. She lived in a bark cabin fourteen by twenty-eight feet; it was divided into two sections by a bark partition, the inner part being her private apartment where she performed mysterious incantations and ceremonies. One of Coo-coo-chee's daughters, Vocemassussia (Isabella), married the Scottish immigrant George Ironside, the wealthiest merchant at the Glaize and one of the leading traders of the entire Maumee Valley. Born in Scotland in 1761, Ironside earned a master's degree at King's College, Aberdeen in 1781, shortly before migrating to North America. By 1789 he worked as a clerk at Miamitown (Fort Wayne) and engaged heavily in the fur trade along the Miami River. His residence at the Glaize was the most impressive establishment in the area: a spacious three-room cabin of hewn logs with a loft, which he used as his store, warehouse, and dwelling. The contrast from living in the modern city of Aberdeen to living at the Glaize, near his Mohawk mother-in-law's bark cabin, could hardly have been starker. Yet Ironside thrived among the Indians in Northwest Ohio. He learned the Shawnee language, participated fully in their councils and ceremonies, and was their advocate in deliberations with the British in Detroit. The Indians embraced him as their brother and friend.

Another daughter of Coo-coo-chee married Simon Girty, a Pennsylvania-born "renegade" who befriended Ironside at the Glaize and was hated by white Americans for his loyalty to Britain and leadership of Indian resistance against American encroachment. Simon Girty was very interesting. He and his two brothers, James and George, were captured as boys in 1756 by a Delaware-Shawnee war party. They lived with their Indian captors for several years, learned

their languages and customs, and with their invaluable knowledge became inter-
preters for the British Indian agencies. Shortly before the American Revolution
James Girty also traded with the Shawnees near Chillicothe, and Simon scouted
for Lord Dunmore during Dunmore's War against the Shawnees in 1774. During
the Revolutionary War, the Girtys, in service of the British Crown, were active in
Indian warfare against the Americans. By 1792, at age fifty-three, James Girty
lived at the Glaize with his Shawnee wife. A legendary veteran of Ohio frontier
warfare, he dressed in Indian clothing, his face was grotesquely scarred from
tomahawk wounds, "his sunken grey eyes shaded by heavy brows meeting above
a flat nose, and a forbidding facial expression." He was known for his rough character and vicious hostility toward captured Americans. He and his brother
Simon still occasionally performed as trouble-shooters for the British Indian
agents based in Detroit, who provided the weapons and ammunition that made
resistance against American encroachment possible.[27]

Though George Ironside knew the Girtys and was related to them by marriage, he was probably repulsed by their roughness and uncouth habits. Ironside himself stood out for his education, culture, and humanity, and he came to
know a great deal about the Indian culture into which he had married. When
the American O. M. Spencer was captured and held as a virtual slave for nearly
eight months by the Shawnees at the Glaize, and was forced to work for his ransom, George Ironside sympathized with him. He educated Spencer about the
Native Americans' history, manners, and customs, and arranged for his early release, for which Spencer was eternally grateful.[28]

Another captive in Ohio during the period was the Englishman Thomas
Ridout. In 1774, at age twenty, he migrated from Sherbourne, Dorset, to Maryland in order to join a brother who had assumed an important position in the
colonial government. Their relationship and his refusal to join the patriots put
his life in danger, so he left to trade in the West Indies and Europe during the
war years. In 1787 Ridout returned to Philadelphia and journeyed west down
the Ohio River, beyond Fort Pitt, with four hundred pounds of merchandise to
trade for Indian furs. Ridout was mesmerized by the views of Ohio that he enjoyed from the summit of Laurel Hill (in southwestern Pennsylvania), the
Ohiopyle Falls, the remains of mastodon skeletons, and other natural wonders.

But serenity quickly changed to horror in January of 1788, when he and his
crew were attacked by Indians who emerged from the Ohio side of the river.
They were "almost naked, painted and ornamented as when at war. About
twenty leaped into our boat like so many furies," Ridout recorded, "yelling and
screaming horribly, brandishing their knives and tomahawks, struggling with
each other for a prisoner. A young man, painted black, first seized me by the

arm." The Indians were mainly Shawnee but included some Potawatomies, Ottawas, and even Cherokees. Most of Thomas Ridout's companions were killed; but Ridout himself was taken from his young captor by "an elderly man, who seemed to be a chief. . . . This Indian was of a mild countenance, and he gave me immediately to understand I should not be hurt, holding me by the hand to show his property in me."

But Ridout's troubles were far from over. He endured a four-month ordeal, including torture, frequent fears for his life, and the memory of seeing his friends slain. However, he also experienced some kindness and regard for his value as property. During his captivity in Ohio, Ridout met another English immigrant taken prisoner the day before he was, from a preceding boat. He was William Richardson, "a decent-looking man of about forty-five years of age" whose property of seven hundred guineas was confiscated by the Indians and was similarly being held for ransom. Richardson was often trembling uncontrollably out of fear for his life.

Ridout was taken north up the Maumee River toward Detroit for ransom by the British. During the journey his treatment steadily improved. Along the way he met Indians who obviously traded with other Englishmen. Upon reaching one village on the Maumee he enjoyed the hospitality of an old chief Kakinathucca and his wife Metsigemewa. An African slave also lived among them. The chief's family used copper kettles and frying pans, pewter plates, and cups and saucers of English yellow ware, from which they drank tea. Ridout was shown favor and respect because he was an Englishman, not a land-hungry American, against whom the Indians expressed a murderous rage. Finally, in the spring of 1788, Ridout and his captors arrived at Miamitown and the Glaize, where they met Blue Jacket, Simon Girty, George Ironside, and other Englishmen by the name of Sharpe, Martin, and Parkes. Here the Indians treated Ridout "with the greatest kindness," and with the help of Simon Girty and Alexander McKee—an agent for the British Crown—he was soon on his way to Detroit, freedom, and a long career with the British government in Upper Canada.[29]

Thomas Ridout, the Dorset immigrant trader who was captured by natives in 1788 and held for four months in Ohio until ransomed in Detroit. From Western Pennsylvania Historical Magazine 12 (Jan. 1929).

As Thomas Ridout observed, the Glaize was a place where natives and British people and cultures mixed and formed something new. In mid-August the Indians held their Green Corn Festival, a harvest tradition observed by Indians in many parts of America. Coo-coo-chee celebrated the festival at her home with her daughter and son-in-law, George Ironside, as well as many other people—both white and Indian. The participants smoked the pipe together and Indian leaders made speeches praising the Great Spirit for the harvests granted to their people. Then they condemned the Americans who continued to encroach on their land and called on the warriors to drive them out. After the speeches were dances and sports contests, a sumptuous feast, and much drinking of rum, apparently provided by Ironside, who was one of the central figures of the festival. Eventually the celebrations got out of hand as the singing and dancing turned to whooping and quarreling until "uproar wild and deep confusion reigned."[30] Still, at the Glaize American Indians and Europeans of mostly British origin or descent got along relatively harmoniously and in a mutually beneficial way.

John Kinzie, son of a British surgeon in the Seven Years' War, also spent a lot of time at the Glaize and other parts of northern Ohio. Though born in Quebec in 1763, his parents were recent Scottish immigrants and his mother imparted their culture upon him so deeply that for the rest of his days he was affectionately referred to as "the Scot." After his family moved from Quebec to New York, Kinzie ran away from home, returned to Quebec, and pursued the jeweler's trade before heading west to trade with the Indians. By the late 1780s he was a regular feature of the fur trade throughout the Maumee River Basin, including the Glaize. As a silversmith Kinzie capitalized on his trade, exchanging brooches, ear rings, and other silver ornaments for skins and furs at a handsome profit.[31]

The silver ornaments that Kinzie and other British traders supplied to Ohio's Indians were highly significant—much more than mere visual displays. They had cultural and symbolic meaning and introduced a new vocabulary of status. Ohio Indian cultures were deeply affected as silver, glass beads, and other ornaments replaced feathers and animal claws as badges of distinction. In effect, their exchange of furs for ornaments democratized the Indians' access to emblems of status, which had previously been governed by the age and achievements of the individual and by ancient cultural tradition. This shift to a market-oriented economy and wider availability of status-bearing ornaments— brought primarily by Britons at this time—changed old traditions of authority and leadership. It also encouraged younger Indian men to hunt for what the market could bring them personally. In turn, hunting as a market response undermined the deeply spiritual nature of the hunt and its traditional restraints by encouraging over-hunting throughout the Ohio River Valley.[32]

John Kinzie was a boon companion of Henry Hay, son of a British Indian agent in Detroit, a native of Pennsylvania, and a British loyalist who traded with the Indians and apparently served the English garrisons in the region. Hay recorded the life of the traders in northwest Ohio during the last decade of the eighteenth century and he provides a fuller picture of early British Buckeyes. At the Glaize, Hay played the flute and Kinzie the fiddle while ladies sang and danced in the homes of other prominent whites. They played for religious services as well. On some occasions Ironside, Hay, and others attended formal balls in which "the Gentlemen & Ladies all appeared dressed in their best bibs & Tuckers, & behaved very descently not one of the men the least in Liquor, & which is mostly the case in this place when they collect together." The group even danced the minuet and sang "God Save the King." They also got along well with the remaining French of the area, sometimes playing music with fellow French musicians.

The Glaize's British settlers also lived harmoniously with various Indians who dominated the valley. The legendary chief Little Turtle (Michikinikwa) often visited them, as did Blue Jacket. Another of their frequent Indian guests was Le Gris, a Miami chief prominent in the warfare with the Americans. Le Gris and Little Turtle frequently stopped in to have breakfast or dinner with Hay and Ironside. Le Gris would return the favor by bringing food, once consisting of "four Turkys, two leggs and two sides of Venison exceedingly fatt." Pacan was another Miami chief who was a good friend of the British in Ohio. Still, the trade between the British and Indians was rather cutthroat: "Rascally Scrambling," Hay wrote, "everyone tries to get what he can either by fowle play or otherwise."[33]

The Britons of northwest Ohio were certainly no strangers to self-indulgent excesses. One night Hay and Kinzie got "infernally drunk" with a trader from Dublin named James Abbott, who, Hay recorded, "gave me his daughter Betsy over the bottle. Damnation sick this morning in consequence of last night's debashe," he continued; but he and Kinzie were still able to play music for the next morning's mass, "as usual," as well as that evening's vespers. Their evening dinners seem to have been as frequent as they were indulgent, at least during the raucous last days of 1789 and the holiday season of New Year 1790. They held a dinner "among us Englishmen here," consisting of "fine newly corned pork." The following night they again "got very drunk"—Kinzie so much so that he could not make it home, though the next morning they played music at mass, surely hung over. If that was not enough, the following night they "got damned drunk."

New Year's Day, 1790, in the Maumee Valley was remarkable. Hay, Kinzie, Ironside, and the other British held a party that included so many Indian friends and continued so late in the morning that Hay and Ironside could not get any sleep. Rum flowed freely, skirting the British ban on providing alcohol to Indians in the town. Over the next two days there was more dancing, music, card playing, and a practical joke involving the stealing of a hog, which produced a good laugh. But the high alcohol consumption did not end after the New Year began. On January 10, Hay attended a dinner party of six persons where ten bottles of wine were consumed, plus an unspecified number of bottles of "Grogg." "We were all pretty merry," he wrote.

Clearly the Indian and British residents of the Glaize got along well together. They were generally trusting and even enjoyed each other's company, a harmonious relationship nurtured by the fact that some of the British had married Indian women and lived with or near their Indian in-laws. Participation in each other's institutions illustrates the depth of their friendship. In early 1790 Ironside and Kinzie established a fraternal organization at the Glaize called "The Friars of St. Andrews." Its rules were written in both English and French and their membership included Indians, among them a Miami chief named J. B. Richardville. Here was a very real if unlikely example of intercultural relations: Indians as members of a society dedicated to St. Andrew. The interaction flowed the other way too. When in March of 1790 the Shawnees decided to construct an additional town for their families, they called a meeting that included the British residents to discuss their plans. In this way the British were involved in some of the important decisions of their Indian neighbors on the Ohio frontier.[34]

The Indians of the Glaize were full participants in other distinctly British institutions and ceremonies, including the celebrations of Queen Charlotte's birthday. Though they got the date wrong, the British made solemn speeches, fired three volleys, and passed the rum. The crowd of celebrants included The Snake, a Shawnee chief whose village was just outside the Glaize, and some of his warriors, all of whom were duly informed about the great significance of the occasion and the "Reason of the Rejoicing." The British and their native friends seem to have found that in spite of their profound differences they had some things in common. They shared an appreciation for nature. When the winters were so harsh that the rivers froze solid and made their trips to Detroit impossible, Kinzie and Ironside took the day off for ice-skating, a sport that amused the Indians but was consistent with their own enjoyment of nature.

Notwithstanding their close relations, the cultural divide that remained was deep. Some of the scenes that Hay, Kinzie, Ironside, and other Britons witnessed

at the Glaize were shocking reminders of the alien qualities of Indian culture.
At one time a Shawnee chief by the name of "Captain Johnny" showed them the
heart of a white prisoner whom the Indians had killed. "It was quite dry," Hay
observed, "like a piece of dried venison, with a small stick run through from
one end of it to the other & fastened behind the fellows bundle that killed him,
with also his Scalp." The very same day a group of Miamis freshly returned from
war performed a victory "scalp dance." Attached to a stick their victims' scalps
flopped in the air to the rhythm of the warriors' dance. The ritual was a specta-
cle grotesque enough to sicken the stomachs of the toughest British adventurer.
Yet that night some of these warriors spent part of the evening at Hay's house.[35]

Other British immigrants were living as missionaries in the area with Indi-
ans as members of their community. William Edwards was one of the earliest
English missionaries among Ohio's Indians. Though raised as an Anglican in
Wiltshire, Edwards joined the Moravians in 1749, migrated to America to work
as a missionary, and became very prominent in his work among Ohio's Indi-
ans. He became an associate of David Zeisberger and took charge of the
Gnadenhutten mission in 1777; the following year he took his converts to
Lichtenau to escape the violence of the Revolutionary War. In 1782 he went to
Sandusky where he served the Indians until returning to the Tuscarawas Valley,
where he died in 1801.[36]

Altogether—and cultural clashes aside—the mixed British and Indian culture of northwest Ohio thrived in the late 1780s and early 1790s. British and Indian people enjoyed a harmony and prosperity that would not be seen again.
They lived together, dined together, and celebrated both native and European
days of importance—like New Year's Day, the British monarchs' birthdays, and
Indian harvest festivals. They danced together at evening ceremonies. They occasionally intermarried, and of course traded with each other, which was the
basis of their relationship. Associations between the British and the Indians in
this part of Ohio were free and easy. Altogether, it was a truly multicultural
frontier community.

But it was also a community of increasing military strength because of its
link with the British garrisons in Detroit. When Matthew Elliott, an agent for
the British government, called a council near the Glaize in early 1792, about a
thousand warriors assembled. The British Indian Agency, sometimes working
through intermediaries like Ironside and Kinzie, provided weapons and ammunition with which the Indians defended themselves against white encroachment. They also provided seed corn from time to time.[37]

The British-supported Indian barrier to white settlement in Ohio became
less and less acceptable for the new American government. The situation

became especially precarious as violence increased between Indians and the whites who were entering the area in greater numbers now that they were free from the restraint that had been imposed upon them by the British Empire. On February 13, 1790, Henry Hay observed that a few days prior, some of the local Indians had gone near the Ohio River and "fell in with a Party of Americans, killed some of them & stole their horses, and took a negro Prisoner." Later that morning another party of Shawnee warriors appeared with a young American prisoner whom they had captured in retribution for a previous American attack, in which several women and children were indiscriminately killed. Ironside and Hay were called to the village near the Glaize to attend the Indian council that was held to hear a "very minute Report of all what passed." Ironside feared that the American prisoner would be tortured and burned to death for revenge of the murdered women and children; instead he was adopted into the tribe. Kinzie arrived to interview the prisoner, who said his name was Mc-Mullen, born in Richmond, Virginia. He had traveled through the Ohio wilderness "to get a debt that was due to him."[38]

A month later, on March 21, the conflict between the Indians of the Maumee River Basin and the white Americans escalated further. This was an ominous trend for both the local British residents and those stationed in Detroit, who realized that the new American government would eventually bring in its military. Ironside and Kinzie feared the worst when more Shawnees arrived with four American prisoners, including one African. The prisoners were taken after the Shawnees attacked a boat and killed twenty-one men and one officer. Several months later the American government responded.

The first attempt involved the ill-fated expedition of the American general, Josiah Harmar, who in the autumn of 1790 set out to build a fort on the Maumee River and pacify the area. He aimed to overwhelm the Indians with the power of the new American republic and prevent the British from trespassing from Detroit. Harmar was especially determined to get rid of "the villainous" British traders who supported the natives through their trade and helped keep the northwestern corner of Ohio a virtual British possession. When Harmar's troops attacked Miamitown, the Indians retreated out of danger, allowing the American forces to burn three hundred Indian houses and about twenty thousand bushels of corn. But the Indians' counterattack was as well coordinated as it was fierce. They killed some two hundred of Harmar's troops. Afterwards, many of the Indian survivors of Harmar's destruction of Miamitown moved to the Glaize, rendering the area an even more important center of trade with the British, and a more significant military target for the Americans.[39]

Ironically, the next general to lead the attack against the Indian and British presence in northeastern Ohio was perhaps the most famous British immigrant in Ohio's history: Arthur St. Clair. He was born in Thurso, Caithness, Scotland, in 1736 to a comfortable middle-class merchant's family and was educated in medicine in Edinburgh. But at age twenty he bought an ensign's commission and came to North America with the British Army to serve in the French and Indian War. He served under General Jeffrey Amherst in the capture of Louisburg and under General Wolf in the storming of Quebec. But as tension grew between the colonies and their mother country in the 1770s, St. Clair shifted his loyalties from Britain to America. In January of 1776 St. Clair became colonel of a Pennsylvania regiment, and then later that year was appointed brigadier general. He was with Washington at Valley Forge and was appointed major general in 1777. He also accompanied Washington at Yorktown to accept the surrender of Cornwallis. With his election to the Continental Congress—of which he was chosen president in 1787—Arthur St. Clair clearly became one of the young nation's most prominent citizens. He was instrumental in the passage of Jefferson's Northwest Ordinance, and was a natural choice for Governor of the Northwest Territory.

And yet St. Clair's most memorable action as Governor and major general was his disastrous attempt in 1791 to lead an army against the Indians who had defeated Harmar's forces the previous year. St. Clair was based at Fort Washington, near Cincinnati, which by this time had nearly a thousand residents and a growing commercial interest. He planned to march his forces of some 1,400 men ninety miles north. Racked with pain from gout and handicapped further by his army of ill-trained soldiers, the general led his troops to disaster at the Wabash River. St. Clair himself was brave, but of questionable military competence. His forces suffered the worst, most humiliating defeat any United States army ever endured at the hands of American Indians. Under the leadership of chiefs Little Turtle (who after Harmar's defeat had moved to the Glaize) and Blue Jacket, the Indian coalition of Miami, Shawnee, Potawatomi, and Chippewa warriors fell on St. Clair's forces with fury. The Indians killed 630 Americans, including 37 officers. Some 300 were wounded. Ignominiously, the survivors panicked and threw down their arms as they fled, it was said, for thirty miles, even though the Indians pursued them for only four. Of about 250 women who had also marched along to accompany their men, 56 were killed and a few others were taken prisoner. The Indian forces lost only 21 braves. To make matters worse the Americans left behind eight cannons and twelve hundred muskets. The battlefield was strewn with the corpses of soldiers, many of them horribly mutilated. Some of the bones lay there until Anthony Wayne's men found them three years later and built a fort on the site, which they named Fort Recovery, to mark the spot where the remains of the Americans slain in St. Clair's defeat were buried.[40]

The disaster infuriated George Washington, though St. Clair himself was exonerated of any wrongdoing by an investigative committee appointed by the House of Representatives. Indeed he was commended for his valor. Yet in retrospect, St. Clair's poor planning and lack of leadership were clearly part of the problem, and his shameful trouncing blighted his reputation and damaged much of the remainder of his tenure as governor. After the debacle, national leaders saw him as irrelevant; and, increasingly ignored in Cincinnati, St. Clair pitied himself as "a poor Devil banished to another Planet."[41]

After St. Clair's defeat the Glaize grew as the headquarters of the Indian confederacy and became more influenced by the material culture of the whites. One of the victorious Delaware chiefs, Whingwy Pooshies, returned to his cabin near the Glaize with his spoils, including clothing from the dead soldiers, guns, axes, horses, and several tents—one of them a fancy marquee in which the chief's family lived for a number of years. The new riches created "much joy among them," and also contributed to the continuing evolution of the Indian community there.[42]

But in reality the Glaize's days were numbered. In 1794 General Anthony Wayne and his army invaded and destroyed all the buildings at the Glaize. Wayne boasted of burning fifty miles of Indian corn fields, but not before most of the residents escaped their own destruction. Some English immigrants fought alongside Anthony Wayne to put down the Indian resistance and the British presence in Ohio. One of them was James Anderson, who had also helped suppress the Whiskey Rebellion. Wayne promoted Anderson to the rank of captain for his effective and meritorious military service.[43]

Wayne established his headquarters, which he called Fort Defiance, on the site of the traders' town.

Arthur St. Clair, the Scot who fought with Washington, served as president of the Continental Congress, and was Ohio's first territorial governor. In 1791 St. Clair led a force that suffered the worst, most humiliating defeat any United States army ever endured at the hands of American Indians near the town known today as Fort Recovery, in northwest Ohio. Portrait by Charles Willson Peale, ca. 1780.

Later that year, at the Battle of Fallen Timbers, he routed the Northwest Indian Confederacy, of which the Glaize Indians had been an important part. Finally, the Treaty of Greenville of 1795 ended Indian independence in Ohio and led to the British forfeiture of Detroit in 1796, and northwest Ohio's British Indian society came to an end.[44]

Up until 1795, then, British immigrants like Ironside—and others in this community whose stories were not preserved—were important cultural intermediaries in Indian-white relations throughout the Great Lakes region. They transformed Indian culture, and were also transformed by their experience. They helped invent a new frontier society and reinvented themselves in the process. British immigrants and traders were part of an intercultural exchange, from which evolved the early Ohio frontier communities that flourished and enabled the population to grow enough to allow statehood in 1803.

After the Treaty of Greenville and the pacification of northwestern Ohio, the Scottish immigrant Arthur St. Clair continued his work as Governor of the Northwest Territory, hoping to live down his humiliating defeat of 1791. As Governor from 1788 through 1802, he played a central role in the history of the frontier and made a particularly significant impact on Ohio in its prestatehood days. His earliest duties consisted of adopting territorial laws and appointing local officials. Through his own insistence, St. Clair claimed the power of veto and struck down eleven out of thirty bills passed during his tenure, an exercise of power that concerned even his most faithful supporters. The governor and his judges saw the need to pass laws that promoted morality and public order. Profanity, drunkenness, and Sabbath violations were targeted along with arson and robbery. And in spite of his humiliating defeat of 1791, St. Clair worked hard to establish peaceful relations with Indians and attempted to ensure that whites who committed crimes against them were duly punished.[45] His attempt to create a moral society reflects his upbringing in a Scottish Calvinist culture. He also set up county government in Cincinnati and helped stop ruthless and corrupt land speculators from acquiring inordinate wealth and power. He remained a British conservative in the Federalist sense, and achieved success in his legislative efforts.

Instead of retiring in 1797, St. Clair pleaded to President Adams for another term. Adams granted him two more, during which he managed to restore his reputation somewhat. But St. Clair's main legacy is not much appreciated today because he deliberately delayed Ohio's move toward establishing a territorial assembly and statehood. Not having fully set aside his old-world pretensions and elitist beliefs that only educated, refined people like himself should govern, St. Clair was convinced that Ohio did not have enough able and educated men for true self-government. He was a staunch Federalist, determined to preserve a strong national authority. He carried from Britain the conviction that good government ought to be provided to the people through privileged and able men like himself. Maintaining civilizing order and preventing mob rule were ideals shared by eastern aristocrats like Alexander Hamilton and other Federalists.

St. Clair was not the political reactionary his opponents and some historians have claimed. He believed that the ultimate source of political power lay in the people. Yet, he did not fully appreciate or comprehend America's emerging popular democracy, and remained convinced that Ohioans were not ready to govern themselves. Again, the Calvinism that permeated Scottish culture imbued St. Clair with the conviction that people had to be restrained, their selfish nature controlled. In this sense Arthur St. Clair was an anachronism in an Ohio growing quickly in population and democratic spirit. In Chillicothe mobs rioted against St. Clair while others petitioned the new president, Thomas Jefferson, to remove him from office, which he did in 1802.

After the end of his public life Arthur St. Clair moved to Pennsylvania, where he ran a tavern and lived out the rest of his life in obscurity. His record is decidedly mixed. He untangled early land claims, passed law codes, kept speculation in check, and brought centralized government to new areas and appointed generally good men to office—no mean achievement for this critical moment in Ohio's history. But his paternalistic nature, snobbery, and lack of competence also showed in the end. St. Clair led Ohio Territory through a transitional phase as it approached statehood; but ironically, he was not a supporter of Ohio statehood and self-government.[46]

During the time of the Constitutional Convention in Philadelphia the floodgates to settlement in Ohio were opened. The Land Ordinance of 1785 was a breakthrough because it set the terms and procedures for the sale and development of the Old Northwest. The Northwest Ordinance of 1787 was also important because it provided secure land titles and a stabilizing structure of law and courts that was based on English common law, familiar to American-born and British-born settlers alike.[47] British immigrants were a large part of the force that transformed Ohio from a territory to a state. Sharing the same language and basic culture with most early white Ohioans, and with an ease of mobility, Britons spread rapidly throughout Ohio. They assumed important positions and served functions that other immigrants did not.

Britons especially provided services in the transportation and sale of goods. John Sutherland, from Caithnesshire, Scotland, was among them. He was born in 1771 and immigrated to Virginia at age seventeen; after a few years he entered Ohio. In 1793 he came to Cincinnati and became a captain of packhorses, transporting goods and supplies to forts and military posts throughout the territory. This was an important and dangerous operation during early Ohio history. After Anthony Wayne effectively eliminated the Indian threat in the region, Sutherland settled in Hamilton, Butler County, and opened his own store to trade with the remaining Indians. He was so successful that by 1820 he was among the wealthiest persons in Ohio, esteemed for his charity and generosity in real estate dealings.[48]

James Reeside was another Scottish immigrant whose business activities helped develop Ohio's early economy. Although his family was poor when they immigrated to Maryland in the late 1790s, Reeside began a successful business of hauling merchandise between Philadelphia, Baltimore, and Pittsburgh—and later between Zanesville and Columbus—early in the nineteenth century. He established his own mail and stagecoach enterprise throughout the region and became good friends with Andrew Jackson, Henry Clay, and other prominent politicians.[49]

Many other British merchants never reached such heights but still were important for establishing communities and enabling the economy to grow. In the 1790s Caleb Thorniley left England with his family and a couple of others and settled on Ohio Company lands not far from Marietta. He wrote that there were already many other English families nearby with dozens more to come. While his son farmed, Caleb ran a tavern and could proudly report that "We are rising fast in riches. . . . We enjoy the fruits of our industry . . . and possess greatness as a Nation and freedom as individuals."[50]

Merchants were especially vital to early economies because they controlled credit and capital. Managing local markets and handling much of the goods, they exercised an influence far greater than their numbers might suggest.[51] Some young men got in on the action, as did John Christmas, who emigrated from Manchester in the 1790s when he was eighteen. After trading for a while in Pennsylvania he moved to Wooster in 1818 where he was one of the area's most prominent merchants. British immigrants seem to have been over-represented among these early pioneer merchants and traders, reflecting their origins in a more highly developed economy that provided them greater access to commercial experience and capital. They helped turn settlements into flourishing towns, accelerate the economic development of Ohio, and push the frontier line further west.[52]

British immigrants continued to be prominent in Ohio's early political development, and none more so than Edward Tiffin, Ohio's first state governor. Raised in the northern English city of Carlisle, where he was apprenticed in medicine, Tiffin immigrated with his parents and siblings to Virginia in 1783.

After further medical training and graduation from the University of Pennsylvania in 1789, he returned to Virginia where he practiced his profession and bought slaves. The young physician rose rapidly within the elite of Virginia society. He married Mary Worthington, the daughter of a wealthy landowner, converted to Methodism in 1790, and two years later was ordained by Francis Asbury—himself an English immigrant.

Tiffin's religious conversion opened his eyes to the sin of slavery. At the same time he saw the economic and political opportunities emerging on the booming frontier. So in 1798 he left for Ohio with his brother-in-law, Thomas Worthington, and friend Robert Lucas (both of whom also became Ohio governors). He also brought along his slaves, whom he manumitted and employed as free labor in his fields near Chillicothe—the political and economic center of the lower Scioto Valley, the future site for Ohio's constitutional convention, and Ohio's first capital.

In Chillicothe Tiffin earned a sterling reputation as a doctor and preacher, who preached "with much fervor and power." And with Worthington and William Henry Harrison (another former Virginian) he became one of the few elite citizens known as the "Virginia Clique," or "Chillicothe Junto," a powerful and able group who dominated Ohio's early politics. Soon Tiffin gained the attention of George Washington, who, in a letter to territorial governor St. Clair, wrote of "Dr. Tiffin's fairness of character in private and public life, together with knowledge of law, resulting from close application for a considerable time." With such a powerful recommendation St. Clair appointed Tiffin to the territorial court of common pleas. However, this did not stop Tiffin from criticizing his fellow British expatriot for promoting an elitist and authoritarian government. In contrast to St. Clair, Tiffin advocated a freer democracy for all white males. He was as staunchly Democratic-Republican as St. Clair was Federalist, and in the opposing viewpoints of these two British Buckeyes and their allies we have the origins of party politics in Ohio.[53]

Tiffin was a natural in Ohio politics. He was a brilliant conversationalist and enjoyed a reputation of the highest integrity. He served as Speaker of the territorial House of Representatives from 1799 to 1801 and in 1802 as president of Ohio's Constitutional Convention. He was possibly the most popular man in the entire Northwest Territory. In 1803, at age thirty-six, he was overwhelmingly elected the first Governor of Ohio, garnering at least 90 percent of the vote. Though his office was granted little executive power—in reaction to St. Clair's authoritarian instincts—Tiffin was still able to dominate much of Ohio's Democratic-Republican Party. Perhaps his most notable action as Governor was his suppression of the Burr-Blennerhassett expedition, for which Thomas Jefferson commended him. Also, Tiffin convinced the legislature that the common law—which St. Clair had adopted in 1795 and which put Ohio Territory firmly in the English legal tradition—was undemocratic and too reliant upon English medieval legal precedents, and that statute law should be adopted. While it helped his reputation at the time, unfortunately for his reputation today, Tiffin cast the deciding vote not to allow African Americans suffrage in Ohio. He resigned in 1807 to accept his election by Ohio's state legislature to the United States Senate, where he was a firm supporter of President Jefferson and promoted Ohio's development by securing appropriations for improving navigation on the Ohio River, extending the mail service, and surveying public lands.

Edward Tiffin returned to Chillicothe in 1809 to serve as speaker of the Ohio House of Representatives and then as Surveyor General. During this time, however, he lost much of his popularity because many voters unfairly saw him as one who talked democracy but practiced corruption with his elitist friends, a reaction that was caused by Tiffin's attempts to remove state judges who had tried to nullify acts of the state legislature. Furthermore, because of lingering elements of his conservative English culture, Tiffin could not keep pace with the growing democratic and egalitarian spirit in the young state. Accordingly, his influence waned. He died in Chillicothe in 1829 after a decade of illness and retirement from politics. Today the town of Tiffin, Seneca County, bears his name.[54]

Another English immigrant in Ohio's Constitutional Convention was the preacher, John W. Browne. He had fashioned his radical stance in England and went so far as to denounce St. Clair as an infidel and ridicule George Washington for his lack of true Christian faith. He became editor of *Liberty Hall* and will be discussed later in that capacity. Levin Belt, a lawyer in Chillicothe who served the Territorial Government, is another example of an English immigrant who held noteworthy judicial functions. Described as "bluff" and "hearty," and "very tall, broad shouldered, muscular, without surplus flesh," Belt was one of the territory's leading Federalist politicians whose popularity attracted the support of many Democratic-Republicans as well. In

Edward Tiffin from Carlisle, northern England, became Ohio's first governor and a member of the "Chillicothe Elite." From The Governors of Ohio, 2nd ed. (Columbus: Ohio Historical Society, 1969).

1802 he became the first prosecuting attorney for Ohio in Ross County. Then he was elected presiding judge of the second circuit, and later served as prosecuting attorney of Scioto County. In 1814 he was elected mayor of Chillicothe and at the same time served as Justice of the Peace, in which capacity his presence was "awe-inspiring."[55]

Wealthy and educated British immigrants like Tiffin, Browne, and Belt helped establish a political and economic elite that shaped and dominated the culture of Chillicothe. As both political leaders and major landowners they led the economic and agricultural development of the surrounding area.[56]

Immigrants from Britain were influential in Ohio's early development in other, less spectacular ways too. Englishman Edward Salt is credited with establishing the first permanent settlement in the township of Franklin, then part of Clermont County, where he built a cabin around 1796 and started a ferry business. In 1798 Englishman Houton Clarke settled in nearby Bethel and raised a family that was "one of the most influential" in the county for the next one hundred years.[57] Barnesville, in Belmont County, was founded by the family of James Barnes, who emigrated from England a generation earlier.[58] And in 1803 Davis Furnas, a Quaker who had arrived from Cumberland to South Carolina back in 1762, took his family into the remote wild forests of what became Wayne Township in Warren County. They suffered great difficulties in their attempt to prosper far from markets—the nearest mill was thirty miles distant—but they hung on and paved the way for more settlers.[59]

Unfortunately the harmony between the British-born and native-born Ohioans suffered a sharp if temporary jolt in 1807, and even more so in 1812. New hostilities emerged between Britain and America as the two nations jostled over control of the Great Lakes. The United States complained of the impressment of their sailors—many of whom were actually former British navy men who had deserted and joined the American navy. And with the anti-British Democratic-Republicans in control of the government under the presidency of James Madison, and the more pro-British Federalist Party—the party of Washington, Adams, and Hamilton—in decline, the renewal of military conflict was perhaps inevitable. The Federalists complained with some justification that the Democratic-Republican "War Hawks" were too eager for confrontation with Great Britain and did not see that the real threat came from Napoleonic France. The other party, however, saw the occasion more in terms of a "second war for independence" necessitated by the unfulfilled terms of the Treaty of Paris of 1783 and the unclear boundaries in the Great Lakes region. Britain, of course, was determined to protect its own interests in the region. The result was the

War of 1812, or "Mr. Madison's War," as the Federalist opponents called it. Bordering Lake Erie, Ohio could not escape the conflict.

As editor of *Liberty Hall*, John W. Browne demonstrated patriotism for his new country by denouncing the British and calling upon the militia to join General William Henry Harrison after the British and their Indian allies attacked Fort Meigs.[60] But for other British immigrants living in Ohio without American citizenship, the war revived the same suspicions of disloyalty that surfaced during the Revolution. Distrust grew after President Madison sent his war message to Congress on June 1, 1812, and declared that British subjects residing in the United States were enemy aliens. Accordingly, the government announced that all British subjects must report to the marshal of the territory or state in which they resided and provide this information: "the persons composing their families, the places of their residence and their occupations or pursuits; and whether, and at what time, they have made the application to the courts required by law, as preparatory to their naturalization." Newspapers published the notice and the alien reports were sent to the Department of State.[61] Though an unnecessary harassment, the alien reports do tell us something about these early British immigrants.

There is no way to determine how complete or accurate the alien reports from Ohio are. But, assuming the reports are accurate and representative, they shed at least a little light on the early British population in Ohio. Fifty-eight British heads of households are recorded—thirty English, seventeen Scottish, nine Welsh, and two described as hailing from "North Britain." Many others were never recorded in the reports; however, from the limited data it appears that the Scots were over-represented at this stage. They comprised nearly 30 percent of the British in Ohio, while they comprised less than 15 percent of the British population in 1821, according to the British census of that year. The data suggest that the Welsh were also over-represented—comprising 15 percent of the British in Ohio, but less than 6 percent of the entire British population in 1821. The English were under-represented—comprising 55 percent of the British in Ohio but about 80 percent in Britain.[62] Though this ratio of English, Scots, and Welsh cannot be assumed to characterize the British in Ohio with perfect accuracy, it does not appear that the English outnumbered the Scots and Welsh to the extent that they did in Britain. During this period the Scots and Welsh were more likely to migrate to Ohio than the English, but the English still dominated.

Exactly half of the fifty-eight heads of households of the British alien families were recorded as "farmers." Of these, twelve were Scots, a significant overrepresentation relative to the ten English who were farmers. Also, six of the nine Welsh were farmers, indicating that they were still predominantly agricultural (the other three were blacksmiths or bakers). In later decades the Welsh tended to come from more industrial backgrounds—especially mining and iron founding. While the Scots and Welsh were mostly in agriculture, only a third (ten of the twenty-nine) of the English in Ohio were farmers in 1812. This is significant. Among the English we see early diversification in occupations, which is a reflection of England's more diversified economy and earlier entry into the industrial revolution.

The nonfarming English in early Ohio came from various occupational backgrounds. There were three shoemakers, three weavers, a distiller, cabinet-maker, house joiner, upholsterer, cooper, tin-plate worker, lime burner, cotton manufacturer, and printer; there was also a tavern keeper. Altogether, a wide variety of British people diversified Ohio's early population. They provided fresh skills and services that promoted economic development.

Another safe generalization about British immigrants is that they were not the poorest of Britain's people. Though some could be characterized as "poor," few were very poor or destitute. Indeed, most seem to have been well above the poorest ranks, as suggested by their occupational diversity and contemporary observations. Many had savings and skills with which they could readily make a living.

During much of the century British immigrants were uniquely influenced by another factor that tended to prevent their poorest members from coming to America: the option for free passages to the colonies—which were mostly taken by the poorest emigrants—left the better-off to choose the United States. This was observed by an English resident in Cincinnati at the time: that the destitute English were sent to the colonies, while healthy and more prosperous workers went to America. And in 1836 the *Cincinnati Gazette* reported that the British immigrants to that city "were not destitute—they were mechanics and small farmers, a class that should be encouraged to come to the United States." Meanwhile, a German immigrant in the same city complained that German immigrants were "the lowest and most ignorant clan which tended to give the natives of the United States a bad reputation of Germany." And the Irish of Cincinnati were seen as "undoubtedly a turbulent element."[63]

British immigrants in Cincinnati who were poor could find aid among their relatively well-off fellow expatriates, who had formed ethnic societies in the city. The Scots established the Scots' Society of Cincinnati (1827) and a St. Andrews Society in Cleveland (1846) in order to assist fellow Scottish immigrants. And the English had established the St. George's Society of Cincinnati by 1837.

But few needed such assistance. They were the type of people that the United States intended to attract with its open immigration policy: self-sufficient, industrious, determined to succeed. Altogether, the British made positive contributions and, in spite of the Anglophobic fears of some Ohioans, they were readily and cordially welcomed.[64] In the nineteenth century, after the Napoleonic Wars ended in 1815 and the last war between Britain and America was over, Britons arrived in the young state of Ohio in truly significant numbers—in virtually every place and occupation.

2

The Nineteenth Century: Migration Patterns and Assimilation

"I consider the people of the United States as the portion of the English people charged with exploiting the forests of the new world."

Alexis de Tocqueville, *Democracy in America (1835)*

BRITISH BACKGROUND

It was the British century. After the final defeat of Napoleon at Waterloo in 1815, Great Britain was unchallenged on the high seas in addition to being the world's undisputed superpower. And though the loss of thirteen American colonies was an expensive humiliation, Britain still had a vast empire in North America, the Caribbean, Africa, South Asia, and other parts of the world. The British Empire was expanding and increasingly based upon trade rather than sheer military conquest. It was the largest empire the world has ever seen—an empire upon which the sun never set.

In addition to being the world's greatest imperial nation, Britain was the first industrial nation and for most of the century the greatest trading power. In the previous century Britain had pioneered modern iron and textiles production, the industrial use of coal, and the steam engine, and launched the industrial revolution that changed the world. While the great changes in manufacturing and technology disrupted countless lives and caused horrific social misery, it also produced new levels of national wealth, more power to the middle classes, and rising living standards for many. After repealing its protectionist Corn Laws in 1846 to become the world's only free-trade nation, Britain became the center of world trade and banking, home to the world's greatest merchant marine and navy. Not until after the unification of Germany in 1871 and the United States' rise as an industrial power was Britain seriously challenged in military or economic might. But even as late as 1880 the United Kingdom produced 41 percent of the manufactures that were traded in the world, compared to Germany's 19 percent and the United States' mere 3 percent.[1]

Under Queen Victoria the nation exuded success and confidence but also harbored some self-doubt as it dealt with the social ramifications of its rapid industrialization and urbanization. Progress was real, but so too were new problems. In the new industrialized economy, many people became victims of technological displacement and unemployment, and sensed that a future in Britain was not good. Others benefited from economic growth and realized they could seize even greater opportunities in America. Both mindsets—but especially the latter—characterize the Britons heading for the state of Ohio during the nineteenth century.

Emigration from Britain to America increased naturally in the early 1820s. In 1815 peace was restored in Europe and the British and Americans negotiated a conclusion to the War of 1812. Travel on the high seas was no longer subject to the caprices of war. In northern England and other textiles centers the end of war meant the end of military contracts for uniforms and other textile products, and the return of demobilized British soldiers stiffened competition for jobs. Many saw this as a propitious time to move to America.

The British had other reasons for coming to America, especially to places like Ohio. The state was getting positive attention in English newspapers, which reported its dynamic growth and potential for opportunities. As early as 1812 the *Times* reported "Great emigrations" to Ohio as people flooded in to take prime land. In the 1820s the newspaper included detailed descriptions of the state's flourishing population and trade, which was "increasing at an extraordinary rate, and on the completion of canals even this rate must be accelerated." They also reported the growth of schools and universities and made Ohio sound like the place of the future.[2] Such reports, when coupled with detailed information from emigrant guides, encouraged prospective emigrants.

More important were personal letters from people already in the state. Immigrant letters created networks of information that facilitated movement. For generations British people had come to North America and in the 1820s the networks of communication acted as funnels for new immigrants. Many British families had some contact with relatives or former neighbors who had emigrated before the Revolution. Expatriot Methodists commonly maintained ties with fellow worshipers in Britain. The personal information made emigration a more immediate and likely option to consider, and British migration to America surged accordingly.

In fact, migration to America increased so much that the United States government finally took steps to keep track of the multitudes pouring in. In 1819
the U.S. Congress passed a regulatory act that attempted to improve conditions
on ships and also required that—beginning in 1820—all captains arriving from
any foreign port must deliver to the collector of customs a sworn list of the
names of all passengers, together with their sex, age, occupation, nationality,
and country of destination. Fortunately for historians, these passenger lists contain reliable data indicating the social and economic characteristics of these
people. Though the lists (with only a few exceptions) do not identify those people going specifically to Ohio, they do offer much information about the British
immigrant population as a whole—the vast majority of whom were going to
northern states. From this information we can make some generalizations
about the British people heading for the Buckeye State.

Detailed research of the passenger lists of 1831 offers some findings that can
be applied to Ohio. Emigration from the British Isles increased between 1829
and 1833. According to official statistics, between eleven thousand and twenty-
nine thousand English, Scots, and Welsh sailed for the United States in each of
these years; but the actual numbers were even higher because many Britons
were counted as Irish, and many others landed in Canada and crossed the border undetected. These years were quite favorable for most British farmers because prices for their produce were comfortably high, though this was also the
time of the Swing Riots, when Britain's farm laborers destroyed the new farm
machinery they deemed threatening to their livelihoods. During these years of
relative agricultural prosperity, farmers were overrepresented among British
emigrants to the United States, forming nearly 20 percent of the adult male migrants but less than 9 percent of the labor force in Britain. Farm laborers—who
were typically much poorer than farmers—were underrepresented on the lists,
though some are probably among those described as farmers.

Like the farmers, preindustrial craft workers (people whose work was not
seriously affected by industrial change—artisans such as building trades workers, miners, woodworkers, and so on) also immigrated in significant numbers
during the early 1830s. So did industrial workers who experienced modernizing
change such as textile workers and iron workers. In fact, about half of the adult
males whose occupation was recorded on the lists were skilled industrial workers. (The figure for Ohio would be less, because many of the industrial immigrants stayed in the more industrial eastern states.) Also dramatic is the movement of families. More than three-fourths of all British immigrants traveled
with family members, a higher figure than for any other immigrant group during the antebellum period.[3] Though these estimates are for the British entering

the United States generally, we extrapolate that immigrants coming to Ohio during this period were varied in their occupational background. A large contingent were farmers. Others were industrial workers (many of whom would farm in Ohio). Many had some financial resources. They could travel as families and afford multiple passage tickets. They were generally not desperate people, but had skills and probably savings with which they could make a successful transition to Ohio life.[4]

During the 1840s British immigrants to the United States came disproportionately from the less developed and more rural areas of the west and south— from counties like Cornwall, Devon, Somerset, Dorset, and Sussex. Preindustrial craftsmen predominated, though farmers and those who intended to farm were still an important part of the migrant stream. The late 1840s, also known as the "hungry forties" for the catastrophic potato famine, food shortages in many parts of the British Isles, and increasing unemployment in some sectors of the textiles industries, saw increased British migration to America (though not on the Irish scale).

But then, at midcentury, Britain entered its famous "mid-Victorian boom," in which the economic troubles of the preceding years seemed to "vanish as if by magic." Thanks in part to free trade, the resulting fall of food prices, and a booming export economy that provided more and more manufactured goods for the Atlantic world, Britain enjoyed one of the most prosperous periods in its history, which lasted for about a generation. The Great Exhibition of 1851, held in the fabulous Crystal Palace in Hyde Park, heralded Britain's primacy. Here the world was invited to display its best products and achievements. The British stole the show with their astonishing array of technological and industrial inventions, but the Americans also displayed impressive labor-saving technical devices, a positive result of the higher cost of labor in the United States. The 1851 Census also showed that Britain had become the world's first truly industrial and urban nation, as over half of its people worked in manufacturing and lived in cities. And remarkably, this period of rapid industrial growth and urbanization was accompanied not by rising crime and social strife, but by less. It was "an Age of Equipoise," in the words of historian William Burn.[5] For most people life was getting better and the future in Britain looked promising, though for others still trapped in urban slums or rural poverty the "boom" was an illusion.

One might expect that during these times of improvement emigration tapered off as people stayed at home to take advantage of the rising social and economic conditions. But just the opposite happened. Emigration increased during the midcentury period. Some farmers found the adjustment to the

falling farm prices difficult, but thanks to free trade they could envision farming in America and exporting food to their old country at good prices. Agriculture in Ohio and other states in the Old Northwest was expanding at midcentury, attracting British people who apparently used their growing prosperity in
Britain as a means to emigrate and buy land. America had so much to offer to
British farmers, especially land.

As for the industrial workers who emigrated during the prosperous midcentury, they do not appear to have been suffering technological displacement or
unemployment. Engineers and skilled machinists, in great demand in Britain,
greatly outnumbered the distressed foundry workers and especially the handloom weavers. Generally the industrial emigrants were not distressed in Britain,
and many of them were motivated by a promising future in America—including the vision of farming one's own land. In fact, an astonishing variety of
British emigrants with little or no prior agricultural experience successfully
took up farming in the United States during this period.[6]

During the late 1860s and early 1870s, and again in the 1880s, the flow and
rate of British migration to America increased. During the later years, especially, more were leaving from urban areas and were composed increasingly of
building trades workers, miners, and unskilled laborers, and most were traveling as single individuals. Those going to Ohio during this period included more
miners and steelworkers as well as building trades workers, but even then surprising numbers ended up on a farm.[7]

The powerful attraction of land explains much of the British migration to
America during the nineteenth century. In Ohio one could buy land for the cost
of renting it for a few years in Britain. And to many people of the eighteenth
and nineteenth centuries, land ownership meant independence and freedom.
They acted upon long-range plans and, even when Britain's economy was ro-
bust, saw a brighter future for themselves and their children across the Atlantic.
Through the first half of the century they migrated overwhelmingly with family members and many had skills or experience in farming. They were capable
and determined to make the most of their lives, and they were willing to endure
a rigorous voyage and journey to fulfill their goals.[8]

VOYAGE AND JOURNEY

Moving from Britain to Ohio in the early nineteenth century was a formative, often traumatic experience that reveals much about the immigrants' self-
sacrifice and character. The financial cost was very considerable, especially as
most of them took family members along. Steerage passages cost about five or
six pounds during the 1820s and 1830s, less for children. Then in the 1840s the

infamous timber ships were built to take American lumber back to Britain. Captains essentially used humans as ballast on the voyage to America at reduced fares, which fell just in time for the Irish and other impoverished people who otherwise could not have afforded the passage. During the midcentury, steerage passages from Liverpool to New York fell to a little over three pounds (roughly seventeen dollars), though provisions were not necessarily included. But there were also other costs: transport to the port of embarkation and to the final destination, not to mention the lost wages during a journey that lasted at least a month and often two or more. And unless they had help waiting for them in Ohio, there were necessary expenses to establish their new home. It seems, therefore, that five pounds (twenty-five dollars) was about the minimum cost per individual. It took at least one hundred dollars for a family of four to get to Ohio. Thus British migration was quite selective: normally the immigrants were not the poorest but those with some skills, resources, and savings. They were just what the young state of Ohio needed for its development.

The experience at the port of embarkation—most often Liverpool—was chaotic and stressful. Accommodations were expensive and cramped. Thieves preyed upon unsuspecting emigrants, many of them "runners" who presented themselves as employees of the shipping company and stole the emigrants' baggage. In such bewildering situations at the port, emigrants could make bad decisions. For the Ohio-bound Beaham family of Worcestershire, leaving for America started out disastrously. Upon reaching Liverpool and boarding their ship, the parents, assured by the captain that the ship would not sail for several hours, did some last-minute shopping for provisions, only to find the ship—and the baby they had left on board in someone else's care—gone on their return. Sailing on the next available ship, the couple took four weeks to make the voyage to New York and another three weeks to find their baby, who had nearly perished. After recuperating for a few days, the reunited family headed for the Cleveland area where they settled down.[9]

In the age of sailing ships the transatlantic voyage was often so long and horrible that it is impossible to comprehend fully today. The average sailing from Liverpool to New York took a month or more, but bad weather or bad ships doubled or even tripled the ordeal. Nightmarish accounts were all too common in the journey from Britain to Ohio in the early nineteenth century. Mary Hemminger was a ten-year-old girl from London when she sailed with her parents in the fall of 1822. Theirs was a terrible voyage. It took nearly three months to arrive in Philadelphia because storms broke the rudder, leaving them "drifting at the mercy of the wind and waves," until some of the sailors managed to make repairs under water, several of them perishing in the attempt.[10]

John Hoyle's ship took an astounding one hundred days to make the crossing and was entirely out of provisions by the time it landed.[11] Elizabeth Mervin took four months to join her husband, John, in 1850 because she was shipwrecked three times before finally making it safely on her fourth voyage.[12] And Sarah and James Willment, a young married couple from Somerset, set sail for America in 1832 and were on the water for eleven weeks—the last three without food. Near Newfoundland they obtained mackerel from fishermen and lived off that for the rest of the voyage, only to land in New York during a cholera epidemic that had all but depopulated the city. After some time in New York they set out for Ohio in a covered wagon and were on the road for twenty-one days before they reached their destination.[13]

Dramatic journeys like these were not uncommon. Some immigrants were shipwrecked and rescued but lost all of their possessions and arrived in Ohio penniless. Others buried family members at sea. And of course most if not all were at some point racked by terrible seasickness. Today it is scarcely possible to imagine what it was like to endure weeks, even months, on a poorly venti-lated, foul-smelling, and dangerously ill-equipped sailing ship, and being sick for much of the time. One Englishman, D. Griffiths Jr., who spent two years in Ohio in the early 1830s and wrote a guidebook to inform prospective immi-grants heading for the Western Reserve, captured the trauma of the voyage in his description:

> Morning comes, but not a word is uttered, much less a joke; not a passen-ger stirs. Hear what a hurly there is above! No hope of lighting a fire such a morning as this. By and bye, a poor fellow, enfeebled with sickness, stag-gers to the ladder, and if he doesn't get beaten back by a breaker, dashing down the hatchway, he gains the deck. But, on deck every thing is wet, cold, and comfortless. He finds no pity there; the waves drench him, the ship shakes him, and the sailors laugh at him: if he has read Milton, he may feel disposed to soliloquize in the language attributed to the fallen Archangel: "Me miserable! Which way shall I fly?"[14]

Understandably, such voyages made permanent emigrants out of some who had intended to return to Britain but could never face boarding another sailing ship. But amazingly, some of the hardier immigrants seemed unaffected by the ordeal. Englishman Thomas Wharton, who sailed from Hull in 1829 to join his father already in Ohio, had some terrible bouts with sickness; still, he recorded —perhaps with a selective memory—that, "in spite of sea sickness, and the weariness of sea-life our time upon the whole passed cheerfully and pleasantly enough." And even Griffiths admitted that in better weather "all troubles were forgotten, . . . good humour revived," and the passengers were able to amuse themselves with a book, some tobacco, or a dance to the fiddle and flute.[15] Still, for most the sailing was a formidable undertaking indeed.

The end of the voyage did not necessarily mean the end of the ordeal because the trip from the port and eastern states to Ohio often had its own perils and miseries. Once people had crossed the Atlantic they could be lulled into complacency that the dangerous part of the sailing was over, only to discover that Lake Erie could be even more terrifying than the ocean. William Babbage, an emigrant from Devonshire, for example, landed in New York in 1834 with only $2.50 in his pocket and with no friends to help him. After working in Rochester as a farm laborer for a short time he left for Ohio via Buffalo and sailed on Lake Erie during an equinoctial storm that terrified him and the other passengers. Many said it was the worst storm ever witnessed on the Lake. The captain was lucky enough to turn back for safety and try again several days later.[16]

From the earliest years of settlement well into the first half of the nineteenth century, the most common way to get to Ohio—especially the southern regions—was to start out in Pittsburgh and float down the Ohio River in an ark or flatboat. The beauty and majesty of the River was appreciated by many and often described in poetic terms. The English traveler and writer Charles August Murray described it thus: "The Ohio is indeed a noble and majestic stream, flowing between high and undulating banks teeming with an profusion of foliage, which includes every verdant hue from the willow to the cedar. . . . This perpetual fringe of verdure, together with the equable and quiet nature of the current, gives a tone of beauty and repose to this river that I have never seen equaled."[17]

The Ohio River journey had its own challenges, though nothing like that of sailing the ocean or hacking one's way through a dense forest. For British travelers it was a mixture of adventure and excitement, but also a measure of tedium and work. William Cobbett, the "radical" journalist who published the *Weekly Political Register* in England and lived in the United States from 1817 to 1819, published *A Year's Residence in the United States of America.* In this famous book he included the observations of his friend and colleague, Thomas Hulme, a successful master bleacher from Yorkshire who detested high English taxation and the reactionary government of the years after the defeat of Napoleon. Hulme traveled to Ohio in 1817 to locate a new home for his family of nine children and recorded his experience on the Ohio River, which was in most ways typical. "Leave Pittsburgh," he wrote in early June, "and set out in a thing called an ark, which we buy for the purpose, down the Ohio. We have, besides, a small skiff, to tow the ark and go ashore occasionally. This ark, which would stow away eight persons, close packed, is a thing by no means pleasant to travel in, specially at night. It is strong at bottom, but may be compared to an orange-box bowed over at top, and so badly made as to admit a boy's hand to steal the oranges: it is proof against the river, but not against the rain." The following day, "floating down the Ohio, at the rate of four miles an hour," Hulme experienced "lighting, thunder, rain and hail pelting upon us. The hail-stones as large as English hazle-nuts. Stop at Steubenville all night. A nice place; has more stores than taverns, which is a good sign."[18]

Along his trip down the Ohio Hulme met other English people and must have been struck by the prevalence and prominence of his fellow countrymen. An English officer was aboard the ark on the early part of the journey. At first Hulme distrusted him, taking him "for a spy hired to way-lay travellers," until being assured of his integrity. Later on the journey the party was joined by a "watchful back-woodsman" who had come from Sherwood Forest to America forty years prior. Hulme found him "a very entertaining companion" and seems to have been fascinated by his transformation into a rough American character. After arriving in Cincinnati at midnight in mid-June and tying their ark to a log along the river, this older English immigrant discovered that the boat had broken loose and saved it from floating far past its destination. When Hulme finally made it to the city he had traveled a total of five hundred miles on the river and had spent only fourteen dollars for all of his costs, after his party of nine travelers sold the ark they no longer needed.[19]

Englishmen were commonly seen floating down the Ohio River to their western destinations. They participated in piloting the boat and procuring food on a very long journey and in the process began their assimilation as British Buckeyes. They took turns steering the ark and shot squirrels and pigeons for their food.[20] Some British travelers on the Ohio were less charitable than Hulme and Cobbett and found their American passengers too rough and uncouth. Englishman Thomas Hamilton described with disgust the eating habits, bluntness, and lack of learning of the American passengers on his boat, but generally, the British and Americans got along well on the journey.[21]

Floating down the Ohio River was not the only option for early immigrants; for many, hiking was the way to go. Some of the poorer immigrants walked the entire distance from the Atlantic port or from Lake Erie if they traveled via the Erie Canal. The strength and courage of these people is remarkable in hindsight and indicates something of the character and fortitude of these new Ohioans. John Parrott emigrated from Somersetshire in 1841 and arrived in Huron

County "with one cent in my pocket," he recalled, "with which I bought a cracker." Parrott then "conquered the dragon of adversity" by working for a local farmer for eight dollars per month, and then by trekking to the gold fields of California, where he earned his money not by digging gold but by working for high wages. Wise investments and hard work enabled him to eventually become one of the wealthiest landowners in Greenwich, Huron County.[22]

The age of sailing ships, then, witnessed migrations from Britain to Ohio that were often heroic. Steamships began to dominate the transatlantic emigrant trade in the late 1850s and virtually took over in the 1860s. By 1867 over 90 percent of the passengers who left English ports for America took steamships. The new ships made a huge difference. They were safer and better equipped—though conditions could still be miserable and dangerous. The steamship that carried the Ohio-bound Middleton family from Kent, England, across the Atlantic in 1869 was wrecked off of the banks of Newfoundland and drifted five hundred miles back toward Europe with three feet of water in the hold until at the last minute they were rescued.[23] But generally steamships were an enormous improvement. Above all they were faster, taking only ten to fourteen days to cross from Liverpool to New York. And though the steamship passage ticket was more expensive, the quicker voyage meant that there was less time in lost wages—rendering the real cost of the voyage cheaper for some passengers. Perhaps most significantly, the shorter and less unpleasant voyage made it more thinkable to return to Britain if the United States did not meet one's expectations. In effect, the steamship lowered the high "migration threshold" that had intimidated prospective migrants during the age of sail.

The new steamships and easier voyage were a major reason for the rising numbers of all immigrants to America in the late nineteenth century. By the 1870s and 1880s, Britons more easily experimented with life in Ohio and other places, knowing that a return was always feasible. The so-called "birds of passage"—seasonal migrants who worked for a period in America and then lived the rest of the year in Britain—also increased in number. Remarkably, British immigrants of all occupations made frequent return trips to Britain in the late nineteenth century: to marry someone from their former village, attend funerals of loved ones who had stayed in Britain, or simply to visit the place of their youth and to see old friends.[24] And of course some returned to Britain for good, having found Ohio not to their liking or because they had a short-term sojourn in mind all along. During the late nineteenth century, perhaps as many as 40 percent of British immigrants to America returned to Britain (a return rate far higher than Dutch or German immigrants), though the percentages for Ohio specifically were probably significantly lower than that. With the exception of miners and quarrymen, many of whom were seasonal migrants, most of those who came to Ohio had come to stay or move on to western states.[25]

Early British immigrants to Ohio frequently used chain migration. Though the English did not have ethnic communities to join in America, they did often use a network of contacts with other English settlers, which allowed them to obtain their first place of residence and occupation with greater ease. Such was the case of the Mighill brothers, who began migrating from Brighton in 1830 to Ohio and went from place to place in the state working for other English immigrants. This strategy gave the brothers extraordinary mobility and occupational flexibility in their settlement in Ohio.[26]

Apparently, a significant majority followed other family members or friends who had preceded them, sometimes using passage money remitted to them from America. The extended family, especially, was the main network that brought Britons to Ohio. Letters to Britain contained detailed information about American life that usually amounted to encouragement. Enticing, almost unbelievable stories about Americans having meat three times a day, earning wages that were double or triple those in Britain, or having a political voice and freedom from high taxes, paved the way for more immigrants.[27]

Some newcomers lived with earlier immigrants and worked for them until they could get established, a strategy commonly used by today's immigrants. This arrangement worked well and enabled many to settle in America effectively with less homesickness and a gradual immersion into American life. Such arrangements, though, could produce their own tensions and problems, especially when the terms for work were not well defined. In the early 1850s, for example, English immigrant John Robinson advanced fifty dollars to Thomas Pepper for his passage from England to Ohio. Pepper agreed to work for Robinson for room and board and twelve dollars per month, but after he allegedly caused the death of a mare and yoke of oxen worth $225, Robinson demanded compensation and refused to pay wages. Pepper left to become a boilermaker's apprentice, sued for his wages, and the court awarded him only five dollars. Conflicts between English immigrants regarding land sales also occasionally showed up in court, as happened with Richard Mosey and John Haywood in 1832. Mosey claimed that Haywood refused final payment on a land contract in order to keep possession, and the case was settled out of court.[28]

Another case of conflict between English immigrants in Ohio involves Philip Mighill, who came from Brighton to Aurora in 1837 and got established by working as a farmhand for an old family friend, George Bartlett. Mighill complained that Bartlett "was allways cross with me. He wanted to play Englishman on me but it would not do here amongst Yankees—I am a Yankee myself. George . . . left me to rake some hay. I did not rake it all before a shower came. When he came home he was cross and told me to look for another place." Later, Mighill accused Bartlett of dishonesty and ingratitude: "George Bartlett kept me to work for him for fore months for witch he never thanked me but when I left him he told people that I worked for him to pay my passage out here. I hope I never shall see the wretches face again."[29] Clearly, the widely used transatlantic network of English immigrants helped many get established, but not without its share of personal problems.

Another problem in chain migration was the tendency of some letter writers to exaggerate America's charms and create images and expectations that were unrealistic, leading to disappointment and regret for the new immigrant. William Corlett, from the Isle of Man, arrived with idealized visions of Ohio. After settling in Newburgh, Cuyahoga County, in 1842, he wrote back to his brother: "This country is a fine country . . . not however so rich as some of our good friends wrote to us the first years when we heard that bread grew on trees & ginger root was the worst weed here."[30] To avoid disappointments like these, many letters contain the disclaimer that persons had to decide for themselves, or that satisfied people ought to stay in Britain. But generally accurate information did get back to Britain and made America practically irresistible—especially when Ohio's rich and readily available lands were described.

Occasionally British immigrants came to Ohio without much prior planning. For the London-born John Adams, who enjoyed life as a British sailor, coming to America occurred quite by accident. His ship was wrecked off the coast of Cuba and Adams managed to swim ashore. From there he made his way to the United States and settled down to farm in Columbiana County. He then moved to Carroll County, purchased eighty acres of government land, and raised a family of farmers who prospered handsomely in Ohio.[31]

But the great majority made long-term plans. When the sources provide details about their migration we find that many planned their migration very carefully indeed, some to the extent of visiting the new country first and making the decision later. Angus McDonald was one of them. A twenty-year-old man from Aberdeen, he came to London seeking his fortune, but found the metropolis a "boisterous maelstrom" and so went to Liverpool where he found work in a foundry. At the great port he could hardly avoid all the excited talk about life in America. So he returned to Aberdeen, married Kate Dinwiddie—a young woman from his native village—and in February of 1840 set sail alone for America "for the purpose of making observations of the country, and with the design of returning to Scotland should he not be favorably impressed." Upon landing in New York he heard great things about Massillon, so he headed there and immediately found employment at good wages working as a foreman in a foundry. Fully satisfied, he sent for Kate and the child that she bore him during his absence, and the family was happily reunited. In Massillon McDonald was viewed as a classic Highland Scot. He wore the kilt and spoke with a heavy Scottish brogue as he expounded the work of Robert Burns and read his poetry in public.[32]

John Bright was an English immigrant who planned his migration to Ohio with great care and a high degree of selectivity, after he was "fired by the impulse" to come to America. Before taking his family to America he made no fewer than four solo trips to North America to scout out the best place. Finally, on his fifth trip he took along his family to stay. Bright chose Ohio, but still his high standards and determination to find the very best place to farm kept him restless for a while. First the family settled in Goshen, in Clermont County, but not being fully satisfied they came to Clinton County a short time later to take up a farm near Martinsville. Still not satisfied, the family bought a different farm near Westboro, where they spent the rest of their days.[33]

It is also evident that women were often at the heart of migration decisions. Unfortunately, sources too often focus on the male heads of households. Women are usually left in the shadows and their roles and personalities obfuscated. But their roles and stories are not less worthy than those of men. Though Victorian Britain and America were highly patriarchal societies, the process of transatlantic migration was very often a team effort between more or less equal partners. Any assumption that British women were passive in migration decisions or were reluctant spouses, being dragged across the ocean by their more adventurous husbands, must be avoided. In fact there are some cases of wives coming to America in spite of their husbands' refusals and lack of courage.[34]

The independence and resourcefulness of women often emerged with the death of a husband. Ann Beelby Wardell farmed in Yorkshire with her husband, but after his death in 1849 she decided to leave England with her children and settle in Pickaway County. She sent her oldest son ahead to find work and the best available land and then followed with the rest of the family.[35]

Many British women in Ohio were enthusiastic additions to the state's population who added color to their communities and exercised a great deal of influence. Amy Wilshire Bright and her husband were Cambridgeshire farmers who settled in Westboro, Clinton County, in 1868. Amy was something of a legend in this part of Ohio. The Brights were raised Anglicans but became Methodists in Ohio and were among the congregation's most ardent members. Amy was a person "of wonderful personality" and "sunny disposition" who was

well known throughout the Westboro area, where she "wielded a strong influence in her community." She also possessed a voice so wonderful that she was
celebrated as an oral reader in the community, reading the Bible, poems, and
literature. As a girl she had entertained "the great ladies of Queen Victoria's
court" because of her wonderful voice and charming manner.[36] And one merely
has to reflect on our story of Mad Ann Bailey (chapter 1) to realize that some of
the British women were tough and formidable and hardly the passive type.
Mary Hemminger, a ten-year-old girl from London who settled with her parents on a pioneer farm near Bucyrus in the 1820s, seemed to relish danger and
hardship. She was known as the "cow-boy" of the family and spent much time
in the wilderness, "many times for days and nights in the woods."[37]

ORIGINS AND SETTLEMENT PATTERNS

Between statehood and the Civil War the British entered Ohio in steady
numbers. According to the 1850 U.S. Census, there were 19,509 English, 4,003
Scots, and 5,045 Welsh in Ohio—a total of 28,557 British Buckeyes. Using the
1850 U.S. Census and the 1851 U.K. Census together reveals some interesting patterns. In 1851, 81 percent of the British population was English, 14 percent Scottish, and 5 percent Welsh. According to the U.S. Census of 1850, 68 percent of
Ohio's British immigrants were English, 14 percent Scottish, and 18 percent
Welsh.[38] By midcentury the Welsh were the only British immigrants who settled
in Ohio in proportions greater than what they comprised in the general British
population. The Scots came to Ohio in proportions identical to what they comprised in Britain at the time, while the English were considerably underrepresented. This can be attributed in part to the fact that the English were showing
a greater interest in other states at the time, most notably Wisconsin and Illinois. They were also settling in eastern states earlier in the century because they
were closer to major ports and could seize industrial opportunities. The English underrepresentation was also observed in the data on British aliens in Ohio
during the War of 1812, as noted in chapter 1.

Meanwhile, the Welsh were still coming to Ohio in overrepresented proportions (as was also observed in the 1812 data) because many Welsh communities
had been established in Ohio and the Welsh were seizing new opportunities in
Ohio's burgeoning coal and iron industries (this will be explored in future
chapters).

Some general observations about the precise origins of the immigrants can
be linked to their basic settlement patterns in Ohio. Because census data and the
passenger lists say virtually nothing about their exact origins, we turn to the

county histories. Much can be learned about who the British Buckeyes were by examining a sample of 602 English, Scots, and Welsh immigrants who settled in Ohio during the late eighteenth and nineteenth centuries and whose biographies appear in the county histories (see the Appendix). Among the English the West Country was well represented in Ohio. Cornwall, Somerset, and especially Devon sent significant numbers to the Buckeye State, as they did to other states in the Old Northwest. Cornish miners were mobile and in search of fresh opportunities, as were Devonshire farmers and artisans, who had a tradition of migration and access to information that made their movement more likely.[39]

Perhaps most interesting is the prominence of migrants from high-wage agricultural counties in southeastern England, particularly Kent and Lincolnshire. This is another reflection of how people with relatively adequate earnings could afford migration, but also an example of how farmers of these heavy soils were vulnerable to the fall in wheat prices that occurred after the repeal of the Corn Laws. And like the West Country, the southeast had a long migration tradition that produced migrants when American opportunities rose and English ones fell.

One of the most dramatic findings from the county histories is the huge representation of people from England's high-wage industrial counties, dwarfing that from the low-wage agricultural counties. Immigrants from Lancashire and Staffordshire were very common in Ohio, as were people from the London area, which offered various industrial jobs at relatively high wages. Immigrants from the northern counties of Northumberland, Durham, and Nottinghamshire were all prominent among the British Buckeyes. Their occupations included even more craftsmen than modernizing industrial workers, and quite a number of those in commerce and the professions.[40] It appears that the more prosperous parts of the country were contributing more of the migrants because generally more people in those places had the resources and perhaps the initiative to migrate.

For the Scots and Welsh as well, some observations can be made that are consistent with those made for the English. Welsh and Scottish industrial counties contributed the great majority of immigrants to Ohio. This was especially true of the Welsh. On the one hand, this is to be expected because the industrial counties had greater population and thus greater numbers of prospective emigrants. But also, these areas contained people who had recently left agricultural areas for industrial ones, and many of these were susceptible to making another migratory step to America. They were likely to have had industrial or other nonagricultural experience; but this did not necessarily mean that they would take up industrial work in Ohio. As later chapters will show, the Buckeye State offered both agricultural and industrial opportunities to Britons from both agricultural and industrial backgrounds. The appeal of both forms of work is noticeable in their settlement patterns in Ohio.

Altogether, the origins of British immigrants in Ohio show some continuity with the four migration waves that marked the colonial era. Eastern and southern counties were still prominent sources of emigrants, as was London, the North Midlands (especially Lancashire and West Yorkshire), northern England counties, and the borderlands of northern England (especially Northumberland) and the Scottish lowlands. The most striking difference for Ohio was the greater flow from Wales. Much had changed since the earlier centuries; but British migration retained much of its origin patterns. The earlier British immigrants were shaped by the great events of their generations, particularly those about religion and the nature of politics, and carried their issues and concerns to America. The later immigrants to Ohio were concerned mainly with modernity and industrialization, and they also carried these issues and their experience to their new homeland.

For the settlement patterns of British immigrants in Ohio we can turn to the work that geographer Greg Rose has conducted with the 1850 U.S. Census. Map 1 indicates where the British were located in 1850. Map 2 is especially revealing because it shows the counties where British immigrants lived in percentages greater than the statewide average. On the one hand, the British—especially the English—settled in patterns not very different than the Ohioan population generally. But in contrast with other immigrant groups—who clustered tightly in areas where their ethnic group had become established, where one's native tongue could be heard and early adjustments could be made—the British were almost everywhere. They were overrepresented in thirty-four of Ohio's eighty-eight counties. Their common language, culture, and relative ease of settlement are apparent.

The maps also reflect the fact that British immigrants were prominent among Ohio's earliest settlers. They hugged the Ohio, Great and Little Miami, and Muskingum rivers, as well as Lake Erie, because these natural highways took them into the interior before there were extensive roads, turnpikes, or railroads. They stayed near the rivers because they were the only means of transporting their goods and themselves to markets and towns. They also settled along the canals, which were built in part by British capital, engineering skills, and to a lesser extent the labor of the immigrants themselves. Along these early transportation routes many of the British established their new homes. These were ideal places to be a farmer or perhaps an artisan.

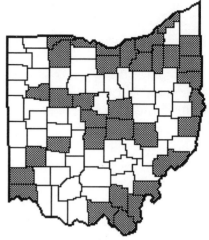

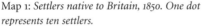

Map 1: *Settlers native to Britain, 1850. One dot represents ten settlers.*

Map 2: *Counties with settlers native to Britain over the statewide average of 4.11 percent of the immigrant population, 1850.*

In some counties at midcentury, British immigrants formed significant percentages of the population: nearly 9 percent in Jackson County (many of these were Welsh), and roughly 5 percent of the population of Cuyahoga and Lorain Counties were born in Britain. Lake, Erie, Portage, and Summit Counties were not far behind, and they show how the Lake Erie route and emerging industries in northeast Ohio drew British immigrants. Gallia and Meigs Counties also had noticeable numbers of British immigrants, especially Welsh, which was a legacy of the Ohio River route and the early settlers who located themselves there.

At midcentury the English were also concentrated in the important towns and cities—especially Cincinnati, Cleveland, Columbus, Gallipolis, and East Liverpool, which were places of commerce and early industry, offering openings to skilled and professional immigrants (see map 3). As the century progressed, these places blossomed and the British became even more likely to fill positions in the professions, commerce, and skilled crafts. And, of course, many farmed in areas near the growing cities. About 40 percent of the English in Ohio lived in the Western Reserve, which shows their cultural affinity with this part of the state, which was most thoroughly New England in character, and where English people might feel most at home.[41]

Map 3 indicates that the English were a little less likely than other Ohioans to be in some of the least developed counties. This may reflect a tendency to be

Map 3: *Settlers native to England, 1850. One dot represents ten settlers.*

Map 4: *Settlers native to Scotland, 1850. One dot represents ten settlers.*

"fillers-in" at more established farming areas where they could obtain cleared or partially cleared land. But surprising numbers did buy unimproved virgin land from the government or took over claims that were minimally improved and went to the Ohio frontier to live lives of incredible hardship, adventure, and often success (see chapters 3 and 4). Clearly, the English were widely diffused in their settlement and made their mark on Ohio history and culture. By midcentury they numbered roughly twenty thousand, which was 13.3 percent of the immigrant population, and their numbers and influence only grew as the century progressed.

The Scots—who in 1850 numbered about four thousand in Ohio—also settled in many parts of the state. Though some retained ethnic characteristics, like their distinctive brogue and sometimes a kilt, their use of the English language enabled them to blend in with the larger society. According to Maps 3 and 4, the English and Scots shared similar settlement patterns, though the Scots showed less interest than the English or Welsh in settling in the Columbus area. This may reflect their greater preference for farming during the midcentury. The Scots were less likely than the Welsh to form clusters, but they still did in certain places. Barlow, in Washington County, was a settlement composed largely of Scots, as was the "Scotch Settlement" near Wellsville in Madison and Yellow Creek Townships of Columbiana County. Most of the immigrants there were

Map 5: *Settlers native to Wales, 1850. One dot represents ten settlers.*

Highlanders and some of the earliest settlers in the region, having arrived in 1802. Also, in 1823 over 150 Scots arrived in Marietta in response to a pamphlet published in Scotland the previous year by landowner Nahum Ward, who extolled the virtues of that part of the state. Unfortunately, they arrived during an epidemic of what was probably yellow fever, and some died. The survivors bought Ward's lands in Wesley and Barlow townships, and more Scots joined them over the next decade.[42]

Welsh settlement patterns reveal just how different they were from the English and Scots, a difference attributable largely to their language and tighter ethnic cohesion. They were less diffuse than the English in their settlement. The English, like other Ohio residents, were concentrated in Cincinnati and Cleveland and settled in many counties. They included both urban and rural people with a wide array of occupations—crafts, industry, mining, mercantile activities, and farming. The Scots were more inclined to stay in eastern counties and along the lakeshore. But the Welsh obviously clustered in central, southwestern, and especially southeastern counties (see map 5). The trend reflects their early migratory history, ethnic clustering around their churches and chapels, and especially their predominance in the iron industry in Lawrence and Gallia Counties, which will be covered in more detail in chapters 3 and 5.

RELIGIOUS CULTURE

One important reason why most British immigrants meshed with Ohio society so readily and settled in so many places was because they shared religious denominations and institutions with the Anglo American majority. With the exception of some Welsh, they did not have to establish new churches or share their religious lives only with fellow immigrants, as did many German, Dutch, Swedes, and others. In the churches there was an instant familiarity and fellowship among Ohioans and Britons. Many British who settled in Ohio were Methodists or some other type of nonconformist. Those who appear in the county histories and had their religion recorded were overwhelmingly nonconformist. A mere 13 percent were Anglican or Episcopal. Over a quarter were

Presbyterian (about half of these were not Scottish and therefore noncon-formists). Fully a third of the others were Methodists—mainly Methodist Epis-copal, Calvinist Methodist, or simply Methodist. One in ten were Baptists; 5 percent were Congregationalist. There were only a few Quakers, Catholics, and Jews. Altogether, about three-fourths of the British immigrants to Ohio were nonconformists and had little official association with the established church.[43]

Their nonconformity helps explain their emigration. Nonconformists came to America more willingly because—especially early in the century—they were sometimes discriminated against with regard to public office, university admis-sion, and land tenure. They emigrated more readily because the ties keeping them in Britain were weaker. Meanwhile, the tradition of Methodist migration to America provided a network of people, information, and assistance to facil-itate the arrival of newcomers. And Methodists were perhaps the best-equipped denomination on the frontier because they had an effective organization, an ea-gerness to help each other get established, and popular doctrines.[44]

British Quakers clustered together because some found it hard to integrate with the larger community. The English Quaker Thomas Shillitoe, born in London in 1754, came to Ohio in 1826 at the age of seventy-two to visit and preach to fellow Friends in Belmont and Jefferson Counties. He and other Eng-lish Quakers in the area maintained their distinctiveness. However, other English Quakers integrated with the larger community. William Maddock was raised a Quaker in Staffordshire and held his beliefs for his whole life, and yet after he settled in Portsmouth he attended the Episcopal Church.[45] Generally, the British had familiar religious institutions and denominations to ease their adjustment into American life.

Religion entailed more than one's relationship with God. It was a cultural, moral, and intellectual framework that affected most things in life, including political behavior. As predominantly Methodists and other nonconformists, British immigrants were pietists, committed to conversion and the reform of society. They did not separate religion from civil government, but rather inte-grated right belief with right behavior. Therefore they embraced reform move-ments, most notably temperance and abolitionism, as well as Sabbatarian laws. This religious culture also affected their politics.[46] (We will return to religion and reform in chapter 6.)

British immigrants in Ohio and most other places in the United States over-whelmingly supported the Whig and later (1854) Republican Parties. According to the county histories, over 80 percent of Ohio's British immigrants were Whigs or Republicans, a little more than 10 percent were Democrats, and the rest were Independents or members of the Prohibition Party.[47] This shunning of the Democratic Party by British immigrants might seem surprising, but is understandable. The Democratic Party was identified with Jefferson and Jackson and committed to goals that were egalitarian, libertarian, and above all, secularist. It was a party that believed in social leveling and a limited government based on self-interest, and so it aimed for a secular state free of church control and was disinclined to legislate social behavior. Believing strongly in ethnic diversity, the Democratic Party successfully attracted most immigrants, especially the Irish and German Catholics. The Democratic Party also included anti-British elements—from Andrew Jackson to Irish Catholics—that did little to welcome British newcomers.

In contrast, the Whig and Republican parties were the natural political home of most Yankee Protestants and British immigrants. It was more elitist, entrepreneurial, legalistic, and it viewed government more positively as a force to promote greater morality in society. It was, according to one historian, "the party of decency and respectability, the guardians of piety, sober living, proper manners, thrift, steady habits, and book learning."[48] Many viewed the immigration of Catholics as a threat and reacted with Nativist tendencies. In fact, some British and Protestant Scandinavian immigrants joined the American-born in organizations like the American Protective Association, which opposed Catholic immigration and promoted a strong state that could control and reform citizens' behavior.

Compared with the Irish and many continental immigrants the British expressed a strong allegiance to the American nation and a faith in the power of government to promote morality. They often joined the American-born in political and religious affiliations to form communities based on Protestantism and the English language. They were also distinct from other immigrants by supporting women's suffrage; over 50 percent did so, in comparison with under 25 percent for other groups in places that have been studied.[49] Thus, in their religion as well as their politics, British immigrants had much in common with their American hosts.

Though the English, Scots, and to a lesser extent the Welsh fit into Ohio's social and economic environment and assimilated to American life with relative ease, not all escaped pangs of doubt, acute homesickness, or any difficulties of adjustment. And they certainly did not blend in perfectly. The Scots, with their characteristic accent, clothing, and reputation for extreme frugality, sometimes stood out as curious additions to Ohio society. This was true of William Steward, from Ayrshire. Arriving in Portsmouth in 1842, he attracted considerable attention because he was "a typical Scotchman whose appearance and speech announced that fact wherever he went." And Scotsman James Westwater, whose kilt was an object of amusement for his fellow glasscutters in a Columbus factory, spent his first earnings on new clothes that helped him fit in with his fellow workers. In the evenings he studied and practiced hard to become more American—"his heart's chief desire." Soon he had American friends who considered him one of them.[50]

For English immigrants in particular, the fact that many Americans were highly nationalistic and wore their patriotism on their sleeves was an irritant. Their constant demands that English people in America agree on the superiority of the United States government, and their quasi-religious regard for liberty was enough to make some consider returning to Britain.[51] And Americans' celebration of independence—with its exaggerated sense of righteousness and bitterness toward England—was an annual institution that many could just as soon do without. It was a reminder that, for some Americans, English immigrants could never be fully part of the family. D. Griffiths sensed this during his tour of Ohio in the early 1830s, when he was invited to a Fourth of July celebration in a settlement in the Western Reserve. "The Meeting House was already filled," Griffiths observed, "and a young Republican was reading an Essay on Independence in which were some harsh invectives against the tyrant of Great Britain, &c, all which I had to bear alone, being the only Englishman present, I would observe here, that this annual repetition of injuries, sustained during the Revolutionary war, is too well calculated to keep alive the bitter feeling of Americans towards the British Government, and to kindle such a feeling in the minds of their youth; and on this account is to be lamented."[52]

English immigrants with upper-class backgrounds and a distrust of unbridled democracy found such adjustments especially difficult, and probably should have stayed home. One such person wrote to the *Cleveland Leader* to express his frustration with what the United States was becoming: "this country is the moral sewer of European society . . . with cities and towns compared with which Sodom and Gomorrah are saintly. I am an uncompromising aristocrat and it was a sad, sad day when Columbus discovered this majestic country to be invaded by the dregs of the world's social cauldron. Two years of intense suffering in this country have made me acquainted with all phases of American life. I am going back to dear old England tomorrow."[53]

Some Americans held suspicions of British immigrants because they had lived under a monarchy. Like Jefferson himself, they believed that such immigrants had to be taught liberty. They feared that they would never learn to be citizens instead of subjects.[54]

The challenges of acceptance into American life were accentuated in the 1840s when Britain and America quarreled over the western boundaries dividing

British North America from the United States. It did not help when Americans elected the aggressively expansionist president James K. Polk. His bellicose slogan, "Fifty-four forty or Fight," and the hatred for Britain that he inherited from his mentor and fellow Tennessean, Andrew Jackson, helped fuel Anglophobia in some places. Yet, even during the tense 1840s most British immigrants and native-born Americans enjoyed good relationships that continued to improve. And after diplomacy settled border disputes, relations improved even more. Britain was no longer a threat to American independence and expansion. In 1852 the Ohio newspaper, *Daily True Democrat,* observed this happier trend:

> There has been . . . a lurking dislike towards Great Britain on the part of many of our countrymen. The causes which produced it and which keep it alive are well understood . . . we have heard her sneer, and felt her satire. . . . But a great change has come over . . . our "blood relations" over the water. Her literature breathes a kindlier tone toward us. Her criticism is more genial. The daily voice of her press is not friendlier only, but positively friendly. . . . Under these circumstances, we should meet this fraternal feeling of Englishmen, with a feeling as fraternal, and prove ourselves men by burying antipathies with the rotten infirmities of the past.[55]

In addition to the improving diplomatic tone of the midcentury, many Americans recognized their historic and cultural ties to the mother country and sensed that they and British newcomers were "cut from the same cloth." By the same token, while acknowledging their cultural debt to Britain, some Americans felt the need to step out of Britain's cultural shadow. As European travel literature makes abundantly clear, some tried to compensate for a lingering inferiority complex by trumpeting their greater liberty and equality; many took personally any failure by a European to see America's superior morality and inherent virtues. Thus, between Britons and Americans there was often a mixture of admiration, affection, distrust, and perhaps jealousy.

The curious cultural relationship between Britain and America can also be seen through the eyes of British literary figures in Ohio. Frances Trollope, the great novelist and travel writer, was one of the most interesting and perceptive. In 1827 she took three of her children to Nashoba, Tennessee, a colony for emancipated slaves founded and supported by British immigrants Fanny Wright and Robert Dale Owen, to work there and provide education. Trollope found the colony's conditions and philosophy of free love impossible to accept, so she moved to Cincinnati, where she established a fancy goods store that eventually failed. Still, she saved enough money to make her famous tour that resulted in the publication in 1832 of *Domestic Manners of the Americans*. This classic book praised America's superior economic system but criticized its low intellectual and cultural standards and exposed its many faults. It also raised the wrath of thin-skinned Americans who found the criticisms offensive and unjust. Trollop's novel, *The Old World and the New* (1849), reveals the impressions of a cultural and refined Englishwoman in the Cincinnati area.

The most famous Briton to tour Ohio in the nineteenth century was also the most famous novelist of his day, Charles Dickens. On his celebrated 1842 tour of America, which furnished the material for *American Notes* and *Martin Chuzzlewit*, Dickens fought off adoring crowds who mobbed him in Cincinnati, Columbus, and Cleveland. Though he spent a total of only eight days in Ohio, the great British storyteller was a sensation. He was wined and dined, forced to meet local dignitaries, and compelled to shake the hands of up to six hundred persons a day. He was the superstar of his time. But a few anti-British and somewhat jingoistic newspapers, especially the caustically patriotic *Plain Dealer* of Cleveland, described his visit in unflattering tones.

Dickens' assessment of Ohio was a mixture of praise and criticism. He complimented the appearance of Cincinnati—"the prettiest place I have seen [in America] except Boston"— and its society, which he described as "intelligent, courteous, and agreeable." He was also appreciative of Columbus, though he poked fun of some of the rougher types, men with cheeks swollen with chewing tobacco, spitting the foul juice, often inaccurately, in public places, or from the front seat of a rapidly moving stage coach. For some reason he found the inhabitants of Sandusky "invariably morose, sullen, clownish, and repulsive."[56] In his visit we see the mutual familiarity between the two nations, their shared lingering cultural suspicion, their sense of competition, and for some Americans a sense of cultural inferiority, all of which flavored the relationships of many Britons and Ohioans. A unique and complex relationship evolved between the native-born and the immigrants. And though for some of the hypersensitive the relationship was prickly, for most it was relatively smooth and often rendered the assimilation of British immigrants quick and easy.

Differences in accents and the use of the English language highlighted the cultural gap between native Ohioans and British newcomers. The Scottish brogue was already familiar and was often a source of amusement. But some English accents, especially those of northern England, were scarcely understandable in some parts of Ohio. The distinct Yorkshire accent, particularly the proclivity for dropping the *h* sound in words, could be a formidable barrier to communication. For instance, one might say that "I 'ate the flies in my 'ouse," which could easily have been misunderstood. D. Griffiths noticed in the Western

Reserve that a Yorkshireman had recently arrived and his American neighbors assumed "he had forgotten all his English."[57] Nevertheless, such linguistic differences were quite temporary and a minor hurdle in the immigrants' assimilation.

Though the English assimilated most easily, they were not necessarily the quickest to become American citizens. Sometimes they retained a pride in their mother country that irked native-born patriotic Americans. But others eagerly became Americans. John Poste, who arrived as a twenty year old in 1853, came to Columbus and immediately fit in; he worked in the state house library and became an American virtually overnight.[58] John Palmer arrived from England in 1848 and naturalized "as soon as the laws on this subject permitted, and was ever afterward a true American."[59] Even the Welsh, many of whom struggled to retain their language and tended to live in ethnic concentrations, were said to be "less clannish and more readily Americanized than many other classes of foreigners."[60]

For many British immigrants the Odd Fellows, Masons, and other lodges or "fraternal orders" were a convenient and important means of maintaining social ties and adjusting to American life. These organizations were created in Britain and transplanted to America, so the immigrants were already familiar with them, probably became members before their migration, and upon arrival could call upon the help and brotherhood of fellow members. Lodges provided a transatlantic network, allowing members to prearrange their employment and to get other assistance if they needed it, so in effect such organizations lowered the threshold of emigration and gave advantages to members over non-members.[61] Of the 602 immigrants in our sample, an amazing ninety-five—nearly one out of six—stated their membership in a fraternal order. These institutions again illustrate the fact that the British and the Americans had much in common and that British migration to the United States was unique for the relative ease of adjustment and assimilation.

Occasionally English immigrants in Ohio articulated well the common Anglo American political heritage and their pride in both England and America. Norton Townshend, legislator and educator at Ohio State University, spoke for many other English immigrants—though with more verve and historical understanding. As a member of the Thirty-second Congress in 1852 he responded to a personal attack by a representative from North Carolina who claimed that no English-born person could love liberty enough to be a loyal American. Townshend declared:

A man does not choose his birth place, so I do not consider it a subject of either glory or shame. Could I have chosen it, I would not have selected any other spot—on one hand was the field of Naseby where that stern apostle of liberty, Oliver Cromwell, overthrew the power of the royal tyrant, King Charles I. On the other hand was the river Avon, whose waters flowed by the birth-place of Shakespeare. Could any spot be more suggestive of all that is heroic and glorious in action, or of all that is true and beautiful in expression? How much I owe to these associations I cannot tell, but this I know, that Cromwell and Milton, and Pym, and Vane, and Hampton, are among the saints in my calendar, and I trust that I cherish something of their hatred of oppression. I think men may understand and appreciate the principles of civil liberty though not born on this continent. . . . Persons born within the limits of monarchy are not necessarily Monarchists. The fathers of the Revolution, Washington, Jefferson, the Adams' and Patrick Henry were born under the same Monarchical Government as myself.

Townshend finished his stirring, impromptu speech by turning the tables on his North Carolinian foe: "The true friend of freedom would scorn alike to be a slave or to own one. . . . For myself I will add that representing a hundred thousand freemen, I shall take the liberty to speak as I please and when I think proper, without asking special permission of any man, and least of all of one who comes here the representative of whips and manacles and slaves."[62] Such brilliant oratory was not characteristic of most British immigrants, but most realized that Americans and English were linked, and that English people could claim American liberty as their own birthright.

The awareness that Britons and Americans had much in common grew in the later part of the century as immigrants with unfamiliar languages and cultures arrived from southern and eastern Europe. By comparison the British were all but American already. Their common language and ability to fit in and perform some of the most highly skilled work made them the most welcome of Ohio's immigrants, in contrast to the hostility that often greeted the so-called "new immigrants" from southern and eastern Europe. During the late nineteenth and early twentieth centuries newspapers, county histories, and other opinionated texts often expressed unabashed pro-English sentiments.[63] Such Anglophilia, which would have seemed strange earlier in the nineteenth century, was partly a result of the fact that by the 1880s British and other northwestern European immigrants were greatly outnumbered by migrants whose culture seemed threatening to Anglo Saxons. Also to blame were the growing influences of social Darwinism and ideas of racial superiority. In this changing social and intellectual climate, the British were warmly received. Of course, not all British immigrants were peaceful, well-adjusted persons contributing to their new society. It is easy to exaggerate the positive qualities of British immigrants because the available sources are biased in that direction.

A different perspective is provided by the Jail Reports of the Secretary of State to the Governor of Ohio from 1851 to 1855, and which were submitted in 1854 and 1855. Although not complete or consistent they provide a glimpse of British immigrants whose legacy to Ohio's history was less than stellar. Englishman James Hile, age thirty-eight, was charged with rioting in January of 1852. Another English immigrant, Samuel Sanforth of Jeffeson County, was guilty of "Surety of the peace," but discharged by the Probate Judge. Edward C. Fowler, a twenty-eight-year-old from the north of England, committed burglary in 1855 and was sent to the state prison for one year. In Wayne County three English immigrants were convicted of rioting in March and April of 1853. Others were culpable of retailing liquor, disorderly conduct, and other minor offenses.

More serious were the crimes of John Sutcliffe, a forty-year-old immigrant who served "5 days on bread and water" for petty larceny but who also had a previous conviction for manslaughter. And Henry Baldwin, a thirty-five-year-old immigrant, was found guilty of "assault with intent to rape," and sentenced to three years. James Parks, already convicted of burglary, was arrested for murder in April of 1853 and therefore sent to Cuyahoga County for trial. Only three Scottish immigrants appear in the reports, convicted of burglary, drunkenness, and "Surety of the peace." No Welsh appear in the reports, which probably reflects the intense religious and moral nature of their upbringing, and that at midcentury most still lived in Ohio's rural Welsh settlements.[64]

It is also instructive to put the criminal British immigrants into a statistical and comparative perspective, though the data do not allow absolute confidence in the findings. A total of 110 persons, for example, are listed in the Jefferson County Jail reports for November 1851 to November 1852, and of them only 2 are British. This is a mere 1.8 percent. In Jefferson County in 1850, English immigrants numbered 343, out of a total population of 29,133, or 1.2 percent of the population. The percentages are roughly equal given the statistical margins of error. The English were no more likely to be convicted criminals than they were members of the county's population. But the Irish in the same county and year comprised 82 of the 110 in the jail reports—fully 75 percent—while the Irish in Jefferson County in 1850 numbered 936, only 3.2 percent of the county's population.[65] Notwithstanding the well known prejudice against the Irish in America at this time, and the bias that put innocent Irish people behind bars, the drastic overrepresentation cannot be ignored or ascribed merely to bias alone. The most frequently listed crimes of the Irish were rioting, drunkenness, surety of the peace, assault and battery, and the like.[66] And as much as the American judicial system victimized Irish immigrants, they apparently committed crimes and breaches of the peace in disproportionate numbers. Jail reports of other counties also show an overrepresentation of the Irish, though not to such an extent.

In addition to the jail reports, court records also occasionally reveal the sinister British immigrants who trickled in with the more law-abiding majority. James and Betty Dickinson, for example, married in England in 1853 and immediately departed for Ohio. There they fell prey to another English immigrant, William Beatson, also known as Edward Gu. Gu stole six hundred dollars in gold from Betty Dickinson, and her husband James retaliated by murdering Gu. James Dickinson, who had his own shady past and was also known as James Parks, was convicted of the crime and executed.[67] But altogether, the criminal element among British immigrants was miniscule. The vast majority were hardworking, honest people who were welcomed by native Ohioans and fit in well with society.

The British immigrants' diffuse settlement patterns, their familiar religious affiliations and political leanings, allowed them to assimilate early and play formative roles in many parts of Ohio. They and most native whites shared a largely Anglo American culture. This was a salient feature that distinguished the British among Ohio's immigrants. The British had more in common with Ohioans than they had differences, and they offered valuable skills and services to Ohio's growing economy and budding industries. In later years they were seen not so much as immigrants per se, but as "cousins" who were in Ohio from the start, helped build it, and helped bring it into modernity.

3

Communities and Settlements

There arrived here by lake steamboats during the past
week 200 emigrants from the Isle of Man. . . . These people appear
to be well assorted with reference to sex and age, and there apparently
is no probability of any of them becoming paupers.
They are principally destined for Stark and Columbiana counties.

—*Cleveland Herald*, August 3, 1827

THE British are a diverse people. Though the political community of Great Britain was created in 1707, sharp cultural, religious, and linguistic distinctions remained. In the nineteenth century the differences between England, Scotland, and Wales were in some ways starker than the similarities. This was also true of the people leaving these countries for America. British immigrants were known collectively for blending in quickly into American society, but this was truer of the English than of the Scots, and especially the Welsh and settlers from the islands of Guernsey and Man, who had cultural and linguistic distinctions and created tight ethnic communities in Ohio. Some English settlers also tried to establish settlements in Ohio, but the fact that they tried and failed tells us a lot about them.

The most notable attempt by the English to establish a settlement in Ohio was led by George Courtauld. He was a descendent of a Huguenot family that fled France in 1688, a few years after Louis XIV revoked the Edict of Nantes and ended toleration for Protestants. Taking refuge in England, the family became merchants, gold and silver smiths, and eventually silk manufacturers. One member, Samuel Courtauld, immigrated to America in the late eighteenth century as a merchant and after moderate success died there in 1821. George Courtauld, meanwhile, served a seven-year apprenticeship as a silk throwster in Spitalfields, a district in East London, and in 1785 made his first of four trips to America. Upon his second trip in 1789, he attempted to take up farming in New

York and then bought a farm in Kentucky. His Irish-born wife, however, could not stand the hard life, so in about 1794 he leased out his American lands and with a few hundred pounds in his pocket returned to England and the silk business. But due to an economic slump in England, quarrels with his partners, and his conviction that America was both politically and economically superior to England, George returned again to America in 1818—this time to Ohio.

The fifty-seven-year-old Courtauld was drawn to Ohio when he heard about the well-publicized English settlement that Morris Birkbeck and George Flower were attempting to establish in Edwards County, Illinois. Inspired, in 1818 he arrived in Athens County where he purchased a large estate for himself and his family, intending to sell land to other English immigrants. He called it "Englishtown." A fast speculative return on his investment did not pan out so he returned to London, where he published a tract extolling the advantages of life in Ohio. He also attempted to form a joint-stock company to give his project an economic boost. In 1820 George Courtauld returned to the Ohio wilderness with his two sons, two daughters, and their spouses. His wife Ruth and eldest son Samuel remained in England to run the family silk manufacture in Essex. But Courtauld was confident: in 1821 he opened a small store that included the Englishtown post office.[1]

Clearing the forests was far harder than Courtauld had anticipated, but he drew strength and courage from an idealized vision of his family gathered around him on a beautiful estate, with other English families nearby with whom they could associate comfortably. The Courtaulds aimed at nothing less than bringing a piece of refined English culture and civilization to the untamed Ohio wilderness; they fully expected the rest of their family and other English settlers to arrive soon. But George's wife Ruth and son Samuel refused to join the others, preferring to remain in England, where the silk trade was improving. Samuel, who began to steer the family silk business toward phenomenal success, had severe doubts about his father's judgment. To him the scheme to colonize Ohio with English families seemed dubious at best. Writing to his father, Samuel told him that he was "quite satisfied . . . that your particular view of business in this country is impracticable." Ruth was even more scornful, explaining to her daughters in Ohio that she could not go to America "under the dread of being sent adrift where your father spent all his money, which experience teaches us would be soon." Such family tensions and the harsh reality of life in the forests of Ohio ultimately doomed the attempted settlement to failure—but not without some interesting developments.[2]

The Courtaulds did have positive moments. George's daughter Sophia expressed delight with the beauty and grandeur of the Ohio River, and became "a wonderful favourite" with most of her pupils when she did some teaching in Zanesville. Her sister Eliza was struck by the beauty of the pristine countryside, and the family was pleased with the beer they brewed, which they proclaimed "most excellent."[3] But that was about it. As Eliza recorded in May of 1822:

> The Mosquitoes are shockingly numerous; I am obliged to wear a pair of Mr. Ash's cloth Gater's to keep them from my legs. When I was in bed in the day time I hear a noise of something falling, and looking on the box I saw a Snake which had entered I believe the roof and fallen down, and the other day I saw a very large lizard crawling on the logs over the bed and as to the mice they run about by thousands. Our garden thrives tolerably well, but being much disappointed in getting men to help us plough are much behind in corn planting: indeed we fear we shall not have any this year.[4]

Six weeks later she recorded a more mixed experience:

> I have sixty two chickens. I am sorry to tell you our best horse died last week: the immediate cause of his death we do not know, but I believe the flies were the primary cause; the other two look most wretchedly for they are absolutely nearly bled to death by them; all new comers are persecuted in the same manner. . . . Our dinner to be sure is soon made ready as it consists of nothing but bread, cheese and fried pork. We have lately fared most sumptuously upon roasting pig and squirrel pudding. We have also brewed a barrel of small beer, holding 33 gallons. . . . I think I am better for it. I am going to try an experiment and roast some bacon to day.[5]

Perhaps the biggest problem the Courtaulds encountered was sickness, particularly ague. Malarial illnesses were all too common on the Ohio frontier, where standing water and rotting vegetation attracted mosquitoes and other insects that infected the pioneers. In September of 1823 reports claimed that more than half of the people within a radius of fifty miles of Columbus were sick.[6] People suffered diarrhea and other symptoms so routinely that many accepted it as an inevitability they could not control. Some Britons found dealing with sickness while practically isolated on the Ohio frontier too dangerous and traumatic and turned back to Britain because of it. And it did not help that when a doctor could be procured he or she might well be a quack whose nostrums did more harm than good—a common problem in antebellum America. For Ronald McDonald of Aberdeen, for example, Ohio lost all of its charms and ap-

peal when he was struck with ague in 1843 while visiting his son who had settled in Massillon. McDonald's illness was a painful and frightening ordeal that
dissuaded him from staying in Ohio. "I would not live here if you would give
me all the country between Zoar and Massillon," he complained. And being
horrified at the treatments prescribed by a doctor, he recorded, "you feed mercury to your people . . . don't I know what mercury is?" He left Ohio in disgust
and returned to Scotland.[7]

For the Courtaulds, sickness was magnified by the stark contrast between
England, where they had professional medical help when they needed it, and
the isolated Ohio frontier, where they were on their own in times of emergency.
One of George Courtauld's daughters-in-law, Kate Taylor, reported to her sister
Sophia in England:

> Oh in sweet England, illness was nothing, absolutely nothing compared to
> what it is here. None, none can know that have not felt the melancholy
> contrast of illness when surrounded by every comfort, every assistance, all
> the attendance that can lighten. And as it is here to us,—without any as-
> sistance,—without the female friend to think of all that could suit the "sick
> man's palate,"—or the cook to execute. The contrast sinks my spirits, nat-
> urally lowered by illness, till every thing assumes even a deeper shade than
> reason would allow.[8]

And then she continued, exposing the heart of the matter. The plan was unrealistic; life in the Ohio wilderness was romanticized to a cruel extreme; the
loneliness and stress that urban English people suffered in the backwoods of
Ohio was grossly underestimated; and George Courtauld's well-intentioned
plan had been a naïve and terrible mistake:

> When those flattering pictures of the *back woods* were sketched, when the
> small but therefore more endeared circle was pourtrayed by fancy enjoy-
> ing after the various occupations of the day "the feast of reason & the flow
> of souls," oh had truth snatched the pencil & shown us that little circle so
> widely scattered o're these boundless woods—how would our hearts have
> sunk within us; but not more than mine often sinks. In England we often
> mourn'd the absence of dear friends, but there every face comparatively
> was the face of a friend. I seem here to have no feelings in common with
> those around me, their sorrows are not my sorrows, nor their joys my joys;
> the very sources of my hopes & my fears are far far away where their wishes
> or their hopes never reach. . . . My feelings have been kept more on the

stretch lately from the circumstances of my disappointments . . . oh could I have for one thought my leaving England would indeed parted us; nothing, nothing should have induced me to leave it. . . . When I think of that fair distant land: In a moment I wish to be there.[9]

Disaster struck in August of 1823: George suddenly died of a fever and the Courtauld settlement began to disintegrate. But as the rest of the family prepared to return to England, another English immigrant picked up the torch and tried to make the project work. James Knight had been a maltster and shopkeeper in Sussex, where he enjoyed relatively high standards of living but lost his assets during the speculative boom of the Napoleonic Wars. Then he and his wife, Sarah Redman Knight, and several other English families joined the Courtaulds. They arrived in 1822 with a small stock of goods about a mile away from the Courtaulds, where Knight erected a few simple buildings, including a small frame store and house, which became the nucleus of the village of Nelsonville, laid out by Daniel Nelson in 1823. Courtauld's Englishtown became known as the Longstreth Addition of Nelsonville. Knight got started by selling surplus produce to his American neighbors. When the Courtaulds headed back to England, Knight determined to bring more English immigrants to Nelsonville, where he visualized an English community prosperous enough in farming to provide food for local people. His letter dated June 4, 1825, reveals a confidence that gave some momentum to the planned English community:

> I had considerable Corn coming into me last year from many families to whom I had supplied some two months or less before they could gather their Crops, by letting them have 3 Bushel to receive four after gathered . . . this is the way you know the Americans live—and how happy they must think themselves to have an English person to provide for them.[10]

James Knight was certainly an energetic and industrious man, a good choice to follow up on George Courtauld's project. By May of 1825 he reported that his "premises have undergone such additions and (I think) improvements . . . that you wd hardly recognize them," and that "several extra families are settling down around us." As an indefatigable booster of Nelsonville he constantly watched the progress of the Erie and Ohio Canal and hoped it would bring prosperity. He and other traders used flatboats on the Hocking River to transport their goods to and from larger markets and enabled the area to grow.

One cold winter Knight's goods saved some people from starvation. Knight also brought from England knowledge about using coal as fuel, and was the first in Nelsonville to burn the mineral—twelve bushels in one winter—for which he paid only four cents a bushel. His efforts to attract outside capital to develop the local coal deposits and inaugurate industry came to naught. But Knight persevered. He was particularly proud of the whiskey he distilled and was happy to share it with his American neighbors, who after drinking to the health of the Courtaulds (who had just departed for England) declared "the English people the best in the World." And when frost ruined the local crop of apples and peaches used to make cider, he had plenty to spare. With fourteen barrels of "pretty good whiskey" from his cellar, Knight began a successful public house in Nelsonville. In one year alone he sold sixteen barrels; but realizing that the liquor was being consumed too heavily and wreaking havoc on some of the local families, he stopped selling it, bought a stack of temperance tracts published in Gallipolis, and handed them out to his customers.[11]

James Knight's efforts to pull more English people into the area were considerable. In August of 1825 he attracted an English family living in Meigs County by offering good, partially cleared land and a cabin complete with a brick chimney. Knight also wrote glowing articles for English newspapers in hopes of attracting more immigrants. Though prospective immigrants often distrusted such published letters, Knight's were convincing. In 1832 forty English people from Wisborough Green, Sussex, suddenly showed up in Nelsonville. Knight had known some of them in England, and they were in dire need of food and shelter. James Knight did what he could, allowing some to stay in his own home or the simple cabins and a warehouse he had built, and he tried to persuade them to buy his lands. But the venture, like the cabins he had built, was already falling apart.[12]

Knight continued to work hard to promote Nelsonville, even after it was clear that it would never become an English community. He helped build bridges, schools, and meeting houses, established Sunday and day schools, and served as Nelsonville's postmaster. He was also the main force behind the construction of the first bridge over the Hockhocking River, and arranged for people to help pay for it through individual grain subscriptions. Thus he was understandably honored as "one of the most active and influential citizens" of Nelsonville, "participating earnestly in the local improvements and social movements of the day." In 1836, at only age forty-seven, he died of a "nervous fever," according to his widow, Sarah, his vision of a large, tight-knit English settlement unrealized.[13]

In the end, the efforts of the Courtaulds and James Knight were doomed to failure—no matter how good the land and amenities or how determined their efforts. What they did not realize was that English immigrants did not need their own ethnic community in Ohio, or any other place in America for that matter; they fit in well enough with native Ohioans. Already sharing a language and culture, they blended in, settled where they wished, found familiar church denominations, and easily associated with locals. They saw no reason to be limited and restrained by living with former countrymen. English communities in Ohio simply did not make much sense—but Welsh ones did.

THE WELSH

Like the English, the Welsh came to Ohio very early and made a great impact on the state's growth and development. Unlike the English, the majority of Welsh—with their distinctive language and culture—established their own inward-looking ethnic communities. The Welsh had many cultural differences with other Britons, and were related mainly by the complex political relationship between England and Wales, which was formed by a unique blend of geography and history. The beauty and austerity of the Welsh landscape is complemented by the staggeringly impressive castles that still ring the country, the legacy of the conquest of Wales chiefly by King Edward I in the late thirteenth and early fourteenth centuries. England's domination deepened when the Statute of Wales imposed English law and organization on Wales in 1284, and again when the Union of England and Wales was enacted by Parliament in 1536 and 1543. By this time Welsh blood also ran in the veins of the Tudor monarchs, including the mighty Henry VIII and the greatest of them all, Elizabeth I. Suppression of their language and culture in later centuries did not endear Britain to the Welsh. Instead they drew together in nonconformist religious denominations that stressed piety, thrift, self-reliance, and obedience to God. And the hard lives lived by the vast majority of Welsh men and women—whether farmers, laborers, servants, miners, quarriers, or ironworkers—turned many heads in the direction of America.

Like other parts of Britain, Wales in the nineteenth century was undergoing vast changes in agriculture, including the imposition of the Corn Laws, and especially industry, as green fields gave way to grimy coal mines, factories, and ironworks. Many Welsh saw themselves as victims of a rampant industrial capitalism that pulled people from their farms to the mines or factories and threatened their piety and traditional ways of life. Many came to realize, paradoxically, that they could preserve their culture and former ways of life by packing up and moving to Ohio. There they could stay on the farm—one they owned, not rented. Or if they preferred, they could continue industrial work as miners or ironworkers at much higher wages, with better prospects for advancement and ownership, and more political liberty as well. Ohio's farmland was an especially strong draw. The Welsh felt at home in the hilly regions of Ohio, which resembled their old homeland. They were experienced with the challenges of farming such lands, and they considered them healthier than the flat lowlands and swamp areas where water stagnated and produced malaria. Besides, the fertile flat land was often too expensive or already purchased by other settlers.

Most of the Welsh in Ohio were Calvinists, either Calvinist Methodists or Baptists and Congregationalists who had retained some Calvinist doctrine and culture.[14] The Calvinist Methodists had followed George Whitefield over John Wesley when a schism occurred between these two leaders of early Methodism in the eighteenth century. Though retaining the organizational structure and bureaucracy and the circuit riders, the Calvinist Methodists shunned the Wesleyan emphasis on free will and stressed a Calvinist theology based on predestination. Most of the Welsh Presbyterians, Baptists, and Congregationalists were also Calvinist in their doctrines of God and their worldviews. They saw a sovereign God in control of the world and believed themselves called to redeem the world for his purposes. They sensed a mission as they tamed the wilderness, and they drew strength and courage from a theological confidence that God was on their side. Their religious assurance and fierce work ethic proved a good match for the Ohio frontier.

Much information about the Welsh in Ohio is available in the county histories and the obituaries found in Welsh publications. Of the 124 Welsh immigrants who appear in the county histories, 99 provided a precise county of origin. Of these, three quarters were from South Wales, especially the major industrial counties of Glamorgan and Monmouth. This southeastern region of Wales had become a vast industrial center for coal mines, blast furnaces, and rolling mills by the 1830s. Montgomeryshire, in the southeast corner of North Wales, was actually the most frequent origin of the Welsh in the county histories. This is best explained by the fact that around the middle of the century modernizing English textile mills undercut the local cottage woolens producers and caused them to look abroad to maintain their livelihoods or become farmers. Meanwhile, they were susceptible to clergymen like Benjamin Chidlaw, who had immigrated to Ohio and returned to Montgomeryshire to encourage more Welsh to join settlements in Ohio.[15]

Cardiganshire was also a common origin. The relatively high rate of migration from this county is explained not so much by the decline of rural industries or enclosure, but to its limited resources being pressured by rising population, and the solid links of information with Cardiganshire folk already in Ohio. As letters from Welsh settlers in Ohio filtered back into Cardiganshire, more realized that a life of marginal farming or seasonal labor in Wales did not

Wales

compare with a life of land ownership and prosperity in Ohio. Attractive guide-books for emigrants written by Cardiganshire-born ministers in America encouraged many to make that important decision.[16]

Clearly, the Welsh entering Ohio came from a variety of agricultural and industrial backgrounds—a reflection of both Wales's and Ohio's economic diversity. The industrial Welsh included many who were victims of declining wages and unemployment in Wales, due to natural economic cycles and the attempt by industrialists to compensate for increasing competition and falling prices by cutting labor costs. At the same time American iron and coal companies were recruiting skilled workers and found some of the best ones in the form of Welsh immigrants. And while those from the rural north were influenced by the hardship of subsistence farming and the security that came with chain migration and the encouragement of local pastors, those from the south—especially the industrial southeast—were influenced more by the challenges and vicissitudes of industrialization. Both groups saw a more promising future in Ohio. Land was a large part of that assessment, especially for those from the northern agrarian and rural counties. But land also drew many from the industrial southeast, especially those who had originally hailed from rural areas before moving into industry. They could always combine industrial work with farming in Ohio.

The wide and sustained Welsh migration to Ohio had its origins in the eighteenth century and was initiated by individuals who established settlements that continued to draw immigrants. One of the first known Welshmen was Reverend David Jones, from Cardiganshire, who first settled in Delaware. He became a missionary among the Shawnee and Delaware Indians in the early 1770s. The first permanent Welsh-born immigrants were Ezekiel Hughes and Edward Bebb, from Llanbrynmair, Montgomeryshire, North Wales, a place said to be one of the most moral and religious in Wales. Originally settling in Ebensburg, Pennsylvania, Hughes and Bebb headed west in 1796. After walking over the mountains near what is now Brownsville, Pennsylvania, they obtained a flatboat and floated down the Ohio River to Cincinnati.

The men were joined by another Welshman, William Gwilym, and squatted on land east of the Great Miami River, waiting for the government to survey the west bank so they could pounce on it, which they did in 1801. Hughes was the first person to purchase land west of the Great Miami River, in Hamilton County; Bebb purchased land farther north in Butler County, where the first Welsh community in Ohio, Paddy's Run, was soon established. In 1798 the men were joined by a couple of others from South Wales, who squatted on land near Blue Creek. Others from Llanbrynmair followed around the turn of the century in Butler and Licking Counties. Like most of the earliest Welsh settlers, they first lived in Beulah, a settlement founded by Welshman Morgan J. Rhys in 1798, in Pennsylvania, about eighty miles east of Pittsburgh. This settlement grew in the late 1790s, but hearing about the better soils farther west, the Welsh left Beulah for Ohio. By 1825 virtually all of the Welsh had abandoned Beulah.[17]

After securing his land, Edward Bebb headed back to Wales to find his old sweetheart and hopefully bring her back as his wife. To his amazement, he met her in Philadelphia, now a widow with a child. The two married and headed out to their homestead. In 1802 they had their first child, William Bebb, the first European born in Butler County, who from 1846 to 1848 would serve as the seventeenth governor of Ohio (as a moderate Whig). Ezekiel Hughes became a justice of the peace in 1806 and helped establish Paddy's Run Congregational Church. Bebb and Hughes traveled back to Pennsylvania to recruit newcomers, and Hughes made a trip back to Llanbrynmair, where people were stirred by his enticing descriptions of the land. As a result, between 1803 and 1820 a more or less constant stream of Welsh headed to Southwestern Ohio, many of them settling at Paddy's Run.[18]

Though Welsh immigrants, especially those from the parish of Llanbrynmair, Montgomeryshire, did predominate at Paddy's Run, the place was never exclusively Welsh. In fact, the settlement was named after an Irishman in the first surveying party who drowned in a local creek. The early years there were very hard; the Welsh "went into the forests and hewed out homes for their families, and had become almost like the natives."[19] For over twenty-five years the Welsh at Paddy's Run were quite isolated and without neighbors. Yet the settlers endured and prospered. An English Congregational minister from Cincinnati, the Reverend J. W. Brown, joined them in 1802 and organized the Whitewater Congregational Church the following year.[20]

By midcentury the Welsh numbered some eight hundred in the community and surrounding area, described at the time in these terms: "The land is well cultivated, it is a good land for Indian corn and wheat. . . . It is a healthy place, and many people live to a ripe old age." As people mainly from Llanbrynmair—a center of literacy and enlightened, profound Calvinist thought—the Welsh at Paddy's Run were devout. Most were Calvinist Methodists. They promoted literacy, abhorred slavery, and maintained their culture well into the second half of the nineteenth century. Many of the immigrants resisted learning English, though by midcentury most of their children spoke English as their first language.[21]

Another early Welsh settlement in Ohio was established by David Pugh, who left Radnorshire in South Wales in 1801 and arrived the next year in

Franklin County to identify and survey a military land warrant held by another Welshman, Dr. Samuel Jones. By 1804 "Radnor," as Pugh called the area
in honor of his homeland, was ready for settlement and in a few years a large
group of Welsh families arrived. These early Welsh immigrants also endured
great hardships and privations. Hunger, cold, and sickness were frequent
dangers. During the War of 1812 they abandoned their homes for fear of
Indian attack.[22]

Meanwhile, other Welsh settlements were also established. As early as 1802
Calvinist Methodist families left Cardiganshire and founded the "Welsh Hills"
settlement near Newark, Licking County. The community had its origins in an
incident in Carmarthen, Wales, in 1787, when John H. Phillips—a son of a
wealthy Welshman—allegedly wrote a pamphlet criticizing the British government for its lack of religious reform and immigrated to America to avoid pun-
ishment. Upon sailing to Philadelphia with his two brothers, Phillips settled
near the city and met up with other Welsh settlers. One, the chaplain for General Anthony Wayne, procured Phillips an appointment on the general's staff.
The sons wrote home to encourage their father to join them, along with neighbor Theophilus Rees and a group of other Welshmen located in Beulah. In 1801
the elder Phillips and Rees purchased two thousand acres near what is now
Granville and Newark, Licking County. The next year the settlers arrived and
began carving their settlement out of the hilly, unbroken forest, and gradually
the community grew. Some of the settlers had been stone masons in Wales and
used their skills in Zanesville, Newark, and Marietta to earn the money necessary for establishing a successful settlement.[23]

Theophilus Rees was considered the "patriarch" of the Welsh Hills. A gentleman, scholar, and deacon in the Baptist Church, Rees was a natural leader during a time of hardship and uncertainty. He helped organize the Welsh Hills Baptist Church in 1808, after the community had used their cabins for worship
during the first six years. The settlement was tight and viewed by outsiders as
clannish—not unlike some German settlements in Ohio—for the fact that the
immigrants knew little or no English and conducted all of their social and religious affairs in Welsh. Only the second generation learned enough English to
break down some of their isolation. But even then the Welsh stuck with their
own. While they headed for their settlement, Virginian Indian scout James
Johnson and his family joined them. Though the Johnsons became founding
members of the Welsh Hills settlement, they did not intermarry with the Welsh
for several generations.[24]

The pioneers at the Welsh Hills settlement endured extremely hard conditions on their edge of the frontier. The earliest arrivals traveled by canoes as far

as Zanesville, and then hacked out roads through the dense forest to get their wagons into that remote part of Licking County. The Samuel Joseph Phillips family, arriving in 1809, traveled in a typical manner—they had two horses and no wagon; one horse was used as a pack horse while the wife rode the other with a babe in her arms. Samuel led the way on foot and the boys drove the cows. They traveled that way for over three hundred miles.[25]

Though not hostile, the Indians still frightened the Welsh. They considered them "not very welcome visitors," because fearful stories of Indians circulated in Wales. But wolves and panthers were a real threat. Theophilus Rees's son was treed by a pack of wolves that nearly shredded the tree in their efforts to devour him. Those who walked from cabin to cabin at night had to carry arms for protection and defend themselves with torches or firebrands. In fact, both wolves and panthers were common enough in much of Ohio during these times that officials in Franklin County offered bounties of one dollar for the head or scalp of each newborn wolf or panther and two dollars for the head or scalp of each adult.[26] The extermination of these animals was seen as necessary for the protection of both people and livestock, and for the Welsh and other British immigrants settling in remote areas the danger posed by wild animals could be quite a shock.

The Welsh succeeded in Ohio by relying on faith and family. The families who joined these settlements were extraordinarily "mature," that is, there were many adult children traveling with their own children under the leadership of patriarchs and matriarchs, an arrangement that contributed to discipline and the coordination of effort. Religion carried the Welsh through their early trials, for faith was central to their lives. The Welsh in Licking County were either Calvinist Methodist, Baptist, or Congregationalists, but they were all, with rare exceptions, Calvinists in their doctrines of God and the world, and they were among the most churchgoing of all people.[27]

For the Welsh, piety filtered into all aspects of life, and education was essential to successful and godly living. They almost universally favored temperance and opposed slavery, and were quick to volunteer for the Union during the Civil War. When the Civil War broke out, the Welsh Hills School contributed twenty-nine soldiers for the Union army. After the war, large numbers graduated from nearby Dennison University. The settlers of Welsh Hills continued to assimilate but they did not abandon their sober and pious living. As one writer described them in 1880, "The present occupants of the Welsh Hills have become considerably Americanized. They are honest, sober, industrious, frugal, free from drunkenness and debauchery, vice and crime which degrade humanity."[28]

Some of the Welsh pioneers were served by gifted immigrant preachers with religious and political influence. One was Thomas "Priest" Jones, born in Radnor in 1778, who emigrated in 1800 because he felt the sting of English hostility to his Baptist tradition. After serving churches in New Jersey and Pennsylvania and naturalizing to become an American citizen, he came to preach in Warren, Wayne County, in 1812. He also served as a state legislator and was one of the early abolitionists of the state, known for the statement, "Slavery is a blot on our National escutcheon." In 1812 he also organized the first Baptist church in Wooster, which was then a tiny settlement, and served as its pastor until 1839, after which he continued to preach throughout the area. He also strongly advocated education and formed an education society in Youngstown.[29]

The story of Thomas Powell, born in Radnorshire, South Wales, in 1760, reveals an interesting insight on the character and piety of these Welsh pioneers in Licking County. Powell settled in Beulah, Pennsylvania, in 1801 and then went to the Welsh Hills in 1805. He was remembered for memorizing most of the Bible and for his stubborn streak. Taking issue with how the Welsh Hills Church was being built, he swore he would never enter it. He kept his word, but every Sunday he sat outside on a nearby stump, listening carefully to the sermon and singing the hymns with gusto—whether in the sun, rain, or snow. He worshipped that way for nearly forty years, until he died in 1848.[30]

The Welsh loyalty to their churches was legendary, and sometimes transcended marriage. This was the case of the Dolbey family, Welsh immigrants who settled in Ohio in 1829. Robert Dolbey was a devout member of the Welsh Calvinist Methodist Church in Washington Township, Van Wert County, all his life, even after he married Elizabeth Thomas. She was also born in Wales and came to America at the same time as the Dolbeys. But she remained a faithful member of the Welsh Presbyterian Church, and so on Sundays the married couple went their separate ways.[31]

The Welsh were certainly industrious and resourceful farmers. Fully nine out of ten of the Welsh Hills community members were literate. Virtually all who came to the settlement had learned a trade before emigrating; and though few had farmed in Wales, they farmed successfully in Ohio because of their extreme hard work and thrift. Their religion and piety affected their farming practices: they farmed every inch of their land and harvested every grain to honor God in their calling to a life of agriculture. Agriculture in the Welsh Hills community consisted of mixing crops with livestock and often mixing farming with other occupations. Some who arrived shortly after the Napoleonic Wars were woolen handloom weavers thrown out of work when military contracts for uniforms were cancelled in 1815. In Ohio they continued to produce wool on their farms and weave it in their cottages. By 1850 they raised corn, oats, hay, hogs, and fruit for market, in addition to their sheep. At least one who recorded his farming techniques "did very considerable manuring" of his fields, treated his corn crops with lime plaster, ploughed his fields deeply—eight to nine inches—and introduced new machinery to the area. These farming methods were advanced for the time and were more labor intensive than the methods used by most native Ohioans, but they worked well in the Welsh Hills. And they persisted in part because the Welsh community was quite self-contained and did not have much immediate interaction with American-born farmers who had more extensive agricultural methods.[32]

The Welsh maintained attitudes and culture in their Ohio communities that distinguished them from most English and Scottish immigrants. But this was not true of all the Welsh. Some of those from the northeast of Wales and the agricultural lowlands of Glamorganshire were highly anglicized and mingled with Ohioans and English immigrants, rather than join Welsh settlements where they would have stood out for their *lack* of Welshness. But these anglicized Welsh immigrants were relatively rare in Ohio.[33] The great majority were distinctly Welsh and exhibited characteristics that defined them in the eyes of most Americans. Few held much patriotic love for Britain, though many were still emotionally attached to their old homes in Wales. Without the sense of loyalty to the king or queen that the English often exhibited, the Welsh were quicker to see America as their "only political mother." Their communal cooperation also became legendary as they organized cabin raisings for newcomers, as well as "choppings," "huskings," and "butchering days," which were great social and economic events.[34]

Though natives of Wales may have been quick to shift their political loyalties from Britain to America, their distinctive language and culture, their tendency to form enclaves, and their intense religiosity naturally led them to assimilate into American culture more slowly than the English or Scots. The primacy of religion and the manner in which it preserved ethnic distinctiveness is evident in the fact that they founded their communities by building their own chapels. Welsh chapels began in the form of a *seiat*, a self-governing religious fellowship society that met in the pioneers' homes, settled religious and civil disputes, and disciplined members who had committed violations. This form of organization contributed to Welsh separatism.[35] Thus, in their inward-looking Ohio settlements the Welsh were able to reestablish and preserve their traditional way of life, which they had felt was threatened in their native land. In this way they were similar to the Dutch Calvinists who settled in western Michigan, Iowa, and northern Illinois.[36]

Even in later years, when Welsh immigrants helped lead Ohio into the industrial revolution, they were known for their overt piety. The Jefferson Iron Company, founded by devout Welshmen in Jackson County in 1854, decided never to operate on Sunday. Therefore the blast furnaces were taken off at 11:59 Saturday night and turned back on at 12:01 Monday morning.[37] Thanksgiving Day was also off-limits to work. And when the Scioto and Hocking Valley Railroad connected Portsmouth and Hamden in 1856, it obtained rights-of-way through the farmlands of Welsh settlers only by a contract that was kept for many years stipulating that trains would never run on Sundays.[38] In the Welsh area of Scioto County it was more than five decades before any Welshman applied for a divorce in court, and the affair was still a "great shock" to the entire settlement. No wonder the English immigrants living nearby referred to them as "Those God Almighty Welsh."[39]

By 1850 there were a little over five thousand Welsh immigrants in Ohio.[40] Their numbers would not have been that high without the encouragement of writers and especially clergymen, who promoted migration as a means of both spiritual and material well being. In this respect they were not unlike the Puritans, who were led by clergy in their settlement of New England two hundred years earlier. In 1851 the Welsh Congregational minister and promoter of Welsh immigration to America, R. D. Thomas, visited most of the Welsh settlements in Ohio and identified nearly forty places where Welsh immigrants were clustered in groups. Most of these clusters were near coal mines and iron works where many Welsh worked. But it was not just the occupations that attracted them. The hilly areas of Ohio attracted many because the land was cheaper there and the beautiful landscape resembled that of their native land. [41]

Women were also instrumental in establishing Welsh communities. They were, of course, essential for making any settlement succeed through their hard physical work and their ability to earn supplemental income for their families with needlework, butter and cheese making, and the like. But they also provided community leadership. The Tyn Rhos area in Jackson County owed much of the success of its Welsh settlements to Ann Richards, a widow who sold her farm in Wales and came to Tyn Rhos with her four children in the early 1840s. There she bought more land and encouraged other Welsh families to join her. Because of her efforts, about twenty-eight other Welsh families joined the community.[42]

Jackson and Gallia Counties contained the largest concentrations of Ohio's Welsh immigrants, mainly from Cardiganshire. The story of how the settlement started illustrates the pioneers' adventures, the influence of Welsh women, and how capriciously the site of a settlement could be chosen. In the spring of 1818 six families from Kilkenin, Cardiganshire, set out for America, heading for Paddy's Run to join former neighbors who had just settled there. After a particularly terrible and perilous seven-week voyage across the ocean, they made it to Baltimore and hired wagons to get to Pittsburgh. They were bound for Cincinnati and from there would go north to Paddy's Run. They bought a flatboat for their journey down the Ohio River.

Because they decided to cut costs and manage the boats themselves, the trip down the Ohio contained more dangers and frustrations than normal. The group ran out of provisions and landed at Gallipolis, Gallia County, where the French inhabitants welcomed them warmly and tried everything to encourage them to settle there instead of Paddy's Run. They pointed out that the land was as good as could be found anywhere. That night a fierce storm hit Gallipolis and in the morning the boat was nowhere to be found. It presumably had broken loose from its moorings during the storm. Some later speculated that their French hosts let the boat go in order to keep the Welsh there, with the intention of "booming" the growing town and inflating their land values. The boat was in fact found a few days later. But by that time the Welsh women had rebelled against further travels, declaring that they had already risked their lives and had no intention of going any further. The additional inducement of available work on the new road being built between Gallipolis and Jackson settled the matter—even though the local soils were of poor quality, making farming more difficult—and thus was born the first Welsh settlement in that part of Ohio.[43]

Still, the early hardships of the Gallipolis Welsh were great. Many from Wales had never used an ax before, and now their survival depended on it. Their early homes were basic shelters—rough log huts that hardly kept out the wind, rain, and snow—and their lives were desperately difficult. They did not send positive letters back to Wales until several hard years had passed, and it was not until 1829 that more Welsh people arrived. Then in 1831 a Reverend Edward Jones came from Cardiganshire and visited the settlement. Upon his return to Wales he published a pamphlet that extolled the rich resources of Jackson and Gallia Counties and declared it the perfect place for Welsh people to settle. And they did.[44]

The Welsh, almost entirely from Cardiganshire, began arriving in large numbers through chain migration in 1834 and found the area promising because they could both farm and perform industrial work, which consisted mainly of charcoal-based iron production. Many had circulated between rural and urban places in Wales and had experience in both farming and industry, so they found this corner of Ohio a rather ideal place of settlement. They were uniquely suited for working and developing its industries.[45]

Most were devout Calvinist Methodists who left Wales in part because they sensed an ungodly commercialism and industrialism that threatened their faith and way of life, while Ohio seemed free from these problems. In their new Ohio homes they actually felt more culturally secure than they felt in Wales, and they kept their religion so paramount in their lives that it guided their very business practices. In an attempt to build a moral economy pleasing to God they adopted low-risk strategies and rejected borrowed money and debt. This actually worked: the Welsh in "little Cardiganshire," as the area was soon called, raised living standards and developed local industry. The Welsh prospered in the area such that by midcentury the largest concentrations of Welsh were in southern Ohio. They formed 74 percent of the foreign-born population in Jackson County, and 57 percent and 20 percent in Gallia and Meigs Counties respectively.[46]

With such high concentrations of fellow Cardiganshire immigrants the Welsh in this area were particularly successful in preserving their culture. So successful was their preservation of tradition—at least for a time—that visitors insisted that the Welsh in Jackson and Gallia Counties were "more Welsh" than the Welsh back in Wales. Like many Norwegian immigrants in Minnesota who were considered "more Norwegian" than those in the old country, the Welsh in Ohio found the freedom to preserve their old beliefs and culture, which people in Wales did not necessarily have during rapid industrialization.[47] Education and music were also very important. They frequently participated in the famous Welsh *eisteddfod*, a choral music competition that showcased their brilliant tradition of congregational singing in four-part harmony. Their speaking and debating societies and mathematics and spelling contests further demonstrated their commitment to education and cultivating the mind. Those who wrote and performed music were the most highly esteemed members of their communities.[48]

It is significant that Welsh immigration to Ohio was highly place-specific. That is, they left certain places in Wales for certain places in Ohio and were thus able to preserve not just their Welsh culture but their local Welsh culture. Paddy's Run was composed almost entirely of people from Montgomeryshire, whereas the Jackson, Gallia, and Meigs Counties settlements were of people from Cardiganshire. In 1833 other people from Montgomeryshire, including some who first lived at Paddy's Run, settled in Gomer, Allen County, which became one of the most prosperous of Welsh settlements in Ohio. There was also the community of Welsh from Radnorshire, South Wales, in Radnor, Delaware County, founded by David Pugh. He purchased four thousand acres there and by 1804 had divided it up into one-hundred-acre lots and sold them to his friends back in Radnorshire—who poured in and made the community thrive. Their dedication to the abolition of slavery and the Union was demonstrated by the fact that the small community of Radnor contributed 161 soldiers for the Union army.[49] All of these tight communities were the result of chain migration based upon the information and encouragement in letters from émigrés, and the personal testimony of the Welsh, especially clergymen, who traveled to Ohio and returned to Wales with their accounts of what they had seen.

Welsh immigrants to Columbus, in contrast, consisted mainly of those who drifted in from the Welsh Hills and nearby Radnor settlements. Already in 1822 a Welshman named Ebenezer Thomas owned and operated a woolen mill there for carding, spinning, and weaving. By 1824 there were enough Welsh in the city to organize a Welsh Baptist Church. And from 1840 to the Civil War more came directly from Wales, especially Montgomeryshire, as economic conditions in that part of the country deteriorated. Religion-inspired migration was also important for the Welsh in Columbus. Samuel Roberts, a charismatic Congregational preacher, championed the poor farmers of his native Montgomeryshire and denounced landlords for their high rents and callous disregard for tenants. His efforts to change conditions failed, but he did stir up the anger of many Welsh, hundreds of whom looked to immigration to Ohio as their only means of improvement. Many of these came directly to Columbus. By 1850 Franklin County had 110 Welsh-born people. The majority of the men were skilled workers, especially carpenters and plasterers.[50]

Another example of a Welsh preacher prompting emigration is Reverend Benjamin W. Chidlaw, who emigrated from Radnor with his parents in 1821. After finishing his education at Ohio and Miami Universities, he served as minister at Paddy's Run Congregational Church from 1836 to 1844, and in 1835 and 1839 he made return visits to Wales to preach there. The Welsh were fascinated by the sermons of this transatlantic preacher who knew both countries well. Chidlaw explained that Ohio had both religious and material opportunities, which made it the ideal place to raise their children and become more independent. This was a powerful inducement for more emigration. One of those whose parents followed Chidlaw's recommendation later recalled the story, which conveys how decisions to emigrate were sometimes made quite suddenly, and by women:

> Rev. B. W. Chidlaw put us in the notion of coming to America. He was a preacher who lived with his mother at Radnor and had come back to Montgomeryshire for a visit. . . . Chidlaw told us of the great advantages for raising children in America. My mother took all of it in for she had

seven children. And she decided then and there to come here. Father objected to coming, but mother prevailed and we came, arriving in Columbus in June 1840.[51]

After the Civil War the character of Welsh immigration to Columbus and much of Ohio changed. They were now predominantly "mill men"—iron and steel workers, including puddlers—whose work still involved much skill. The Steel Rail Company of Columbus imported a Welshman to become superintendent, knowing that he would take many other Welsh workers with him, mostly from South Wales, where the industry was advanced and had much to offer the new mills in Ohio. Between half and three-fourths of workers at the Steel Rail Mill Company were Welsh. Another Columbus company that relied heavily on Welsh skills and labor at the time was the Hayden Company, which also proved to be a good stepping-stone for the immigrants to secure better, white collar jobs in the city. Ohio's heavy industries would not have developed as spectacularly as they did without the Welsh, as we will see further in chapter 5.

THE GUERNSEY SETTLERS

Shortly after the Welsh began establishing their settlements in Ohio, British people with a French Norman language and ethnic identity began doing the same. They were from the island of Guernsey, one of Britain's Channel Islands, and they were coming to what would soon be called Guernsey County, in southeastern Ohio. The county's name itself indicates the extensive influence of these unique people, whose culture was an interesting blend of French and English. Located sixty miles southwest of England and about twenty-six miles west of northern France, Guernsey is a twelve-mile-long island that covers an area of about fifty square miles. With the other Channel Islands, Guernsey fell under English control after the Norman Conquest. In the Middle Ages possession of it switched back and forth from England to France six times. Over the centuries the people of Guernsey had developed their own language, which set them apart from most other British immigrants and led them to form a distinctly ethnic community rather than to blend "invisibly" into American society.

Like many English immigrants, those from Guernsey were Wesleyan Methodists, Methodism having arrived on the island during the 1780s. They carried certificates of "good moral and Christian character," which explained that these people were leaving Guernsey because of "the fall of trade." This economic depression was due mainly to Napoleon's threatened invasion of England in 1805–06 and the strict embargo that England placed on the island. One immediate problem caused by the embargo was that England's allied Russian

Cossack soldiers, about six thousand of whom were stationed on the small island, plundered Guernsey's farmers for food and supplies. Furthermore, the
men of Guernsey were subject to English press-gangs that forced them into military service. The Guernsey migration to Ohio, then, was a classic case of multiple "push factors" leading a community to reestablish itself in the Ohio backwoods, where greater freedom and future opportunities existed.[52]

The first Guernsey immigrants to Ohio were led by the Sarchet family. The
leader was Thomas, a licensed Methodist preacher who owned a large stone
house with fourteen acres on which he grew fruit and vegetables for the market.
He was thirty-six when in May of 1806 he set out with his artisan brothers and
cousins and their wives for a better life in the New World, free from the English
and French militarism that was engulfing the Channel Islands. Altogether there
were twenty-six men, women, and children. The families boarded a ship commanded by a son-in-law of Peter Sarchet, who was "a gentleman of leisure and
means." Once out of the English Channel they flew an American flag to protect
them from French cruisers. But the French were not the only problem. During
an eight-day calm in midocean in which the ship remained totally stationary,
one of the children died. And after a terrible storm that followed, the captain was
so drunk and violent with rage and fear that the Sarchets took command,
chained the captain in his cabin, and brought the ship safely to America.[53]

Once in America the Sarchets headed overland along Zane's Trace—the
path blazed through the wilderness from Wheeling to Chillicothe, which many
of the first explorers and pioneers traveled in the eighteenth century. In Ohio
they came upon the new settlement of Cambridge, which had recently been laid
out by three families who were eager for others to join them. And while the Sarchet men were determined to proceed to Cincinnati, the women met privately
and told their husbands they would go no further; the exhausted men agreed.
Like the Welsh women who refused to go beyond Jackson County in the 1830s,
the Guernsey women were aware of their power and exercised it above the
protests of their husbands. So it was the women who shaped this episode in the
history of Ohio by establishing the place of the Guernsey settlement in southeastern Ohio, rather than in Cincinnati, as envisioned by the men.

The day after their arrival being a Sunday, the Guernseyites observed the
Sabbath by holding their own service and singing hymns. The women wore
large frilled caps, short dresses and gowns, and the men were dressed in frocks
and short breeches and long stockings, with white broad-brimmed woolen hats.
They were a strange sight for the few other white settlers, but the Guernsey immigrants were appreciated for what they were bringing to the new settlement.
In March of 1810 a new county was created out of portions of Belmont and

Muskingum Counties, and it was called Guernsey because its identity was already associated with the Channel Island of that name, and because other settlers came to regard the people from Guernsey so highly.[54]

Thomas Sarchet, the only Guernsey immigrant who could speak English upon arrival, assumed leadership of the community in Cambridge. His goal was to develop the economy of the nascent settlement, so he journeyed to Pittsburgh with packhorses to obtain salt and then made another journey to Philadelphia for goods with which he opened the first store in Cambridge, in 1808. He also sank wells in brine water for making salt, a crucial commodity on the frontier for preserving meats and making food flavorful, and rode on horseback to Marietta to procure seeds for the first orchards and nurseries of the county. The trees included the English Pearmain and English Belleflower varieties of apples. As a licensed preacher he took the lead in establishing the Methodist Episcopal Church of Cambridge and held the first service in his cabin. Itinerant preachers also held services in the Sarchet home. Local people referred to their Sunday school meetings as "French meetings" because they were held in the Guernsey language. Later, Sarchet and the Methodist Episcopal Church split over the issue of life tenure for bishops, when Sarchet—tired of the "kingly prerogative" of the old country—advocated lay delegation rather than life tenure for bishops. And after the split in 1832 he built the first Methodist Protestant Church in Cambridge at his own expense. He also brewed beer and distilled whiskey.[55]

In the true fashion of chain migration, the 1806 party was followed by other Guernsey settlers the next year. It was known as "the hard year of 1807" because the lack of food forced the settlers to survive on corn pone and mush, as well as the squirrels who were decimating their corn and wheat crops. The winter was also so cold that, as was remembered, the settlers kept warm in two ways. "One was to chop and carry wood to keep up the fires day and night, the other was to carry water from the distant springs to throw on the chimneys to keep the cabins from burning up."[56]

Among the arrivals of 1807 was Thomas Ogier, whose reasons for emigrating were unusual. Seeing a Russian soldier steeling his apples, Ogier shot him in the legs. The soldier managed to escape and make a report, but then he died of his wounds and Ogier became a fugitive of the authorities who tried to arrest him for murder. The terrified and remorseful Ogier escaped to Jersey and took a ship to America. Hearing about opportunities west, he joined the Sarchets in Ohio and wrote letters back to family and friends to encourage them to come.[57] Another early Guernsey immigrant was John Robins, who first came to Coshocton in 1807 to develop the salt industry there. In 1810 he proceeded to

Guernsey County and bought twelve hundred acres of land that eventually brought him great profit. He also served as justice of the peace.[58]

This "second Guernsey colony" was followed by other families a few years later, and Guernsey immigrants continued to trickle in after that, along with other Britons and Americans. As late as the 1830s people were still arriving from Guernsey, such that by 1835 there were more than fifty families. Among the notable ones was Edward Matthews, who arrived in 1833. After a few years digging for gold in California in the early 1850s, Matthews went on to pursue his education. He graduated from Cincinnati Law School in 1860 and in the mid-1880s was appointed by Governor George Hoadly to the Court of Common Pleas. He also was elected mayor of Cambridge, got involved with railroad promotion and real estate, and became president of the Central National Bank. Throughout his long career he did much to shape public opinion and provide leadership in civic affairs.[59]

Rarely do the historical records of the nineteenth century include people like Guernsey immigrant Sophia Gibaut, a transsexual who was born in 1812 and came alone to Guernsey County in the late 1830s. Gibaut arrived by stagecoach dressed in black, was about six feet tall with masculine proportions, but kept to herself and spoke little to people. Sophia lived her entire life in Ohio in disguise but made valuable contributions to the community at Cambridge. She earned her living by cleaning houses, nursing, pulling teeth, and serving as a midwife. For about thirty years she kept her true identity hidden. She had no friends, was seen by others as mysterious, and after she died suddenly of a fever in 1865 it was discovered that she was in fact a man.[60]

By the 1820s immigrants from other parts of Britain were joining the Guernsey settlers and helping to develop the county in important ways. Naphtali Luccock, for example, was apprenticed as a grocer and ironmonger in Cheapside, London, and had acquired some education in Cambridge, England, when he emigrated in 1821. After several years in Philadelphia he proceeded to Liberty, Guernsey County, where he prospered as a merchant and farmer. It was said that his experience with the "squalor and slum in Cheapside" had inspired him to be an active citizen in the United States and do everything to "advance the people in morals, religion and politics." He was Liberty's "model business man," and served twelve years as justice of the peace. He also served as Liberty's first postmaster, and when the postal department ordered him to rename the settlement (on account of there being too many Ohio towns named Liberty), Luccock chose the name Kimbolton, after his ancestral home in Huntingdonshire. Here was yet another example of British immigrants providing place names in Ohio. Luccock also led the formation of the local Methodist Episcopal Church, which was an offshoot from the church at Cambridge, and became its first class leader. In 1849 he ran as a Whig candidate for state representative and was defeated. One factor in Luccock's defeat was the fact that he had distant relatives who were slave owners in South Carolina, and during the campaign he admitted candidly that if he had come to South Carolina rather than Ohio he might own slaves too. The local Free Soil candidate, John B. Mitchell, and the Democratic candidate and victor, Matthew Gaston, used the statement to destroy Luccock's chances.[61]

The 1850 Census recorded that Guernsey County had 135 English-born residents (it does not indicate how many of these were from Guernsey) as well as 23 Scots and 4 Welsh, out of a total of over 30,000 people. This included 1,246 immigrants, nearly 1,000 of them Irish.[62] Considering how relatively few British immigrants there were in Guernsey County at midcentury, it is remarkable that they had such a profound influence in the county, providing it with its very name. Their influence was far greater than mere numbers would suggest. After the Civil War there was a new surge of British immigrants in the county—not from Guernsey but from the industrial centers of England, Scotland, and Wales. Among them were many highly skilled and experienced persons who helped transform Guernsey County into an important industrial area, especially in mining, iron and steel, and tin plating. We will turn to them in chapter 5.

The Manx

Another group of British immigrants who formed a close-knit community in Ohio were the Manx, from the Isle of Man. With their distinctive culture and Gaelic-based Manx language, they resembled other European immigrants by migrating as communities to the Western Reserve, near Cleveland, in the 1820s and 1830s. Here they formed the largest concentration of Manx in the United States. They also exhibited a clannishness that commonly marked non-English groups. They limited their social contacts largely to other Manx, felt little pressure to assimilate, and created mutual aid societies for Manx newcomers. In this way they managed to keep their culture and language alive in Ohio.

The Isle of Man has always been a distinct and separate part of the British Isles. Set in the middle of the Irish Sea, the 227-square-mile island developed its own culture and language, derived from Celtic and Norse influences. On a clear day England, Scotland, Wales, and Ireland are all in view. Until 1266 the isle was owned by Norway, though it had its own king. In the fourteenth century it became part of the realm of England's King Edward III, but in 1405 his descendent—Henry IV—gave it to the Stanley family. In 1765 it was finally sold to Britain for seventy-thousand pounds, and it became a self-governed dependency of the British crown within the Commonwealth.

The Manx were seafarers and fishermen, farmers of the thin Isle of Man soil, as well as shepherds, producers of wool and linen, and smugglers. In the eighteenth and nineteenth centuries, Methodist missionaries converted much of the island's inhabitants. But unlike other parts of the British Isles, Man had virtually no industrial growth to absorb immigrants as the population grew and pressed the limited availability of land. Social pressures intensified at the turn of the eighteenth century. There was much resentment over increased taxes to fund the wars against Napoleon, and in 1817 a new tithe levied by the British government resulted in rioting on the isle. Finally, with the decline of the fishing industry and the inherent hardships of farming stony soil, many Manx looked to other places for procuring good land and improving their livelihoods. They found the ideal place in the area around Cleveland.

The story of Manx settlement in Ohio is a classic one of chain migration through an informational network. It started when Dr. Harrison, a Manx physician for the British Army, visited the legendary Niagara Falls and the southern shore of Lake Erie sometime in the early 1820s. Upon his return to the Isle of Man his enthusiastic reports of what he had seen in Ohio unleashed a pent up desire for emigration. In 1826, William Kelly, a local school teacher from Kirk Michael, with his wife Eleanor and two children, together with two other Manx families—Patrick and Ann Tear, and William and Mary Kneen—set out for Cleveland, then a town of only six hundred people. They settled in Newburgh, about six miles south of Cleveland, where Kelly leased fifty acres before purchasing it from the Connecticut Land Company. His letters back to the isle were published in Manx newspapers, widely read, and became the catalyst for more immigrants. "A man can earn thrice as much here in America per day and provisions are thrice as cheap, as in the Isle of Man," he wrote, with perhaps some exaggeration. "It is worth while to come out, let every many judge for himself, but if we who have come were in the Isle of Man we would all come to the plentiful country again."[63]

Along with Kelly's letters, those of Thomas Tear, another Manx settler in Ohio, were published in the *Manx Advertiser* of February 15, 1827. Some of the more enticing details stirred the Manx readership:

Taking into consideration, the way of living among the lower class of people in the Isle of Man, compared with the same sort of people here [Ohio], give as our decided opinion, that a laborer can live as well here, as a man

that has from 20 to 30 acres of land in the island. Mechanics and tradesmen, equal to a great many of your farmers. Farmers can live as easy here
as they desire, once they get their land cleared, they can raise all the neces-
saries of life here in abundance. Having no tithes to pay here as they may
desire, once they get their land, only a tax of one dollar per 100 acres of
land. . . . The country is so well watered, and found in all things, necessary
for comfort and conveniences of life. The inhabitants, for the most part a
civil, enlightened and religious society. . . . Sugar maple is plentiful on our
farm, and had produced some sugar this season already. In the spring of
the year they make up their yearly stock. There are a great many shrubs
and herbs, which serve as substitutes for tea. . . . We are all very satisfied
that we came to this land of liberty and opportunity. When we consider
how easy it is for a man to live here, enjoy the luxuries of life. But we often
lament that so many of our countrymen have not the means of emigrating here, and it would give us the greatest joy to see them here.[64]

In the Manx towns and villages, letters like these were "passed from hand to
hand" and they "produced great excitement" as the descriptions of Ohio
reached fantastic proportions—"deer and turkeys running at large," "forest
trees distilling sugar," and "land to be got for the asking." The more astute realized that "the more sober colors of the picture were left out." Yet, the letters from
Ohio had a hypnotic effect on many readers. At Kirk Andrews—a village on the
northern end of the Isle—lived the Radcliffe family, who received so many letters from Ohio that their house became known as "the Ohio Cottage." People
from other parts of the island came to hear the letters recited aloud and then
considered coming to the state to try a new life there as well.[65]
As poor Manx men and women heard more and more about Ohio, their
thoughts sometimes turned to little else. Daniel Caley recalled the cold Manx
winters sitting around the turf fire and the conversation almost always turned
to Ohio, especially as the fifteen-year lease on their land was nearing expiration:

They tell me, Mother, on the market and at the fishings that land is cheap
there; that its fields are fertile and acres are boundless, that the son of the
poor man has the same chance as the son of the rich. Our fifteen year lease
will soon expire. Shall we renew it or go to far-off America, what shall we
do? After much deliberation, deciding as most true wives would, she said,
"We will go. We will leave our friends, and acquaintances, our relatives and
neighbors. We will leave *mannin veg veen* (our Dear Little Island) with its
green hills by the sea and seek a new home in a new country.[66]

In the early summer of 1827, after the flood of enticing publicity washed over the Isle of Man, migration began in earnest. About seventy families headed out, the following year about the same number joined them, and conveniently took the newly opened Erie Canal to Buffalo and then a boat to Cleveland. Many of them spoke no English, and during the early years their conversations and religious services were conducted in their own Manx tongue.[67]

Among the Manx immigrants of 1827 was forty-four-year-old William Corlett, whose family had worked an unenclosed farm of about forty acres near Peel, on the Isle, for five generations or more. To finance the migration Corlett sold the farm, on which he found it hard to provide for his six children. The family left with fifty other Manx and went directly to Newburgh township, where the nucleus of the Manx community had been established the year before. The Corletts leased fifty acres and then purchased land that had already been cleared, the second purchase from the Connecticut Land Company. The steady flow of additional Manx families in subsequent years enabled the Corletts and other Manx immigrants to succeed as commercial farmers, and though Corlett was not interested in land speculation, his farm was valued at $3,300 in 1860. His migration was apparently economically motivated rather than political, as he did not bother to become a citizen until 1836, a full decade after his migration. Corlett also donated land for the community's new log schoolhouse in which the Manx children could be educated in their native language and learn English.[68]

On several occasions William Corlett wrote to his family, and his letters from Newburgh to his brother Thomas in Kirk Michael reveal much about the local conditions, their enthusiasm for Ohio, and their desire to have other family members join them:

> All my neighbors does very well and encreasing every day. We are about ninety person in the neighbourhood, all from the little Isle of Man, and we all attend to hear the Gospel preached every Sabbath Day. . . . I do prefer this country for my own part; and if I should be in the old country now I would soon come out. I would be very glad if some of my relations would be here; but I don't encourage any person to come. Let every person make their own mind up about that. I have thirty-two acres of improvement, with acres under wheat and 12 acres ready to sow.[69]

Eleven years later Corlett wrote again to his brother on the Isle of Man, with more encouraging descriptions that included political matters. "I know of no one of the Manks who are not doing well," Corlett claimed. "I believe they have plenty of work and pretty good pay. There is no regular wages established yet. I believe the wages for shomakers, joiners & other tradesmen is from one dollar to one & a half per day." In 1842, reflecting on the prevailing economic depression and new friction between the United States and Britain, Corlett remained very optimistic: "Money is getting better and the prospect is that in a few years the money will be good. All the disturbances between this government & Great Britain is settled and now universal harmony and peace reigns through the States. Crops has been very good this year." Corlett also put his faith in the local religious revivals that were sweeping the country, known collectively as the Second Great Awakening. "The country is growing more & more healthy, the state of society more & more moral. There are great revivals all over the country & thousands are turning to the Lord. The Lord is working powerfully in all this land. Temperance sweeps all before it. Millions have joined the tee-total temperance society."[70]

Interestingly, none of Corlett's siblings joined him. The Manx economy improved due to emigration and the growth of English tourism, and the other Corletts also found opportunities closer to home, in Manchester, Liverpool, and London. But many other Manx responded to letters from Ohio, detailing what life in the Buckeye State could offer them, and the migration continued quite steadily into the 1890s.

The early Manx settlers—described as "strong, independent and individualistic, deeply religious as well as ambitious"[71]—faced a very different environment than the one they had left behind. Whereas the Isle of Man had been settled and developed for many centuries, northern Ohio was still a daunting virgin land. The Manx in Ohio recalled the "terror" caused by the "long howling of the wolves," the roads made of "bottomless mud" and "new fields covered with stumps," and of a "weary stretch of quagmire and country" near Warrensville. And "almost without exception" the Manx in Ohio "encountered the ague and fevers incident to a new country," and "in some instances the heads of families were taken away."[72] Angus Munn Cowle, a Manxman of Scottish descent, found himself surrounded by Indians pointing at him in a way that petrified him. Like many other British immigrants, Cowle had heard stories of Indian cruelties; but the Indians were simply amazed to see a person with red hair—which they had never seen before.[73]

The early difficulties and perceived dangers did not stop other Manx from coming. Soon there were over 3,000 Manx immigrants and their children in the Cleveland vicinity. Bound by their own language and experience of migrating through networks, they produced a clannishness uncharacteristic of most other British immigrants. In 1851 the Manx established the Mona's Relief Society, dedicated to assisting their fellow immigrants. The society's impressive work reveals the dedication of the Manx community toward their fellow expatriots: from 1876 to 1886, 268 persons applied for relief, and a total of $1,746 was distributed. Some of that was paid to the families of people who died without means for a proper burial.[74]

The Manx of Cleveland contributed significantly to the economy and society. The *Cleveland Leader* claimed that "no class of citizens are more respectable, industrious, or worthy than those whose nativity was in the Isle of Man," and that "Manxmen make good citizens everywhere. They are lovers of home and of freedom and possess manly characters. It is seldom that we find a beggar among them. They have a spirit of independence among them, which they maintain socially and politically."[75] Thomas Quayle, a master shipbuilder among the earliest arrivals of 1827, built some of the finest ships that plied the waters of the Great Lakes during the nineteenth century, and he became known as "the father of Cleveland Shipbuilding." William Kerruish became a famous Cleveland lawyer. And John Gill, who arrived in 1854, established the building firm of John Gill & Sons, which built many of the city's finest buildings, including the Terminal Tower.

Generally, the Manx were not slow to shift their political loyalties to America. They were widely known for leading enthusiastic celebrations of the Fourth of July. They also participated prominently in Cleveland's Annual Festival, providing "excellent music, a bounteous supper, and giddy mazes of the dances."[76] And Manx immigrants continued to prosper in later years. Their prominent cultural organization, the Manx Choral Society, was organized in 1926, and the Cleveland Manx cultivated closer cultural ties with their homeland.

In addition to the settlements of the Courtaulds, Welsh, Guernseyites, and Manx, there were notable frontier communities founded by British pioneers. One example is that of Samuel Coates and his son, also named Samuel. They were raised in the northern city of Leeds before it was an industrial giant. There the Coates attempted and failed in business so they came to the United States in the 1790s to start over. When in 1799 a mail route was established along Zane's Trace, which was scarcely a road at this time, the elder Coates was appointed postmaster at crossings on the Hockhocking River. Here in 1800 the Coates father and son team erected the first log cabin and post office and the settlement of Lancaster was born. The elder Coates remained postmaster until his death in 1808, after which Samuel Jr. took over the job until 1814.[77]

Other English immigrants became the founders or early settlers of Ohio towns by virtue of their appointment as new postmasters, as land surveyors for the government, or as the first suppliers of provisions. All three were true of the

Larwill brothers, of Kent. William Larwill emigrated in 1793 and landed in Philadelphia during the height of a yellow fever epidemic. After his quarantine there he lived in Pittsburgh until 1802, when he moved to Columbiana County. Two years later he was appointed the first postmaster in Fawscettstown, before it was renamed East Liverpool. At the same time William's brother, Joseph, was in Wayne County "running the county off in sections for the federal govern- ment," and he was joined by yet another Larwill brother, John, who was hired by the government to provide the surveying party with fresh provisions. John, only fifteen at the time, had to cut down trees to bridge streams over which he carried his provisions, while forcing his horse to swim.

Soon the Larwills moved into farming and business. In 1809 Joseph and John planted the first corn and mowed the first grass for cattle in Wayne County. In Wooster, William Larwill erected the town's first frame dwelling house with a broadax and a drawing knife, a building that he used to store pow- der, lead, and tobacco for trade with the Indians. The same house was expanded into the first store when in 1814 Joseph and John ordered goods from Philadel- phia and sold them in William's parlor. Later they teamed up with a couple of Philadelphians and built a large store that provided for the growing commu- nity. In 1820 John Larwill was elected justice of the peace for Wooster Township and held that office for six years, a reflection of his role as the town's most im- portant founder and developer.[78]

The immigrants who were among the first in the region were subject to the uncertainties and hazards that came with exploration, and frequently had to make adjustments during their early years of settlement. John McCafferty, from Sweet Avon, Scotland, was one of the first settlers in Cincinnati, having arrived there in the 1780s when it was just becoming established. McCafferty unfortu- nately had chosen land that was too swampy and infested with malaria, so in 1790 he moved to Chillicothe, which at that time consisted of but a few cabins. Here the McCafferty family found better land and prospered. They got along well with local Indians, enjoyed their company, and frequently went on hunting expeditions with them. The McCaffertys were among the first settlers of Chil- licothe, who saw it grow from a small village with a large Indian population to a prosperous, strategic town, and the first capital of Ohio.[79]

There are many other cases of British pioneers establishing communities and then entering commercial and professional roles as the communities devel- oped. The family of Joseph and Ann Newlove emigrated from Newton, York- shire, in 1821 with their fifteen year-old son, Joseph. They were among the first pioneers of Clark County and founded a settlement near Springfield. At age twenty-one Joseph Jr. set out on his own, purchased a farm, expanded his land holdings, and became an important player in real estate and banking. By 1852 he was elected county auditor and was manager of the Marysville Bank. Then after the Civil War he established the Farmers' Bank and managed that for the rest of his career. He was remembered as an "estimable gentleman" from England, quiet, unostentatious, a good neighbor, and an esteemed citizen.[80]

British immigrants in Ohio were indeed a mixed group of people. Though most were individuals and families who filtered into the population, some—the Welsh, Guernsey settlers, and Manx—had linguistic and cultural distinctions that led them to attempt to form separate communities. They did have some important things in common. All were subjects of the British Crown at the time of their migration. Also, most—particularly before the Civil War—felt a strong attraction to Ohio's rich farm lands, and many attempted to farm it and make it their own.

4

Agriculture

I bought a 40 acre lot of land
at 1½ doller per acre with a county road and a
stream of water runing through it.

William Morris, formerly of Lancashire,
in Washington County, December 30, 1838.[1]

HROUGHOUT the nineteenth century, British immigrants in Ohio
filled a wide variety of occupations, especially as cities grew and industries expanded. The widening opportunities in Ohio are evident when
Ohio is compared to other states in the Old Northwest. The 1870 census reveals
that in Wisconsin, Illinois, and Michigan—where industries were less well developed—the English and Welsh were more heavily concentrated in agriculture.
Ohio's more diverse economy and growing industries beckoned. And yet Ohio's
farmland maintained its powerful grip on the minds of many. During the first
half of the century in particular, farming attracted a majority of the British immigrants to Ohio.[2]

According to the county histories there was a surge of British immigrant
farmers to Ohio in the late 1840s and 1850s. This was related to Britain's historic
repeal of the Corn Laws in 1846, which ended tariffs on imported grain. The
protective tariffs had begun during the ultraconservative, reactionary phase of
British politics in the aftermath of the Napoleonic Wars. In effect the Corn Laws
were a subsidy to the landed classes and the farmers who owned or rented land,
and were a clear example of the government's bias in favor of the aristocracy
and food producers. But the Corn Laws also raised the price of bread and made
the hard life of the urban poor and industrial workers even harder. As bitterness
between the classes became more palpable, and as some politicians feared the
revolutionary unrest that was building up on the European continent in the

1840s, action was finally taken. The anti–Corn Law League and the rise of the more moderate Tory faction in Parliament, led by Robert Peel, were finally able to dismantle the laws as the potato famine demonstrated that grain imports were necessary. They convinced Parliament that free trade would lower food prices and diffuse social unrest and that liberalizing the economy in this way would also bring benefits to manufacturing and industry. Britain opened its economy to food imports, and prices of grain and food fell significantly.[3]

British farmers had some adjusting to do. As grain prices fell, farmers had to compensate by increasing production, either by expanding their acreage, employing more advanced "scientific techniques" that included new fertilizers, or by engaging in mixed farming and animal husbandry. Some adjusted by migrating to Ohio. According to the limited data, Lincolnshire, Kent, Cambridgeshire, and Yorkshire saw the greatest numbers of their farmers depart for Ohio during the postrepeal period. These counties had clay soils that were hard to improve and make more productive. Additionally, there was a long tradition of migration to America from these counties, and some farmers had been entertaining for some time the thought of joining friends and neighbors across the sea. So when prices fell many took that as the occasion for their move.[4]

Paradoxically, the immediate effect of the repeal of the Corn Laws on the Ohio grain market was to depress prices. Ohio farmers had been exporting grain to Canada for milling, and during the Corn Laws Canada enjoyed trade preferences due to lower tariffs. Without protection, Canada lost part of its market to Europe and curbed imports of Ohio grain.[5] But the longer term proved beneficial to American producers, especially those in highly productive states like Illinois and Wisconsin.

LAND ACQUISITION

During the antebellum period especially, Britons on or near the frontier experienced the full range of harsh rigors that came with pioneer life. Extreme hardship could be a shock for those who believed in the "agrarian myth" and expected a life of idyllic self-sufficiency in the wilderness. Yet, for some the frontier was ideal because they knew what they wanted and what they could expect there. William Berryman and his sons left England because of their love of hunting and their numerous arrests for poaching in their native Devonshire. Arriving in the backwoods near Dayton in 1820, they immediately purchased ninety-three acres on which they could kill game to their heart's content.

Within five years the Berrymans sold their farm and moved to the even more unsettled parts of Logan Township where they continued to live as true pioneers and practiced their formidable hunting skills. Their new home was surrounded by Shawnee Indians. One of the Berryman sons, Russell, learned the Shawnee language, befriended them, and often joined in their feasts and sports. Russell became so fluent in the language and familiar with Shawnee culture that he was employed as an interpreter. Later in life he entertained his friends by performing Shawnee dances and recounting Indian powwows and other important rituals. He also told stories of Indians, their interaction with white settlers, and their tragic addiction to alcohol. Russell Berryman relished pioneer living and the unlimited opportunities for hunting. Once he shot seven deer before breakfast, and at another time after a two-day hunt he and his brother produced four large barrels of dressed and packed venison. One winter the Berrymans killed twenty-seven deer, gutted them, let them freeze, and then loaded the carcasses onto a sled and pulled them to Dayton where they traded their kill for supplies of salt. On their many forays into the wild parts of western Ohio, the Berrymans lodged and ate with their Indian friends. They had truly found their paradise in the backwoods of western Ohio, where they flourished and could hunt without restraint.[6]

But few British immigrants intended to live the kind of life that the Berrymans created for themselves in western Ohio. Some expected to live on the frontier with ample leisure time and little hard work. Such unrealistic ideas may have come from books that glorified nature, a popular literary genre of the day. Perhaps they had read books such as Hector St. Jean de Crevecoeur's *Letters from an American Farmer* (1782), which idealized American nature and the agrarian life that supposedly offered independence and happiness. More likely, people simply underestimated the contrast between living in English towns or cities and living on the isolated Ohio frontier. This was a place and time when one had to be sure it was safe to fetch a cow in the evening, whether "a cry for assistance was a neighbor in need or an Indian ambush," when no one ventured far from one's cabin unarmed.[7] Thus, there was a distinct difference between most American-born and British-born pioneers: for most of the former, frontier life was a continuation of what they had known; for the latter, life on the frontier entailed a profound life change.

Some immigrants actually left busy and sophisticated urban areas in England for the virgin wilderness of Ohio, as did the Joseph Pearson family, Londoners who settled in the wilds of Clark County in 1832. The contrast between Europe's largest city and the backwoods of Ohio was a shock. The Pearsons felt threatened by wolves and Indians, even though by this time American Indians were no longer much of a threat and had much more to fear from white settlers, who were forcibly removing them to the west. By 1825 there were only 2,350

Indians in Ohio, and they held but a half a million of Ohio's seven and a half million acres.[8]

The William Green family of London also settled in a remote part of Ohio in 1846 when they arrived in Wood County, which still had enough Indians and wolves to frighten most Londoners. They were among the first settlers in Plain Township, and spent their first years in a "rude log hut" while they struggled to carve a farm out of the wilderness. Ten years later John Marwick, a drover from Cambridgeshire, came to the same area. He walked from Toledo to Bowling Green, and still found the area a "wilderness" where life was "hard and uncongenial."[9]

John Smalley from Lincolnshire also came with his family to Wood County to work on the Ohio Canal until he could afford to buy eighty acres. He built a log cabin ten-by-twenty-four feet, without windows or a proper door, in which his family of six lived a desperately hard life for a number of years. Other Lincolnshire families arrived in the county at the same time and lived in similar conditions. That fellow English families also struggled and generally succeeded in the same undeveloped corner of Ohio must have brought some comfort and reassurance. And they must have sought each other out from time to time, when their limited social lives allowed it, to help each other in time of need, to share hopes and visions for a future in Ohio, and perhaps to reminisce about England. Remarkably, many other British immigrants left modern urban environments in Britain to take on the Ohio frontier, clear land, and endure alien and difficult conditions.[10]

Scots also met the challenges of taming the frontier, including Archibald and Agnes Grieve, who were early settlers in Greene County. Having emigrated from Selkirk in 1812, the thirty-seven-year-old couple and their children spent two years in New York, then pioneered in Warren County for a while, and finally moved on to Greene County, where they bought one hundred acres of wild land. They sensed a danger and isolation on the frontier that proved highly challenging for the transplanted Scottish family. They even felt a need to bar the door of their little log cabin to keep out the wolves. Archibald was a good enough shot to eliminate the wolves and provide venison for the family, and he cleared his land at a reasonable pace. They raised nine children who helped tame their piece of the Ohio frontier.[11]

Most of the British who farmed in Ohio bought land that needed at least some clearing. Those who went to the frontier, of course, had much clearing and logging to do. Coming to untamed parts of Ohio in the early nineteenth century from a country largely denuded of its forests, the British immigrant would be stunned. There was the dense, encompassing forest with the awesome trees, but also the daunting reality that without removing them there would be a depressing lack of sunlight, fear of the unknown lurking in the thick woods, and no hope of making a living. Clearing land was an enormous task that few seem to have appreciated fully until they began the work.

There were two general methods of clearing: the "southern method" involved girdling a tree by cutting a ring around the bark to deaden it, causing the leaves to drop, which allowed the immediate planting of crops. But its drawbacks included the potentially dangerous falling of limbs and the later removal of trunks, as well as a ghastly appearance. The other was the "New England method," which required the immediate felling and burning of trees, and therefore more immediate intensive labor. Those lucky enough to take up cornfields previously owned by Indians had much less clearing to do. Most of the British farmers in Ohio took up land that required substantial clearing, and they tended to use the "New England method."[12]

Unfortunately, the British had little experience at wielding an ax, in stark contrast to their American counterparts. English observers like William Cobbett were in awe of the Americans' proficiency with the ax, which he ascribed to the notion that they were "born with an ax in one hand and a gun in the other." Describing Americans along the Ohio River he noted that "An ax is their tool and with that tool *cutting down* trees or *cutting them up*, they will do ten times as much in a day as any other men that I ever saw. Set one of these men upon a wood of timber trees, and his slaughter will astonish you."[13] At best a newly arrived Englishman could clear about five acres of woodland a year, while an expert Ohio axman could clear an acre within three to seven days. One former cabinetmaker from England was able to break and clear only two acres a year near Gallipolis—and that was mostly prairie land. Stephen Bewick left England to purchase eighty acres of timberland in Ohio but was so overwhelmed by the task that he returned to England to work there. Eight years later he migrated again—this time to Wisconsin, to settle on the treeless prairie.

A few others were more successful. In Stark County one English immigrant cleared twenty acres in five years. John Smalley, son of a Lincolnshire laborer who arrived in Akron in 1848, had almost no schooling and started out in Ohio binding wheat for 37½ cents per day. He then worked on the Ohio Canal near Chillicothe for a couple of years for between $10 and $17 dollars per month, with which he bought eighty acres in Portage Township for $450 dollars. Smalley cleared his farm bit by bit during the winter months while the canals were frozen over, and continued to combine canal work with farming as a means of ready cash. Other British immigrants relied on their skills as craftsmen to earn money and hire others to clear their land and then took up farming once the land was ready, but most had to clear the land themselves.[14]

Some British pioneers faced greater challenges while clearing their plot of Ohio forest and succeeded against the odds. John Thomas was a particularly determined British pioneer. He left Wales in 1835 after an accident required his leg to be amputated, a procedure that he watched with nothing—not even alcohol—to dull the pain. In Portage County he still managed to clear his virgin farm while also working both as a blacksmith in his community and temporarily for the Ohio and Pennsylvania Canal. His resilience and ability to transcend his handicap were an inspiration.[15]

All British immigrants found clearing the land a hard task, and for those from professional backgrounds without much experience with hard physical labor, the challenge was especially serious and often insurmountable. Yet even among these, there were some who found clearing land was possible, though difficult. William Kinmont, a Scot who emigrated in 1824, was a "highly educated man" who taught languages in an academy in Cincinnati until 1835, when he moved to Champaign County to buy heavily wooded land on which to farm. He managed to clear eighty acres in four to five years—a rate equal to that of most hardy Ohioans—though he had the help of his four sons.[16]

Merchants and people with backgrounds in the professions and unaccustomed to hard physical work were especially susceptible to idealized notions about pioneering life. Some abandoned their advantageous positions to make their own attempt as pioneers—only to return to their original occupation when reality hit them in the face. An example is George Morris, one of the pioneer merchants of McConnelsville, Morgan County, who arrived from his native Trowbridge, Wiltshire, in 1817. Morris started out in life with some fortunate advantages. His father was a well-to-do merchant and a "man of some prominence" who provided his son with an excellent education. He intended to watch him rise within the academic profession and climb the social ladder of English society. George, however, heard "the glowing accounts of the new country and the opportunities offered for the acquirement of property and position," and disappointed his parents by migrating to Marietta with his brother in 1817. Here George started out by teaching and his brother worked at his craft of coppersmith. Though the brother found Ohio falling short of his high expectations and returned to England, George stayed and found a superb tract of land in Bloom Township in Morgan County.

George's letters home were so glowing and persuasive that in two years the entire family joined him. The Morrises had every reason to feel encouraged, because other English pioneers were thriving in the area. Among them were George and Martha Corner, well-to-do middle-class people who emigrated from Cheshire. They had prepurchased eleven hundred acres of land in Kentucky and then emigrated in 1795 with their large family, only to find the title in dispute, so they settled in Morgan County and prospered. There was also an Englishman named Edward Miller, who pioneered in the area and became a successful farmer. But the Morrises were not up to such a task. For them clearing was so new and so frustrating that they leased out their lands. George fell back on the family mercantile tradition, turned to salt production, and did very well. He then took up tin ware, then the hardware trade to provide farmers and settlers with their necessities.[17]

Altogether, the Britons who came to the Ohio frontier were quite diverse in their socioeconomic backgrounds. In fact, some wealthy people from elite heritages or aristocratic aspirations settled in undeveloped parts of the state and made a significant impact on the local landscape, society, and economy. Particularly noteworthy was Thomas Robinson, a widower, "a man of wealth," whose "views and ideas differed widely from those held by the average pioneer." He came from England in 1820 and settled near Mansfield, Richland County, where he bought a quarter section of land that he soon expanded. Here he built "Robinson castle" on Big Hill, a home so spectacular that it became a tourist attraction. The building and what went on there amazed the simple pioneers who were still clearing land in the area and barely surviving as subsistence farmers. The juxtaposition of English-style aristocratic luxury with small clearings and log shanties sheltering poor pioneers must have been stunning. The "castle" was actually a very large house built of oversized bricks; but its architectural style resembled that of aristocratic, stately homes, and it stood like a castle on the summit of the hill. It had several wings and wine cellars arched with carved stonework.

Not much is known about Robinson's background. He hailed from Derbyshire and came with money to live "imperious in his style and lordly in his manner." He "adhered to the old style of dress," which evokes images of knee breaches and powdered wigs. He was a real character who must have shaped or confirmed many stereotypes of an English gentleman. More important for the economic development of the Mansfield area was Robinson's sense of noblesse oblige. He was a major benefactor to his community by giving ready employment to many people on his estate. Furthermore, he paid his workers very high wages—in cash—which people greatly appreciated at a time when money was scarce and much local business was done via bartering and payment in kind. When some local settlers found it impossible to pay their property taxes, they obtained the money by digging out stumps on Robinson's land. Not having the patience to let the stumps rot, which other people usually chose to do, Robinson hired men to dig them out at great expense. As stories of his generosity and eccentricity spread, and as fabulous rumors of his immense wealth began to circulate, people traveled for miles to work for him. Robinson reportedly gave work to all who applied. On average, he had at least a dozen men working for him year round.

After his Ohio estate was cleared, Robinson returned to England to find a suitable wife. He was absent from his Ohio estate for fully seven years before finally returning with her. He never explained the surprising length of his absence, and no one dared to ask him about it. His wife was also the epitome of the English upper-class woman, but when she died after eight years in Ohio, Robinson buried her in Milton cemetery, and in 1843 he returned to England and died within the year. By midcentury the castle's arched foundations gave way, a wing collapsed, and over time the rest fell into a mass of impressive ruins, which continued to attract tourists from far and wide. Some tourists traveled by train to see the ruins and paid guides to tell them the story of the castle and its eccentric English owner, who was known as "King Tom."

But the legacy of Thomas Robinson did not die with him. "King Tom" had a brother, Francis, who joined him in Ohio and settled nearby. And Francis had a son, James S. Robinson, who helped organize the Eighty-second Regiment of the Ohio Infantry and served as a colonel and brigadier general. He led the 2,800 men of his regiment in the battle of Gettysburg and allegedly suffered the highest casualty rate of any Union troop: only sixty-five escaped death or injury. General Robinson himself was wounded but survived to serve in the state legislature and as secretary of state.

It is hard to exaggerate the impact of Thomas Robinson on what was then a remote section of central Ohio, even though the memory has faded. Not only did he contribute to the economy by supporting local workers; his estate added a rare element of refinement and grandeur to a part of the state that was just beginning its economic and social development. Furthermore, his eccentric behavior and generosity created local perceptions of the English. For years people talked about "King Tom" and his "castle" on a hill on the Richland County frontier, and how would-be aristocrats did not really fit into the Ohio cultural landscape.[18]

Some other British immigrants from nonagrarian backgrounds also brought new traditions and artistic sensibilities to the Ohio frontier. One well-known pioneer, John Robinson—no relation to "King Tom"—was the son of the famous London artist who superintended both the construction of the interior of the

House of Lords and the throne of Windsor Castle. John himself was raised in London, educated in a French Protestant College, and inherited both money and talent from his father. But after a fire destroyed his London house, which was worth forty thousand dollars, he moved to New York City in 1833. Within a short time he traveled to Delaware County and purchased four hundred acres. He soon doubled his acreage and built up an especially fine, highly cultivated farm. Thanks to his upbringing and natural artistic talent, Robinson furnished his large home with elaborate carving and ornamentation that he created. He was also a highly skilled painter. Local people often stopped by to see his artwork, which was a rare and welcome addition to the Ohio frontier.[19]

There were many other memorable British settlers who contributed much to the culture and the success of the growing frontier communities. Many of them were women. Because the British on the Ohio frontier consisted largely of family units, men and women were often in balanced partnerships, sharing equally important tasks and challenging experiences. The burden on women was enormous, beyond what they could have imagined in Britain, and could reach crisis proportions in times of emergency. Soon after Rebecca Burlend and her family left England and settled on the Illinois frontier in 1831, her husband fell sick and she was forced to harvest the crops while also caring for three children, one of whom she was still nursing.[20] In addition to burdens such as these was the need to maintain the simple frontier home, which required constant attention to keep out the elements.

It is hard to overestimate the value of women like Mrs. Homes, born in Kent in 1799, who immigrated to Saybrook, Ashtabula County. She and her family transformed wild, unbroken land into a farm. She was a true pioneer, doing all forms of work except holding the plough. In addition to her duties, she "took the place of a regular physician," often traveling from her home for days at a time to attend to the sick and needy—an important and demanding task for which she never received any compensation. But the physical and mental demands took their toll on Homes. The "unnatural life of those days ruined her health," and for the last twenty years of her life until her death in 1866, she was an invalid.[21] The life story of this British woman, who perhaps gave too much of herself to her neighbors, is a poignant reminder of how difficult it was to create a farm on the American frontier.

Caring for the sick was a common task for British pioneer women. Scotswoman Jane McRitchie, affectionately known as "Grandma Ritchie," was a very welcome addition to the northwest Ohio frontier. In the words of her biographer, she "endured all the hardships of an early settler near Port Clinton,

performing the various arts of kindness which one in that situation finds it possible to do. She attended the sick and cared for the suffering, when care was not
easy to obtain, and was indeed one of those remarkably pure and good women
with the strong character that only this kind of hardship can develop."[22]

The travels of Mrs. Homes and Grandma Ritchie through the most remote
parts of Ohio also illustrate a mobility that must have brought them into contact with fellow British expatriates who were sharing their immigration experiences. Above all it was the common language that allowed British women to in-
teract with others in these important ways. For, whereas many other European
women immigrants never learned English and remained cut off from the larger
community, English women as well as Scots and many Welsh could communi-
cate immediately and not feel like total strangers in a strange land.[23]

English immigrants to Ohio were remarkably diverse not only in their variety of backgrounds and experiences but also their motivations. For many—
probably a larger proportion than any other immigrant group—it was mostly
the "pull" of Ohio that set them in motion, not any negative "push" factor in the
old country. Among the immigrant farmers, especially, there were some who
were prosperous in England, with bright futures there, too. But they could not
rest until they saw Ohio for themselves. Apparently, some of these well-to-do
immigrants had neighbors or relatives who settled in Ohio and had written letters describing the opportunities to own large estates.

John Harrison was one such person. He owned an "excellent farm" of 114
acres near Otley, Yorkshire. But in 1814 he made his first trip to America and traveled as far as Pittsburgh before returning to England. Two years later he left for
America again with his family and they became the first English pioneers in
North Township, Harrison County. But life on the edge of the Ohio frontier was
harder than he had anticipated, so in 1823 he returned to England where he lived
out the rest of his days. His son Joseph, however, stayed in Ohio as the benefici-
ary of his father's experience as an immigrant, and probably his capital and expert farming knowledge as well, because he became the largest landowner of the
township and the most successful stock farmer, on over seven hundred acres.
Not only did Joseph Harrison become the leader of the county's dairy industry,
he also introduced the first mowing machine to the area, manufactured and installed the first drainpipe in the township, and supplied much of the drainage
pipe for other parts of the county. His careful practice of scientific farming and
his expertise in drainage was admired by many. His fame grew when he raised
the largest steer the county ever saw—one that weighed 3,250 pounds. His success as a farmer and citizen led him to serve as township trustee.[24]

It is highly interesting that, like the Harrisons, another farmer from Otley also made repeat migrations to North Township at roughly the same time. He was John McLandsborough, who came to Harrison County alone in 1831 and purchased 106 acres near the Harrison homestead. He then returned to England and in 1834 brought his family along and pioneered successfully enough to expand their holdings to over 500 acres. Such repeat migrations were apparently common ways for English farmers to seek out the best land in Ohio. It is all but certain that the Harrisons and McLandsboroughs knew each other in their small village in Yorkshire and in their fledgling township in Ohio, and that the Harrisons had informed the McLandsboroughs and encouraged them to join them.[25]

Selecting the right land in the right place and financing the purchase were perhaps the most important decisions that the British in Ohio could make—after the migration itself. Making repeat migrations and traveling the state in search of the best lands was how some of the English made that decision. And once they found their land they used a variety of means and strategies to make the purchase. A few arrived with enough capital to buy it outright. J. B. Downing, a "well-to-do" Devonshire man who arrived in 1869 with "considerable money," immediately purchased two farms in Wood County. A fair number of Britons could draw on loans or subsidies from family members when buying land in Ohio.[26] On the other end of the spectrum, a minority pulled themselves up from poverty, having worked for years just to purchase their passage ticket and arriving with little or no money. They required considerable time to become landowners.

Perhaps most arrived with capital but still had to work before purchasing land. Many worked at some other occupation first—such as coal mining or a craft—to accumulate the necessary capital, or they started out as farm laborers for wages that were high in comparison to Britain's. During the 1830s Englishmen on the Old Northwest prairies were well known and sought out for digging sod and ditch fences for American farmers, and for using their earnings to buy land themselves.[27] The British were especially likely to start with a former occupation before turning to agriculture, or combine farming with some other work. Examples abound of merchants, blacksmiths, barristers, brick makers, teachers, miners, lace makers, tanners, sailors, and many others applying their craft in Ohio before turning to agriculture, or combining a trade with agriculture in order to succeed.[28]

NOVICES AND THE LURE OF LAND

It is significant that Britons, more so than any other immigrant group, included large numbers of newcomers to farming, many coming directly from urban or industrial backgrounds. This is understandable. Many people left rural areas in search of work in Britain's cities and industries, and did not necessarily shed their love for the land or a determination to farm. For much of the century many of Britain's urban and industrial people were in frequent and intimate contact with the land and maintained a deep cultural desire to own it. Especially during peak harvest times, urban artisans and industrial workers were frequently recruited to supplement the agricultural work force. For them the transition to farm life in America was not a totally alien experience.

Furthermore, urban and rural spaces were not always mutually exclusive places, and even after the middle of the century Britain's cities were not fully urbanized in the modern sense. London and Manchester, both surrounded by countryside, had open spaces and supported allotment cultivation—complete with pigsties and chicken coops. Among the many who found their way into Britain's cities, land and agriculture still represented some measure of freedom, independence, and an escape from the gritty reality of urban industrial life. The prospect of exchanging the grime and smoke of factory life for the clean air of the frontier was highly alluring—even redemptive. For those actually raised on farms before entering industrial or urban work in Britain, emigrating to agricultural life in America could be a way of returning to their roots.[29]

In addition to urban people with rural roots came others who had never lived on a farm, had never gotten their hands dirty working in the soil. No other immigrant group in Ohio agriculture included so many who were partial or complete novices to farming. It is not surprising, therefore, that of all people on the frontier the British were most vulnerable to believing in the idealized agrarian myth, which died hard. When Andrew and Jane Morris wrote to their brother in Lancashire from Aurelius in 1842, they admitted that after more than ten years in America they still lived hard lives in "rude log houses." And yet they insisted that once they cleared their farm they would "do very well by working one half or two thirds of the year."[30]

Through the letters of James Martin, an Irish-born resident of London who emigrated to a farm in Crawford County, we can appreciate some of the difficulties and success that these people experienced. Martin had no real farming knowledge and yet went directly to the Ohio backwoods in 1821, where he found the task of turning raw forested land into a farm much harder than he had anticipated. Even after fourteen years of work most of his farm remained unimproved. To make ends meet he combined preaching with farming while his wife and children spun and wove at home to supplement their meager family income. Apparently Martin never really felt at home in the new republic and was critical of some of its inhabitants, preferring New Englanders to Ohioans and Pennsylvanians—whom he referred to as "the basest race of people." Yet the struggling Martins hung on and James witnessed the rapid development of the area during the 1830s, and was soon "surrounded with a very dense population." He died in 1840.[31]

After facing the reality of what American pioneering life was really like— and what agricultural life was becoming as the Jeffersonian ideal of subsistence farming gave way to surplus production for the market—some left agriculture, gravitated to towns and cities, or returned to Britain. But surprising numbers stuck with it and succeeded, people like John S. Mahony, who was "entirely new" to farming when he left Liverpool and settled in Wood County in the late 1840s. The early days did not go well for Mahony. Years later he admitted, eu-phemistically, that his "first attempts at plowing will never be forgotten." Per-haps he experienced what some other English immigrants did when they tried to learn plowing on the job: being chased by their enraged oxen so far into the forest that they got lost. It's also possible Mahony was plowing prairie, as there were some large prairie areas in parts of central and western Ohio that were difficult to "break." Nevertheless, Mahoney persisted and eventually developed an excellent farm.[32]

Francis Donaldson's story is even more remarkable. Born in London and educated at St. Andrews and Cambridge Universities, Donaldson became a re-spected and prominent barrister in London. But he decided to take up farming without any prior experience. After briefly trying it out in Durham and Wales he took his well-educated family to Clermont County. With the advantages of wealth they managed to overcome the disadvantages of limited experience by hiring help, and the family prospered. They also found time to provide leader-ship in the local abolition movement.[33]

Through the remarkably detailed story of the Morris family we gain a clearer appreciation of what many immigrants experienced and thought of the relative merits and challenges of life in southeastern Ohio during the 1830s and 1840s. The Morris saga is also of special interest because it is about a family of handloom weavers who were determined to reinvent themselves on farms in Ohio, though they had no prior agricultural experience. They hailed from a part of Lancashire that was changing too fast for them, the village of Heath Charnock, which contained about five hundred people. Nearby was the town of Chorley, booming in the 1820s because of the industrial revolution. Like many others in the area, the Morrises entered Chorley. John, the father, with his eldest son Jonathan, pursued their craft as a carpenters and joiners. The other children worked in the expanding cotton industry. The younger sons—Andrew, Thomas, and William—became fancy weavers, as opposed to unskilled power-loom weavers increasingly composed of cheaper female and Irish workers.

Hardship in Lancashire did not drive the Morrises to Ohio, but rather the perception that England lacked a bright future for them and their children. After sensing a declining social standing in England they saw hope in achieving higher status and a better living by farming their own land in Ohio. They also desired to be free of "kings, priests and tyrants," but their main motivation was the promise of land ownership for themselves and their children. The Morrises also hoped to become prosperous enough to have a leisurely life and farm without doing a lot of work, something that neither Ohio nor any other state could offer them.[34]

Andrew Morris and his wife Jane paved the way to America in 1829, at about age thirty-two. They first went to Philadelphia to weave for comparatively high wages and accumulate earnings to buy land in Ohio. The following year Thomas arrived with his wife, also named Jane, and went ahead to buy land and settled in Aurelius Township, Washington County. Andrew and Jane's letters urged the parents and the rest of the family to join them, revealing confidence as well as considerable resentment toward England. Meanwhile Thomas and Jane Morris also wrote back to the family with a highly positive assessment of Ohio that included not just a better material life, but greater educational opportunities too:

> I am very sorry that you are yet in an oppressed countrey. It is pitty that such a pritty, senseable, goodlooking boy as Thomas, my nephew, is should be kept to the loom every day, and I may say every night too almost, wile boys in this country of 15 or 16 years old are going to school.... You say he talks of coming to America if he lives; but how long must he live before he comes.... We are glad to hear that our brother Henry and sister Alice are going pretty well, but we think the would do better in this country.

Thomas and Jane also reported that they contacted Andrew, who was still weaving in Philadelphia, and encouraged him to join them. Perhaps attempting to persuade their brother to make the move, they even insisted that Ohio had fewer problems with biting insects and flies than England, though most letter writers saw it the other way around:

We have had 2 letters from brother Andrew and he seems to be doing very well. He did talk of coming to us in one letter but in the latter he had changed his mind. He wants to get money with weaving and then come out here and buy land which I think he will manage in a year or two. In his last letter he sent me a coppy of your letter to him of the date of March 18th in which you informed him that Samuel Marsden is not coming to this country, of which I am very sorry to hear. You seem to take notice of what Henry Marsden said about never going to bed on account of the bugs and muskities. I have never seen nor felt a bed bug since I have been in America, niether a muskitte. There are a few knats on a fine summers evning, but I have never felt them near as bad as I have in England.

Jane and Thomas Morris appealed urgently to their family not to miss the opportunity of a lifetime. The couple also made the preparations and journey sound less formidable than in reality, emphasizing the assistance they would provide and the comforts the family would enjoy. Perhaps the letters glowed because they were so desperate to see their loved ones again:

You said in your letter to my brother Andrew that you did not know wether it would do for you and William to come to this countrey or not. You are afrade to leave your sick club, but if you will take my advice you will not hesatate 1 day. If you can by any meanes get as much as will buy your sea stores and pay your passage over I would advise you and my mother and William to come, the sooner the better. You never had has good a chance in your life. If you could sail for Philadelphia your would have your own son [Andrew] within 5 miles to receive you. . . . Yes, if you will come to us I can promis you shall never want common nessersaries of life wile I have health to rase them off my own land. You used to say you could like to occupy land of your own. If you will come to me you may have as much as you can make use off wile you live. If you will come to me you may ether live with us or I will build you a house to yourselves . . . and you may have free access to our vituals and you may have as much timber to work at or to burn, or you may have . . . coal to burn as we have plenty very good to get, as you pleas. Bring nothing with you but your cloths, beds, and beding . . . and Bible and a few choice books. You may think you are too old but there was older looking men and women than you [on the ship] with us and did very well.

Politics also entered the family's deliberations about joining Thomas, Jane, and Andrew in Ohio. The impending Great Reform Bill of 1832, which increased the English electorate and corrected structural abuses in Parliamentary representation, was feared by the aristocracy as too radical, though it did little for the common person. The House of Lords stalled the bill and was therefore dismissed by Thomas and Jane, even though the father had put some faith into it:

> You talk of better times in England and a reform bill, but I see in my news paper that the Lords rejected the bill and disturbances and mobs began and are still incrasing. As for me and my wife, we are very well satisfied that we are got to this happy country and would be still glader if all our ralations and friends were hear also.

Then Thomas and Jane turned to the more important matter of economic independence; they proudly described their living situation and the crops and livestock they raised in Ohio:

> We live in our own house on our own land. We have cleared a little land. We raised about 100 bushels of corn and about 40 bushels of potatoes and about 8 bushels of cucumbers and about 10 bushels of pumkins besides beans, peas, turnips &c. last year and I erned 21 bushels of wheat with mowing & reaping, &c. at 10 bushels per day. We have 2 cows, 2 bull calves, which I intend to have for a yoak of oxen if the have luck, 2 sheep and 14 hogs and 3 we have killed for our winter and spring meat and 13 head of poltrey and a dog and cat.[35]

With letters like these it is not surprising that the rest of the family, except for Jonathan, soon followed. They joined Andrew in Philadelphia for five years to weave and acquire capital. The women worked on the power looms while the men manned the handlooms, doing plainer work than in Lancashire. A sister, Ann, arrived with her husband, a farmer, in 1832. Later that year the parents arrived with their son William, their daughter Alice, and her blacksmith husband. Jonathan remained in Lancashire; but the rest of the family was finally reunited in Ohio during the financial panic of 1837.

The combination of good land and water, adequate river and road transport, the nearby market towns, and the healthy environment drew the Morrises to Washington County. Federal land was readily available even though the country was past the frontier stage of development. The spot seemed ideal.

But the clan did not prosper as envisioned. Clearing the land took much longer than expected and their livestock were slow to grow and multiply. So Andrew, Thomas, and their brother-in-law John Birchall, did what many other farmers were doing in that hilly part of southeastern Ohio. They became tobacco farmers. In the mid-1820s it was reputedly the county's most profitable cash crop. Though labor-intensive, tobacco required little capital, so shifting to tobacco made sense at the time. However, so many other farmers did the same that prices plummeted, sometimes too low to pay the cost of shipping to market in Baltimore. By midcentury, growing tobacco in eastern Ohio was a questionable enterprise, though the Morrises still devoted much of their land to it.

Because Jonathan Morris was content to stay in Lancashire as a carpenter and joiner, the Morrises continued their correspondence from Ohio to England, which provides additional details about their experience of becoming American farmers. In 1838 William Morris went to Steubenville in Jefferson County to work in a woolen factory because there was none in Washington County. There he wove "sattennet, flannel, and casemeer." But he also kept his farming interests alive and bought forty acres near Marietta—close to where his parents settled. He described his land positively: "The land here is hilly and broken. It runs in high ridges and deep gutters but it is rich and productive and there is generly enough of good laying land on a place for ploughing and the steep is very good for grass or woodland and there is good water, cole and limestone." Nevertheless, William eventually decided to get out of agriculture: "I have given up the notion of agriculture for my imployment and think I can live easer by working at the manufacturing buisness." So he continued to work in the woolen mills of Steubenville. Still, he reported farming in Ohio in very positive terms to his brother Jonathan, hoping to lure him across the sea: "We should all be very glad to see you in this country and think it would be advantageous for you and especially your childran." But, he was quick to add in all honesty, "there is so many homesick complaining English folks in this country that we do not wish to advise."

By mid-1841 William moved to Barnsville, in the western part of Belmont County, where he did "reasonably well" in a weaving factory run by steam engines. But, writing back to Jonathan in Lancashire, he reported that "Times has been rather dull in America for this last 4 years and some macanics have been out of work at their own trades," a reflection of the depression that followed the panic of 1837. In William's eyes the economic stagnation threatened to become worse because of new developments in American politics, particularly the great divide over slavery. "There is two great politicle partyes," he wrote, " called the Whig and Demacrat parties and people of the same intrests are very much devided in opinions and party spirit runs very high before the elections. There are also a party in favour of the abolishion of slavery and a party oposed to the abolishion of slavery. Theese contending parties makes the prospects of American manufactures somewat uncertain and changeabale." Although he still put his faith in America, William admitted that England was the right choice for his brother: "But I think you have done right in not changing certientyes for uncertantyes for I belive it is best to be satisfyed as long as you are doing well, but if not doing well to be redy to come."[36]

A year later, in August of 1842, Andrew and Jane Morris also wrote to their brother Jonathan in Lancashire during the height of the depression afflicting both Britain and America. And though the couple acknowledged that times were tough in Ohio too, Britain's workers were necessarily worse off because of England's social inequality and the notorious exploitation of laborers by the rich and powerful. The Buckeye State remained the place of the future:

> We are sorry to hear that times is so bad in England and that their are so many people out of imploy, but it is nothing but what we expected, knowing as we do the smallness of the island and emance population and that all the property belongs to the rich and they having the making of the laws can consequently do as they pleas with the working class. . . . Things is very different here although times is wors than ever they was known to be through bank failurs and scarcity of money; yet there is an excelent prospect for both the presant and riseing generation.

Then, in response to questions posed by their brother Jonathan in his own letters to them, Andrew and Jane painted a vivid picture of their life and thoughts on the young but developing corner of Ohio:

> You ask if we have good roads. Our roads are good considering the newness of the country. You ask are we far from a town or vilidge. We are 20 miles from Marietta, a very nice town on the bank of Ohio River at the mouth of the Muskingam River. It is pleasantly situated and has 2 market days in a week. We can go with a wagon in half a day. The market hours are from daylight until 9 oclock Wednesday and Saterday. We frequently go in the night with butter &c. in the wagons, sell out in the morning and come home the same day. . . . You ask if the country is pleasant. What is pleasant to me is unpleasant to another. It is broken or rowling and a great deal of the land is prity steep. So we answer it is pleasant for a broken country. You ask if there any farms on sale part

cultivated, to wich we answer Yes, plenty. You ask can we sell our produce and get money for it, to wich we answer yes . . . though at presant
it is very low. You ask can we injoy society, to wich we answer Yes. You
ask is there any railways near, as to wich we answer No. You ask is it considered a healthey spot, to wich we answer Yes. You ask are we much
trubled with reptiles or wild beasts or bugs or fleas or midges, to wich
we answer No, there are no wild beasts except some wild turkeys and a
few dear; bugs are not as bad as in England. Fleas we have none and
midges are not near as bad here as there. We have some snakes but not
many.

Through it all Andrew and Jane Morris were satisfied with their migration
to Ohio. But they were also aware that during the mid-1840s Ohio lost population through westward migration to fresher lands and wider opportunities. And
they contemplated joining the westward movement, to sell their Ohio lands for
fresh, cheaper, and larger lands that they might sell again. The cash nexus entered their lives, and like so many Americans of their time they considered buying land not as an estate for their children, but to sell at a profit. Their attitudes
appeared more American all the time:

You ask do we consider we have made a good choice. We should think so
if we did not hear of so many other parts that is so much supearier, but if
times gets better we shall very likely some of us go and look and if we like
sell our property here and go. You ask do we live in rude log houses. We
answer Yes. When people buys Congress land in the woods they build what
they call temperary log cabins untill they get a farm cleared and fenced
and cultivated so as to grow produce enough for there own use and some
for market.

In early 1844, nearly two years later, Andrew sent another letter to Jonathan,
reporting on the improving economy and again making comparisons between
Britain and America. He acknowledged that it was probably wise for Jonathan
to remain in England. But Andrew was quick to add that he had no second
thoughts, and it apparently had as much to do with politics and class distinction as his material well being:

For my part I could not live contented in England were there is so much
distinction between the working class and the rich, so many people in a
state of starvation or beging from door to door, and besids there is very

little prospect for the preasant generation, and for the riseing generation there is absolutly none allthough there seems to be great exsitement on the subgect of reform and the Irish repeal, but I do not think they will make good times for the working class long at once.[37]

The Morrises were in many ways a typical British immigrant family searching for a better life in Ohio. Material and economic improvement, and especially land ownership, was the main objective. Owning land in its broadest context meant an independence and fulfillment that was much harder to achieve in Britain. The political dimension mentioned by some of the Morrises was real enough, but secondary to economic considerations.

Yet British immigrants in Ohio expressed political differences with such frequency and passion that America's greater freedom must have been a significant part of their migratory decisions. Political and economic freedom were essentially intertwined. Most were enthusiastic about American politics and the greater equality and opportunity. The fact that one did not have to doff one's cap to a person of higher social standing was sometimes reported in letters. Yet, some found American politics a fraud and little more than a license to pursue material gain. James Martin, who settled in Crawford County in the 1830s, found American political freedom hollow. Writing back to his family in England he reported: "Our politics here are nothing but jargon of every body's self-interest—there is nothing desirable here above England except that a poor industrious man can obtain land & become very independent. I think that America is the acropolis of the whore [of] that great City that reigneth over the Kings of the earth. There is one eternal ring in your ears of *trade* and Speculation."[38]

Such negative expressions against American politics, however, were relatively rare. At the opposite extreme was Robert Bowles, a substantial English farmer who was settled on a farm in Hamilton County by the early 1820s. For him life in Ohio was much more than an opportunity to become a landowning farmer. It was an escape from aristocratic tyranny and decadence and refuge in liberty and equality—Alexis de Tocqueville's "twin pillars" of American democracy. Like some of the more politically conscious immigrants from Britain, Bowles scoured the works of William Cobbett, the English "radical" journalist who, after spending time in the United States, published the *Political Register*, which called for reform and defended the cause of the working classes. Bowles believed that England was in moral and political decline; without major reforms a radical and violent revolution in the French fashion would occur. He also thought that the ongoing commercialization and industrialization of Eng-

lish life would bring only destruction to people like himself. He fled English oppression to find freedom in Ohio. At least that is how he portrayed it to his
brothers back in England in 1823.

Robert Bowles remembered England with palpable bitterness. He deeply re-
sented his native land for not providing the social and political equality he now
enjoyed in Ohio. He was more strident and radical in his thinking than the
Morris brothers, for he jettisoned his Englishness to become fully American as
soon as possible: "I begin to rid myself of many foolish English ideas—and view
these things with a philosophical eye. Here I see no princely piles, or gorgeous
palaces to mock my humble cabin—If I had ever so fine a house [in Ohio] I
should be met with no more respect."[39]

Bowles's brother sent Robert a copy of the *Farmer's Journal*, a highly politi-
cized English publication that reported the difficulties that English farmers
were enduring in the early 1820s. A typical article from 1822 reads: "Calamity has
advanced with more rapid, more destructive strides, than imagination could
have conceived . . . there is scarce a corner of the United Kingdom that is exempt
from it. . . . Already the evil reaches of the landowner will, ere long, more
forcibly grasp [the farmer]. . . . Such is the power, such is the means of levying
taxes, that as long as there is a cow, a sheep, a shilling, a bed, the tax-gatherer
will, must seize it."[40] Such hyperbolic stories of poverty, rising crime, and vic-
timization by landlords and government stoked anger toward Britain and seems
to have touched a raw nerve in Robert. He became progressively more stridently
convinced of his narrow escape from economic and political destruction:

> We receive much ammusement from perusing the Farmer's Journals, you
> so kindly sent to us . . . but instead of causing an _____ pang that I am not
> there now, I feel happy . . . that I have escaped that land. . . . In reading the
> Farmer's Journal I cannot help contrasting it with the publications of this
> Country. . . . To talk of coming back again under such circumstances
> would be worse than insanity. Never did I feel so happy in this country as
> I have since I have perused the Farmer's Journal . . . I feel the blessings, I
> profess, and rejoice that my flight allowed me to escape destruction.[41]

Bowles admitted that his early days in Ohio were hard. He was one of the
comparatively few without "migration chains" laid by acquaintances, for he
came to a corner of Ohio absent of friends or relatives to welcome him. During
the early years he must have seriously doubted his decision to emigrate; but he
had made it through the worst of it:

'Tis true that for some time we had great inconveniences, and made many
sacrifices. We had trials to undergo . . . and [were] wanderers in a new
country, in search of a home, without friends or acquaintances to apply to
for instruction or advice, and with the consideration that one false step
might prove inevitable ruin—But all these trials are over and gone, I have
now a home, and a comfortable one seated in a fine country, where freedom reigns and distress is unknown, and where Liberty, Happiness and
Peace alighted when they flew from Europe.

Bowles's initial struggles were apparently worth the effort, for he returned
again and again to the triumph of escaping British tyranny. With considerable
exaggeration and not a little venom, Bowles declared to his brother how he saw
the British government after living as an American farmer in Ohio:

You are ruled by a set of rascally miscreants, the very scum of the country,
and nothing but the Dread of popular commotions makes them bear your
complaints of misery and starvation caused by themselves—were it not
for that you would have the Sword for a breakfast-a Bayonet for a dinner,
and a musket ball for supper.

Bowles extended his rancor to his fellow Englishmen when he declared—so
unlike the great majority of British immigrants in Ohio—that he did not want
more countrymen to follow him. He saw them as too sentimentally patriotic
and attached to their mother country, and not even worthy of life in America.
"I have no wish for many Englishmen to come here," the immigrant continued.
"I know their weaknesses so well, that I am certain they would most of them
cause me much more plague than pleasure. . . . Englishmen are I suspect the
most prejudiced to their own Dear country of any men in the world—and
therefore to leave it is considered to be *compleat* exile."
    Robert Bowles based much of his faith in the American political system on
the freedom of the press. In a previous letter to his brother he praised what he
experienced in Ohio:

The liberty of the press is here enjoyed in its greatest perfection and is
considered by the Americans in its true light, viz. *The Bulwark of Liberty*.
So long as the liberty of the press remains (and they are too proud of it
to allow its curtailment) Vice must certainly shrink from the severe ordeal which the attainment of all high offices necessarily subjects the can-

didates to, I have before told you that all public offices are chosen by the people, and their public conduct is closely investigated that it is almost impossible for a vicious character to obtain an office of consequence. There is scarcely a town equal to an English village but what has a News-paper published in it, and those of any size have several. Cincinnati has 4 every week.[42]

Though Bowles focused on the political dimension of his move to Ohio—almost as though to convince himself and his brother that he had made the right decision—he still put most of his time and energy into farming. But ulti-mately, the land he owned and cultivated, by which he fed his family and earned income, was most important. In that regard, at least, he was a typical English immigrant in Ohio:

I am daily more and more pleased with my emigration—I highly ap-prove the purchase I have made here. I know not the persons with whom I would exchange situation[s]—I know of no small farm that has so many advantages as mine has . . . I begin to see the good effects of my labours and in about 7 years it will be exactly what I always hoped to be master of—abounding with fruits of all kind, with every other sort of luxuriant vegetation, surrounded with everything that I can wish for and chiefly the offspring of my own industry—Independant of the world. . . . My present stock consists of 2 cows—one young calf—1 year-ling steer—two horses—1 sow 3 pigs 4 large store [?] pigs, about 250 hens and chickens and 40 Ducks with about 1/2 a dozen young Turkies.[43]

Whatever their background and political ideas, British immigrants in Ohio agriculture showed a knack for "climbing the tenure ladder" by renting land, then buying unimproved land to expand and bring it into cultivation. A classic example is William Cotterill, who arrived from Lincolnshire in 1851 and began by renting a farm near Kenton, Hardin County. The next year he purchased forty virgin acres, partially cleared them while living in a log shanty he had built, sold the land for a profit, rented a larger farm, and then with his earnings purchased eighty acres, which he gradually brought into a high state of cultiva-tion.[44] In the many examples of immigrants working with all their might as la-borers, renters, farmers—often combining farming with another trade for extra income—we see remarkable resourcefulness and a tenacious determination to own their own land.[45]

George and Orange Slade were English farmers struggling in Coshocton County who wrote back to their family in Devon in 1841. They had a miserable seven-week voyage, and George worked for an English immigrant for a dollar a day in Kingston, Ontario, before proceeding to Ohio. Here they joined friends, only to suffer severe fever and ague in the winter of 1840. Then they went to Coshocton, where they managed a farm for fourteen dollars per month, "rent free fire wood the keep of a cow and pigs. Raise as much Poultry as we like and have as much new milk as we like now while our cow is Dry."

The Slades were satisfied by the better diet and opportunity to earn money for land purchases. "You well know we are far better off here then [sic] we should have been in England," Orange wrote to her brother. "George says he should be better off here and work Two Days a week then [sic] he would be in England and work every Day." However, their separation from family in England tempered the couple's excitement about starting in Ohio agriculture:

> We are all Disappointed to hear that no one is comming out this summer. I am glad to hear that you have some Thought of coming here for I assure you it's a Good Country. . . . I hope Mother will not grieve about our coming to America for I'm sure we are all better off here. I only wish all the family was here. I wish it was possible that I could send my dear old mother a pound of Tea and Father a pound of Tobacco. The winters are Longer and Colder and the summer are verry hot and so that the crop is brought on in a short time and in abundance. Everything is plenty and cheap. I wish father and Mother was here. They would live well in there [sic] old age. They might suffer first from ague but there is no one ever known to die from it. . . . Our children are growing verry fast. And they do not wish to see England again.[46]

Scots made similar observations in letters back to the mother country. A fairly large number formed the "Scotch Settlement," near Wellsville and East Liverpool in Columbiana County. Most were Highlanders, some of the earliest settlers in the region, having arrived in 1802. Some had fled in order to escape impressment into naval service. By 1850 the county had 379 Scottish immigrants, the largest number of any Ohio county.[47]

One member of the settlement, Charles Rose, wrote a long and detailed letter in 1822 to his nephew, John Rose of Inverness, who requested information about Ohio. Some of the excerpts reveal a pride in his new home in Ohio and a sense of relief that he no longer lived in Scotland:

Dear Nephew . . . you wished me to give you my opinions of this country. . . . This is a good country let who will say to the contrary but every
good has its own evil in this world where there is no perfection. . . . This
is the best time that ever was for any person who has money to come
here, they can buy land very cheaper than in the woods or cleared land
. . . and once you pay that no man can dispossess you again like those
Tyrants in that Country [Scotland]. . . . The price of clearing an acre of
the land varies so much on account of being hard or easy to clear but I
believe from four to six dollars per acre will make it ready for the plough
. . . cattle is very cheap . . . horses from 30 to 60 dollars sheep one dollar,
I hold only 162 acres and each of my Sons the same, my horses consists
of five head my cattle at present 13. . . . If you use both economy and industry with what money you said you have you may depend on a better
way of living here . . . it would be my warmest desire that you all would
come if you find freedom in your own minds . . . the January is long and
difficult but he who overrules all things can safely conduct you both by
sea and land if you trust in him.[48]

Eight years later Rose also wrote to his brother in Scotland, and gave details
about life in the Scotch settlement and how to become a citizen. Rose noted that
some British immigrants naturalized slowly for religious reasons, because of the
"secular nature" of the Constitution and its acknowledgment of slavery. "There
are a great many of the British that refuses to become naturalized," Rose observed, "for the reason that the constitution does not admit of the existence of
God, that there is no provision made for the maintenance of any negroes and
. . . that there is no religious test required for holding the most important office
in the government, therefore that a Christian has no pre-eminence over an Infidel, of which there are a great many in this country and that they hold office
of importance to the great danger of the Christians."

Rose also explained that some British immigrants did not "like to subjugate
their native country, in the manner that it is required." He referred to the American law that British immigrants at their naturalization were required to swear
an oath in which they "forever renounce and abjure all allegiance and fidelity to
every foreign prince, potentate, state, and sovereignty, whatsoever and particularly to the Queen of the United Kingdom."[49] But the main thrust of his letter
provided an honest assessment of what agricultural life in Ohio entailed, and
for farmers in Scotland, Rose's descriptions were enticing. "This is an excellent
country for a poor man with a large family," he concluded. "A man with a strong

family . . . will not require much assistance from any other hand . . . he many have for himself & his family plenty of the necessities of life."[50]

EXPERTS: FARMING METHODS AND ADJUSTMENTS

Despite early trials and initial doubts while struggling to clear the land of trees and breaking the virgin soil to establish farms, most British farmers in Ohio succeeded. The conventional frontier wisdom that lives were too short because it took a farm couple their whole lives to create a farm, only to die before reaping the fruits of their labor, does not apply to all the British farmers in Ohio.[51] The available historical sources are certainly weighted toward successful immigrants. But even allowing for those who failed at farming, the widespread success is clear. This is especially impressive in light of the fact that many had little or no prior experience in farming yet still managed to build a farm out of virgin land with enough time left at the end of their lives to enjoy their reward. They prevailed by working hard, adopting local farming methods, and learning quite quickly how to survive and prosper.

Though there were British novices in Ohio agriculture, there were also many who were experts with long and successful agricultural traditions. In fact, English farmers in Ohio had a reputation as some of the best, most "scientific" farmers in the state, who helped raise the standard of cultivation. And that might be expected. The English and the Dutch developed "advanced methods" of "high" or "scientific" farming and new practices for raising livestock; those methods founded the agricultural revolution of the late seventeenth and eighteenth centuries. During the half century following Independence, America received much of its inspiration for innovative agriculture from England. During that time the Philadelphia Society for the Promotion of Agriculture encouraged dirt farmers to use English techniques of crop rotation to avoid soil erosion. And Ohio agricultural publications often featured advice from England and Scotland. The English influence can also be seen in the fact that in America advanced farming was commonly referred to as "English agriculture" and early clovers were called "English grass." As late as the 1870s the American Institute, an important organization dedicated to disseminating the latest and most efficient agricultural methods, featured speakers who had toured English farms and advocated their techniques of crop rotation and use of nitrogen-fixing root crops, advanced drainage, new plows, and manure.[52]

It is not surprising, then, that English farmers were often disgusted with what they considered sloppy, inefficient, and crude American practices. William Amphlett, an Englishman in Ohio who wrote his "Emigrant's Directory" for prospective migrants, warned readers in 1819 that the English emigrant-farmer will not . . . behold a mode of agriculture pursued, that will excite his envy or admiration. The appearance of the farm-house and yard, the implements of husbandry, and methods of using them, with the neglected state of the live stock and the corn-fields, will excite in him much wonder and disgust; more indeed than he will have any right to indulge in, after a farther acquaintance. But he will see at once how much industry may accomplish in this country, when carelessness and inattention thrive so well.

At the same time Amphlett warned his readers that there was much poverty and even misery on the Ohio frontier: "What most excites an Englishman's surprise, if not his contempt, is the slovenly-built log-cabins, which have all the outward appearance of wretched penury, and within but little show of cleanliness or comfort."[53] That quite a number of British immigrants in Ohio lived in precisely that kind of setting, at least during the first few years of carving a home out of the wilderness, highlights the jarring adjustment that often had to be made on the Ohio frontier.

But no matter how expert the British farmers were, most faced a new environment requiring them to make changes. The Ohio woods forced English agrarians to adjust or even abandon their previous methods and attitudes. They came from a land whose depleted timber resources were treasured, and now were in a new land whose superabundance of timber could hardly be comprehended. It could be shocking to see the inclination, even necessity, of settlers to clear it away and destroy so much of it. Observing the clearing of forests, Amphlett remarked:

> Among these living hills . . . one striking, melancholy feature obtrudes itself at every step we take: it is the incredible quantity of fallen timber in every stage of decay; the surface of the earth is literally covered with it, so as from that cause alone to make the woods impassable where there is no thicket or underwood. The trunks are many of them of so enormous a size, that it is an Englishman's constant lamentation that they lie here rotting and useless while such a value is set upon them in his native land.[54]

Such dismay at the shoddy appearance of early Ohio farms and the desolation of pristine forests was echoed by D. Griffiths, who toured the state in the early 1830s and still found the contrast with England's ancient, well-tilled fields enormous. "What a contrast to the beautiful and fragrant hedge rows of Old England do the bare zigzag wooden fences of Ohio present! And how disfigured its luxuriant crops by the half-burnt black stumps that show their unsightly heads in every part! Yet even these are not so alarming as the hollow trunks of trees through which the flames are still bursting; or, otherwise their black ruins present such dubious shapes to the lonely traveller, that it requires but a little superstition to convert them into fiends and hobgoblins."[55] Another English observer in the early nineteenth century thought that Ohio farms were a full century behind those of England, in matters of cultivation, livestock, and general appearance.[56]

British immigrant cultivators in Ohio, then, had to adjust their perceptions of timbered land. No matter the value of timber in Britain, in Ohio it was in the way and expendable. They had to realize that clearing land in Ohio was a time consuming and laborious task, and that conserving labor was often more expedient than conserving land. George Washington acknowledged this in a letter to Arthur Young, the great English agricultural expert. Somewhat embarrassed by the reckless methods of American farmers, Washington explained that their aim was "not to make the most they can from the land, which is . . . cheap, but the most of the labour, which is dear; the consequence of which has been, much ground has been scratched over and none cultivated or improved as it ought to have been. . . ."[57] Not surprisingly, much soil exhaustion and erosion resulted from these practices, which troubled English immigrants with well-developed ideas about "proper agriculture." But most found it hard to rely solely on their traditional English methods.

"English methods" were based on an efficient blend of livestock farming and raising mixed crops with labor intensive–techniques. Instead of "mining" the soil through repeated plantings, as typically done in America, the labor-intensive English methods maintained soil's fertility by rotating crops with nitrogen-fixing legumes and soil-conserving grasses, weeding the fields, providing drainage, and by applying manure for fertilizer.

Many American farmers considered manuring fields ineffective, too labor intensive, and therefore too costly. Thomas Jefferson himself recorded in 1793 that he did not use manure on his plantation "because we can buy an acre of new land cheaper than we can manure an old one."[58] It is no wonder that Jefferson's neglected plantation did not produce an adequate income for his retirement. But to neglect manuring was unthinkable for most English farmers. They were appalled at the failure of American farmers to enrich the soil in this way. As one Englishman in America observed, "the Yankee farmers are the most careless in their operations of any agriculturalists I ever saw. They would not lay in their manure, as they said it would fill their fields with weeds."[59] In contrast, many Lincolnshire farmers actually valued their cattle foremost as "manufac-turers of manure."[60]

Sheer economic reality, however, eventually forced most English farmers in America to change, to assimilate. In particular, the high cost of farm labor and the comparatively low prices for crops were a sobering reminder that agricul-tural life and practice were different in America and that their old ways were not always practical. In fact, by the late 1870s a leading prize-winning agricultural expert cautioned Wisconsin's dairy farmers *not* to use the practice of "English soiling"—feeding green fodder to cattle in the stalls during summer—precisely because the requisite labor costs were too high in relation to land costs.[61] These market realities usually forced English immigrant farmers to lay aside their old methods and attitudes and adopt American ones. For the English this usually meant less manuring, having a much lower ratio of labor to land than they were accustomed to, and using methods that exploited the land in order to maximize production.[62]

Thus, most attempts at transplanting English methods wholesale in Amer-ica usually failed. The labor-intensive English methods, highly appropriate in Britain where labor was plentiful and land relatively scarce, were less so in the United States—where labor was scarce and land was abundant. America's abun-dance of land made soil exhaustion seem a minor problem easily remedied sim-ply by moving on and buying fresh land, and land that needed drainage was easy to avoid.[63] English farmers who stubbornly stuck to their old methods and crops in Ohio often paid the price until they adopted American ones. As we have seen, the Morris family in Washington County turned to land-intensive American methods of tobacco cultivation in an attempt to succeed. Generally, English agricultural methods did not survive long in Ohio.

Another reason why English farmers in Ohio did not cling to traditional farming practices as much as many German, Dutch, and Scandinavian immi-grants did in various parts of the Old Northwest is due to their culture. These continental newcomers lived in tight, inward-looking ethnic groups and in that setting were more likely to retain their culture, including their attitudes toward agriculture. As we saw in chapter 3, the Welsh also seem to fit this pattern. The English, not having formed their own ethnic enclaves, interacted more quickly with Ohioans and adopted their methods and attitudes.[64]

Still, the British made a deep and lasting impact on Ohio agriculture. Amer-icans widely recognized them for being some of the "progressive" or "leading farmers" of their township or county, whose farms were exceptionally neat, well managed, and under the highest state of cultivation.[65] One observer perceptively noted that the reason why the English "rank among the most skilled farmers in the world" and have "complete knowledge of husbandry" was because England's limited land resources had forced "prudent habits" upon them.[66] And according to later historians like Milo Quaife, they deserved such accolades.[67]

Some Scots were also recognized for agricultural expertise and innovation. One excellent example is William Crichton, a native of Perthshire. After gold mining in California he settled down in Porter Township, Scioto County, to farm for both profit and "esthetic recreation." He developed expertise in wheat farming and raised up to thirty bushels per acre without commercial fertilizers. Also aware of the potential to increase production through new technology, he introduced the new McCormick reaper to his area. Crichton became known as the pioneering farmer who made that section "one of the famous wheat producing districts of the State." Others made similar contributions to the state's fruit production.[68]

One prominent English "scientific farmer" who made it to Ohio and advanced the farming standards in his community was John Symons, from Devonshire. In Clinton County his neighbors considered him among the "better trained in the science of agriculture," one who was "quite far in advance of his day in the practice of scientific farming." His farm in Jefferson Township was so highly developed that other farmers traveled for miles to see and learn from it. Symons introduced large-scale potato farming to the county and his hogs were regarded as the best in the community.[69]

Knox County's agricultural progress was also led in part by English immigrants. Moses Colwell Bone was one of them. He left his native Cornwall in 1854 at age twenty-one and came to Gambier to work at his craft as a wagon maker before turning full time to farming in Miller Township. There he purchased 375 acres, which he "cultivated by up-to-date methods" and made "one of the most desirable properties" in the county. Though he seems to have developed his agricultural expertise in Ohio, he apparently brought agricultural experience and knowledge with him from Cornwall as well. No one could "more justly be termed an agricultural expert" than Moses Colwell Bone.[70]

The English contributed especially to improving animal husbandry throughout the Old Northwest. The entire region's growing agricultural industry owed much of its success to English breeds and techniques to improve livestock. In 1834 the Ohio Breeding and Importing Company began importing cattle breeds directly from England to the Miami and Scioto valleys, which became Ohio's prime stock breeding region. Nineteen cows and bulls of the Durham and Shorthorn breeds were purchased from England's most celebrated breeders of the time, and the Company's profits soared. Devon cattle, English Short-horns, Herefords, and many others were also brought in at midcentury, some of them by Thomas Aston and John Humphreys, two English immigrant farmers who settled in Elyria. Herefords in Lorain Country were said to be owned ex-clusively by English immigrants for about a decade. Ayreshires were shipped from Britain in 1848, and after the Civil War Jersey and Guernsey cows were also directly imported to enhance Ohio's dairy industry.[71]

As Ohio's farmers began to develop agriculture and gear their livestock op-erations for the growing marketplace, they often looked to English experts who had recently arrived and could apply their experience to improving the breeds. In Madison County farmers found a wealth of knowledge in Jonathan Farrar, an English immigrant who was one of the first settlers in Oak Run Township in Madison County in the early 1820s. Because he was esteemed as a "fancier of thoroughbred stock" and had acquired valuable knowledge about breeding in England, local farmers appointed him to lead the Madison County Stock Breed-ers' Association, in which capacity Farrar returned to England to purchase fine-blooded stock for importation.[72]

Not surprisingly, sheep were also imported from England, where sheep breeding and wool production thrived for many centuries. In 1834 English im-migrant Isaac Maynard introduced the first long-wool sheep—Southdowns, Cotswolds, Leicesters, and Lincolns—to Coshocton County. These sheep were not well suited to the harsh conditions of the area, but Maynard stubbornly per-sisted in his enterprise.[73] After the Civil War, as Merino sheep became less prof-itable, Ohio's farmers turned to the sheep Maynard introduced, all of which produced superior wool and mutton. (Significantly, each of these breeds brought into Ohio's vocabulary English place names that also represented the origins of many of the English immigrants who were settling in the state.)

As for the swine industry, Ohio was a major producer. Cincinnati was dubbed "Porkopolis" early in the century, and English breeds of pigs con-tributed to the development of Ohio's pork business. The Berkshire and Sussex, Suffolk and Yorkshire pigs were regularly imported from England by the late 1830s and 1840s and contributed to the important modernization of the pork industry. Essex hogs were imported first to Ohio, in Massillon in 1839, by an English immigrant who was a leading agriculturalist in his community.[74]

Along with English breeds of animals came English farmers who were ex-pert breeders and brought skills and experience that proved essential for Ohio's developing animal-husbandry industry. In addition to the aforementioned Thomas Aston and John Humphreys, James Hammond arrived from Yorkshire in 1848 with a mere twenty-six dollars in his pocket. He eventually became one of the most successful livestock breeders and dealers in Northeast Ohio and was duly elected president of the Summit County Agricultural Society. Also in Summit County, George Davis, an 1845 Lincolnshire immigrant, was the largest stock dealer in Bath Township and became well known for the cattle, sheep, and fine horses that he bred.[75] Others specialized in breeding Norman horses and Merino sheep.[76]

The Welsh were also among the top animal breeders in Ohio. Thomas Jones, who arrived in 1823, came to own two large farms in Union County where he became a leading stock raiser. He specialized in shorthorn cattle and French Norman and Clydesdale horses and was the first to introduce them into the county.[77] Other Welsh immigrants were admired for their high standards of agriculture and innovation, especially those who arrived with capital and education and made noticeably fine additions to Ohio's farming community. David Pugh, an early Welsh settler in Delaware County, sowed "Welsh clover" taken with him from Wales and found that it provided "most excellent pasturage."[78] And John Gordon, son of Welsh farmers "in comfortable circumstances," emigrated after the death of his father in 1870. He was well educated and bought a large farm near Bucyrus, which he steadily turned into one of the finest farms in the county. His material advantages in Wales probably enabled him to succeed as well as he did in post–Civil War Ohio.[79]

In addition to their expertise in animal breeding, British immigrants brought important skills and experience in drainage techniques, perfected from England's extensive need for drainage.[80] For centuries the English had struggled to drain the fens of East Anglia, Lincolnshire, and other places. Early on they had the help of Dutch immigrants and engineers, who had developed techniques and equipment that were the product of their long history of reclaiming land from the sea. This heritage of land drainage was a godsend to those on some of America's wetter soils. Newspapers published in the Old Northwest frequently featured articles on advanced

Thomas Jones, the Welshman who arrived in 1823, became a leading stock raiser in Union County, where he owned two large farms and introduced shorthorn cattle and Clydesdale horses. From Ewing Summers, Genealogical and Family History of Eastern Ohio.

British drainage methods, which the English introduced to the Illinois prairie early in the century.[81]

English immigrants settled on some of Ohio's swampland and used their famous drainage skills to bring it into cultivation. Henry Sarvis, for example, emigrated to Canada and then Ohio in 1844. Making his way to Wood County, he joined a group of other settlers struggling on an area of heavy wet lands called Hull Prairie. Sarvis took charge, got a "ditch law" passed, and drained the Prairie; it was "transformed into a most valuable and productive tract of land, its farms being now unrivaled in excellence and richness." In nearby Liberty Township, Lincolnshire native John Herringshaw purchased eighty acres of swamp land that he also drained and turned into a richly cultivated field. Thomas Crosse, who left Hereford for Ohio in 1874, transformed his wet land in Wood County by tiling and ditching it.[82] Further south, Scotsman John Weatherspoon also improved his Belmont County farm by providing sophisticated underground drainage.[83]

John Bright was another English farmer with specialized knowledge in drainage whose contribution to Ohio agriculture was particularly great. He was raised on a farm in a Cambridgeshire village where drainage techniques had been highly developed during the long tradition of draining the Cambridgeshire fens. Bright emigrated in 1868 with his wife, Amy, and six-year-old son, William, after he had made several trips alone to find the best place to farm and put his drainage expertise to use. He found it near Westboro, Clinton County, where he was immediately recognized as "a systematic master of drainage." In addition to draining and improving his own farm, he laid hundreds of miles of tile drains in the county and other parts of Ohio and helped many other farmers to prosper. Because of his valuable skills in drainage John Bright was "a man of large usefulness in his adopted country" with "a reputation throughout county second to none."[84]

Among the first to settle on the prairies, British immigrants also helped to dispel Americans of a prejudice against prairie soils—the faulty assumption that land without trees was not fertile enough for profitable farming. Already in 1817 Morris Birkbeck and George Flower selected a section of prairie land in Edwards County, Illinois, for their settlement and took the fertility of the land for granted. They also drained wet lands that Americans had previously deemed impossible to farm. Other English immigrants arrived later in Illinois and helped to open up the prairie to cultivation.[85] Ohio had less prairie than Illinois or Indiana, but the English opened up prairie land there as well. The family of Henry Robertson from Edinburgh was one of the first to settle on Hull Prairie, where they took up eighty acres of virgin land to create a "highly cultivated farm."[86] And George Brim, a poor immigrant from Devonshire, came to Wood County in 1855 and eventually converted 360 acres of prairie land in Plain Township into a large, prosperous farm.[87]

Thus, despite the fact that Ohio's agricultural and labor environment forced most British farmers to adopt American methods and strategies, immigrants still used the skills and knowledge they had brought with them to raise the standards of cultivation. They were especially helpful in advancing livestock breeding, drainage techniques, wheat and fruit production, and opening Ohio's limited prairie land to settlement. Improvements in those areas became increasingly important for Ohio's agricultural prosperity in the post–Civil War period, when Illinois's expansion in wheat production forced Ohio's farmers to diversify in order to stay profitable.[88] English immigrants, and American-born farmers of English stock, also influenced Ohio's agricultural landscape by erecting the distinctive "English barn"—notably in places like Geauga County.[89] British immigrants made an impact on Ohio agriculture that was invaluable to the state's economic development.

British farmers certainly made their biggest impact on Ohio agriculture in the first half of the century, but Ohio agriculture still had great appeal after the Civil War. The golden age may have been over, but the opportunities were not. The John and Mary Guess family, for example, had farmed successfully in Kent for many years; but in 1884 they immigrated to Huron County where they bought land, improved it, and brought it under a "high state of cultivation" with "progressive and up-to-date methods." They clearly capitalized on the high farming standards and scientific methods that they had developed in England to succeed as large landowning farmers in Ohio. Another English farming family moved into the area shortly thereafter and similarly succeeded. William Clements, who was born in Somerset in 1854, emigrated in 1889 with his wife, Martha, and four children. They came directly to Ridgefield Township, Huron County. William worked as a farmhand for four years, and farmed on shares until 1905, when he purchased a 134-acre farm. Clements steadily improved it and became a successful farmer late in Ohio's agricultural history.[90] As relatively late English immigrant farmers settling in the same part of Huron County, the Clements and Guess families likely knew each other and other English settlers in the area as well.

After the war, Akron was a place where immigrants could still effectively combine farming with business. Thomas and Edward Putterill did this. They came to Akron as young men in their twenties and thirties in 1872, following friends who had settled there before them and informed them of the area's opportunities. The Putterill brothers immediately found work and after five years purchased an omnibus line, which they sold after a few years to buy a farm of 114 acres in Stow Township. While they improved their farm they also made money manufacturing cement blocks for Akron's thriving building industry.[91]

NORTON STRANGE TOWNSHEND

One individual stands out in Ohio's agricultural history for his singular contributions to the scientific and academic study of agriculture and for bringing it into its modern state. He is the English immigrant Norton Strange Townshend, the "father of agricultural education in America" and one of the founders of Ohio State University, where he was the first professor of agriculture. Townshend was born in Northamptonshire in 1815, the only son of successful tenant farmers Joel and Rebecca Townshend. They were Congregationalists, with a net worth of about a thousand pounds in 1810, and were well respected for having a good education and a substantial library. Norton started formal education before age five at a boarding school in Bitteswell, in Leicestershire, for which the parents paid seventeen guineas annually. But adversity led the Townshend family to turn their attention to America. The agricultural economy in England slowed after the Napoleonic Wars such that livestock were hard to sell for profit, and their sheep became infected with rot, all of which reduced the family's income and cast their future into doubt.

Though Norton was only fifteen when he emigrated with the family in 1830, he was imbued with an English culture and upbringing that remained with him for life. As his grandson recalled forty years after Townshend's death, "In spite of his early arrival in this land and his militant American patriotism, he remained to his dying day essentially and immutably an Englishman." He understood the essentials of English "scientific" farming well, and inherited a love and respect for education and books—especially scientific ones—from his father and mother. The family settled on a farm in Avon, Lorain County. While only nineteen, Townshend taught school in Ohio, and began to study medicine at the Medical College in Cincinnati in 1837. There he confronted slavery for the first time when a southerner visited Cincinnati with his slave girl Matilda, who ran off, was captured, and brought to trial—which Townshend attended. The young Salmon P. Chase defended Matilda and during the trial developed a lasting friendship with Townshend that flowered during the Civil War and brought a new chapter to Townshend's career as an army medical inspector. (See chapter 6.)[92]

After earning his MD in New York in 1840, Norton Townshend sailed to England to attend lectures in medicine and to represent Ohio at the World's Anti-Slavery Convention in London that year. He then returned to his hometown of

Avon to farm and practice medicine. But agriculture and agricultural education and improvement remained his main abiding interest. In 1844 Oberlin established the first American agricultural college, and they called Townshend to be one of their first instructors. He taught there for three years and lectured in Cleveland as well. Later Townshend's leadership in abolitionism got him elected as a member of the 1850 Constitutional Convention, which framed Ohio's new constitution.[93]

Then he was elected representative in the Thirty-second Congress in Washington. There he distinguished himself as an opponent to the black codes and a foe of slavery, and helped get Salmon P. Chase elected to the Senate. After one term in the House he was elected to the Ohio State Senate in 1853. As a state senator he made lasting contributions by introducing measures that established schools for needy children and asylums for the mentally ill. He also worked indefatigably to grant suffrage to Ohio's women, but to no avail. His origins as an English farmer and continued passion for agricultural improvement and education led him to serve as a member and president of the state Board of Agriculture for many years. With other leaders in the nation he was also instrumental in passing the Morrill Land-Grant Act in 1862. In 1873, after serving as a Union army Medical Inspector during the Civil War, Townshend was appointed Professor of Agriculture for the new State College at Columbus: the Ohio Agricultural and Mechanical College. After it became Ohio State University, the trustees appointed him Professor of Agriculture, Botany, and Veterinary Medicine. He held that position until his death in 1895, at age eighty.

Townshend's role in Ohio State University's establishment, particularly the agricultural college, is significant. Already in 1873 he inaugurated agricultural experiments on how to rehabilitate farmland in light of Ohio's growing problems with soil exhaustion. His inclination to develop agricultural experiments was inspired by experiences in his native England.[94] In 1880 he proposed an agricultural experiment station, an institution the likes of which only Connecticut and North Carolina had at the time. So in 1882 the general assembly of Ohio established the Ohio Agricultural Experiment Station. Two years later Townshend toured Britain and Ireland to examine the sophisticated experimental work being conducted at the various agricultural and veterinary schools and botanical gardens, and he returned with ideas and methodologies applicable to Ohio's new experiment station. He saw the station's greatest tasks to be determining the best breeds of cattle, developing the best fertilizers and crop varieties, and fighting crop diseases and parasitic insects.[95]

As a trustee, Norton Townshend believed that the College should remain a practical institution with an emphasis on agriculture, whereas other trustees advocated the liberal arts. Townshend, who saw farming as a profession rather than a business, wanted the station to be a part of the University; he quarreled with those in favor of a comprehensive liberal arts institution with an independent experiment station. Townshend and his supporters lost those battles. The Experiment Station became a separate institution; the Ohio Agricultural and Mechanical College was changed to the Ohio State University, and it became a major state university rather than a land-grant university. But he continued his tenure as professor of agriculture.

Townshend's appointment remained a crucial link between Ohio's farmers and the University, and that relationship preserved the vital financial support that came from the Morrill Act funds. Thus it is ironic that Townshend, who foresaw Ohio State University as an A&M College, still played an important role in the effort to make OSU into a world-class, comprehensive research university. Townshend Hall, a memorial building dedicated to agricultural education in 1898 and built at a cost of $155,000, still stands in honor of the English immigrant. And though it is now the home of the Department of Psychology, it maintains the memorial plaque, which reads: "To the Memory of Norton S. Townshend 1815–1895, Beloved Physician, Friend of the Cause of Freedom, Wise Law Maker, one of the Founders of the University and its First Professor of Agriculture, the Students of Agriculture and Veterinary Medicine have placed this tablet. AD 1909."[96]

5

Crafts and Industry

During a five-day period early this month,
1,500 emigrants, principally from Great Britain,
arrived in New York and many others are on the way.
Most of these persons are artisans, and are precisely
the men we are in want of for our manufacturers.

—*Cleveland Herald*, May 25, 1827

O HIO's economic development over the course of the nineteenth century was spectacular. As the frontier gave way to productive farms linked with growing towns and villages by a market economy, there was a great demand for people skilled in various crafts. And as industries took root there was a special need for people who could provide the latest technology and know-how. Those who made or fixed the essential household items or provided important services were vital to economic growth and community development and in high demand, and they were in relatively short supply in a state as dynamic as Ohio.

British immigrants helped fill this need. Perhaps a third of those who settled in Ohio before the Civil War were skilled in traditional "preindustrial" crafts not drastically changed by industrialization.[1] Blacksmiths, butchers, tailors, shoemakers, wagon makers, cabinetmakers, bakers, carpenters, and miners were especially common. These were generally not novices trying out a new occupation; young ones with limited experience were outnumbered by those who were more mature, had apprenticeships, or at least some degree of mastery. Artisans with well-developed skills seem to have predominated. Some younger ones also developed their existing skills or adapted them to meet the particular demands of the American labor market. Richard Jones, for example, was an apprenticed carpenter who at age nineteen emigrated from Liverpool, but he "completed the mastery of his trade" in Ohio. Then he worked on the buildings of Denison University, the Union Depot in Columbus, and even Fort Custer only a year after the massacre.[2]

Many British craftsmen arrived with enough skill and experience to get work immediately and then go into business for themselves. One of them was Henry Vincent, an apprenticed butcher who left London in 1849 and quickly established his own thriving meat business in Portsmouth.[3] Shoemakers, bakers, and blacksmiths similarly established their own businesses with apparent ease. If the county histories are representative, it would appear that as many as half of the artisans who arrived during the first half of the nineteenth century also became farmers—either exclusively, after applying their trade, or in conjunction with their trade. Working at one's craft was an ideal way to accumulate money to pay for farm labor or to supplement farm income. William Miller did so. A tailor by trade, he emigrated from his native Soham, Cambridgeshire, in 1842, worked at his craft for a few years in his shop in Medina, and then came to Wood County where he purchased a farm and successfully combined farming with tailoring.[4]

The demand for blacksmiths was especially great in the early years. In 1799 there was no blacksmith within twenty miles of Dayton, but throughout the region there was a huge demand for people with these skills.[5] Because most blacksmiths served the needs of farmers and rural communities they were intimately connected with farm culture and often had agricultural experience themselves. British blacksmiths found it especially convenient to use their skills in America as a means of turning to farming their own land. As a result, they often made excellent farmers in Ohio and yet kept their hammer and anvil handy. James Cobban, for example, was a poor Scottish blacksmith who emigrated from Aberdeenshire at age twenty-one to New London, Huron County, Ohio, in 1835. There he opened shop and worked until he could afford to move to Richland County and purchase farmland. He combined blacksmithing with improving his farm, and though he never solicited for any business, his neighbors gave him plenty as the high quality of his smith work became known. As a farmer he also used extensive tilling and other improvements to make his farm one of the most desirable in the county. Both the blacksmithing and tilling skills brought from Scotland served him well in Ohio.[6]

Many other types of British craftsmen successfully farmed in Ohio through similar strategies.[7] Some intended to farm but fell back on their craft because they found that more profitable, as did one Lancashire blacksmith who tried farming in Washington County.[8] And others continued their trade to move into other work altogether. Thomas B. Jones, a shoemaker in his native Cardiganshire, emigrated in 1856 "without means," to join his two brothers who preceded him to Youngstown. Here he prospered making boots and shoes, eventually employing fourteen workers. From that success he went on to serve on the state appraising board, the board of education, and board of commissioners for Mahoning County.[9] Altogether, most British craftsmen were well prepared to enter Ohio and pursue advantages that awaited them in crafts, farming, some other occupation, or a combination of these callings; the common language and similar culture they shared with most Ohioans made this transition relatively easy.

Canal work was another way in which British immigrants entered farm life in Ohio. Working as a digger—or navvy—was a ready option. Some took on supervisory and technical roles. That is not surprising, given England's canal-building boom in the eighteenth and early nineteenth centuries, when much of the modern methods and technology associated with canal construction were developed. England's engineering achievements were breathtaking and the envy of the rest of Europe, as were the higher living standards they helped achieve. In 1761 the Duke of Bridgewater's canal to Manchester boasted an aqueduct over a valley and tunnels that bored through hills. By 1858 Britain had over four thousand miles of inland waterways.[10] Thus among Britons in Ohio were some who knew how to build and supervise canals, although those who did so were likely intending to become farmers.

William Babbage found canal work a convenient way to get started as a Buckeye farmer. Having arrived from Devon after an adventurous crossing with only a couple of dollars in his pocket, and "with no friends to help him," he walked from Toledo to Defiance in 1836 to work on the Miami Canal, which was being constructed at the time. But Babbage was not going to work as a navvy, sweating in the trenches while flinging dirt and mud for a dollar a day. Rather, he took the position of superintendent of several sections. With his relatively high wages he soon purchased 120 virgin acres and built a log cabin in the middle of the woods. And the Mighill brothers, who began arriving from Brighton in 1830, found personal independence and adventure, as well as handy cash, working as boatmen on the Miami and Erie Canals and other Ohio waterways. Richard Mighill in particular enjoyed steering canal boats between Dayton and Cincinnati for 15 dollars per month, and reported that he was "dewing very well."[11]

But even common unskilled work on the canals was convenient for some young British immigrants who needed money. John Blackburn found the work an expedient way to start life in Ohio. After his father died, he and his seventy-five-year-old mother emigrated from Lincolnshire to Ohio. He was twenty-three, and upon his arrival in Boston Township in Summit County he worked on the Ohio Canal for three months for ready cash. He then chose to work for a farmer to gain agricultural experience, rented a farm, and then purchased his own 155 acres in 1864.[12]

Most immigrants who combined their craft with agriculture did so to become full time farmers, but some did the reverse, taking on agricultural work to establish their trade. Charles Hornby, an apprenticed tailor who left Lancashire in 1856, came directly to Little Sandusky with only forty cents to his name. He had no capital with which to start up his own tailoring business, so he worked as a farm laborer for seven years. Finally in 1863 he set up a small shop with his earnings and gradually built a merchant tailoring business so successful that by the 1880s he typically carried three thousand dollars worth of stock.[13]

POTTERY

By transferring important skills and technology directly from Britain to America, British immigrants were instrumental in the inception and development of Ohio's crafts and industries. Perhaps the clearest example is the pottery industry that blossomed in East Liverpool. Potting necessitated much skill and artistry, but comparatively little investment and machinery. It also required considerable experience to identify native clays, form, throw, turn, and fire the clays, make molds, and decorate the final product. And no one did this better than the famed potters of Staffordshire.

The first kiln in East Liverpool was fired in 1839 by James Bennett, an expert craftsman who had worked in a Derbyshire yellow ware factory. Bennett emigrated in 1837 to work for Henry Clews, a Staffordshire potter who came to Kentucky and then Indiana to start potteries there. Clews failed because of poor clays and the lack of an adequate workforce and capital. So Bennett struck out on his own and headed back east by foot in search of employment. On his way he discovered clay along the banks of the Ohio near East Liverpool that he recognized as perfect for the kind of pottery that he had made in Derbyshire. He soon obtained the necessary financial support from a local man to build a kiln and started firing simple yellow ware mugs, which he sold by hauling wagonloads to show local settlers. With a profit of $250 by 1841, Bennett was "getting on famously in the business," and sent for his three brothers, also potters, who were still in England. Their partnership was the foundation of a local industry that flourished and made eastern Ohio one of America's premier pottery centers.

By concentrating on the cheap yellow table and toilet ware, which required less skill than the highly decorated blue and white Staffordshire ware, the potteries of East Liverpool successfully competed with imports from England. Soon Staffordshire potters came pouring in, attracted mostly by higher wages,

Potteries in East Liverpool, 1887. This scene was familiar to immigrants from Staffordshire, who brought the pottery industry to Ohio. From Henry Howe, *Historical Collections of Ohio,* vol. 1.

the prospect of land ownership, and for some the promise of a meatier diet. The frequency with which British immigrants in America wrote enthusiastically to family members in England about how often they ate meat—even three times a day—is a good indication of how significant this aspect of American life was.

Though the immigrant potters had to adjust their work practices to make a mass-produced, more mechanized product, they achieved a higher standard of living and enjoyed a better future in Ohio. And, very significantly, all of this happened in a community of fellow English immigrants, many of whom knew each other in the old country. Neighbors, friends, and family members crossed the Atlantic Ocean, traveled west, floated down the Ohio River, and reassembled their community in East Liverpool. By 1879 twenty-four potteries existed in East Liverpool, employing some two thousand men, women and children—nearly all English immigrants and their families—and the town boasted itself as "the pottery capital of the world."[14] As late as the turn of the century East Liverpool remained essentially a transplanted potting town of Englishmen. The vast majority of the fifteen thousand inhabitants were English immigrants and their children—many of whom thrived and rose to positions of local leadership.[15]

A breakthrough occurred in the East Liverpool pottery industry in 1862, when the U.S. Congress slapped a 40 percent tariff on imported earthenware. This protectionism drove English pottery out of the American market and brought unemployment to many Staffordshire potters, who then migrated to East Liverpool, where they could resume their occupations at good wages among fellow countrymen—a good example of the interconnectedness of the two economies. This protectionism against a free trade Britain not only precipitated a fresh flow of British immigrants but also enabled Ohio to manufacture new products for the first time. In 1873 the potters of East Liverpool began to produce the white granite ware, which had been a virtual British monopoly up until that time. It was the protectionism and immigration of the skilled British workers that made the new product possible.[16]

Some immigrants from Staffordshire, especially youngsters, learned or honed their skills in East Liverpool. Samuel Cartwright arrived as a boy and went to the potteries where other English immigrants taught him the craft. After serving in the Union army during the Civil War, Cartwright and his brother established their own pottery business, which was incorporated in 1897. The same network allowed young immigrants like Edward Devon from Devonshire to emigrate alone at age sixteen and come directly to East Liverpool, where he developed his skills and worked at increasingly demanding tasks for various potteries in the city.[17]

Immigrant potters from North Staffordshire outside a pottery in East Liverpool, Ohio, mid to late nineteenth century. They were skilled, tough, and determined to be their own masters. Courtesy East Liverpool Historical Society and the Ohio Historical Society's Museum of Ceramics.

Scottish potters also came to East Liverpool to work for the English who dominated the industry. George Carlyle learned the craft in Glasgow before leaving in 1849. After working in East Liverpool, Zanesville, and Cincinnati, he started a business manufacturing terra cotta sewer pipes—the first of its kind in America. His training in Glasgow and work in East Liverpool under English managers prepared him well and he built a "vast business."[18] Another Scot, John Wyllie of Edinburgh, showed the amazing mobility that many potters enjoyed. For many years he worked at his craft in Scotland, various places in England, the Netherlands, France, and then Staffordshire before settling down in East Liverpool. Such a well-traveled and experienced person made an interesting addition to the community.[19]

The Staffordshire potters brought their craft to other parts of the state as well. Akron was particularly important. In 1848 Enoch Rowley, a potter from Stoke-upon-Trent, Staffordshire, arrived in Akron with his family and established the city's first pottery. He was very successful and later became city councilman.[20] Another important founder was Staffordshire potter William Robinson, who first went to East Liverpool and worked there until 1856. Then he moved to Akron, where he saw even greater rewards for his skills, and developed the city's extensive pottery and sewer pipe industry. He went on to become one of the most important early businessmen of industrial Akron when he formed the Robinson Clay Product Company. His son served as president of the company as well as president of the Second National Bank of Akron.[21]

Other Staffordshire potters left East Liverpool and came to Akron to continue their craft and become owners in the industry. George Whitmore did, as did Joseph Cook. He was born in 1847, the same year that his parents settled in East Liverpool with other English potters. Joseph was reared as a potter there, enlisted in the Union army, and then shortly after the war headed for Akron where he pursued the pottery business. Eventually he became president of the Akron Stoneware Company and the Akron China Company, and later was connected with the Cleveland China Company.[22] As a leader of Akron's stoneware and pottery industry Joseph Cook surely knew another English immigrant who filled a similar role: J. M. Willis, president and superintendent of Akron's United States Stoneware Company.[23]

MECHANICS, ENGINEERS, AND MILLERS

British immigrants in Ohio were also conspicuous as mechanics, engineers, millers, and artisans who made tools, machines, mills, and various other mechanical devices to meet specific needs. Ohio had a great demand for these skilled workers because Cleveland and Cincinnati were the machine tool centers of the United States. As the world's first industrial nation, Britain had a large share of its working population with industrial and mechanical skills— many on the cutting edge of their field.

Most British immigrant mechanics and engineers entering Ohio appear to have had full apprenticeships or at least extensive experience and training. Some made quite an impact on the developing state. Thomas Cotton Lewis, an apprenticed machinist, draughtsman, and millwright from Merthyr-Tydfil, South Wales, went to Ohio after erecting mills in New York and Pennsylvania— including the first American mill that rolled bar iron from blooms. In Portsmouth in 1832 he erected the main mill for Glover, Noel & Company and with his son built and operated another foundry a decade later. Interestingly, in 1850 Lewis gave up his prosperous business to settle on a farm in nearby Wheel- ersburg—a good illustration of the primacy of agriculture for many of the an- tebellum British immigrants.[24]

John McTammany exemplifies how young, mechanically gifted immigrants channeled their talents into various mechanical occupations. Born near Glas- gow in 1845, at seventeen he emigrated to Uniontown (between Canton and Akron) with his family. He started out repairing agricultural equipment and designing improvements for the reaper and other machines. In 1863, only one year after his migration, he enlisted in the 115th Ohio Volunteer Infantry, out of dedication to his new country and opposition to slavery. McTammany was wounded near Chattanooga and during his convalescence began repairing mu- sical instruments and music boxes. Later he invented a player piano for which he was awarded patents. He also built a voting machine used in Massachusetts in 1896. McTammany invented many other devices, including a census tabulat- ing machine and other musical instruments.[25]

Milling and mill building were especially important for Ohio's developing agricultural economy, because they allowed farmers to go beyond subsistence farming and produce for the marketplace. Mills were so necessary that in 1798 the Connecticut Land Company offered generous bounties or loans to those who would erect them in the Western Reserve. In 1823 English immigrant James Martin, writing from Crawford County, Ohio, to relatives in England, reported that he had to travel forty-four miles to obtain flour, indicating the dire need for local mills in any community.[26] But there were problems in the early milling business. Millers had reputations for being dishonest or incompetent. Honest, experienced millers were an asset to any community.[27]

Many of the important millers and millwrights in early and mid-nineteenth- century Ohio were British immigrants. Most were mature adults with experience in milling and mill building, coming to Ohio to seize the greater opportunities available to people of their caliber. The promise of becoming independent millers was especially alluring and a very realistic goal. John Hadley, a Scottish miller who came directly to Marietta in 1854, began as a head miller and then became superintendent of several mills, a mill builder, and then owner of the Newport Mill in Washington County.[28]

Others went from miller to mill owner and even further to become significant business leaders. Roger Heath, born in 1840 to a large family of millers in Devonshire, used his rich milling tradition to rise to such heights. For generations the Heaths were expert millers and mill owners in southwest England. After his father's death Heath was apprenticed to his uncle as a miller for seven years. At age twenty-one he set out as a journeyman miller, working in various places throughout Britain, where he earned a good reputation and high wages. But "he believed that the business opportunities in the New World were superior to those that he could secure in his native land," and so he headed for the United States in the 1860s.

Heath first came to Akron, then Kent, and finally to Shelby, Richland County. He started by purchasing a mill, rebuilding it, and bringing it "into harmony with ideas of modern milling." He also formed a partnership with his brothers who followed him to Ohio, and together they increased the capacity of their mills such that they were recognized as the best millers in northeast Ohio. The brothers had more modern machinery than any other mill of that size in the entire state, and mill manufacturers often sought Heath out for his opinion on how to improve machinery. Heath always aimed to build the highest quality mill possible, and he became known in the region for raising milling standards. He was so successful that he expanded his interests, became president and director of the Citizens Bank, and became one of the leading businessmen of the county. He helped establish the Shelby Steel Tube Works, the Shelby Bicycle Works, the Automobile Works, the Shelby Printing Company, the Land Improvement Company, and the Shelby Foundry Company. In the meantime he also served in numerous local public offices.[29]

British millers and millwrights in Ohio commonly flourished in the milling industry and then settled on a farm. Many succeeded spectacularly at their trade and helped advance the industry, only to move to farming as though that had been the goal all along, a pattern that underscores again the importance of agriculture to people of many different backgrounds. For Robert Turner, an apprenticed miller in his native Norfolk, farming his own land was a proper and respectable way to end his days. The day after his arrival in Akron in 1852 he was hired as head miller for the Allen-Perkins Company. After ten years he bought a steam-powered flour mill, which he operated for another ten years. Afterward he bought a woolen factory and converted it into an oatmeal mill. Finally, in 1881, he sold out, bought a farm of ninety acres, and devoted his time to agriculture.[30]

Other British millers arrived with advanced skills and experience, branched out into new or related fields, and then went into farming. John Chapman left his native Cornwall at age nineteen in 1831 with a thorough knowledge of mill building, and within a year was in Akron, building the town's first mill. He made the first flour in Akron and worked on every aspect of mills and their construction, and he was an accomplished wheelwright. He worked as a consultant and superintendent of mill construction throughout Summit County. But with all of this success it was land that he ultimately sought, so he bought a farm in Tallmadge.[31]

With their knowledge of milling and the mechanics of mill construction, British millers and millwrights had skills that could be transferred to other occupations. After building mills some applied their talents to related mechanical construction. Experienced millwrights like Joseph Palmer were talented, resourceful young men who adapted their skills to related trades to pursue other opportunities. Settling in Akron in 1836, Palmer was hired to build the locks in the Ohio Canal. After that he also assisted in building mills, but in 1854 moved to a farm in Medina County for a life of full-time agriculture.[32]

Like mill building, toolmaking was a particularly important skill that British immigrants brought to Ohio. Henry Warwood, an expert toolmaker who arrived from Birmingham in 1848, made tools and cutlery in Cuyahoga Falls and then Martin's Ferry. There he erected a factory to produce tools of all sorts that were sold throughout much of the United States. Engineers and toolmakers also had the skills and often the capital to make relatively easy changes in occupations, to become merchants, or take up farming. This was especially true as Ohio continued to industrialize after the Civil War and yet remained an important agricultural state. Some found work on trains, which was a dangerous occupation in the nineteenth century. In 1874, a boiler explosion killed Welsh immigrants William Hutchins and his father while they ran trains between Delaware and Columbus.[33]

Certain parts of Ohio were especially attractive for English machinists. Many went to Crawford County to work for the railway industry in Bucyrus. The clustering of machinists there suggests a sharing of information among English mechanics and a network that paved the way for others to join them. James Thorpe, for example, had learned the machinist trade in Bradley, Yorkshire, by the time he left for America at age eighteen in 1848. Shortly after his arrival the Toledo & Ohio Railroad in Bucyrus offered him the highly paid position of general foreman. The same company also employed a Scottish machinist, David Christie, who arrived from Fifeshire in 1852. Others local companies hired more British immigrants who had become expert machinists before their migration.[34]

After the Civil War, Ohio continued to offer rich opportunities for skilled British machinists. J. M. Davidson, who completed a full apprenticeship in his native Scotland, came to America in 1878 and went to Akron, where he worked for the Akron Iron Company for fifteen years. Then he went into business himself as a general contractor and coal dealer, employed a large workforce, and was awarded many lucrative contracts in the city. Some English machinists and machine makers who came to Ohio after the war used their expertise to achieve a level of success that almost certainly would have eluded them in England.[35]

George Wadsworth became famous in foundries throughout Ohio and many other parts of North America for the machines and devices he invented. As a boy in Liverpool he showed a knack for mechanical things, and after some education he entered the Great Western Railway shops at Wolverhampton, which were on the cutting edge of the industry at the time. He served a six-year apprenticeship in the fitter and turner trade, and in 1880 at age twenty-three he immigrated directly to Cleveland to work at the Cleveland Bridge and Car Works.

Wadsworth moved rapidly from company to company, exploiting his skills to their full potential. From the Cleveland Bridge and Car Works he moved to become the first toolmaker for the National Cash Register Company. Then he entered business for himself in Findlay, where he created and ran a machine shop, Wadsworth, Sheesley & Company. Afterwards he returned to Cleveland and superintended the Avery Stamping Company until 1894, when he moved to Chicago for a short time to direct a machine shop. But he soon returned to Ohio. In 1901 he set up his own company again and invented a core-making machine as well as the Wadsworth Portable Core Oven—devices soon used by most foundries throughout the country. In 1902 he also became general superintendent of the American Motor Carriage Company. At the same time he oversaw the Falls Rivet and Machine Company in Cuyahoga Falls, with three hundred men under his supervision. With such an impressive array of experience in the machine industry, George Wadsworth was by the turn of the century renowned for his significant contributions to Ohio's modern industry.[36]

Some truly expert engineers arrived late in the century. One of them was Harry Pounder, who was born in Staffordshire in 1862 and graduated from the Technical Department of the Government schools in Hull as a marine engineer. After working in Hull, the Portuguese Government recruited him, made him a citizen, and sent him to Africa to work on engineering projects in the colonies. An engineer at the top of his profession, who had seen much of the world, Pounder could probably find lucrative work virtually anywhere. He returned to England in 1883 and then moved to Buffalo, New York, where he worked as a chief engineer. He finally moved to Cleveland to do the same for the Forge & City Iron Company. In 1890 he became vice president of the Galion Lumber Company and exercised much influence as a leading member of the business community.[37]

Though most of the transfer of technology and technique from Britain to America occurred early in the century—while Britain remained well ahead of the United States in economic and industrial development—skilled British immigrants still came to Ohio later in the century and made important additions to the labor force. Consider the case of Robert Mitchinson Reay, an apprenticed blacksmith and mechanic in Durham, England, who migrated directly to Massillon, Stark County, in 1869. Though he started out as a blacksmith, his mechanical skills enabled him to run a forge and then become superintendent of the Massillon Bridge Company, a major manufacturer of railroad and highway bridges.[38] And William Siddall, who served a "rigorous apprenticeship" as a mechanic in Birmingham, saw wider opportunities in Ohio. So in 1888, at age twenty-one, he went to Cleveland and then Columbus. After a stint as chief engineer and master mechanic of the Duquesne Mills in Pennsylvania, he returned to Ohio to become master mechanic at the Bellaire Works of the National Steel Company in Belmont County, and supervised everything mechanical in that huge plant.[39]

A final example of the disparate roles played by British engineers in Ohio is Alexander Winton, who trained as a marine engineer in the Clyde shipyards near Glasgow before immigrating to Cleveland in 1885, at age twenty-five. With his skills and background he was appointed superintendent of the Phoenix Iron Works. He then organized the Winton Bicycle Company, making fifty high quality bicycles per month during the heyday of the new American pastime, around the turn of the century.[40] Altogether, the immigrants' inventiveness and entrepreneurial spirit served Ohio well.

COAL MINERS

If Ohio's pottery, milling, toolmaking, and engineering trades benefited from British talent and experience, the coal mining industry was virtually founded upon it. From its very inception, all the way through the nineteenth century and into the twentieth, British colliers, mine operators, and managers were at the center of Ohio's important coal industry. The Welsh explorer and cartographer, Lewis Evans, first located and recorded the existence of coal in Ohio, near the Hocking River, in his 1755 "Map of the Middle British Colonies in America." Evans had previously reported information from Indian traders that there was a fire on a coal outcrop near the head of the Muskingum River in 1748.[41]

The first reported coal mining in Ohio occurred in 1800, three years before statehood, and the industry grew slowly but steadily in the first half of the century. When Thomas Hulme traveled down the Ohio River in 1818 and passed Steubenville, he noticed "several fine coal mines" that were within fifty yards of the river bank and about ten yards above the water line.[42] These were simple exposed coal seams that allowed even unskilled laborers to dig out the coal and bring it to market. Some of these early mines were developed by English immigrants working as families, much like they had done in the old country.

The Heatherington family was especially interesting. The father, John, and his four sons arrived in Belmont County in the 1820s and began developing a coal bank near McMahons Creek. They loaded coal out of the banks in wheelbarrows and dumped it through board screens, making a terrible noise that infuriated the neighbors, until they saw the wealth and business the operations generated. The family's musical talents also provided entertainment that made the Heatheringtons the most popular folks in the valley. The Heatherington legend grew when one of the sons, Jacob, set out on his own, bought eight acres of coal land, and worked it with his mule, Jack, who was more a partner than a beast of burden. Jacob built a mansion—said to have cost $35,000—with a likeness of Jack over the doorway, and Jack frequently could be found in the house. When Jack finally died at age forty, Jacob's grief was indescribable, and for the rest of his life he solemnly showed visitors the mule's grave and told tales of their days together in the coal mines.[43]

Soon after the accessible coal seams were exploited, deeper mines were opened up, mines that required much more sophisticated operations. Like the pottery industry, advanced mining required experience to find the raw, extractive materials and skilled hands to make it useful. And in coal mining, as in other industries, skilled British immigrants brought much of the knowledge and technology, though they also needed to adapt to a new environment.

Coal mining before the onslaught of mechanization in the late nineteenth century was still a skilled craft occupation. Miners not only had to dig out the coal by hand, they had to do it safely. Timbering the shafts and coal seams, ensuring adequate ventilation, and if necessary pumping water were essential skills. Miners needed to prevent catastrophes caused by suffocating poisonous gasses emanating from the seams. And of course every miner's nightmare—the

JACK.

Jacob Heatherington and his mule, Jack. This eccentric English immigrant teamed up with Jack to open the coal mines of Belmont County in the 1820s. From Henry Howe, *Historical Collections of Ohio,* vol. 1.

collapse of the mine wall and the deadly cave-ins that took so many lives during the century—had to be prevented. This required an intimate knowledge of mining environments and the ability to extract coal without weakening the tunnels. In these respects the British were ahead of the game, since mining in Britain dated to before Roman times. An extensive coal industry stretched back to the Middle Ages, when Britain's forests were being depleted. Thereafter, the British were always on the cutting edge of new techniques and technologies. Great Britain—essentially an island built on coal—contained many very deep mines; some of them plunged a thousand feet or more below the surface and stretched far beneath the seabed. There miners honed their skills and became experts.

Thus, the British developed the modern coal mining industry and transplanted the craft, complete with the latest techniques of hewing, timbering, and mine draining, to the United States in the nineteenth century. During the 1850s alone, roughly 37,000 British miners came directly to the United States and many thousands more came via Canada. So prominent and important, they soon dominated the ranks of authority in the industry as overseers, mine operators, and owners. According to one historian, "in the pre–Civil War days, every mine boss in the anthracite region was English, Welsh, or Scottish."[44] The 1880 census reveals that of all of Ohio's miners, over five thousand were born in Britain, but only forty-five in Ireland, forty-one in the United States, and two in Germany.[45]

A combination of powerful "push" and "pull" forces drew them to Ohio. The pull to America began as early as the 1820s, when British miners were recruited to exploit anthracite seams in eastern Pennsylvania and then heard of newer opportunities further west in Ohio. The push out of Britain manifested itself in a number of ways: conflicts with coal masters, uncertain and falling wages, or just the gritty and dangerous routine without prospect for change. Economic depressions in Britain's coal fields, like those that hit Wales in the 1840s and Scotland in the 1860s, were especially important as they resulted in thousands leaving the old world for the new. Many went to Ohio, perhaps first mining in Pennsylvania.[46]

But even during relatively good times, and though miners earned substantially more than laborers or most skilled craftsmen, life in British mines was hard and dangerous. British mines were initially more dangerous because they were deeper than their American counterparts, though American mines were typically more primitive and getting increasingly dangerous as well. In addition, British coal mines typically paid on a piece-rate basis. Therefore a younger man in his twenties or early thirties was usually at the peak of his earning power, while earnings usually diminished in middle age—along with options for the future. But with relatively high wages, British miners were mobile, willing, and able to find the highest reward for their skills and the dangerous underground work they performed. And by the 1830s Ohio was an ideal place. There were fresh mining opportunities in relatively shallow mines, the discovery of new mines, the prospect of mine ownership, and, important for many, rich farmland. By the Civil War, coal miners in the Mahoning Valley earned as much as $220 per month, much more than miners made in Britain.[47]

The higher cost of American goods diminished the higher American earnings; not enough, however, to eliminate the advantages of working in Ohio mines. David Griffiths was a Welsh immigrant working near Steubenville during the Civil War and he reported back to his friends in Aberdare the costs and benefits of being an American collier: "We get four cents a bushel for cutting it and each car holds twelve and a half bushels and we fill six cars a day and so we earn $3 a day that is 12s. 6d in your money. We work very hard while we are working but we leave every day about three to four o'clock. I like it here very much; it is so much better than being a fireman in Wales. . . . You have to pay for tools for our work and four cents a day for sharpening them. . . . Clothes are very expensive, calico (5½d. a yard in Wales) is forty-five cents here, shoes are very dear and the best are poor as they have all been pegged."[48]

Along with their higher earnings, British newcomers rose quickly to positions of leadership and authority in Ohio's coal industry. Typical was C. R. Thompson, a Northumberland miner who left home at age twenty-eight. After working in the Pittsburgh coal industry for four years, he proceeded to Steubenville, where his experience opened the doors of various companies, and he became superintendent of the largest coal company in Jefferson County. Welsh immigrant Roger Ashton had a similar meteoric rise to mine superintendent and social prominence in Belmont County, as did many too numerous to mention.[49] Scotsman John J. Hill, who left Lanarkshire in 1864 with modest savings from mining coal there, was immediately appointed as a superintendent of mines in Haselton and then Nebo because the mine owners prized his experience.[50] Josiah Wells entered the mines in his native Cornwall at age fourteen, and emigrated after his father died, leaving his mother behind until he could afford to send for her. He started out mining in the Lake Superior region of Michigan, and after the Civil War went to Nelsonville, and then New Straightsville when it was composed of but three or four houses. He was elected corporation clerk a few years later, and in 1880 became superintendent of the Straitsville Central Mining Company.[51] One reason why British immigrants were quickly appointed as mine bosses was because they were experienced at wringing more work out of miners at less cost. This characteristic was not appreciated by other British immigrants like Welshman David Watkins, who was mining coal near Youngstown during the Civil War. Referring to his authoritarian mine boss, a Scot, Watkins explained in a letter back home: "Some of them are set up as bosses over us because they have just come from the Old Country and are more used to oppressing the workmen by carrying the work on at less cost. It is like this with us at the moment, as the owner of the works has sent some creature from Scotland here; but I think that he regrets it because we have had two or three strikes against him already and we will have some more to put him in his place until he leaves. If one of the bosses utters a harsh word to one of the workmen it is quite likely that there would be a strike against him the next day."[52]

But the relative equality of America provided British immigrants with a good environment in which to push for better conditions and organize their labor. Though there was a long way to go, the greater egalitarianism that Ohio offered was not lost on many British immigrants. As Watkins also remarked: "It is wonderful to live in a free country where the rights of men are upheld, one weighing as much as the next in the scales, with no difference between rich and poor and if you happen to meet the two on the street it would be difficult to say which was the gentleman. There is none of the pride or the inferiority of the workman here."[53]

As attractive as Ohio's coal industry was, many British immigrants used mining only as a stepping-stone to other occupations. John Lomax was an impoverished miner from Lancashire whose meager possessions were stolen upon his arrival in America. After this inauspicious beginning, he mined and quarried to earn sufficient money to become a grocer and hardware storeowner in Lowellville, Mahoning County.[54] Though entering business in such a fashion was the goal for some miners, land ultimately attracted most of the British immigrants who started out mining in Ohio—especially before the Civil War.

In Britain, farming and mining often occurred together naturally. In Ohio, then, shifting to farming after sufficient earnings had been accumulated was natural and quite easy. Such was the story of Francis Redfearn, who farmed and mined lead in Muker, in the Yorkshire Dales, and took his family to America in 1830 to mine coal in Pottsville, Pennsylvania. With their coal earnings they proceeded to Washington Township, Hancock County, where they were among the earliest settlers. To reach their land they cut a path for their wagon through the dense forest and crossed the Sandusky River by floating their wagon and forcing their terrified cattle to swim. After living for a few years in a crude log shack that scarcely protected them from the elements, the family moved to Wood County and became some of the most prominent pioneers of the area.[55]

Even for those at the top of the coal industry, farming proved an irresistible, ultimate goal. Thomas Johnson was only eight years old when his family emigrated from England to Ohio in 1862. By 1880 he and his three brothers established their own business as coal mine operators and distributors, and Johnson became the owner of several coal companies and corporations in several states. But after his retirement in 1915 he turned his full attention to a fourteen hundred-acre farm he bought in 1898 and developed an extensive cattle-breeding operation—a source of both profit and recreation. Johnson realized a dream that was fantastic in England.[56]

British experience and technology were particularly important to the coal industry of the Steubenville area, where the Steubenville Coal and Mining Company sunk its first shaft in 1857. Plagued by inadequate experience and backward technology, the company suspended operations until miners from Durham and Newcastle imported the "Durham System." The system involved new methods and equipment for mine drainage, ventilation, and coal extraction that had been developed by John Buddle, one of Britain's ablest mining en-

A poor Lancashire miner, John Lomax emigrated in 1854 at the age of thirty-one with his first wife, Margaret. After she died, John returned to England to marry his cousin Alice (shown here) and resumed life in Ohio. After mining and quarrying, John became a grocer and hardware storeowner in Lowellville, Mahoning County. From Ewing Summers, Genealogical and Family History of Eastern Ohio.

gineers. This direct transfer of British methods and technology transformed the coal industry of Steubenville and enabled it to flourish.[57]

Some immigrant miners were well educated in the science of mine engineering. John Morris, whose family combined mining with farming for many generations, was an expert mining engineer with an Oxford University education before his emigration from Cumbach, Wales, to Youngstown in 1845. There he worked with a cousin who operated the Chippewa mines in Franklin Township until he was killed in a mine accident in 1854. John Morris's son, Mordecai, joined him in the mines at an early age to drive mules and benefit from his father's experience. After serving in the Union army Mordecai mined in various parts of the United States and became a mine superintendent in Indiana. In 1873 he returned to Summit County, where he became superintendent first of the Johnston Coal Company and then another coal company in Massillon. In 1882 he retired from mining and devoted his attention to his farm and real estate in the family tradition.[58]

After the Civil War, as Ohio's coal industry expanded to meet the growing demand of industrial America, British immigrants continued to dominate positions of authority. Robert Bell, an experienced coal miner from Cumberland who migrated directly to Ohio in 1867 at age thirty-five, moved around the state in search of the highest wages and most responsible work. Eventually the governor appointed him mine inspector for eight counties.[59] And J. W. Blower was a miner in his native Staffordshire before emigrating at age nineteen in 1881. After a few years in Pennsylvania he came to Ohio to study mining and engineering at Ohio State University. The education prepared him well to be superintendent and operator of various mines before becoming superintendent of all the mines for the Pittsburg & Lake Erie Railroad. Blower then purchased his own mining property in Athens County and organized the Hisylvania Coal Company. He was also president of the Colburgh Coal Company, and by the early twentieth century Blower was "widely recognized as a most prominent and prosperous representative of mining interests" in Ohio. He probably knew the family of John T. Carding, also from Staffordshire, who arrived in Ohio a year earlier and organized the Carding Coal Company at Columbus, which blossomed to include other coal companies and real estate.[60]

Other individual British immigrants made notable contributions to the history of Ohio's coal industry. Thomas Pirt is certainly one of them. Born in Craulington, Northumberland, in 1841, Pirt was not yet eight when he entered the mines of northern England. Apparently he acquired some education because he signed his marriage certificate when he married Anna Mark in 1860. In his early twenties he decided to leave for America—while bound by contract to work for an English coal company for another year. It was a bold and illegal move. Pirt was arrested on the ship *Louisa Ann* just as it set sail, tried for quitting his contract, but acquitted. He nonetheless returned to work in the Northumberland mines and suffered an injury that disabled him for half a year. Finally, he boarded the same *Louisa Ann* and sailed for America, but the misadventures continued. Four days from port a terrible storm wrecked the ship, which was towed back to Queenstown, Ireland. In spite of such numerous setbacks, "the fever of emigration was still burning" in Pirt's mind, so he sailed on the *City of London* and landed in New York in 1862, while the Civil War raged.

In America, Thomas Pirt capitalized on his skill and experience. He first went to Wilkes-Barre, Pennsylvania, where he sank a coal shaft that earned him nearly five thousand dollars in less than two years. Declaring his intention of becoming a United States citizen, Pirt then returned to England where he assembled a crew of men to take to Prussia, where he sank several shafts. After returning to England for a couple of years he returned to Wilkes-Barre and then went to Steubenville and from there to Nelsonville, Ohio, where he became president of the Miners' Union. Finally in 1881 he moved to Columbus to superintend the Ohio Central Coal Company in Corning.[61]

Though British miners in Ohio in the post–Civil War years were most conspicuous for their roles in leadership and ownership in the industry, many of humble backgrounds and modest achievements continued to arrive and contribute to the rapidly expanding industry. They were part of a large migration of English and Scottish miners to America, inspired to some extent by Chartists who had emigrated before the War. Chartists advocated Parliament's enactment of the People's Charter, which was first published in 1838 by the London Working Men's Association. The Charter called for the secret ballot, universal male suffrage, the end of property qualifications for election to Parliament, yearly Parliamentary elections, equal electoral districts, and salaries for members of Parliament. The Chartists who moved to the United States were often politically motivated and maintained contacts in Britain. Some wrote back to encourage miners to join them and establish unions.[62]

The postwar surge of collier migration was also inspired by Alexander McDonald, the famous leader of British miners. McDonald urged men to leave for America because there they could mine for higher earnings and then buy farmland to escape mining forever. In addition, the departure of miners to America was seen as a way of reducing the labor supply in Britain, raising both the wages and bargaining power of the miners who stayed. By 1870 there were over eighteen hundred English, over seven hundred Scottish, and nearly two hundred Welsh coal miners in Ohio, and their numbers grew in the following decade in part due to the efforts of McDonald and the ambitions of British miners.[63]

Though the Scots preferred to join coal mining communities in Illinois after the war, some Welsh and English miners chose Ohio. Among them were a twenty-eight-year-old miner and his Welsh bride, Hugh and Jane Oram Green, who left the village of Frampton-Cottrell (near Bristol and the Welsh border) with Hugh's brother Joseph, for Ohio in 1868. They were miners in England, but the local mines had become virtually exhausted. The Greens arrived in the mining village of Coshocton, located on the site of an old Indian village in the hills where the Muskingum and Tuscarawas rivers meet—the same place where the English trader and adventurer, Nicholas Cresswell, lived with the Indians nearly one hundred years earlier. By the 1870s nearly two hundred people lived within the town limits, and the Greens pursued their work in this relatively prosperous community.

The Greens arrived with virtually no possessions, but with much skill and pride in their craft. They were members of a working elite: not laborers but skilled pick miners. British miners like the Greens brought pick mining to America, and as surface mining in Ohio gave way to underground mining, workers like the Greens became more valuable to the industry. But the Greens also brought with them a tradition of trade unionism. They ardently supported Britain's miners' unions and realized that miners in America needed to organize—a realization lost on most native and other foreign-born miners. They also brought a solid religious faith acquired in the Baptist Church, and their religious conviction grew stronger as they struggled with adjusting to their new American home and culture.

The Greens found the initial adjustment to mining conditions in Ohio quite challenging. Their mining site, Hardscrabble Hill, was a primitive and filthy jumble of shacks, where most of the miners were foreigners—even though most Coshocton residents were native-born. Conditions were very harsh and unsafe. Because American coal operators often engaged in cutthroat competition and produced more coal than the market demanded, employment was unsteady and wages were lower than many expected. Miners were often idle for fifteen weeks in the spring and summer, and their pay might come in the form of company scrip—which sometimes failed to pay their bills at the company store. The Greens never fully accomplished what Alexander McDonald envisioned for emigrant miners. Though Hugh Green did manage to own a small plot of land by the time of his death in 1925, it was insufficient to provide a farmer with a living.[64]

The Greens probably came to know John Bigrigg, a collier from Cumber-land who emigrated in 1870 at age forty-two. After a couple of years mining in Pennsylvania and New York, he joined other British miners in Coshocton, where he also became a member of the Baptist Church. In 1849, Bigrigg married Anna Malkingson, daughter of a flax dresser, and both John and Anna signed their marriage certificate with a mark—showing their lack of literacy. In Ohio, he continued to explore various mines and settled in Shawnee, Perry County, to mine the rest of his days. Lacking education, he never rose to management level. Nor did he ever become a farmer. But mobility did allow him to find the best rewards for his work.[65] In the Shawnee Valley Bigrigg likely met James Heppell, who had mined coal in Northumberland since age nine and came to that part of Ohio at about the same time Bigrigg did to mine coal. Heppell was known for his narrow escapes in English mines: once he was trapped for two days in an old shaft sunk in 1799 that was seventeen hundred feet deep, where the first steam elevator was successfully established. After mining in Ohio Heppell de-cided to change jobs and became an engineer on the Baltimore & Ohio Rail-road, an occupation not much safer than mining.[66]

Other immigrant miners of modest means and economic achievements in the Shawnee area still made important contributions to the community. Enoch Oldroyd, for example, was born in Thornhill, Yorkshire, in 1842 and entered the mines before he was ten years old. In 1866 he married Patience Almond, and though she signed the marriage certificate with a mark, Enoch wrote his name. Early in 1870 they sailed for America, where he mined first in Maryland, then Pennsylvania, and then in 1873, in Shawnee. He remained a miner, but also preached in the Primitive Methodist Church, served as a local trustee, Sunday school teacher, and superintendent. For immigrants like Enoch Oldroyd, min-ing in the Shawnee Valley was much more than a self-centered attempt at mak-ing a living and achieving economic self-sufficiency. It was also a life of service to his faith, his neighbors, and his community.[67]

By the 1870s mining centers like Shawnee became a virtual melting pot for miners from all over the British Isles, many coming and going as they tried out various parts of the state for the highest wages. Harry Kear, born in Gloucester-shire in 1854 to a mining father and a mother, Elizabeth, who was at least liter-ate enough to sign her name on the birth certificate, left England in 1873. Kear joined other British immigrants in Shawnee to mine coal in 1875, after mining in Pennsylvania and Maryland for a couple of years. He also mined in Iowa, where he sank several coal shafts, and then went back to Pennsylvania to work for an iron ore company. Kear prospered enough to take a six-week trip back to England to visit his hometown and London, before returning to America and settling again in Shawnee to pursue business with his brother. For immigrants like Kear, mining in Ohio opened doors to travel, adventure, and profitable business.[68]

Thomas Phillips had perhaps too much adventure before he settled in Shawnee. He was born in Forest of Dean, Gloucestershire, in 1821, and mined by the age of ten. Phillips and his brother sailed for America in 1847, during the height of the potato famine, rising unemployment, and social misery in Britain. Landing in Philadelphia, Phillips traveled toward Ohio with seventeen other persons in a horse drawn coach. While crossing a bridge in Pennsylvania, the bridge collapsed, sending all persons and horses crashing into the river twenty-one feet below. Some people and horses died, and Phillips broke all of the ribs on his right side. After recuperating at an uncle's house, Thomas Phillips mined coal and sank shafts in Pennsylvania, Tennessee, and Alabama; in 1861 he had difficulty escaping from the newly organized Confederacy. After returning to Pennsylvania, Shawnee attracted him too, and the Shawnee Valley Coal and Iron Company made him its bank boss. He probably knew William Wallace, a Scottish immigrant who became bank boss for the New York and Straitsville Coal and Iron Company at about the same time, also in Shawnee.[69]

In many ways Shawnee evolved into a British enclave, so prominent was their leadership in the local economy and society. William Davey was a pillar of that society. Born in 1841 in St. Neots, Cornwall, Davey spent five years in the British Navy, three of them off the west coast of Africa. At about twenty-three he immigrated to Athens County, and served in the Civil War for the 18th Ohio Volunteer Infantry. After the war he moved to Shawnee and was elected mayor in 1876. He was reelected for several more consecutive terms, and also served as justice of the peace.[70] Also, the Methodist Church in Shawnee relied heavily on the tireless work of English immigrant preacher Reverend John Mason.

The Welsh were also prominent in the Shawnee Valley after the Civil War and filled many prominent positions. John Williams, a blacksmith from Llanfachreth, Anglesey, North Wales, began work in 1872 at the Shawnee Valley Coal and Iron Company and opened his own smithing shop in 1879. And William Williams of Carmarthenshire mined coal in Scotland as a youth and also worked in a tin shop and foundry before he sailed for America in 1869, settling in Shawnee in 1872. Within a few years he set aside mining and pursued business as a tinner and sheet-iron maker in the local coal and iron industry. Reese E. Williams also arrived in Shawnee that year. He was raised in Breconshire and was a mine-shaft foreman for about six years in Glamorganshire before immigrating to America in 1863. After mining in several places he joined the other Welsh and English miners in Shawnee, where he immediately became mine boss.

Other examples of leadership include David Davis, a Welsh puddler who migrated to America in 1857 and settled in Shawnee where he mined and served as school director as well as township trustee. Another David Davis, also from Carmarthenshire, came to America in 1863. After working as a mine boss in Coshocton he came to Shawnee, where he became superintendent of the Ore mines.[71] Thus, during its period of rapid industrial growth and development during and after the Civil War, British immigrants dominated the Shawnee Valley mining community in virtually every leadership position and their culture prevailed for many years.

Just east of Shawnee, in Rendville, British immigrants also led the development of the coal industry. Among them was George Plant, from Keele, England, who was born in 1849, started mining at age nine, and took charge of a high-pressure engine at the mines at eighteen. Plant and his bride, Maria Parks, both signed their marriage certificates at their wedding in 1870. The couple immigrated to America in 1879. They first went to West Jefferson, Madison County, and then to Rendville, where George worked as an engineer for the Ohio Central Coal Company.[72]

Just southwest of Shawnee, in the town of New Straitsville, English immigrants also filled positions of authority. One was Thomas Weatherburn, who was raised as a miner in Northumberland and married Mary Ann Wilson in 1869. Both signed their marriage certificates. The very next year they came to Ohio, and after laying track for a couple of coal companies, Thomas was hired to be the mine superintendent of W. P. Rend & Company. At the same company, Welshman David S. Williams, who entered the mines in Wales at the early age of seven and immigrated to America in 1860, served as mine boss. In New Straitsville Samuel Raybould also made an interesting name for himself. An immigrant from Staffordshire in 1869, Raybould mined in various parts of the United States before buying an interest in a coal mine in Athens County. After selling out he served as foreman for a coal yard and foreman of the St. Louis Water Works in Missouri. Then he returned to Ohio and took up butchering in New Straitsville, where he also became the proprietor of an opera house.[73]

Though the Welsh contributed most significantly to the early development of Ohio's coal industry, they continued to arrive in the late nineteenth century to seize opportunities commensurate with their skills and background. In the 1880s Ohio's thriving industry attracted Welsh families with traditions in the coal business. Stephen Selway, from a family long involved with the coal trade of Glamorganshire, took his wife and ten children directly to Ohio in 1881. At Massillon he and his three eldest sons became successful coal operators and mine owners, capitalizing on the experience that the family had gained in Wales

over the years. Selway perhaps knew another Welsh immigrant, Evan Jones, who
arrived in Carroll County in the 1880s. He was from a family of tenant farmers
who longed to own their own land, but with little chance of ever doing so,
turned to coal mining in North Wales and mastered all aspects of the industry.
In Carroll County, Jones utilized his experience in the industry to purchase
farmland, which had been beyond his reach in Wales. He became one of the
county's most substantial farmers.[74]

Also important to the technological development of Ohio's coal industry
was awareness of the growing dangers of working in an increasingly mechanized industry, in deeper and deeper mines, and the need to pass the legislation
necessary to regulate conditions and organize labor. Again, British immigrants
led in this development. When businessmen recruited skilled British miners to
develop the industry, they seemed unaware that many of the miners had experience in the Chartist movement and trade unionism. Many Britons carried a
class consciousness and determination to reform the system and improve workers' conditions. For in fact, though the United States was ahead of Britain in political democracy, Britain was miles ahead in industrial democracy. Parliament
began to devise safety codes and inspection systems in 1850, in response to the
miners' agitation. British miners in Ohio determined to do the same and
shaped the American labor movement profoundly.[75]

In about 1845 British immigrants formed local and district union organizations, which consolidated into the American Miner's Association in 1861, and
established itself in Ohio in 1863.[76] Especially after the Civil War, when
steamships made frequent or even seasonal migration across the Atlantic more
feasible for miners, the nearly constant back and forth movement of British colliers guaranteed solid contacts between Ohio and Britain's trades unions. During the 1860s British miners in America called on their state governments to follow British models. By the 1870s, Ohio's miners—mostly British-born—began
to organize and demand an amelioration of increasingly horrendous mining
conditions.

In September of 1869 the ghastly Avondale mine disaster in Luzerne County,
Pennsylvania, claimed 110 lives, shocked Ohio's colliers, and incited those in the
Mahoning and Tuscarawas valleys to demand state intervention. British immigrants led the movement. Among them were William Thomson, a University of
Edinburgh graduate who settled in Mahoning Valley, and John Pollock, born in
the north of Ireland but raised in Scotland. Pollock mined in Scotland since he
was nine years old and was active in unionism there before his emigration to the
Tuscarawas Valley at age twenty-four in 1863. The most important British immigrant in that episode was Andrew Roy, born in Lanarkshire, Scotland, in 1834.

He mined in Scotland from age eight until his family emigrated in 1850. Roy mined in Maryland, Arkansas, and other states until the Civil War broke out. He enlisted, served under McClellan, was severely wounded at Gaines' Hill and left for dead by his retreating comrades. Confederate soldiers found him barely alive and sent him to Libby Prison, and after his parole he moved to Ohio. He settled in Youngstown and immersed himself in the study of mining engineering and the British system of mine inspections. Roy proceeded to lead the safety movement and became the father of Ohio's mining laws. He also wrote one of the finest early historical accounts of the American coal mining industry.[77]

The barriers that reformers faced were truly formidable. Ohio businessmen and coal mine owners were notorious for rejecting any safety provisions that cost them money. In their search for higher profits they even rejected adequate timbering for supporting roofs and measures to improve ventilation or to prevent flooding. And most outrageous to the miners, they refused to build the double entries that provided an escape in the event of a disaster; the lack of a double entry doomed the Avondale miners. Incredibly for the miners, the mine owners viewed such basic safety measures as nothing more than a threat to their profits. And in an age and culture that celebrated *laissez-faire* government and survival of the fittest, and saw government intervention in the businessman's world as abhorrent, lowly British immigrant colliers faced an uphill battle to protect themselves deep in the bowels of Ohio's coal mines.

In the winter of 1869–70, after increasing agitation among Ohio's colliers, Andrew Roy wrote a bill for submission to the state legislature in Columbus. It explained the miners' concerns for safety and proposed to provide inspection districts and two mine inspectors appointed by the governor to enforce safer conditions. Enforcement provisions allowed inspectors to prosecute offenders in the local courts. Roy optimistically assumed that the coal operators would support the bill, if for no other reason than to dilute the agitation of the colliers. He also reminded the Senate about the success of much of Britain's efforts to improve safety. "We want mine inspectors," Roy exclaimed to

Andrew Roy left Lanarkshire to mine in America in 1850. He was wounded in the Civil War and then led Ohio's mine-safety movement. In 1874 Roy was appointed as Ohio's first State Inspector of Mines and became known as the father of Ohio's mining laws. From Andrew Roy, *A History of the Coal Miners of the United States.*

the Senate with a rhetorical flourish, "to see that good and sufficient ventilation is provided, and an escapement shaft sunk for the withdrawal of the men in case of accident to the main opening. Every mining country in Europe makes such provision by Law. Are the miners of Ohio not entitled to equal protection? . . . We ask for a mouthful of fresh air amidst the mephitic blasts of death which surround us; and for a hole to crawl out when the hoisting shaft is closed up, as was the case at the Avondale shaft a year ago, when the whole population of the mine was killed when the shaft took fire."[78]

But Roy did not fully appreciate the coal operators' disregard for miners' safety, or the power of their lobbying efforts—the bill was killed. Yet the Ohio Senate did introduce a resolution, soon passed, which established a mining commission to investigate conditions further and recommend legislation if deemed necessary. The commission was the genesis of true reform and improvement in the safety of Ohio's coal mining industry and the organization of the colliers, and immigrant miners from Great Britain played a large part in it. In 1874 Governor William Allen appointed Andrew Roy as Ohio's first State Inspector of Mines, a position that he continued to hold until he retired in 1884.

As Ohio's miners began to organize and form unions they found themselves under the leadership of British immigrants who had brought along their experience with labor organization from the mother country. The Miners National Association (MNA), established in 1873, was founded and led by its president, John Siney, who was born in Lancashire, and by its secretary John James, who had hailed from the Glasgow area. James was particularly interesting. A miner since childhood, he had met Alexander McDonald, joined the local union, and was blacklisted for agitating for a Parliamentary mine inspection bill. During the 1850s he tramped in Scotland for work and continued to get in trouble for his complaints against management until 1865, when he sailed for America and with Siney founded the MNA. Siney attempted to settle a dispute between Ohio's coal operators and the miners through arbitration in 1875; but when a strike broke out and was crushed, he was arrested on charges of criminal conspiracy and was ousted from the MNA, even though he was eventually acquitted. Still, the importance of British immigrants to miners' union organization in Ohio was clear to the men in the pits.[79]

THE GOLD RUSH MINERS

When gold was discovered in California, British immigrants in Ohio and elsewhere caught "gold fever" as quickly as anyone else. In fact, they participated in the gold rush at a greater rate than Americans because, after making their arduous voyage across the Atlantic, a trek to California seemed just another long step in their migration. Cornish and Yorkshire lead and tin miners working in the upper Mississippi River Valley, upon hearing about the gold, went to California in droves, to the extent of depopulating the towns they left and causing local economic recessions. Similarly, many British immigrants in Ohio mining coal had skills and experience that could be readily applied to gold.

The combination of mining skills and mobility made people like William Benjamin Williams especially susceptible to gold rush fever. Williams left Glamorganshire as an adventurous youth with his family in 1839 to work in the coal fields and rolling mills of Pennsylvania and Tennessee before settling in Portsmouth to take charge of a furnace. There he was "smitten with the gold fever." So Williams and a group of others had wagons made in Portsmouth, which they shipped down the Ohio River to St. Joe, Missouri, and from there they made a strenuous five-month overland trek to the gold fields. Williams mined gold for a year and then returned via Panama with his money to supervise the Portsmouth mills. But in 1853 he went back to California via Panama, mined again for a year, and then returned again to Portsmouth and worked there until serving as a captain in the Civil War. One gets the sense that forty-niners like Williams enjoyed the adventure of it all.[80]

Sometimes the adventure got out of hand and reached nightmare proportions. George Pugh completed his apprenticeship as a blacksmith in his native South Wales and emigrated in 1841—at age twenty-three—to Radnor, Delaware County, to work at his trade. By 1850 the many reports of people getting rich in the gold fields convinced Pugh that he should seek his own fortune in California. So he joined a party of men who packed up five wagons full of supplies and headed out on foot to Eldorado, leaving his Welsh-born wife, Ellen, and children behind. But the men underestimated what trekking across a continent entailed. Half way through the journey the companions ran out of rations. On their march through the arid western states they survived on flour mixed with water and baked into cakes on hot rocks in the sun; the occasional field mouse supplemented their diet. Every day starvation stared them in the face.

Then matters got even worse. For some reason one of Pugh's companions, Billy Patterson, shot and killed an Indian woman. Upon hearing the gun shot, other American Indians appeared, surrounded the half-starved group of gold-seekers, and demanded the guilty person. While Pugh and his horrified companions looked on, the Indians flayed Patterson alive—his skin slashed into long strips and removed, until he slowly died. Still the ordeal was not over. The remainder of the party was held captive until they could barter for their release. George Pugh himself had to sacrifice a multicolored silk vest made by his wife, Ellen. The Indians fed them dog soup, which they could hardly eat, hungry as

they were. After their release, Pugh and the other members of the party resumed their journey and finally staggered into California—half-dead from starvation and thoroughly traumatized.

After all of that, George Pugh's bad luck continued. He failed to find gold.
So he turned to what he could do—blacksmithing—and was paid in the gold
that eluded him as a miner. In 1853 news of his wife's death reached him and he
returned to Ohio to care for his children. Pugh remarried four years later in
Delaware County and built a brick house with some of his gold, and took on
student boarders to help clear some of the debt. Finally, in 1868 Pugh bought a
farm in Radnor and continued smithing on the site until he died in 1891, at age
seventy-two.[81]

Other British immigrants failed to find gold in California but fell back on
their skills to acquire enough money to return to Ohio and take up farming.
This pattern seems to have been common. Scottish immigrant William Crichton lived in Porter Township, Scioto County, for fifteen years until the gold rush
mania. Enthralled by the idea of digging gold out of the California soil, he
trekked overland to try his luck; not finding any, he turned to the carpentry
trade and made good money erecting buildings in San Francisco. But he soon
tired of California and concluded that Scioto County "was good enough for
him" and returned there to farm.[82]

Though perhaps most of the Britons who left Ohio for California returned,
a larger proportion either remained in California or settled in other places,
compared to other immigrants. Many applied their mining skills in other
places, such as the lead regions of the upper Mississippi River Valley, the iron
and copper fields of upper Michigan, and the silver mines in the Sierra Nevada
and Rocky Mountains. But also, the British shared language and culture with
most native-born Americans, which enabled them to blend in more places and
take advantage of a mobility that many other immigrants did not have. The di-
aspora of British miners was vast and wide, and the state of Ohio was prominently included.

QUARRYMEN, STONECUTTERS, AND BUILDERS

Quarrying and stonecutting were other significant industries in Ohio, especially for the building boom that occurred after the Civil War. And with their
long experience in quarrying and stonecutting in the British Isles, the immigrants helped establish and develop the industries in Ohio. Both were demanding crafts that the British had perfected over several centuries because of the
vast quarrying done since the Middle Ages. By the early nineteenth century
North Wales, Scotland, and many places in England—including Derbyshire,

Cumbria, and Yorkshire—were centers of extensive quarrying and stonecutting, developing and using the latest methods and technology. British stone cutters who came to Ohio, then, often carried invaluable skills and experience that reduced the time and cost of developing the state's industry. Examples abound. Robert Hancock mastered the quarrying and stonecutting trades under his father, a quarry merchant in Wiltshire, by the time he migrated to Columbus in 1870. He soon proceeded to Mansfield, Richland County, where he became a contractor, a master cutter, and conducted huge operations. He owned and operated Hancock and Dow and built churches, banks, school, jails, other public buildings, and lavish private homes. Later he became president of the Barnes Manufacturing Company and was admired as a progressive businessman.[83]

Quarrying expanded during the 1860s with the help of an English immigrant, John Worthington, who once worked on the Houses of Parliament. He employed hundreds of Scottish quarrymen in his huge sandstone quarries in northern Ohio. Ambitious people like Thomas Colpitts, who came from a long line of stonecutters, left England in 1856 in order to "better his fortunes." Locating in Barnesville, Belmont County, he opened his own tombstone business and established a "large trade." The Scots also brought much experience in stonecutting to Ohio. William Stewart, a stonecutter from Ayrshire, came to Portsmouth in 1842, built a stone sawmill, and pursued quarrying and stone sawing. When his health declined, he turned to market gardening with the earnings from his business. Other Scots were apprenticed in marble cutting and used their experience to make a rapid transition to business in Ohio.[84]

The Welsh were perhaps even more endowed with experience in quarrying and stone masonry and made very significant contributions to the industry in Ohio. The "Welsh Hills Settlement" in Licking County was founded in large part by stonemasons whose earnings in Marietta and Newark made the settlement possible, and whose skills quite literally built the settlement.[85] The largest blue limestone quarries in central Ohio were owned and operated by John Evans, who came with his family from Wales in 1862. His business, near Columbus, provided much of the lime and stone for the surge of building that occurred in Marion County in the late nineteenth century.[86] And Welshman J. H. Griffith, a highly skilled marble cutter from Radnorshire, came to Delaware, Ohio, in 1859 and built some of the finest cemetery monuments in the county.[87]

Like the quarrymen and stonecutters, immigrants in related building trades were rarely novices. In fact, many used their experience to jump quickly to leadership of Ohio's building industry. This is what William Fish did. Emigrating from Lancashire in 1849 after serving seven years as a stone mason's apprentice, he worked as a journeyman for a few years in New York, and then proceeded to

Cleveland and Akron to work as a builder. He contracted to build Ascension Hall in Gambier, and the residence of Bishop O'Dell. After nine years of building in Gambier, Fish moved to Columbus where he erected Trinity Episcopal Church, the City Hall building, three major banks, as well as the state penitentiary. During those prosperous years Fish owned his own stone quarries in various places; in 1868 he built the first stone sawmill in Columbus, where he cut the stone for his buildings. This particular skilled building trades worker immigrated to the right place at the right time and rode the building boom wave to the top of his profession.[88]

In the years following the Civil War, Ohio experienced a building boom that drew many tradesmen from Great Britain. Skilled brick workers found especially rich opportunities in Akron. Among them was William Cooper, who mastered brick making in his native Staffordshire before emigrating in 1865 at age twenty. In Akron he mined coal, and after returning to England, went back to Akron to manufacture brick. Cooper made the best bricks in Akron and formed the Cooper Brick Company with his brothers, Samuel and Joseph—also highly skilled brick makers from Staffordshire. William employed many skilled workers and ran the company successfully until he retired in 1905. Other English immigrants came to Akron in the postwar period, learned the brick-making trade there, and then succeeded in the business.[89]

Brick making was especially important to Akron's postwar economy, and British immigrants were essential for that industry. The brick and pottery industries were closely related, so it is not surprising that some of Akron's brick industry leaders hailed from Staffordshire. The president and manager of Akron's Windsor Brick Company, William Windsor, was born to a Staffordshire potter's family, and immigrated to Ohio in 1880, already fully trained in the brick industry at twenty. He established his company in 1896 with forty thousand dollars of capital stock, and became a general contractor to construct buildings. Windsor built the City Hospital in Akron and other important buildings. The Windsor Brick Company even returned to England to build the Diamond Match factory in Liverpool, which contained nine million bricks, because no English contractor could undertake the gigantic two-year contract. This is a good example of how British skills built industries and companies so successful that they were able to return to Britain to take up lucrative contracts.[90]

William Windsor surely knew other English immigrant brick workers and company owners in Akron, including bricklayer John Crisp, of Nottinghamshire who came to America in 1872. Within two years he was in Cleveland building a large church in Painesville. In 1878 he came to Akron and with his brother formed Crisp Brothers, the leading contracting firm in the city for fourteen years. John Crisp became a city commissioner and then superintendent of other companies and banks. His building firm went on to build the Flatiron Building, several school buildings, and other pieces of Akron's architectural heritage. He also trained his son in the trade and raised him as a business partner. By the turn of the century John Crisp & Son was one of Akron's leading business firms and highly prominent in the city's commercial life. Another important building contracting company in Akron, Hunt & Wigley, was founded in 1901 by Joseph Wigley, a Staffordshire man who emigrated in 1882 at age twenty-three after thoroughly learning the building trade.[91]

Like the coal miners, British building trades workers in Ohio also advocated greater labor organization. One prominent leader was William Barnett, who was born in Exeter and served a full apprenticeship in the brick and stone mason trade. He immigrated to Akron in about 1871 and worked on important buildings, including Schumacher House, Buchtel College, Market House, and many others. He helped organize Akron's first bricklayers' union and was treasurer of the body for eight years. He also served as their delegate at the convention to establish the nine-hour system. And Barnett was not a pushover; in his spare time he was an expert boxing instructor. He eventually even became affluent enough to visit Europe twice.[92]

TEXTILES

The industrial revolution is closely associated with innovation in textiles. The change from producing yarn, thread, and cloth by hand to machine was indeed one of the great watersheds in history that improved the lives of consumers while revolutionizing the lives of producers. After James Hargreaves invented the spinning jenny (1764), Richard Arkwright the water frame (patented in 1769), Samuel Crompton the spinning mule, which combined the jenny and the water frame (1779), and Edmund Cartwright the power loom (patented in 1785), the textiles world would never be the same. All of these momentous innovations occurred in England, launching the country fully into the Industrial Revolution. The transfusion of textiles innovation flowed quickly from Britain, via emigrants like Samuel Slater, an apprentice to one of Arkwright's partners, who emigrated in 1789 and set up his own factory in Pawtucket, Rhode Island, in 1793. Then there was Francis Cabbot Lowell, who toured British factories in 1810, memorized what he saw, and set up similar if less sophisticated machines in Lowell, Massachusetts, in 1814. But even in later decades Britain still had much to offer to America's textiles industries.

During most of the nineteenth century Britain was still by far the world's greatest producer and innovator in textiles. At midcentury Britain had some

50,000 handloom weavers and about 250,000 power loom weavers, and British innovation in cotton, woolens, silk, and other fabrics was famous throughout the world. Consequently, British skilled operatives were recruited in the United States, while others capitalized on their reputation for being the most competent and skilled workers.

So great was their reputation that American employers sometimes were duped into hiring Britons who actually had little to offer. John Curtis, an Ohio abolitionist and businessman, together with his associate Richard Cobden—Member of Parliament and free trader—was investing in American textile mills. In May of 1844 Curtis wrote from Ohio to Cobden and reported his frustration: "We engaged an Englishman who had good recommendations and who made large professions of ability to erect a small establishment for manufacturing [silk] and to superintend its operation but he proved entirely incompetent and we were obliged to throw his machinery away as worthless."[93] Still, that such a reputation existed underscores the fact that British immigrants had a lot to offer to the young American textiles industry.

Ohio never had the appeal for British textile workers that New England and Pennsylvania did because the state was never a major producer of textiles. Most who did find their way to Ohio emigrated precisely to leave textile work and farm or follow some other occupation instead. But some did persist in textiles, or, like Edward Phillips, a cotton handloom weaver from Shropshire, adapted to Ohio's economic environment and learned new skills to manufacture woolens.[94] Textile machine makers also came to Ohio, and though their numbers were very limited they were instrumental in the diffusion of British textile technology. One was Isaac Hodgson, who emigrated with his four brothers from Manchester in 1811. He first settled in Delaware, but by 1820 was at Woodburn, Washington Township, in Montgomery County, Ohio. He had five thousand dollars worth of equipment and made "all kinds of Cotton & Woollen Mushinry," which were important for Ohio's budding industry.[95]

Ohio did offer some opportunities for textile operatives. Already in 1809 Cincinnati had a cotton factory that was patterned after ones in Manchester. And Steubenville was a significant center of carpet weaving, thanks in part to the immigration of people like Alexander Mickle, who left his native Ayrshire, Scotland in 1828 because high American tariffs caused stagnation in the trade. He worked in Connecticut for a couple of years before coming to Steubenville in 1831. Mickle became the "pioneer carpet weaver" of the city and maintained his business for more than fifty years. Other immigrant weavers kept at their trade and established their own businesses, or moved into some other work.[96]

Steubenville became an important center for woolen-cloth manufacturing because of its proximity to the sheep-raising region of eastern Ohio. The city had five woolen mills by 1845 and attracted immigrants with the appropriate skills. James Wyatt apprenticed in the dyeing trade in Manchester before immigrating to New York in 1830. After a few years in Philadelphia he proceeded to Steubenville to take charge of the dyeing department of the Orth & Wallace woolen mills. After seven years in that position he started his own dyeing business for wool and cotton goods to become one of the city's prominent businessmen.[97]

The Scots seemed especially adept at using weaving as a stepping stone into the business world. Andrew Dobbie and his father wove carpets in Bannockburn before the family immigrated to Lithopolis, Fairfield County, Ohio, in the 1850s. After a brief stint producing carpets, he turned his full attention to the dry goods business in Columbus and became one of the city's leading merchants and a director of banks and corporations. And Scotsman James F. Morrison left his trade as a woolen manufacturer to pick up the tea trade in Bellaire, Belmont County, in the 1870s.[98]

Most of the British immigrants in the industry had considerable experience by the time they arrived in Ohio. Robert Aspinall was quite typical. He was raised in Leeds and served seven years as an apprentice in the woolen business, for which he received no wages except his room and board. In 1822 he immigrated to Logan County to establish his own business and prospered during a twenty-five year career. He also trained his son William to follow in his footsteps. William Aspinall established his own woolen business in Carey at only age twenty-three. In 1876 he purchased his own mills, which he improved to increase their capacity. He spun 160 spindles per day, and each held up to seventy-five pounds of woolen yarn. Aspinall specialized in stocking yarn, but he also built machinery that produced up to three thousand handles each day for various uses.[99]

Some of the English weavers' success enabled them to branch off into other industries in a way that was much less likely in Britain. William France, for example, was a highly skilled weaver of fancy fabrics in Leeds who immigrated directly to Northfield, near Cleveland. He worked there about a year until he sent for his wife and three children, one of whom perished on the voyage and was buried at sea. After about five years the family proceeded to Lucas, Richland County, where William established his own woolen mill and ran it successfully until he passed it on to his son Enoch, who had learned the craft at his father's side in Leeds. Enoch France expanded and diversified his operations to meet the great demand generated by the Civil War. He produced cloth, blankets, yarn, and other woolen goods, but then with his capital turned to supplying wooden ties to railroad companies. He also purchased and developed stone quarries to furnish crushed limestone to railroads and other industries, a business that grew to "mammoth proportions" in the latter part of the century.[100]

Finally, some immigrants with mechanical skills contributed to the development of Ohio's textiles mills. Quakers had a long history of mechanical expertise in England, and some brought their skills to Ohio. Staffordshire potter William Maddock came from a prominent Quaker family of porcelain ware and pottery makers, but also learned to be a founder and machinist before emigrating in 1824. First locating in Maine and then Detroit, he continued to wear the "conventional Quaker dress." Within two years he came to Portsmouth where, with his savings and some borrowed money, he established a woolen and gristmill. Later he built a foundry and machine shop, the first of its kind in the city. He was so successful that for a time he practically monopolized manufacturing in the town.[101]

IRON AND STEEL

As with pottery, mining, and textiles, Ohio's iron industry was built upon skills, experience, and technology developed in Britain and transferred to Ohio—extensively by British immigrants. The practical experience and knowledge that migrants brought with them often proved invaluable to both them and the industry alike. As with other industries, Great Britain pioneered and developed modern iron and steel production and was virtually unchallenged in these industries until the latter part of the nineteenth century. Abraham Derby first produced coke from coal for fuel on an industrial scale in 1709, and when this breakthrough, combined with Britain's vast iron ore supply, her human ingenuity, secure government and markets, and the advent of steam power, it unleashed rapid and extensive industrialization. In 1828 the great Glasgow chemist and engineer James Neilson invented the hot-blast furnace and revolutionized iron smelting because the heated air of the blast resulted in much more efficient coke consumption and massively increased output, especially when it utilized Scotland's rich Black Band ore. Discoveries like these reduced the amount of fuel necessary to produce iron and raised profitability and propelled Britain further into the lead of the industry. By midcentury Britain was producing about half of the world's pig iron, and it was just beginning its fastest growth period ever to meet the insatiable demands of a booming economy. Then, after Henry Bessemer invented his converter in 1856 Britain made yet another giant leap that changed the world. It is not surprising, then, that Ohio's iron and steel industries were intimately connected with immigrants from Great Britain.[102]

The connection between Britons and Ohio's iron goes back a long time. In 1770 an unnamed English engineer and explorer was the first person to report iron ores in what became the state of Ohio.[103] Ironmakers of British ancestry from Pennsylvania, the Carolinas, and other eastern states established the earliest iron furnaces in Mahoning, Licking, and Adams Counties about the time of statehood. Welshman Thomas Cotton Lewis built America's first mill for puddling and iron rolling in 1817 and shortly thereafter built several others in Pennsylvania and Ohio. John Means, grandson of a Devonshire immigrant by the same name, built the first Ohio furnace in Scioto County's Hanging Rock district in 1826. English immigrants also made Ohio the first state to manufacture high-grade crucible steel. Dr. William Garrard and John H. Garrard, brothers who left England in 1822, built a steel works on the bank of the Miami and Erie Canal in Cincinnati, in 1832. William Garrard was the inspiration and "master spirit" of the entire enterprise. The business suffered a setback during the panic of 1837 but did thrive thereafter, producing the best steel available for saws, springs, knives, files, axes, and tools.[104]

William Firmstone, known as "one of the outstanding iron masters of the country," was a truly central figure in Ohio's early iron industry. A mill manager from a family of ironworks managers who left Wellington, Shropshire, in 1835, Firmstone first used the hot-blast system in Ohio, in 1836, in Lawrence and then Scioto Counties. He also established the first such furnaces in Pennsylvania. Firmstone was instrumental in producing pig iron with coke, an important stage in the Industrial Revolution. He also helped build and develop furnaces that could produce high quality iron with uncoked anthracite coal.[105]

Another important example of a single British immigrant making revolutionary contributions to Ohio's iron industry is John Lewis, who left Monmouthshire and settled in Mineral Ridge, Trumbull County, in 1854. One day while digging a hole in the floor of his work place he noticed a "blackstone" that was similar to the blackband ore he had mined in Wales. He and James Ward, a Staffordshire immigrant, exploited the ore and from those humble beginnings started the iron industry of Niles. Ward later became the owner and president of the James Ward & Company rolling mill and was known as "the man to whom more than any other the industrial development of Niles is due." He was not only the first to utilize the blackband ore, but also the first in the region to smelt pig iron using raw coal.[106]

With such rapid progress in the iron industry, Ohio, Pennsylvania, and other states soon found themselves in the same league as the British producers and began to challenge their supremacy. The largest iron furnace in Jackson County at midcentury—the Monroe Furnace, built in 1854—produced twenty tons daily. This capacity actually drew iron makers from England "to see this monster furnace, not believing it possible to produce so much iron in one day."[107] As with other industries Americans rapidly caught up and in some cases surpassed Britain. The migration of skilled workers from Britain to Ohio and other places made such progress possible.

The year 1870 marked a new phase of Ohio's growing iron and steel industry, when Charles Burgess arrived from England. Described as "modest and unassuming," he patented several ideas and revolutionized Ohio's industry. Settling in Ironton, Lawrence County, Burgess introduced himself to John R. Williams, superintendent of the Ironton Rolling Mill, and demonstrated his new process on how to change iron into steel. By adding certain materials to molten iron at the last stages of puddling, high-grade steel was produced that proved superior for plows, boiler plates, boiler flanges, wagon parts, and especially for machining and welding. Williams and Burgess, who alone knew about the process, sent a bloom of the new "Burgess Steel" to Sheffield—the center of England's steel-making industry—where English cutters turned it into cutlery and pronounced it equal or better than their own product. The new process in no way threatened the puddler, as would later processes, so the workmen accepted Burgess steel without complaint.

The pair thrived so much that in 1871 they purchased their own mill and formed their own company; the Burgess Steel and Iron Company, in Portsmouth, became operational in January of 1872. Burgess, the English immigrant, was superintendent. But in 1873 he sold his interests in the plant and returned to England with his fortune. Thus a temporary English immigrant played a pivotal role in the iron and steel industry of Ohio.[108]

A few years later another English immigrant advanced Ohio's steel industry. William Kent, born to family of Staffordshire ironworkers, ran away from home at age ten to work in a rolling mill owned by his godfather. After twenty years gaining valuable experience on the cutting edge of England's fine steel industry, he immigrated to Cincinnati in 1877, where he saw great potential. He brought leaves of extremely fine sheet steel to impress the Americans with the abilities of England's steel producers, and to serve as a standard according to which Americans could raise the quality of their own production. Kent's significance to Ohio is hard to exaggerate. As a carrier of the latest technical ideas, Kent quickly found himself at the center of mill construction and improvement. He built and improved iron mills in Youngstown and other industrial cities and invented methods to conserve time and energy in the process of melting metal. He invented the "Welded Cast Metal Process" and the "Hot System Sheet Rolling Mill," which earned him the backing of New York financiers.[109]

Other immigrants who built Ohio's iron and steel industry also hailed from Staffordshire. Among them was Jeremiah Holloway, who learned his trade as a sheet-iron roller in the mills of Brierley Hill, Staffordshire, and left with his family in 1868. He worked at various locations before proceeding to Piqua, Miami County, with his son William, where they applied their expertise to the rolling mills.[110] Others arrived at the same time with similarly high levels of skills and quickly filled positions of leadership. As with those in the coal industry, British immigrants in Ohio's iron industry enjoyed advantages of experience and culture that raised them to positions of power and authority in the community. Levi York learned roll turning in the mills of England before he joined his brother in 1868 in Akron, where he assisted him as roll turner and machinist. During the next thirty years York served as superintendent of various mills and built blast furnaces in Ohio, California, and even South America. Finally he became president of the Portsmouth Street Railway and Electric Light Company, in Scioto County.[111] York probably knew other British immigrants developing the iron industry in Portsmouth, including Welshman John Morgan. He left Cardiganshire in 1848 and rose from bookkeeper to become superintendent and director of the Tropic Iron Company while residing in Portsmouth.[112]

James Henry Nutt fully learned the iron trade in his native Worcestershire by the time he emigrated in 1868 at age twenty to work in the mills of Pennsylvania and New York. In 1876 he came to Youngstown to take the position of "heater" with the Brown-Bonnell Iron Company. Fifteen years later he was appointed city commissioner of Youngstown. A year later, in 1893, he took over as commissioner of labor for the Association of Bar Iron Manufacturers West of Pittsburg. He knew many of his fellow expatriates in the industry, such as George Huggins, who left his native Staffordshire two years before Nutt and similarly used his skills to become assistant superintendent of the same Brown-Bonnell Works. That company attracted many other British immigrants of various capacities, who seemed to have a knack for entering local politics and gaining positions of power.[113]

Well after the Civil War, British foundry workers who learned the industry at remarkably young ages still came to Ohio and used their skills to advance quickly. Walter Wainwright, for example, entered the foundries in England at the age of nine, and though he was very poor and lived a hard life, he soon became an expert. After his apprenticeship he sailed for the United States in 1881, and when only seventeen years of age he was made the foreman of the Walker Manufacturing Company in Cleveland—a position he held until 1897. He then went to Massillon and built the foundry for the Massillon Iron and Steel Company, of which he became a superintendent.[114]

In the area of Shawnee (which as we have seen had a thriving coal industry dominated by British immigrants) iron production flourished after the Civil War too. And in Shawnee's iron industry British immigrants had advantages in their industrial experience and mobility. Men like John Johnson, born in Durham and brought to America as a boy of thirteen in 1840, were highly mobile. Johnson worked in iron works in virtually every state that had them, and also worked as an ore miner, cattle driver, lumberman, and fisherman. He also found work as a sailor, which took him to many European ports. But he never lost his love for Ohio, so in 1875 he finally settled in Shawnee. There his knowledge of ore quality led him to oversee the construction of furnaces and become superintendent of laborers.[115]

Though most of the British immigrants who worked in Ohio's mills and foundries arrived with skills and experience, others learned the occupation in Ohio and used that as a stepping stone to better things. W. J. Smith, who was born in London in 1866 and immigrated to the United States at age seventeen, entered the foundry business in Detroit for five years and learned the business "in every detail." He then went to Chicago, Toronto, and then Piqua, Ohio, where he organized the Ideal Stove and Foundry Company. He also bought out a foundry company in Youngstown and established the large Enterprise Foundry of Troy, Ohio.[116]

As some British immigrants succeeded in industry and became economic and industrial leaders, they became natural political and social leaders too. Welsh immigrant Thomas Hughes, who became secretary and treasurer of the Jefferson Furnace Company and held much of its stock, was a truly prominent person in Jackson County. He served the public as a justice of the peace, county commissioner, and as a member of the state legislature. He was well educated and wrote the first life of Christ published in the Welsh language.[117]

As we already noted, Welsh immigrants made disproportionately great contributions to Ohio's industry, a result of South Wales being a world center of innovation in iron production. The Welsh Furnaces in Jackson County are particularly interesting for what they tell us about the Welsh and the industry that they dominated. The Cambria Furnace, for instance, accumulated its capital from local Welsh settlers, who traded much of their belongings, lands, even their homes for shares of stock. Welshmen built the Madison Furnace and the Jefferson Furnace in the early 1850s. The latter was the most successful and famous furnace of midcentury because it furnished products for the railroad building boom. Its capital totaled fifty thousand dollars worth of shares valued at five hundred dollars each, and again, the Welsh—"sturdy men of the soil"—traded their lands for stock but retained the right to cultivate what they had cleared. The firm's construction stipulated that only men of Welsh birth could hold stock, and that the Furnace must be closed on Sundays. The stack was most impressive: hewed out of the solid rock of a hillside, it towered thirty-six feet high.

The Jefferson Furnace produced superior iron (hauled to market by oxcart) especially suitable for car wheels and machinery, and it became the standard of excellence for all furnaces in the Hanging Rock region. During the panic of 1857, when railroad building virtually collapsed, the Jefferson Furnace suffered along with the others, but not before many of the Welsh investors sold off their stock at nearly double the purchase value. Thus the Cambria and Jefferson Furnaces show us that the Welsh immigrants who built, worked in, and lived near them on their farms participated widely in their ownership and influenced operations with piety and hard, disciplined work. They were also quite shrewd as they secured shares of stock and sold them in a timely and profitable fashion.[118]

Welsh immigrants also erected some of the first furnaces and mills in northern counties; they built the first rolling mill in Newburgh, near Cleveland, and made an early impact in Youngstown as well. Though many Welsh were experts by the time they migrated, others arrived as youngsters with their families, gained experience and training in Ohio, and then ascended to the ranks of superintendents and presidents. For instance, John Rogers left Monmouth in 1868 as a boy and became secretary and treasurer of the Youngstown Steel Casting Company. The president of the company was another immigrant from Monmouth, Ebenezer Lawrence. He immigrated a few years before with some experience, but started out as a roller in Girard, Trumbull County.[119]

Though the Welsh dominated iron production in the Hanging Rock region, some Englishmen were also involved. J. Blodgett Britton had experience in metallurgical analysis. And Edward White conducted ingenious pattern work for furnaces in the region; but his family was most remembered for being "conspicuous for their intense loyalty to England." They must have been, for their Welsh neighbors were "ardent Americans." Unlike the English, the Welsh had "no patriotic love for Great Britain, and America is their only political mother."[120]

The Scots also brought considerable experience and labor to the industry, and some individuals are outstanding for their historical significance. The most important and successful was Henry Chisholm, son of a Scottish mining contractor, who left Lochgelly, in Fifeshire, at age twenty in 1842. He arrived in Montreal almost penniless. But there he flourished as a contractor and developed contacts with the Great Lakes region, such that in 1850 he contracted to build Cleveland's railroad breakwater on the lakefront. Chisholm performed so well that he was commissioned to build piers and docks. But what struck him most was Cleveland's potential as a capital of Great Lakes iron production. So in 1857 he teamed up with two other British immigrants, David and John Jones, ironmakers in Pennsylvania, and invested $25,000 to form Chisholm, Jones & Company, which produced railroad and bar iron in Newburgh. He also brought in new partners, including his brother, William. Reorganized, expanded, and incorporated as the Cleveland Rolling Mill Company with Chisholm at the helm, the company in 1868 was the first in Ohio to use the Bessemer process of steel production. This process of mass-producing steel with blasts of hot air is most closely associated in the United States with the Scottish immigrant, Andrew Carnegie.

The similarities and contrasts between Chisholm and Carnegie are remarkable. They had parallel careers. However, unlike Carnegie, Chisholm refused to sell raw iron or steel to unrelated manufacturers. And whereas Carnegie obsessed over lowering the costs of production, Chisholm focused on waste and pioneered the use of Bessemer scrap from rolling mills. He also was the first to successfully roll rods and wires from Bessemer steel, and produce the first Bessemer screws in 1871. The industrialist directed operations at Cleveland Rolling Mill, had financial interests throughout the Cleveland area, and controlled much of the Lake Superior ore production that his companies relied upon. Significantly, his workforce was very largely composed of British immigrants, which increased the level of skill and experience in Ohio's steel industry and the numbers of British residents in the Cleveland area.

Chisholm was comparatively benevolent and paternalistic with his workers—another contrast with Carnegie. He paid his rollers up to seven dollars per day, his laborers $1.65. He also built the Erie Street Baptist Church on Euclid and Huntingdon Streets, its name later changed to Euclid Avenue Baptist Church. Henry Chisholm continued to expand his interests in steel and related industries in Cleveland and Chicago, so that by 1875 he had invested about ten million dollars. His name became the most prominent in the history of Cleveland's iron and steel industry. At his death in 1881, at age fifty-nine, Chisholm was one of America's mightiest steel men. On the day of his death the men at the Cleveland Rolling Mill laid down their tools and went home to mourn the great industrialist who nevertheless remained a "simple man, unspoiled by wealth."[121]

Welsh immigrants were also important for Lorain's steel industry. Arthur James Moxham, born to a landscape painter and engineer in South Wales, emigrated to Kentucky in 1869 at age fifteen to live with his aunt and uncle who owned and operated the Louisville Rolling Mill Company. He became not only an accomplished ironmaster, supervising the flow of operations for his uncle, but also held several patents for iron-strengthening techniques. Moxham's career continued to blossom in Kentucky and Pennsylvania, where he accumulated capital by producing steel tracks for horse and cable cars. He sold his production throughout the country and even exported some of it to England. In 1894 Moxham came to Lorain and constructed a huge blast furnace and rolling mill complex that became the Lorain Steel Company. His business interests spread into Canada as well, but his main contribution to the evolution of the industry was to convert street rails from iron to steel and produce custom-designed track work for electrical trolley systems.[122]

The oil industry, which figures highly in Ohio's economic history, was also shaped by British immigrants. This is evident in the life of John Roberts, born in Montgomeryshire in 1872, who emigrated in 1889 after his parents died. Roberts lived with an uncle in Van Wert County and assisted him in his dry goods business. With his natural abilities and business sense he soon became a merchant in his own right, and within a short time he bought up other local businesses. At the turn of the century Roberts anticipated the promising future of the internal combustion engine and its effect on the oil business. So in 1902 he leased eleven hundred acres of oil land near Venedocia and formed the Cambrian Oil Company with some fellow Welsh immigrants. They started with $300,000 of capital stock; Roberts served as manager and treasurer. After achieving great success Roberts invested in the emerging automobile industry.[123]

Roberts knew David W. Evans, whose parents brought him from Wales to Ohio back in 1839. Evans's father was a manager of the Cambria furnace in Van Wert County and accumulated six hundred acres of prime farmland as well. But after his accidental death at the furnace in 1854, his estate was divided among his sons, and David Evans received 106 acres, which he soon expanded. Then in 1896 he discovered oil on that land and within the decade had nineteen wells in operation. With his fortune Evans ventured into related industries and real estate. As a wealthy landowner and industrialist, Evans became involved with virtually all of the public issues and developments of York Township. He served as president of the school board, justice of the peace, and secretary of the Welsh Presbyterian Church in Venedocia.[124]

William Dow, whose family established the Dow Chemical Company, is one of the most famous names in the industrial history of Ohio and the nation. He was born in Kinross, Scotland, and received his education before coming to America at age twenty. He started out in New York but came to Cleveland and then to Mansfield, where he prospered as a general contractor. In 1903 he and his sons established the Dow Chemical Manufacturing Company, with Dow as president. Concurrently, he was president of the Ideal Electric Company, a director of the Bank of Mansfield, and director of the Barnes Manufacturing Company. He was even involved with coal and timber companies in West Virginia.[125]

THE INDUSTRIALIZATION OF GUERNSEY COUNTY

In the history of Guernsey County we see how the economy of one part of the state was transformed in a relatively short period of time by a limited number of British Buckeyes. Guernsey County not only shows the influence of the immigrants, but how interconnected certain parts of American and British industries were. As we have seen, the large numbers of skilled British immigrants were highly significant because they helped transform Ohio into one of the nation's leading industrial states. In places like Guernsey County that transformation was quite sudden and dramatic. As noted in chapter 3, Guernsey County was settled by farmers from the Channel Island of that name during the first decade of the nineteenth century. It remained predominantly agricultural through 1860. But the rising demand for industrial goods that came with the war, and the economic growth that followed, created incentives to exploit the county's resources and develop its economy, especially in the heavy industries of coal mining, iron and steel, and the tin-plate industry. To a great extent British immigrants accomplished that goal.

The coal mining industry in the Guernsey Valley area owed much of its existence to William H. Davis, who was born near the collieries of South Wales in 1851 and entered the mines at age seven. In 1864 the Davis family immigrated to Ohio. William mined in several parts of the state and in 1888 opened up the Pioneer Mine at Byesville, which became an important coal-producing center largely through the skill and energy of Davis. He then developed the nearby Farmer Mine, opened several others, and became one of Ohio's most successful coal mine operators and businessmen. He employed and supervised nearly three thousand colliers. Davis's importance to the region grew further when he became an officer of the First National Bank of Byesville. In 1907 he merged his many mines under the Cambridge Collieries Company and remained the general superintendent until spleen cancer took his life in 1909. Throughout his meteoric rise in Ohio's developing industrial economy Davis retained much of his Welsh character and upbringing, including his love of Wales, participation in Welsh choral music, deep piety, and dedicated participation in the Welsh Baptist Church.[126]

The mining industry in Guernsey County attracted many other British immigrants who were experts and prime candidates for foremen, engineers, and superintendents. Like William Davis, George Shaw had been a child miner, having worked twelve-hour days in the deep Durham mines since age ten. In 1879, at age thirty-two, he emigrated and mined for six months in Pennsylvania before coming to Bellaire to mine for a year. Then he went to Scott's Mines in Guernsey County, where he made his home and sent for the family he left behind in Durham. After five years at Scott's Mines Shaw moved to Byesville to work in the mines of William Davis, and was made a foreman. In 1900 he became superintendent of the Ideal Mine with four hundred colliers under his control. His son was also a mine engineer there.

Scottish miners also came into the Guernsey County region after the Civil War and took important leadership roles. The family of James Black went to America before the Civil War, during which four of his five sons fought and died for the Union army. James Black returned to Scotland a broken-hearted man. But in 1873 the rest of the family, including son Archibald, returned to America to escape Scotland's glutted mining labor market and take advantage of the numerous opportunities awaiting them in Ohio and other states. Archibald Black effectively applied his skills and quickly rose to positions of authority in several mining regions in the state. In 1908 he moved to Guernsey County to superintend the Trail Run Mine in Jackson Township and supervised nearly three hundred men.

Another Scot who led Guernsey County's coal industry was James Henderson, from Fifeshire. He entered the mines in childhood and then in 1880 at nineteen emigrated with his family to mine in Pittsburgh. In 1893 he passed the examination for mine foreman, became a mine boss in 1896, a superintendent in 1901, and then he came to Guernsey County to superintend the Walhonding Mine for William Davis's Cambridge Collieries Company in 1909. Here Henderson was known for handling his men "in such a manner as to get the best possible results and at the same time retain their good will."[127]

The English also came to Guernsey County long after the Civil War to assume high positions in the coal industry. Denis Conroy was born in Lancashire in 1863 and entered the mines at age nine. Early on he heard other miners talk about the richer opportunities in America, so when he turned twenty-one he came directly to Guernsey County—arriving in Byesville in 1884. He quickly became a foreman and then a superintendent of the Trail Run mine. Then he became superintendent of the Puritan Mine in Valley Township. His work and experience were "of inestimable value" to these firms; and, like James Henderson, he too coaxed the most out of his men while retaining their loyalty.[128]

That Henderson, Conroy, and many other British immigrants made superb superintendents reflects their origins. As miners in Britain they knew what kind of management was best for miners, and their experience with miners' trade union organizations acquainted them with the need to maintain the dignity of the workers. Their transatlantic perspective, then, was an invaluable quality that made them highly effective leaders of Ohio's industrial workers. The Welsh, English, and Scots dominated the positions of power and leadership in Guernsey County's flourishing coal mining industry, as they did in many other parts of Ohio. Many must have known each other, and probably reflected on their remarkable success in America, while the British industry would probably have kept them "where the sun never shines," picking away at a coal seam.

Migrants in the iron and steel industry duplicated the story of the postwar migration of colliers to Guernsey County. Like the migrant miners, those in iron and steel often began their work as children and mastered their occupation at an early age—which made them beneficial to industrial Ohio. For instance, William Evans, from Nantytlo, South Wales, was seven years old when his father died, after which William entered the local rolling mills. He learned the details of the industry quickly, and at age nineteen, in 1878, he came to Niles, Ohio, to work in its iron mills. In 1891 he proceeded to Cambridge, Guernsey County, as one of the first employees of the Cambridge Iron & Steel Company, where his expertise helped make the new company a success. Evans found his work highly rewarding. He purchased a nice house in Cambridge and also a fine 157-acre farm in Jefferson Township. He used it as a place of leisure, gradually turning the land into a model farm with high-grade livestock.[129]

In the 1890s the tinplate industry evolved into an important arena in Guernsey County, other parts of Ohio, and the United States where skilled British workers immigrated and transplanted the industry. The British tinplate industry dates back to the seventeenth century, and South Wales alone produced most of the world's tinned sheet iron in the nineteenth century before the industry was transplanted to America. Around 1871 Welsh tinplaters set up a plant in Pittsburgh, though they posed but a minor threat to producers in Wales. But then in 1890 the McKinley tariff all but eliminated Britain's American market—which took around 70 percent of what South Wales produced. This ruthless protectionism virtually forced the industry to relocate to the United States. As the workmen sat idle in Wales's sixty tinplate mills, unable to tap the American market, American companies imported Welsh materials and machinery, not to mention the workers themselves. The transatlantic migration of the tinplate industry was wholesale. Some Welsh manufacturers even moved their plants to the United States. The new American tinplate industry relied almost exclusively on Welsh technology and skills. However, in the twentieth century, after the Americans made improvements in the techniques, they no longer found Welsh workers indispensable, and even found their tendency to unionize too troublesome.[130]

The Welsh tinplaters who came to Guernsey County had experience and skills invaluable to the new Ohio industry. Some were raised within the industry. David Jenkins was born in 1862 to the superintendent of the Beaufort Tin House, in Morristown, Wales. The family was comfortably middle class. David was well educated there; one of his relatives was even elevated to the peerage in 1897 and became a member of the House of Lords. At age thirteen David began his training and became a master of all the steps of tin rolling. In 1890, after the new American tariff's deathblow to the South Wales industry, Jenkins left for America with his wife and child. He first worked in Pittsburgh for eighteen months before coming to Irondale, Jefferson County, and then to Cambridge in 1895. There he became the first roller in the Morton Tin Plate Works and enjoyed a long career as head roller. He adapted quickly to American life, held no grudge against American protectionism, and he and his wife were "thoroughly Americanized" immigrants who loved their new country. Still, they made several visits to their old home in Wales.[131]

John Reynolds was another Welsh tinplater who made his mark in Guernsey County. Born in Cardigan in 1863 to a farming family, he became an ironworker in 1872 for the local Landore Tin Plate Company, where he mastered every job. In 1892 he also came to the Irondale Tin Mill in Jefferson County, performing the same work he had done in Wales. After two years he joined the Morton Tin Plate Company in Cambridge. He was one of the first skilled workers there, employed as a heater and roller in charge of a large crew of men. He was highly respected for his expertise in all of the tasks. He also Americanized very quickly and made a trip to Wales early in the twentieth century.[132]

The Morton Tin Plate Company thrived by recruiting expert rollers from other parts of Britain. One example is William Upton, born in Staffordshire in 1863, the son of a skilled puddler who never made it to America. William began working in England's iron mills when he was only nine years old and became a skilled sheet roller. In 1892 he arrived in Pennsylvania to work in the mills there, and then two years later the new plant of the Morton Tin Plate Company recruited him to Cambridge, where he rolled the first trial piece in the mill. He became head roller and was in charge of the mill's operation, being "an exceptionally expert roller" who also became active in the local Amalgamated Association of Iron, Steel and Tin Workers. Twice he afforded a return trip to England, though he too had become "thoroughly Americanized" and an "ardent supporter" of American institutions.[133]

The tinplate factories of Guernsey County also drew Scots. James Boyd Peters was born in 1874 a short distance from the birthplace of Robert Burns and forever held the "banks and braes of bonny Doon" in his heart. Raised on a farm, he moved to Glasgow where he learned hydraulic engineering at the huge Blochairn Steel Works. But at only sixteen years of age he left for Pennsylvania to make hydraulic machinery, and after ten years came to Cambridge to take a senior position as an expert shearman at the American Sheet & Tin Plate Company.[134]

In Guernsey County, as in many parts of industrial America, the British immigrants who developed industries and took important positions of authority were also drawn into labor organization and government service—especially as reform legislation in the early twentieth century became more and more urgent. These roles were prominently filled by David and John Morgan. David was raised as an ironworker in the mills of Wales until he brought his family to Newark, Ohio, in 1869, and then to Cleveland, where he found similar work at higher wages. His son John, also born in Wales, worked with him and became a sheet roller. In 1890 David and John Morgan came to Cambridge to work in the new Morton Tin Plate Company, where they worked under the direction of the English immigrant William Upton.

John Morgan was soon respected for his natural political leadership and his concern for the workers' welfare as much as for his technological expertise, because in 1895—only five years after his move from Cleveland to Cambridge—he was elected to the Ohio Senate. He served two years and became chairman of the labor committee. In 1901 Governor George Nash appointed him chief inspector of the department of workshops and factories and reappointed him after four years of highly regarded service. Under his leadership a major child labor bill was passed and enforced, and female district inspectors were appointed to supervise inspection over factories that employed women and children. Morgan also produced other regulations that protected workers, and he was known for being uncompromising in his support for workers' trades unions. He also served as vice president and then trustee of the Amalgamated Association of Iron, Steel and Tin Workers. He helped lead the organization of the Guernsey Valley Trades and Labor Assembly as well, and became its first secretary. This kind of leadership in both technical expertise and labor organization and protection could only come from Great Britain, which led the world in industrialization and industrial democracy during the nineteenth century.

Eventually Cambridge, Ohio, became best known for its fine glass industry. It, too, owed some of its early success to British immigrants like Arthur Bennett, born in Middlesex, north of London, in 1866, to a merchant who provided him a liberal education. He worked as a clerk and then apprenticed in the glass business in London. Aware of the advantages offered by America, he immigrated to Boston in 1886 to work in sales for a glass manufacturer, after which he came to New York as a partner in a china-importing house. In 1902 he came to Cambridge to accept the position of president and general manager of the new Cambridge Glass Company, which made its first glass in that year. He also oversaw the completion of the plant, which concentrated on fine grade cut tableware and medical glass. It was a great success; the plant was the only one in the city that continued to run at capacity during the panic of 1907, and in 1910 it grew to include another factory in Byesville. It exported glass all over Europe and South America and employed first-class skilled artisans. Bennett also became president of the new Cambridge Country Club and was known for his love of golf and gardening.[135]

It is remarkable and significant how a relatively small number of immigrants made such an impact on the industrial and economic history of Guernsey County. Other parts of the state were similarly transformed, if not to such an extent. Throughout the state the newcomers from Britain blended in quickly. They exercised an astonishing mobility—not only geographic and social mobility, but an occupational mobility. Even more than native-born Americans, British immigrants moved quickly through Ohio, taking or creating many of the best opportunities in the state, and on a per capita basis doing more to develop Ohio's industrial economy than any other group of people. They fit in so well so early, and became social and economic leaders, that their status as immigrants seems to have been lost. It was indeed a transatlantic industrial revolution that spurred Ohio's development more than any other factor.

Altogether, it is hard to think of Ohio's industries without remembering the roles played by British immigrants. Though we must certainly not overlook the importance of American innovation and the contributions of other immigrants, the British experienced industrialization early and offered the know-how, which, when combined with Ohio's wealth of resources, helped make Ohio one of America's leading industrial states. As we will see in the following chapters, British immigrants were similarly essential in Ohio's professions and the development of its political and religious history.

6

Religion and Reform

Sarah Dixon was my name
England was my nation
America my dwelling place
And Christ is my salvation

Tombstone in Pike Township, Perry County[1]

IN nineteenth-century America religion was central to most people's lives. This was true of native Ohioans and British immigrants alike. As already noted, the British in Ohio were overwhelmingly nonconformists. Methodists predominated, but whatever their affiliation, they found familiar denominations in Ohio, thanks to previous British immigrants and their descendents who established these churches in the east and brought them west as the United States expanded. Francis Asbury established regular circuits of Methodist preachers in Ohio as early as 1798. Baptists, Presbyterians, and Congregationalists soon followed.[2] Therefore, even some of the earliest British immigrants found familiar churches in Ohio.

For most British Buckeyes the church was for worship and fellowship, but also a place and experience that allowed them to feel grounded in their new country. The sermon provided a familiar moral code that brought a sense of stability and purpose. It gave them a sense of belonging and enabled them to identify with their community and the larger society. And when they heard sermons and sang hymns with American-born church members in the same language, the cultural distance between them and the Ohioans shrank. They were members of the same family of God. In the church they assimilated more fully into American life.

During the first half of the nineteenth century especially, immigrant clergy from Britain were important for setting up new congregations and providing educated ministry to people on the frontier. But though they preached familiar doctrines, the frontier church environment was often crude and could be bewildering to the newcomers. Scotsman James Miller, who arrived in the backwoods of Greene County with his family in 1804, organized a "praying band" for the first Reformed Presbyterian Church of Ohio, near Clark Run. Soon educated Scottish clergy arrived, along with other Scots and people of Scottish heritage. At first they worshipped in homes, but in 1812 the congregation built its first church on James Miller's farm. It was a "rude structure, twenty-two feet square, built of round logs, the cracks closed with clay, the roof of clapboards four feet long, fastened down with weight poles." They used this simple building for twelve years until they could afford to erect a larger structure.[3]

In early Ohio the lack of biblical preaching was a serious problem for some English immigrants. James Martin, who emigrated from London to Crawford County in 1821 and combined farming with preaching, remarked that "I have heard the missionaries once or twice here & the picture of ignorance they exhibit is truly awful . . . a total ignorance of the word of God."[4]

For the Bible Christians—a Methodist denomination that seceded from the Wesleyan Methodist Church around 1815 and became established in Cornwall and Devon—the absence of familiar preaching and religious services was a serious drawback as they established a community in Orange, near Cleveland, in the 1830s. One of their first to arrive was John Stoneman, a man of means, who traveled in America to find the right place for the settlers. He found New York too expensive, Michigan too unhealthy, but Ohio a fine place. He purchased a 243-acre, partially cleared farm, with buildings, for $4,840. His letter was published in the *Western Herald*, the newspaper of Shebbear, Devon, in 1837. After making comments about the soil and climate, the inadequacy of American farmers, and the joys of making one's own maple sugar, he emphasized that religious life in Ohio had its drawbacks: "As to our religious privileges, they are not so great as in the old country; when we came to this place there was no meetings near us, and we knew not where to go for several weeks, till we had meetings in our house; an Englishman came and preached at our house 11 or 12 Sundays. We have now joined the Protestant Methodists, and have the travelling preacher once a fortnight, and they seem to be a loving, zealous people, and are very friendly; but I cannot feel that attachment to them as to our friends at home; and when I grieve for having left my native country, it is when I think of the people of God whom I sincerely love."[5]

A decade later the *Bible Christian Magazine* reported from Devon that the spiritual difficulties in Ohio remained: "Emigrants certainly ought seriously to consider, before they determine on leaving their native shores, whether they are not likely to lose in religious advantages, more than they will gain in worldly possessions. . . . Some of these are situated at a great distance from any means of grace, and others who have been connected with christian [sic] churches at home, feel the want of their own people, even if they are located where there are other sections of the Church to be found. This has been the case with many of our members who have left England for America at different times."[6]

To address the problems the denomination sent a preacher, J. H. Eynon, to ascertain "the spiritual necessities of the friends who had emigrated thither." Eynon left in 1845, and though afflicted with ague and fevers, he visited members in the Cleveland area, including Orange and Chagrin Falls. Though the immigrants were prospering economically, they felt spiritually deprived. "Some of my dear sisters were ready to cry for joy at the sight of what they called one of THEIR OWN preachers," Eynon reported. His preaching was effective. "The power of God was manifestly in our midst. I felt some increase of the Missionary spirit, and many of the congregation felt the presence and power of God. I led the class after preaching; some shouted, and others wept for joy." Under Eynon's guidance, they agreed to support a preacher to be sent from England.[7]

The next year Brother G. Rippin was sent from Canada to Orange, to follow up on Eynon's mission. Rippin preached and reported that "the state of religion here, is certainly most deplorable." He alluded to the fact that many Ohioans, including preachers of other denominations, worked on Sunday, and that the Orange community desired "a purely gospel ministry and a scriptural discipline, which they considered they had not found since their arrival in this country." But with Rippin's help, they built a chapel at a cost of $200 and hired Reverend Keast, a former Wesleyan preacher from Launceston, Cornwall. "He has been to these sheep without a shepherd a valuable friend," said Rippin. By this time the Bible Christian community in Orange numbered eighteen families—all English except for one. The Bible Christian community at Chagrin Falls—four miles from Orange—had another sixteen families, and they bought a schoolhouse twenty-eight feet by twenty-two feet for $150 in which to worship. Rippin considered about half of Chagrin Falls' population "unbelievers."[8]

As the Bible Christian communities near Cleveland illustrate, the English did not always have a smooth transition in Ohio when it came to religious practice. Some yearned for a familiar liturgy and theology, and preachers who could deliver them. Though British and American religious cultures had much in common, some differences developed, especially in the more remote parts of Ohio. The isolation of the frontier and the lack of a formal or hierarchical religious authority produced a new religious environment that made some British immigrants feel like aliens in a strange land. This is how D. Griffiths felt in the Western Reserve during the 1830s:

> There are Sabbath scenes in some of the thinly settled districts of Ohio, that would present a novel appearance to an Englishman. The place of worship, situated on the side of a road, newly cut through the midst of the woods, is none other than a log-house of the rudest description . . . the bare ground serves for a hearth within, which is furnished with two or three large stones. . . . When the sun's elevation indicates the time of meeting, the inhabitants of the township may be seen issuing from the woods in every direction, some on foot some on horseback; but most of them in ox-waggons. . . . During service, the horses are *hitched* to the trees about the Meeting-house, and in wet weather, the saddles are brought inside. . . . With regard to the accommodations for worship inside, the minister is provided with an old chair and table. . . . The congregation, too, have a singular appearance . . . and were it not for the tobacco chawing and spitting, every thing might be said to be done decently and in order.[9]

If the crude and primitive accommodations and facilities of Ohio's early churches did not shock British immigrants, the distinctively American style of theology and liturgy probably did. James Martin had noticeably fundamentalist religious beliefs. And yet what he saw in 1833 at several of the "camp meetings" in Ohio shocked him. The camp meetings defined the Second Great Awakening, the antebellum revival that breathed new life into American Evangelicalism. But Martin saw a resemblance between Ohio's camp meetings and the gaudy, theatrical fairs that he had attended in Barnet, London, where he once lived. Clearly, Martin found it hard to accept this characteristic of religious life as he saw it in the Ohio backwoods, near the town of Bucyrus:

> We have camp meetings here in the woods lasting six or seven days and some have been protracted to 30 days as I have been informed. . . . At the camp meetings many thousands meet together and live in tents like Barnet fair people. Sometimes, considering the number of people, they are considerably orderly, protected by the Law. But their very order is complete confusion—preaching, praying, shouting, groaning, hallooing, all frequently at the same time. There is a large stage erected upon which the preachers (for sometimes they are many) stand, in the front of which is their prayer ring, a space of ground enclosed into which those that

want religion enter when they are prayed for. This is a scene that I cannot describe, some lying apparently lifeless as you would think, some you
would think were dancing for joy, some tossing, some tumbling, some
screaming, whilst others you would think were drawing their last breath.
Many honest, well-meaning people are entangled in these things.[10]

Martin was echoed by other English observers of camp meetings, most notably Frances Trollope, who toured America during the 1820s and published her
observations in *Domestic Manners of the Americans.* Accustomed to high church
Anglican services, the refined Trollope found the camp meetings near the Ohio
and Indiana border both fascinating and disturbing, a vision more of hell than
of heaven: "But how am I to describe the sounds that proceeded from this
strange mass of human beings? I know no words which can convey an idea of
it. Hysterical sobbings, convulsive groans, shrieks and screams the most ap-
palling, burst forth on all sides. I felt sick with horror. As if their hoarse and
overstrained voices failed to make noise enough, they soon began to clap their
hands violently. The scene described by Dante was before me."[11]

Though camp meetings magnified the differences that existed between
British and some American religious expressions, ultimately the similarities in
denominations and religious culture were greater. Even the American camp
meeting did not appear alien to all British immigrants. This was true of the
Primitive Methodists. This denomination was founded in England in 1811 by
Wesleyan Methodists inspired by American evangelists who had participated in
camp meetings on the American frontier. But Methodist church authorities
deemed their style of worship too emotional, referring to them as "Ranters,"
and expelled them. Many members of the new denomination—both laity and
clergy—saw the United States as a better place for their religious beliefs and migrated there in significant numbers during the antebellum period. They started
coming to the United States in 1842, when a convert from Teesdale, Joseph
Grieves, settled in Galena, Illinois, and others soon came to Ohio. The Primitive Methodists felt more at home at an American camp meeting. Among
British and American Methodists, especially, religion was something they had
in common.

Another English religious culture in Ohio was the United Society of Believers in Christ's Second Coming, or the Shakers. They came from Manchester to
America under the leadership of Mother Ann Lee Stanley, in 1774, and entered
Ohio in 1805 when 370 members founded a community at Union Village, north
of Cincinnati. Convinced that the millennium was near, the Shakers danced and
trembled during worship as a sign of being filled with God's spirit. They be-

came quite prosperous through trade with their neighbors and established several other communities in other parts of Ohio. However, their refusal to recognize marriage as a Christian institution and their doctrines of celibacy and communal ownership of goods made them suspect in the eyes of many of their neighbors and kept their numbers small, as did their pacifism and inclusion of women as preachers.[12]

Just as the Shakers illustrate how English religious sects successfully filtered into Ohio, the Church of Jesus Christ of Latter-day Saints, or Mormons, illustrate the reverse, and how British and American religious culture had some common trends and impulses. The Mormons were a deeply American religious movement that touched a chord with many Britons who shared with the Mormons a common interest in the millennium. Mormon missionaries first came to Britain in 1837, and three years later significant numbers of converts began the most important religiously-inspired British migration to America since the Puritans. Between 1848 and 1851 more than five thousand British saints made the journey, and between 1853 and 1856 about sixteen thousand more followed. By this time they were headed to Utah, whose 1870 population included nearly thirty-eight thousand English-born people, or 18.5 per cent of Utah's total population. That was the highest percentage of English-born people anywhere in the United States.[13]

The experience of British Mormons in Ohio was limited. Although Kirtland was the headquarters of the Church of Latter Day Saints, this was during a period before missions in Britain produced immigrant converts. Yet by 1835, a year before the dedication of the Kirtland Temple, there was interaction between Mormons and Britons. In June of that year, religious leader John Hewitt, from Barnsley, Yorkshire, met with Joseph Smith in Kirtland to discuss a possible merger of their two movements. Hewitt was a mathematics professor and pastor of Barnsley Independent Church, who after his excommunication came to represent a group of dissenters known as the Irvingites. These dissenters were the followers of Reverend Edward Irving, a Scot born in 1791 who studied for the ministry, began preaching a millennial doctrine, and called his movement the "Catholic Apostolic Church." Refusing to recognize the legitimacy of other denominations, the Irvingites understandably provoked tensions in England and were harassed from time to time. When Hewitt heard about Mormonism—a similarly harassed group not accepted by mainline Christian denominations—his congregation agreed to send him and his wife to Kirtland to talk with Smith and learn more about his organization, in hopes of seeing common ground and uniting the two movements. Hewitt planned for a long stay, for he bought a home in Fairport, on Lake Erie. But apparently the meetings did not go well, even though there was some promise at the start. Smith was, of course, willing to accept more converts to his faith, but was unwilling to bend his teachings to accommodate Hewitt. Thus, the Mormon Church recorded that "this Mr. Hewitt did not obey the gospel, neither would he investigate the matter," and Hewitt's mission came to naught. However, he did open a school in Painesville, Ohio—a reflection of his resources and religious dedication.[14]

The Mormon Church in Kirtland gained a more fruitful connection with Britain a couple of years later. In 1837, when Kirtland faced economic troubles and an internal crisis was splitting the Church, Smith called Heber C. Kimball and Orson Hyde to start a Mormon mission in England. Kimball's family was destitute at the time, yet he accepted the call. Accompanied by two recent recruits, Kimball and Hyde left Ohio for England on June 13, 1837. Carrying no money, the small group joined up with three Canadian converts in New York City and set sail. After only twenty days at sea they arrived in Liverpool.

The Mormon missionaries found fertile soil for their mission in Britain. They focused on small villages suffering some of the most unsettling changes associated with the Industrial Revolution, especially technological unemployment among textiles workers and declining living standards for people whose livelihoods depended on a preindustrial, rural economy. Mormons offered new hope and purpose for the desperate and the dispossessed. After only nine months of work, Kimball, Hyde, and their small team set sail again for America, leaving behind fifteen hundred converts and enough momentum to ensure the movement's survival.[15]

By the time British Mormons began immigrating to America, the Mormon Church moved from Kirtland to Nauvoo, Illinois, because of financial problems and the possibility of mob violence. Therefore there never was a large contingent of British Mormons in Ohio. However, the state was still the home for some British Mormons. Some remained in Kirtland because they did not have sufficient funds to carry on to Nauvoo, or later, Salt Lake City.[16] Welsh Mormons clustered along the banks of the Ohio in Syracuse, Meigs County.[17] They also settled near Columbus, where some heard the inspiring preaching of another English convert to Mormonism, John Taylor. Taylor came from Milnthorpe, Cumbria, and worked as a skilled woodworker in Liverpool before he converted to Methodism and migrated to Canada at age twenty-four to preach in Toronto. His belief that he had to discover the "full truths" of the Bible for himself steered him away from orthodoxy; consequently, he was no longer allowed to preach. He then met Parley Pratt, an itinerant Mormon preacher from the Cleveland area who converted Taylor and baptized him and his wife.

Taylor rose swiftly in the church hierarchy to lead the Mormon Church in the Toronto area. Upon instructions to move to Missouri, he traveled through Ohio in 1838, preaching on his way. Near Columbus a crowd threatened tarring and feathering if he preached, but he did so anyway—demanding the right through America's constitutional freedoms. Defying the mob, he dramatically tore open his vest and declared that "if tarring and feathering was the gift bought with the fathers' blood, then he was the offering for their 'goddess of Liberty.'" That silenced the crowd, so Taylor preached passionately for several hours and made converts. Eventually he became the third president of the Church of Jesus Christ of Latter-day Saints. Thus, Ohio's immigrant Mormons from Britain show that the religious culture between Britain and America flowed both ways and that the cultural connection between Ohio and Britain was vibrant.[18]

Many immigrant clergy from Britain made a deep impact on Ohio's religious life. Among them was John Swanel Inskip. Born in Huntingdon, England, in 1816, his family migrated in 1820, and John was about sixteen when he was converted at a Methodist meeting. Licensed as a preacher a few years later, Inskip became a successful clergyman and evangelist. In 1846 he accepted a request by the Ninth Street Church in Cincinnati to become their pastor and for six years he served Ohio Conference churches in several cities, including Dayton and Springfield. During that time Inskip promoted "family sittings," which allowed women and men to sit together in church. Many considered the practice heretical, and when he went so far as to publish his views that separate seating was not necessary, the Ohio Conference voted to "admonish him of his error" in 1851. However, at the following year's General Conference Inskip appealed the decision and defended his position so brilliantly that the former ruling was reversed.[19]

Bishop Edward Thomson was a particularly noteworthy English immigrant preacher. He had been an enemy of Christianity but after his conversion became one of its most effective exponents. He was born in the seaside town of Portsea in Hampshire to a family "in easy circumstances," his father being a successful druggist. The elder Thomson took his family to the United States in 1818—when Edward was a boy—and settled in Wooster. Edward studied medicine at the University of Pennsylvania and practiced his profession in Wayne County. Though his family consisted of devout Baptists, Edward Thomson developed a deep skepticism about Christianity and made a "labored effort" to disprove it. But a sudden conversion led him to Methodism. In 1832 he was licensed to preach and soon "displayed intense zeal in the cause." His efforts were highly effective because his sermons attracted large crowds and occasioned many conversions. He was also an effective teacher and headed Norwalk Seminary. When Ohio Wesleyan University was chartered in 1842 Thomson was elected to be its president and guided it to growth until he left the position in 1860. During and after his tenure he also edited the *Christian Advocate and Journal*. After his presidency he was made a bishop in the church.[20]

Primitive Methodist clergy also formed links between Britain and Ohio. The most important was Reverend John Mason, born in 1851 to parents affiliated with the Primitive Methodist Church in Cumberland. Raised as a miner, from 1873 to 1877 he worked as a "deputy" in charge of men in the region's deep shafts. Licensed as a Methodist preacher at eighteen, he immigrated to America in 1877 and served in the ministry in Tennessee and then Steubenville. But in Steubenville there was insufficient financial support for a minister, so Mason returned to mining until he was sent to Shawnee—where there were many British miners of the Methodist tradition. Upon his arrival Mason found the church "in a confused condition," with only five regular members. Through great effort Mason managed to multiply the membership. During a revival in 1881, eighty souls converted and the church grew to nearly two hundred members. Mason was also given charge of the church in Straitsville, where he led a successful ministry.

The shared religious beliefs of British immigrants and native Ohioans, and the immediate participation of the former in American religious life, did not always have harmonious results. In the city of Lorain the post–Civil War influx of British immigrants led to some friction within the religious community. The newly arrived Britons joined Lorain's Methodist Church in such numbers and entered positions of leadership so quickly that the Church's character was given "a distinctly British Methodist slant" in style and liturgy. This created some resentment among the original members, many of them old pioneers who still harbored suspicions of the British from the War of 1812 and the Anglo-American tensions of the 1840s. Some broke off to form a Congregational Church in 1872, which only made the English more dominant. And after a Mrs. Whitehouse was elected treasurer of the Ladies Aid Society soon after her arrival from England, older members complained: "that foreign woman will never be able to understand our money," and "the English [are] running our church." Some also complained about the English accents. The English replied that they ensured the success of the church and filled a vacuum in leadership. "Others were born here," they explained, "and couldn't help themselves but the English came because they wanted to, and if the others were as interested in working in the church as the English were, the English would not be left to run it their own way."[21]

After the confrontation and some adjustment on the part of the Ohioans, the English immigrants of Lorain were accepted as full members of the congregation. The story actually underscores how similar native Ohioans and English newcomers were. Except in a few short-lived instances they were not really seen as foreigners. Precisely because many English jumped right in and got involved in native denominations, some native Ohioans in the church were initially concerned about being overshadowed by them. Common denominations allowed an easy transition and explain why so many British immigrants became prominent in Ohio's churches and seminaries. Among them was William Henry Roberts, son of a Welsh Presbyterian minister, who immigrated with his family in 1855. After studying at Princeton Theological Seminary and serving as a pastor in New Jersey he moved to Cincinnati in 1886. There he assumed the chair of practical theology at Lane Theological Seminary, where he was a conservative voice supporting biblical inerrancy.[22]

TEMPERANCE

During the antebellum period, Ohio, like much of the United States, experienced a "ferment of reform" as evangelists and others associated with the Second Great Awakening began to address the social and economic problems of Jacksonian America.[23] At the same time, reform movements swept through Great Britain. These transatlantic reform movements were rooted in common religious traditions because the eighteenth-century Evangelicalism—especially Methodism—from which most of the great reform movements sprang, was transplanted from Britain to America. Naturally, there was much cross fertilization between the two nations' movements. The evangelical devotion to reform found in many parts of Ohio was familiar for British immigrants and provided them with immediate opportunities for community involvement. Many British immigrants, already aware of the reasons and nature of reform, eagerly participated. Because the Ohio general assembly passed and strengthened "blue laws" that outlawed profanity, gambling, cockfighting, horse racing, Sabbath breaking, and drunkenness, reform-minded British immigrants took heart in a state that was aiming for higher public morality. Religious enthusiasm and piety inspired both Britons and Americans in Ohio to reform society.[24]

The overconsumption of alcohol was one obvious target. In America especially, whiskey was cheap and abundant, partly because the undeveloped transportation system made it more profitable for grain farmers to distill their grain rather than transport it at great cost. England had its own struggles with the effects of cheap gin, as captured by the famous Hogarth engravings of the eighteenth century. Britain made progress through higher taxation of alcohol and the promotion of tea, but serious problems remained. Thus, temperance was a common cause for many British immigrants. It served to unite much of evangelical Protestantism in Ohio, and it lessened the distance between British immigrants and Ohio's Protestants of British descent.[25]

The wide participation of British immigrants in temperance movements might be expected because so many were Methodists or Presbyterians, who were more likely to pledge not to drink alcohol. But there is a larger significance here. The temperance issue was a cultural rift in nineteenth-century America that was based on differing beliefs on whether the state should get involved with social issues. Generally, temperance and other reform issues were embraced by American-born Protestants, many of whom feared the massive immigration of Irish and German Catholics that began in the 1840s. They had a faith in the role of government, that it should actively reform society and establish a higher morality. These intellectual formations characterized both northern Yankees and British immigrants, which again underscores the basic cultural similarities between American-born people and most British immigrants.[26]

Of course, British immigrants were not all teetotalers. Miners and factory workers were known for being overly fond of their beer and for taking "St. Monday" off from work to recover from a weekend of heavy drinking—and some brought the habits to America. But the British were still the most common immigrants in America's temperance movement and many were prominent leaders. Welsh-born Morgan Evans was an indefatigable worker in the Newark Presbyterian Church in Licking County, where he was passionately dedicated to temperance. In the words of his biographer, he "labored earnestly all his life in putting before the people the evils incident to the liquor traffic, and endeavored as far as possible to influence all with whom he came in contact to assert themselves on the side of the temperance movement and become active in trying to effect the abolition of the saloon."[27] James Miller, who settled in Wood County from his native Cambridgeshire in 1854, was active in the Prohibition Party and converted many local people to temperance.[28] And Scottish immigrant John Hill, a mine superintendent from Lanarkshire, supported the Prohibition Party and did "much to eradicate the terrible scourge of the liquor traffic."[29] For some immigrants alcohol was one among many substances that were being abused in an affront to God. Henry Butts, writing from Goshen, near Cincinnati, back to family in Devon in 1855, proclaimed that the chief problem in society was "man who perverts nature, who indulges in Tea & Coffee & Tobacco . . . wines & liquors & highly seasoned dishes; it is man not God who has turned blessings into curses."[30]

Abolitionism

British immigrants affected other realms of American moral life, most notably the abolition of slavery. Quakers and Methodists launched abolitionism in England in the eighteenth century, making it the world's center for the antislavery movement. Many Presbyterians, Baptists, Congregationalists, and Anglicans were also staunch abolitionists, but Methodists were especially effective. Overrepresented among Britons entering America, they took their antislavery fervor with them. With the help of their dedication, there was much cross-fertilization between British and American abolitionism.

Perhaps the first English immigrant in Ohio who took a stand against slavery was John W. Browne, a Congregational minister from Derbyshire who came to Cincinnati in 1798. He was pastor of the Whitewater Congregational Church, at Paddy's Run, which he organized in 1803. Browne was an enthusiastic admirer of William Cobbett and the founder and editor of *Liberty Hall*, a newspaper that condemned slavery, and he was an outspoken delegate to the first Ohio Constitutional Convention—one of two English immigrants, Edward Tiffin being the other. At the Convention, Browne was the most outspoken opponent of slavery, and of the twenty Republicans there, Browne left a record that was "easily the most favorable" to African Americans.[31] Paddy's Run was also an early center of opposition to slavery, because the Welsh who dominated the area were intensely abolitionist. The same was true of the Hanging Rock Iron region, where the Welsh were, "almost in a body," abolitionist in spirit.[32]

The antislavery convictions of British clergy in Ohio stretch back to the time of statehood. Reverend Robert Armstrong, who received a classical education at the University of Edinburgh and studied theology under some of Scotland's leading Presbyterian theologians for ordination in 1797, is a prime example. At that time church leaders in New York and Pennsylvania applied to the synod of Scotland for more clergy to serve the needs of the people heading west. So Armstrong was sent to Kentucky in 1798, and installed the following year to serve three congregations. However, he deemed slavery so contrary to his religion that in 1804 he and his three congregations uprooted themselves and settled in Greene County, Ohio, where they formed the Massiescreek and Sugarcreek congregations. Armstrong preached there for seventeen years. He also made frequent journeys of up to two hundred miles through the Ohio wilderness to supply vacant pulpits and organize new congregations. Throughout his years in Ohio he battled what he saw as religious fanaticism springing up on the frontier during the Second Great Awakening. He also fought to defend the Calvinist doctrines of his religious heritage against the "New Light" secession movement, which taught that faith was the product of human power. Most important, Robert Armstrong always condemned slavery.[33]

In addition to the abolitionist tendencies of many immigrants, British-based abolitionist groups also shaped Ohio's opposition to slavery. British female antislavery groups were especially influential and inspiring to their American counterparts. As William Lloyd Garrison informed Americans in the *Liberator,* women's antislavery organizations were effective in pushing Britain toward the abolition of slavery in the Empire—which was finally achieved in 1833—and they were setting a good example for the United States. They were also a source of aid. Usually working independently from male societies, they raised funds, issued propaganda, and circulated petitions—some of which was sent to the United States. American women learned much from their British counterparts, for in Boston, Philadelphia, and other cities, women held British-inspired fairs to raise funds and trumpet the cause. The fairs received goods for sale—including some all the way from Birmingham and Glasgow, as well from Hudson, Ohio, and other places in America. Through both British and American fairs, then, Ohio's abolitionists were connected with the larger antislavery world. The aid from British women solidified the international dimension of Ohio abolitionism and encouraged the hope that abolition could happen in America as well as in the British Empire.[34]

Transatlantic connections between British antislavery societies and Ohio involved considerable contact and personal visits of their leaders. In 1834 William Lloyd Garrison brought to the United States George Thompson, one of the most important leaders of Britain's movement. Thompson, with his lengthy American visit financially supported in England, helped establish over three hundred branches of the American Anti-Slavery Society in Ohio and other states. His activities and speeches were so bold that some considered him a threat to the Union. Andrew Jackson and others who held the Union as sacred denounced him as a dangerous radical. In 1835 mob violence in reaction to Thompson was so great that he felt compelled to flee and return to England. But he returned to the United States in 1851, after being elected a Member of Parliament for London, and again during the Civil War, when he was given a public reception in the House of Representatives in the presence of Lincoln and most of his cabinet.[35]

The inspiration that American abolitionism received from Britain was reinforced by the immigration of increasing numbers of Britons who were willing to fight against slavery. British immigrants, of course, were hardly free of racist beliefs; but the vast majority did have a deep loathing for an institution that they considered a violation of God's law and the ideals of the nation they were adopting. With relatively few exceptions, British immigrants in the United States viscerally opposed slavery. This was one reason why they avoided the South and settled in free states. In Ohio, which bordered slave states, British immigrants made no small contribution to abolitionism. Though not all of the immigrants opposed to slavery were abolitionists, considerable numbers were.

Abolitionism and higher education were often intertwined movements in Ohio, and one of the most influential leaders of both was the Scottish immigrant, Robert Hamilton Bishop. Born in 1777 to a family of devout Presbyterian tenant farmers near Edinburgh, Bishop entered the University of Edinburgh in 1793. He showed such promise that his professors supplied the financial help necessary to complete his studies, and he earned his AB in 1798. At Edinburgh, Bishop also developed a liberal social outlook. After completing his studies at the church's seminary in Selkirk, the presbytery of Perth licensed him, and in 1802 he accepted a call to serve in the United States. Bishop was first assigned to Kentucky, where he was temporarily suspended for libel as a result of a critical article that he published with other reform-minded clergy. During his period of suspension—from 1815 to 1820—he preached nearly every Sunday to African Americans and organized the first Sunday school for blacks in Lexington. That experience was one of his most enjoyable and helped make Robert Bishop a committed abolitionist.

Bishop's role in Ohio history began in 1824, when he became the first president of Miami University in Oxford and served as professor of logic and moral philosophy, later of history and philosophy of social relations. In 1825 he was awarded the doctor of divinity from the College of New Jersey (later Princeton) and reorganized the Presbyterian congregation at Oxford. His most important work was *Elements of the Science of Government* (1840), which placed civil and religious liberties ahead of obligations to government. He also encouraged self-government among Miami University students and defended their right to explore their own ideas—astonishing student freedoms

Robert Hamilton Bishop. After earning his college degree from Edinburgh University, Bishop emigrated in 1802 and in 1824 became the first president of Miami University, where he also served as professor of logic, philosophy, and history. This portrait was painted in 1830. From James H. Rodabaugh, Robert Hamilton Bishop. *Courtesy Miami University Archives, Oxford, Ohio.*

for the time. During Bishop's presidency, Miami became one of the Old Northwest's leading universities.

While president of Miami University, Robert Bishop helped establish the local Colonization Society (1827) and the Antislavery Society (1834), in which he was highly active. Bishop also supported evangelical abolitionists and befriended Lyman Beecher. When the Presbyterian Church split into the Old and New School branches during the 1830s, Bishop—partly through the influence of Beecher—sympathized with the New School while most of the Miami trustees were Old School clergy. Bishop worked hard to overcome the division, and was blamed by some as going too far to reconcile the branches. Furthermore, he, like other vocal abolitionists, was seen by many as an antagonist to the South and a threat to the Union, which cost him some important University allies.

In 1844 Bishop was dismissed from the presidency because he failed to provide discipline among students and supported the antislavery movement too vigorously. Bishop moved to Pleasant Hill, near Cincinnati, and helped establish Farmer's College—later the Ohio Military Institute. He taught and preached there until his death in Coffee Hill, Ohio, in 1855. He was known for his quick temper as well as his liberal ideas. His students affectionately knew him as "the grand old Scotchman," and his likeness is preserved in a sculpture that portrays him as a Roman senator. He effectively combined his multiple roles of educator, preacher, and abolitionist. And he is rightly acknowledged as "a great influence in the cultural development of the early West."[36]

Bishop knew another Scottish immigrant whose life and contribution to Ohio education and religion had striking parallels, as well as differences, with his own. He was Walter Scott, a brilliant student at Edinburgh University. Upon his graduation in 1818 Scott joined an uncle in America and began teaching at an academy run by George Forrester, a nominal Presbyterian lay minister who was leading a movement to "restore" the worship of the early Christians. Scott accepted these ideas and Forrester re-baptized him by immersion. Upon Forrester's accidental death, Scott assumed the leadership of the school and developed a working friendship with the Scotch-Irish immigrant, Alexander Campbell, who later founded the Disciples of Christ.

In 1826 Walter Scott came to Steubenville to start a new academy there, and later that year Campbell urged him to attend the annual meeting of the Mahoning Baptist Association in Canfield. Though Scott never became a Baptist, he did agree to become an evangelist and preached throughout Ohio to "restore the Gospel"—which he believed was all but lost by tradition. He taught that all rational people were able to respond to the gospel, and his message spread rapidly. In one year alone, the Mahoning Association membership jumped from six

hundred to sixteen hundred in response to his preaching. Some said he converted an average of one thousand per year over the next thirty years.

In 1830 the Mahoning Baptist Association dissolved itself because many
members no longer considered it scriptural or necessary, and Campbell began
his Campbellite movement and the Disciples of Christ. The two evangelists developed a bitter quarrel after Campbell charged Scott with plagiarizing his
views. Scott moved to Cincinnati where he started the *Christian Evangelist*, a
monthly periodical he published almost continuously between 1832 and 1844.
During that period he also lived in Carthage, Ohio, and toured extensively to
preach in Ohio and other states. In 1834, the Ohio legislature appointed him as
a trustee for Miami University. He served until 1837, while Robert Hamilton
Bishop was president. Scott also served as a pastor of two congregations in
Pennsylvania, and finally moved along the Ohio River, in Maysville, Kentucky,
where he finished his long and distinguished career in the ministry. Scott was
important for popularizing Campbell's theology, for his highly effective evan-
gelism, and for countering some of the emotionalism behind the movement.[37]

Higher education and abolitionism often meshed for British immigrants in
Ohio. Thomas Vickers, a Yorkshire immigrant who served as professor of history and president of the University of Cincinnati, devoted much of his time
and energy to abolitionism. He was a close friend of Wendell Phillips, William
Lloyd Garrison, and other leaders of the cause. On one of his return trips to Europe, he took with him a letter from Garrison that introduced him to the leading abolitionists in the British Isles.[38] Vickers probably knew the family of Henrietta Ramsden, also natives of Yorkshire, who were widely known for their fight
against slavery in Salem, Ohio. Henrietta's passionate opposition to slavery
began in England as a Yorkshire girl when she had sold the first book in England on the life of Frederick Douglass. In Ohio the Ramsdens became close
friends of Phillips, Garrison, and other leading abolitionists, and from time to
time provided them lodging in their home.[39]

Kenyon College, in Gambier, Knox County, is another testimony to the link
between British abolitionists and university education in Ohio. It was founded
in 1824 by Philander Chase, the first bishop of the Protestant Episcopal Church
in Ohio, whose desperation for funds led him to England. There his antislavery
principles brought him in contact with leading English abolitionists with deep
pockets, including Lords Kenyon and Gambier. Chase was given a staggering
five thousand pounds, some thirty thousand dollars, which funded the first
buildings and a joint faculty in theology and the arts.[40]

For James Simpson, religious conversion naturally led to zealous abolitionism. In his early life in Nottingham he had been "an infidel" and "had used the

power of large intellect against the Christian religion." Then, like St. Paul, he converted and spread the religion he had opposed so determinedly in the past. Simpson left England in 1840 and preached in Canada before becoming minister at the Big Darby Baptist Church in Madison County. He served there for twenty-five years and became a radical, Garrisonian abolitionist—insistent on immediate emancipation. He worked with the Underground Railroad in Madison County and helped many fugitive slaves to escape into Canada. Simpson was highly intelligent and known for his oratory. He debated throughout Ohio; some debates lasted seven days.

James Simpson imparted his uncompromising abolitionist views to his son, John, a child at the time of immigration. So when the Civil War came, John volunteered out of his commitment to take part in ending slavery. He served as an officer of the color guard and was wounded while carrying the flag at Kennesaw Mountain. After witnessing two previous color bearers being killed, he raised the flag only to be shot himself. His wounds never fully healed, and after thirty-two years of suffering great pain from a running wound, he had the limb amputated. In spite of that, John Simpson managed to become a progressive farmer and developed the "Honest John" variety of corn. His sons also became leading stock raisers of the county.[41]

Robert Wilson was an Englishman whose objection to slavery determined his place of settlement in the United States. An immigrant weaver of the early 1800s, Wilson first came to Maryland where he had pre-arranged his employment. He married the daughter of his employer, who was kind and prosperous, but owned slaves. Wilson could not tolerate the situation, and though the father begged them to stay, the couple packed their bags and headed north for Ohio, eventually settling in Miami County. There Wilson bought heavily timbered land, even though he "knew nothing of farming" and "could scarcely hitch a horse." His sons cleared the land while he wove to earn capital for the farm.[42]

British immigrants with antislavery convictions soon realized that abolitionists were not necessarily appreciated in Ohio. Racism and the prospect of freed slaves crossing the Ohio River to compete with white labor caused many Ohioans to view abolitionists as dangerous radicals who threatened their way of life. It often took courage to support abolitionism publicly. William Crichton, who came from Perthshire in 1833, was one of only two persons in Porter Township, Scioto County (just across the Ohio River from slave-holding Kentucky) who publicly supported abolition.[43] He felt the animosity of other Buckeyes who wanted to maintain the system that kept blacks in the South. James Westwater, a Scottish glasscutter who arrived in Columbus in 1832 and established a successful firm with his father, suffered the same predicament. Columbus citizens widely condemned him as "the nigger lover" because he "was the only one who, having the courage of his convictions, dared to face his unsympathizing audience in his arguments against slavery." Westwater also became a philanthropist, an active member of the Underground Railroad, and a friend of Ben Wade, Chase, and Giddings.[44]

Some British immigrants found themselves walking a fine line between their antislavery convictions and their loyalty to their adopted country. James Brownlee, a Glaswegian who arrived in Youngstown in 1827 and achieved wealth and reputation as a major cattle dealer and early supporter of the Whig Party, was one who found himself in this difficult situation. When the Fugitive Slave law was passed as part of the Compromise of 1850, requiring people of free states to apprehend and return runaway slaves, Brownlee went too far even for some abolitionists. He led an "indignation meeting" in Mahoning County and drew up a resolution that struck some as treasonable. Brownlee's resolution declared that "come life, come death, come fine or imprisonment, we will neither aid nor abet the capture of a fugitive slave; but on the contrary will harbor and feed, clothe and assist, and give him a practical God-speed toward liberty." Brownlee managed to get the resolution passed through his stirring speeches and charismatic leadership; but opponents saw such a radical defiance of the law as something one might expect from someone from Britain—someone who could not be a true loyal American. Brownlee proved his patriotism during the Civil War, however, when he continued his efforts by recruiting soldiers and forming companies at his own expense.[45]

The Francis and Anna Donaldson family made a very real and historic contribution to Ohio abolitionism after they left London and settled in Clermont County in 1821. Francis was a former barrister who took up farming, and Anna was described as "a lady of great intellectuality, of singularly gentile disposition, but of strong convictions." She demonstrated them by becoming a leader of the Ohio Anti-Slavery Society and stirring up antislavery passions. When mobs in Cincinnati attempted to tear down the printing press of James G. Birney, publisher of the abolitionist paper, the *Philanthropist*, Anna and her sons gave Birney refuge in their home. When an ugly mob of anti-abolitionists attempted to break the door down and murder Birney, Anna stood in their way and rebuked them with such defiance and conviction that they turned away.[46]

Another activist English family was that of Samuel Blackwell, a prosperous sugar refiner from Bristol who came to realize the link between his business and Caribbean slavery. He and his family arrived in the United States in the early

1830s to promote abolitionism and other reform movements. He was a perfectionist, who believed that through reform, education, and spiritual regeneration humans could create a just society on earth and usher in the second coming of Christ. In 1838 the Blackwells settled in Cincinnati, a center of revivalism and abolitionism. Samuel died shortly thereafter, but his family of young adult children lived on the grounds of Lane Theological Seminary, where they developed close ties with evangelicals and abolitionists—including Henry Ward Beecher and Harriet Beecher Stowe. Son Samuel married Antoinette Louisa Brown, the first woman formally ordained as a minister in the United States. Son Henry Brown Blackwell and daughters Elizabeth and Emily supported the local antislavery movement and became close friends of the movement leaders, including some New England Transcendentalists who settled in the city.

Elizabeth Blackwell earned a medical degree in New York in 1849, the first woman in the United States or Europe to do so, and then returned to England. Emily followed her sister's example, and studied medicine at the Medical College of Cincinnati in 1848. In 1852 she attended Rush Medical College in Chicago but finished her training at the Western Reserve Medical School in 1854, which had just begun to admit women. Her brother Henry Brown Blackwell moved east and became an ardent supporter of women's rights. In 1853 he was elected secretary of the National Women's Rights Convention in Massachusetts, and he married the great reformer Lucy Stone. But abolitionism brought the Blackwell family back to Ohio and launched them on their careers working for enslaved African Americans and the rights of women.[47]

Richard Realf is another notable example of an immigrant who developed his antislavery convictions in England and worked with important abolitionists in Ohio. Born to a poor family in Sussex in 1834, Realf worked in the fields as a boy and started writing poetry at age fifteen. At seventeen he moved to Brighton, where he worked as a secretary for Mrs. Parnell Safford, who introduced him to the classics, the ideas of the abolitionist and social critic Harriet Martineau, and those of Lady Byron—the widow of the great romantic poet. In 1853 she allowed Realf to live on one of Byron's estates in Leicestershire, where he managed the estate and developed his literary skills. While there, he fell in love with a woman whose higher social class made marriage impossible, and whose pregnancy led to a scandal. After his humiliation, Realf decided to live where his "democratic and republican instincts" could flourish. He arrived in America in 1854.

The young man arrived just in time for the passage of the Kansas-Nebraska Act, which opened up the west to slavery, and the violence that followed. At that instant Realf became a "radical abolitionist," as he called himself. He went to Kansas in 1856 to help settlers to keep slavery out. Then in 1857 he met with John Brown to discuss plans to liberate slaves in the South, which ultimately culminated in the Harper's Ferry raid. Realf liked Brown's plan, agreed to recruit former slaves in Canada, and Brown appointed him secretary of state in Brown's intended revolutionary government.

At this point Realf happened to read Francis Wayland's "Limitations of Human Responsibility," which led him to abandon Brown's violent movement. Instead of carrying out a military mission he sailed back to England to lecture on literature and temperance. He even considered becoming a Jesuit priest, so he returned to the United States in 1859 and attended the Jesuit College at Spring Hill in Alabama, and studied further in New Orleans. While Realf was in New Orleans Brown and his men attacked the federal arsenal at Harper's Ferry. Richard Realf testified for the United States Senate committee investigation on Brown's raid, and afterwards came to Ohio. In March of 1860 he joined the utopian Shaker community of Believers at Union Village, Ohio, a millennial sect that required celibacy of its members. Realf served as their public speaker and attracted large and enthusiastic audiences when he preached reform and abolitionism. In 1862 he joined the Union army and during the war wrote romantic poetry in the style of Shelly and Byron, some of which appeared in the *Atlantic Monthly* and *Harper's Monthly*.[48]

Some British immigrants were important local leaders and helped create city and state emancipation organizations. One was Reverend Thomas E. Thomas, who left Chelmsford as a boy in 1818 with his family and settled in Cincinnati and later Venice, Butler County. Thomas graduated from Miami University, where he developed his abolitionist views. He and some fellow students formed the Miami Anti-Slavery Society in 1834, pledging their "hearts, heads, and hands," to the cause, and declaring that, "let slavery be annihilated, let justice be done to the oppressed." The next year he also founded antislavery societies at Hamilton and Rossville, and after some mergers established the Butler County Anti-Slavery Society in 1840. Thomas was also a delegate to various antislavery conventions and corresponded frequently with other Ohio abolitionists. He taught in various schools and at Miami University and in 1849 was elected President of Hanover College in Madison, Indiana. As an ordained pastor of the First Presbyterian Church of Dayton from 1856 to 1871, he also took a faculty position at Lane Seminary. But up through the Civil War, Thomas devoted most of his time and energy to the fight against slavery. At the General Assemblies of the Presbyterian Church, Thomas E. Thomas successfully urged the

Church to adopt a resolution declaring that "slavery is utterly inconsistent with the law of God, and totally irreconcilable with the spirit and principles of the Gospel of Jesus Christ."[49]

Other examples of antislavery British immigrants in Ohio abound. Alexander McBeth, a stonemason in Scotland until he emigrated with his wife and children in 1831, settled in Columbiana County. There he became an elder in the new Wellsville Presbyterian Church and the family assisted fugitive slaves. Alexander's daughter Susan, only a year old when brought to America, developed a passion to become a missionary to American Indians. In 1860 the Board of Foreign Missions of the Presbyterian Church sent her to Oklahoma to teach and evangelize the Choctaw Nation.[50] There she became known for racially egalitarian beliefs. And Norton Townshend (whose important contributions to Ohio agriculture and the establishment of Ohio State University have already been noted) spent much of his career as a state congressman passionately advocating for the equal rights of African Americans in Ohio—including suffrage. Townshend persevered in this mission during his service as Medical Inspector for the Union army in the American Civil War.

THE CIVIL WAR

When the war came and Lincoln issued his call for volunteers, British immigrants came forward in greater proportions than any other immigrant group, and with an enthusiasm second to none. Several factors explain their remarkably wide participation. Unlike other immigrants, some sensed a lingering American suspicion that their loyalty remained with Queen Victoria. Proving steadfastness to their adopted land was important and sometimes achieved by painting enormous American flags on their barns, or making other conspicuous displays. Volunteering for the Union, then, was a perfect opportunity to declare their Americanness. Britons' quick assimilation also explains their wide participation. Sharing the same language and many of the religious and political ideals that prevailed in the northern states, the British saw the war as an opportunity or obligation to act on those ideals. It is telling that while there were many ethnic regiments, there were no British regiments in the American Civil War, save a minor Scottish one that included non-Scots.[51]

But in a deeper sense Britain and the United States were bound by a common history of slavery and abolitionism, and Britain followed the tragic events that unfolded in America with a sense of a shared experience. Harriet Beecher Stowe's *Uncle Tom's Cabin* sold seven times more copies in Britain than in the United States during its first year of publication, and Queen Victoria and many of her subjects wept when they read it. British working classes had an especially

deep revulsion for American slavery. They were most likely to have relatives in
America and many saw their own fight for greater freedom and equality in
Britain as part of a larger international movement that included abolishing
slavery.

Thus, the Civil War gripped people's attention in Britain. Members of Parliament like John Bright, the liberal Quaker for Manchester and later Lancashire
and Birmingham, as well as freetrader Richard Cobden, saw the American Civil
War in universal terms—especially after Lincoln's Emancipation Proclamation
ennobled the war and lifted it to a higher cause. Freeing African slaves was related to extending the franchise and moving from aristocratic to democratic
government.[52] For others the war was evidence of the frailty of American
democracy and the superiority of the British constitution. But few in Britain ignored the American Civil War, especially as the end of American exports produced the "cotton famine" in northern England and created widespread unemployment. The London Times even claimed in 1862 that "the Civil War in the
United States affects our people more generally even than the Indian Mutiny"
that occurred five years earlier.[53]

For most British immigrants in Ohio regiments the primary and most immediate reason for taking up arms was to rid their new country of its deepest
stain. William J. Inwood fought out of a commitment both to free the slaves and
show loyalty to his new country. Born in Warwickshire and raised as a sailor, Inwood emigrated with his wife in 1848. He was a devout member of the Evangelical Association and despised slavery, so when the war came he volunteered and
served until he was seriously injured in a train wreck near Chattanooga.[54] For
some, preserving the Union was as important as abolishing slavery. Welsh immigrant George Edmunds first settled in Missouri, but as a "Union man" found
it impossible to stay there when the war broke out and moved to Ohio.[55]

The dedication and enthusiasm of British immigrants was evident from the
start of the conflict. The British were among the very first Ohio volunteers. Former Liverpudlian John Mahony resolved "to aid his adopted country in her
struggle to preserve the Union," and literally left his plow standing in the field
to become one of the first members and captain of Company K, 21st OVI. At
Chickamauga he was taken prisoner and never fully regained his health—even
after he returned to his fields.[56]

The honor and sacrifice of William and Elizabeth Pearson was equal to that
of any American-born family. They raised their children in London before immigrating to Ohio in 1832. They had four daughters and six sons, each of whom
"testified to his loyalty to the Union by serving in her defense." One son was
killed at Vicksburg; another died of battle wounds; the other four fought

bravely in Ohio regiments. Before the war son Joseph had traveled in the South and witnessed slavery firsthand, so after Fort Sumter he recruited a company of soldiers from his community in Clark County. He, too, was wounded in battle. Their mother, Elizabeth, who worked for a commission to send supplies to the front, earned fame as well when she exclaimed at a public meeting, "I thank God that I have six sons defending the Stars and Stripes." These are remarkable words for an English immigrant who lost two sons to the war.[57]

British immigrants served in every imaginable capacity in the American Civil War. Though most were soldiers, many served as military carpenters, engineers and mechanics, supply officers, buglers, and medical officers. The physician and politician Norton Townshend served another important role: Union army Medical Inspector. During the Mexican War, seven Americans died of disease for every one killed in action, and in 1861 it appeared the disaster would repeat itself without new hospital organization and thorough reforms. So in 1862 the Medical Department appointed sixteen inspectors to the staff of the Surgeon General, all at the rank of lieutenant colonel, and Townshend was one of them. The sanitary conditions of all hospitals, prison camps, and soldiers' quarters were their responsibility. Some of the inspiration to improve the soldiers' health care came from the scandalously wretched medical conditions that the British Army endured during the Crimean War of the previous decade, and that Florence Nightingale and others addressed with considerable success. By 1854 the death rate among British soldiers in the Crimea plummeted from 203 per thousand to twenty-five—thanks to new sanitary measures. Britain offered America yet another lesson from their own experience with war.[58]

Norton Townshend, from Northamptonshire, served many roles in Ohio. As the "father of agricultural education in America" he helped found Ohio State University, he served Ohio in the Congress and State Senate as an advocate of abolition and women's suffrage, and he was a medical doctor and medical inspector for the Union army during the Civil War. From Charles William Burkett, *History of Ohio Agriculture.*

Townshend was a good choice. Though retaining the love for agriculture he acquired in Northamptonshire, he pursued medical education at some of the finest institutions of the time, receiving his MD from the College of Physicians and Surgeons in New York City in 1840. The following year he gained further education and training in Paris, Edinburgh, and London. Furthermore, his experience as a member of the House of Representatives and a state senator gained him political clout and the ear of Senator Salmon P. Chase. And his campaign as a congressman to repeal the oppressive "Black Laws" and extend equal rights to African Americans left no doubt about his dedication to serve in a war that by 1863 became a struggle to end slavery. The Englishman thoroughly absorbed the best causes that the Union stood for.

Townshend visited camps, prisons, and hospitals in New Orleans, Pensacola, and Baton Rouge. Because the inspection work was fairly routine, he was able to take a leave of absence to Ohio, where he tried to catch up on his duties as president of the State Board of Agriculture, an important and prestigious position concurrent with his military appointment. During another home leave in 1864, he sought a location for an asylum for the mentally disabled after the Ohio legislature had provided funding.

The most notable quality about Townshend's service as Union army Medical Inspector was his concern for justice for slaves and former slaves, in addition to military and medical matters. Not fully understanding the political constraints upon Lincoln, Townshend was exasperated that the Emancipation Proclamation applied only to those states under rebellion and not those in Union control. The fact that people remained in bondage irked him greatly. "The exception from its effects of all parts of Louisiana held by Union Troops is a great injustice," Townshend wrote to Chase about Lincoln's Proclamation. "It applies to all locations where we have no means of enforcing it, while every place were [sic] we could enforce it is excepted." He also emphasized that Reconstruction was pointless and immoral without the black vote—something he campaigned for repeatedly as an Ohio Congressman. "I trust no attempt at reconstruction will be made in Louisiana or any other state without considering the interests & rights of the colored people slave & free," Townshend wrote to Chase in September of 1863. "I don't believe that God will show himself on the side of this nation until all our oppressions of the African race have been repented of & reparation to some extent made." Thus, Townshend anticipated the concerns and agenda of the Radical Republicans, who dominated Congress after the 1864 elections and imposed their version of Reconstruction on the South from 1867 to 1877. Townshend's piety and outrage were rooted in a long-held commitment to abolitionism and the rights of African Americans, as well as to his English heritage. Lincoln and other Republicans shared his conviction that all men, regardless of race, should be able to rise as high as their abilities could take them. Liberal and evangelical spirit cut deeply on both sides of the Atlantic.[59]

Many other British immigrants in Ohio served in the Civil War with distinction. Some had prior military experience and training. Emanuel Constable, the son of a Herefordshire weaver, served for eleven years in the Royal Welsh Fusiliers. He helped suppress the Montreal riots of 1849 and fought in the Crimean War. He even participated in the battle of Balaklava, immortalized by the ill-fated "Charge of the Light Brigade." Constable settled in Ohio just in time to enlist for the 111th OVI, though he was eventually discharged for disability.[60] Col. Robert L. Kilpatrick was another immigrant soldier with extensive military experience in Britain. He was born in Paisley, Scotland in 1825 and at the age of sixteen joined the 42nd Highlanders, better known as the "Black Watch" regiment, perhaps the most famous in the British Army. Kilpatrick was stationed in Malta and the Bermudas for ten years, much of that time as a non-commissioned officer. After settling in Cincinnati, he organized a company of other Scottish immigrants to form the Highland Guards, who wore the Highland costume. This became the nucleus of the 5th Ohio, which Kilpatrick commanded in six pitched battles and twenty-eight engagements. At Chancellorsville he lost an arm, and in 1870 he retired from the military with the rank of colonel.[61] Such immigrants with experience in British wars were comparatively rare. The vast majority were raw recruits with all the enthusiasm and sense of adventure so quickly shattered by the reality of war.

It is truly remarkable how some immigrants volunteered within such a short time after their arrival. Archibald Harvey Thomson, a veterinarian from Edinburgh who settled in Akron in 1859 and clerked for the Empire Hotel, enlisted in the Company G 19th Ohio Infantry as soon as it formed. He reenlisted for three more years, participated in thirty-seven battles, was made a captain, and was wounded three times.[62] And Thomas Blackburn emigrated from Lincolnshire when he was twenty-five, and enlisted in September of 1861, a mere three years after his arrival, serving Battery D, 1st Ohio Light Artillery. He reenlisted in 1863 and served through the war's remainder.[63]

Some enlisted virtually upon their arrival during the war. Stories of bravery and sacrifice by Britons in Ohio are common. They served in every major engagement and participated fully in the war's drama and horror. Some never made it out of the infamous Andersonville Prison in Georgia. Others were captured and made dramatic escapes that stagger the imagination. Some formed their own company of soldiers and rallied Americans to the cause. And at least one British Buckeye led black soldiers in the war. John Cartwright, from Shropshire, served as captain of Company A of the 27th United States "Colored" Infantry. He died while leading his troops at the legendary "Battle of the Crater" during the Siege of Petersburg, Virginia, in July of 1864. His regiment was hon-

ored for the way "it distinguished itself for unsurpassed gallantry and good conduct upon the battlefield," and for providing "heroic service." Cartwright's two
brothers also fought in the war and were lucky to survive.[64]

A number of other stories reveal the character and experiences of British
Buckeyes in the Union army. Some young Englishmen came to America and
underwent amazing adventures both before and during the war. James Facer, an
immigrant from Northamptonshire, came to Ohio alone in 1847 as a seventeen-
year-old boy. After working as an engineer on ships on the Great Lakes and surviving several narrow escapes from shipwrecks, Facer enlisted in the Union
army in 1862 and fought in some of the legendary battles. The war proved to be
more than Facer bargained for, however. He was captured and spent over fourteen months in Andersonville Prison; guards subjected him to treatment that
included not being permitted to stand erect for six months—torture that crip-
pled him for life. An even worse fate remained for his brother William, who followed him to Ohio in 1859 and enlisted in spite of his brief residency. He was
also imprisoned at Andersonville but didn't make it out alive.[65]

Other stories hold great poignancy when we consider what some immigrants endured for the cause. Albert Haworth, from Manchester, volunteered as
a private, suffered wounds, but after the war was killed by bushwhackers near
Chattanooga while he headed home. The chaos of the time prevented the per-
petrators from ever being brought to justice.[66] The Morris family, of Cumbach,
Wales, contributed much to the Union army. Having immigrated to Ohio in the
1840s to mine coal and superintend operations, David Morris had twenty children, and five sons fought in the war. One of them used his training as a mine
engineer very effectively—as he was the one who blew up Fort Hill, Vicksburg—but died from wounds received in the operation. A cousin, Mordecai,
volunteered at age sixteen.[67] Even as the war ended the celebrations turned
tragic for James Thorpe, who had emigrated from Yorkshire in 1848 and served
as a railroad machinist in Bucyrus. He was an enthusiastic supporter of the
Union cause and was given charge of a cannon used to celebrate the victory. It
exploded prematurely and took off Thorpe's right arm; the accident horrified
the city and "checked the festivities."[68]

Some of the heroes awarded the Congressional Medal of Honor hailed from
Britain. Charles Stacey, from Earith, Cambridgeshire, came to Ohio in 1854 with
his father, worked on farms, and completed the education he started in England. In September of 1861 Stacy enlisted for Company D, 55th regiment of Ohio
Volunteer Infantry. His regiment was attached to the Army of the Potomac and
fought in the thick of the battle of Gettysburg. While his regiment was being
annihilated by sharpshooters, Stacey volunteered to go beyond the lines as a

sharpshooter himself. He succeeded under impossibly dangerous conditions, killing the Confederate sharpshooters and saving his regiment. But on the night after the second day of the historic battle, rebels took him prisoner and sent him to Libby Prison. Later exchanged for Confederate prisoners, he participated in other great battles, was recognized as a war hero, and awarded the Congressional Medal of Honor. He commanded the Congressional Medal of Honor Legion of Ohio, and after the war became a leader of the temperance movement and promoted the public welfare in various ways. His fame gave him the notoriety to urge the improvement of public highways and buildings. He also promoted a progressive school system supported by higher taxation.[69]

Not all were heroes struggling for a good cause. In 1864, the *Cleveland Leader* reported a speech in Parliament accusing the United States of placing on emigrant ships recruiting agents who got Englishmen drunk on arrival in order to enlist them unwittingly into the Union forces.[70] Some immigrants fought for the pay or government bounty. James Davis, a Welsh immigrant who arrived from Swansea in 1841, did rather well in the coal transport industry in Coshocton County. He was proud that he could pay twelve hundred dollars for a substitute to fight for three years in his stead.[71] And occasionally their letters reveal the racist attitudes that prevailed among whites at the time. For example, one Welsh miner wrote in 1868, "Almost all the Welshmen are on the radical [Republican] ticket and I would be so myself except for the nigger quality which does not agree with my views that the Creator never intended them to be equal to the white man."[72] Yet, for most it was still a noble cause to preserve the Union, and, for many, to expunge slavery from their new land. In later years British immigrants recalled the Civil War as the most important event that shaped them in their new land and made them Americans, not just Britons in America.[73]

7

The Professions, Arts, and Civil Service

*"Mr. Oscar Wilde, the professional English 'aesthete,'
has come to this country 'to diffuse beauty.' We hope he
will lose no time in coming to these parts."*

—*Ohio State Journal*, February 5, 1882[1]

THOUGH the majority of British immigrants to Ohio were farmers or manual workers of various kinds, significant numbers of professionals and merchants also came to the state. Roughly 7 percent of the adult males who arrived in American ports from Britain in 1851 declared professional or commercial occupations. The figure for those who appear in Ohio's county histories and had their British occupation recorded was about twice as high, though this may reflect a bias in the sources.[2] But, even taking the lower figures, no other immigrant group had such high proportions of professionals and merchants. Britain's more developed economy produced more potential emigrants from the professional and merchant backgrounds. And the Britons' extensive networks of communication across the Atlantic, their common language and heritage, and long tradition of migration to America made it relatively easy for them to enter American life—or at least to try it out for a year or two.

As a nation growing rapidly in geography and population, the United States needed people who could provide medical services. This was especially true in an age when professional and official credentials were not required and medical "quacks" were in the business with nostrums that often did more harm than good. And as Britain had come to lead the western world in medical training in the eighteenth century, there were many physicians who carried their skills and experience to America.

The country doctor was one of the vital figures in pioneering life and most of the English and Scottish physicians in Ohio filled that role. But some surgeons with the highest training and skills available also came to Ohio. Watson Lawrence King, educated at Cambridge and the Royal College of Surgeons in London, immigrated to Ohio in 1870 and studied further at the Cincinnati Medical College. Then, after returning to Britain for a medical degree at the University of Glasgow, he returned to Ohio. King became the leading physician and surgeon in Licking County, an important contribution to a still relatively undeveloped profession in the community.[3]

A number of accomplished British physicians served the medical needs of Ohio's pioneers, though not always with happy results. Daniel McPhail was fully trained as a physician and chemist in his native Scotland and settled in Wooster, Wayne County, in 1818 to become the pioneering physician of the area. He successfully practiced medicine there for twelve years, providing services scarce on the frontier, until he was sued for malpractice. Judge Charles Sherman—father of General William T. Sherman—defended him in court and he was fully vindicated. But McPhail was so shaken by the ordeal that he moved to Tennessee where he established a highly successful practice and earned a sterling reputation.[4] One of the best known doctors in Fayette County was Dr. William H. Jones. He was raised in Wales to a farming and milling family, but upon his father's death went to Cincinnati to prepare the way for his mother and siblings to follow. His mother died at sea, so William raised his siblings. In Ohio, Jones combined medicine with farming, and after retiring as a physician at age seventy he returned to his farm to finish his days there.[5]

Other young immigrants arrived with some medical education and finished their training in America. Richard Gundry, for example, was born to privilege in Hampstead, London, where he received a "classical education" at a famous private school. After emigrating in 1845, he studied medicine in Canada and then graduated from Harvard Medical College in 1851. He soon moved to Columbus and in 1855 became a physician at the Ohio Lunatic Asylum. Gundry eventually became superintendent of the State Hospital for the Insane, which opened in 1874. The doctor was a medical supervisor in Columbus. He gained a national reputation as an "alienist," who emphasized the humane and rational treatment of patients and called for the name "lunatic asylum" to be replaced with the title of "insane hospital." Gundry finished his distinguished career as professor of the College of Physicians and Surgeons in Baltimore.[6]

British-born women also made some highly visible contributions to the field of medicine in Ohio. As noted in previous chapters, some served as physicians on the frontier, and English immigrants Elizabeth and Emily Blackwell were the first women to take medical degrees in America. Another pioneer in women's medical training was Myra King Merrick, born in Hinkley, Leicestershire, and brought to America as a child by her parents in 1826. In 1841 the Kings moved to Cleveland where Myra worked as a nurse for several area physicians and decided to pursue medicine for her profession. After marrying a builder, Charles Merrick, in 1848, the couple moved to Connecticut. Myra studied under physicians at Yale University, after which she gained admission to the Central Medical College in Syracuse. She graduated at the top of her class in 1852 and returned to Cleveland the next year. Myra Merrick was one of the first female members of the American Institute of Homeopathy, and when the Cleveland Homeopathic Medical College suddenly decided to exclude women in 1867, Merrick and others founded the Cleveland Homeopathic Hospital College for Women. There she served as professor of obstetrics and female diseases and became president of the board of trustees. Thus, Merrick made two essential contributions to Ohio's medical professions: the further study of women's diseases and health issues and the promotion of women in the medical profession.[7]

Late in the nineteenth century and beyond, British immigrants continued to fill important positions in the field of medicine in Ohio. In 1912 the Western Reserve University in Cleveland invited Thomas Wingate Todd, a well-known anatomist and physical anthropologist from Manchester, to fill its chair of anatomy. Todd was only twenty-seven at the time, but had already served as house surgeon of the Royal Infirmary in Manchester, was a fellow of the Royal College of Surgeons, and had become an expert in the development of the human skeleton. He remained at the Western Reserve University teaching and directing the university's Hamann Museum of Comparative Anthropology and Anatomy until his death in 1938.[8]

Other professions in Ohio benefited from British immigration. Early America's legal profession, notoriously plagued by inconsistent training and a lack of professionalism, raised its standards with the help of people like Levin Belt, one of the most prominent lawyers and judges in early Ohio during the Territorial Government. A staunch Federalist, he also served as a prosecuting attorney and mayor of Chillicothe. Many immigrants trained in America and contributed greatly to the various professions. Several important university presidents and professors were mentioned in the previous chapter. And Yorkshire immigrant Thomas Vickers studied theology, philosophy, philology, and history in Pennsylvania and the Universities of Heidelberg and Zurich. He knew eleven languages and served as pastor of the First Congregational (Unitarian) Church in

Cincinnati. In 1878 Vickers became president of the University of Cincinnati and professor of history and distinguished himself further as a prominent author and superintendent of Portsmouth Public Schools.[9]

Some teachers arrived from Britain with better training than most American teachers of the time. Mary Harris Williams, for instance, was well educated in her native Glamorganshire and apprenticed as a teacher for five years, and even earned the Queen's certificate by recommendation of the local school board. Before her immigration to Perry County she taught for eight years and every two years her teaching was evaluated to ensure its quality.[10]

John C. Robinson received a good education and served as a teacher in England before he settled in Madison County, Ohio, in the early 1830s. He erected the first saw mill in Oak Run, but sold it to resume his teaching profession. While teaching in Kentucky he was stabbed to death by one of his students.[11] And Edward C. Benson, son of a barrister in Thorne, Yorkshire, emigrated with his father as a boy and graduated from Kenyon College in Gambier in 1849. He taught Latin there during the early 1850s, and after another degree served as professor for thirty-one years.[12]

British teachers seem to have acquired knowledge about the opportunities or lack thereof in a given community and located themselves accordingly. This can be seen in the letters of Thomas Read. Writing from New York state back to family in Middlesex, north of London, in 1834, he expressed his intention to proceed to Cincinnati, where he heard "Teachers are in request." Read had taught for a while in Buenos Aires, so he had traveled widely and had unusual experiences that would serve him well in the classroom.[13] Altogether, Britons with professional and educational backgrounds and aspirations made notable contributions to the development of Ohio.

English immigrants contributed quite significantly to the cultural landscape of Ohio in the visual arts as well. The first recorded arrival of an important artist in Ohio was that of Englishman Jacob Beck, who came to Cincinnati in 1795. And the great landscape painter from Lancashire, Thomas Cole, immigrated in 1818 and a year later came to Steubenville where he began his remarkable career as a portraitist. Cole then returned to Philadelphia where he earned greater fame; but his life along the Ohio River must have inspired his love for nature that eventually made him early America's foremost painter of Romantic landscapes and founder of the influential Hudson River School. One English artist who remained in Ohio was John R. Carroll, who opened a studio in 1812 in Pittsburgh where he painted portraits and gave painting and drawing lessons. The next year he established his studio in Cincinnati. Advertisements appeared in the Zanesville newspapers of March 10, 1813, that "Mr. J. Carroll, *Artist* and *Portrait* Painter from London, a Student of the Royal Academy," was available for commissions, and that he was "a first rate artist, and entitled to encouragement from an enlightened public. He paints Portraits of all sizes in the most elegant manner, and executes every branch of that pleasing art in Oils, Crayons, or Water Colors, in a masterly stile. . . ." Later, Carroll became an active member of the Cincinnati Thespian Society and painted scenery for many stage productions.[14]

Not surprisingly, the English—with their long and brilliant tradition of theater—contributed greatly to Ohio's theatrical arts. One of the first was Samuel Drake, an English actor and theatrical manager, who immigrated to America with his talented family in 1809. Several of his children were also accomplished actors. Though based in Albany, Drake and his new American company—which included his children—toured America with their own backdrop scenes and props and occasionally confronted Indians and heard the howl of wolves. But they relished touring up and down the Ohio River and brought performances to Cincinnati by the early 1820s, where Drake helped establish theater as respectable entertainment.[15]

One of the most celebrated actresses in nineteenth-century America was Mrs. Trowbridge, born in England, who performed widely in Cincinnati and Columbus in the 1830s and 1840s and won "universal acclaim" from her audiences. She played all of the leading female roles and was extremely versatile, often taking a different role every night. Trowbridge gave 105 performances in a single year. She was especially known for her Lady Macbeth and her Adine in *Faustus*, but she also sang popular songs and gave recitations. Her fans hailed her as the best actress in the country. A compatriot, Mrs. Pritchard, also played in Columbus theaters during those years, and amazed audiences with her portrayal of Richard III.[16]

Another well-known English actress who performed many classical roles for Ohio's early theater audiences in the 1850s was Anne Hartley Gilbert. She and her husband were also successful ballet dancers who toured England extensively before they decided to immigrate to America in 1849 to become farmers—a truly remarkable example of how farming one's own land proved irresistible for people of every occupational background. The Gilberts invested their very considerable savings in land near Milwaukee, but Anne returned to the theater in Chicago and became so popular that she toured the Midwest theater circuit and performed regularly in Ohio.[17]

Professional, artistic, and better-educated immigrants included some who attended the finest schools and universities in Britain. Appreciable numbers were well-read scholars, lovers of poetry and music, and had traveled widely. A few had aristocratic ties.[18] Though greatly outnumbered by others who were less refined and more concerned with earning a living than reading or writing books or music, these more privileged British immigrants are also worthy of our historical memory for contributing some refinement to Ohio's culture. One notable English architect is Alfred Bult Mullett, whose parents came from Somerset to the Cincinnati area to farm in 1845. Alfred attended Farmer's College (now the University of Cincinnati) in the early 1850s, and then joined the architectural firm of Isaiah Rogers in Cincinnati in 1857. In the boom years following the Civil War, he designed many federal buildings all over the United States, including some in Cincinnati.[19]

Jim McCormick is perhaps the best-known immigrant in Ohio sports. He left Scotland as a child when his family immigrated to New Jersey. In 1873 he started a baseball club in Patterson, New Jersey. As a successful pitcher McCormick soon drew attention from other teams around the eastern United States, and in 1877 he joined the Columbus Buckeye team in the International Association. Over the course of his career, he played on a number of other teams, as well.[20]

The common language and cultural tradition shared by Britain and America allowed immigrant artists and actors to engage the arts readily in Ohio and make these notable early contributions. The same was true for those who shaped public opinion through the publishing world. English immigrants especially influenced Ohio's early intellectual and publishing traditions, particularly with newspapers and political commentary. John W. Browne, member of the first Constitutional Convention and an important early abolitionist, was also the founder and editor of *Liberty Hall* in Cincinnati in 1804. His newspaper was wide in scope and contained not only liberal editorials but lengthy and sophisticated contributions on agriculture, biographies of notable people, and works on philosophy, science, and poetry. He also gave ample opportunity for people of different points of view to voice their opinions. Browne had developed his liberal politics in England and carried them to Ohio. He was fearless, even caustic in his editorials, and he clearly showed his admiration of Cobbett and other English radicals.[21]

The most important early publisher in Chillicothe and Columbus was John Bailhache, born on the Channel Island of Jersey in 1787 to a family with Norman origins and ancestral lands. Rejecting the farming life in Jersey, he instead became a printer's apprentice. In 1810 he accompanied his uncle, a native of nearby Guernsey Island, to Guernsey County, Ohio. After a brief stint in the family salt-making business, Bailhache joined the staff of the *Fredonian*, one of Chillicothe's first newspapers. He eventually bought a half interest in it, merged first with the Republican *Scioto Gazette*, and then with the Federalist *Supporter* in 1821. In 1825 his firm bought the *Columbus Gazette* and reorganized it into the *Ohio State Journal*, which he edited until 1835. After serving as mayor of Columbus, he moved to Illinois.

Bailhache's legacy to Ohio journalism is significant. A Whig and staunch supporter of William Henry Harrison and Henry Clay, Bailhache took very seriously the responsibilities of a free press as an essential forum for a free republic and brought high literary standards to the *Ohio State Journal*. He also promoted toleration for Catholics—something lacking in much of American society at the time—and helped establish the tradition in Ohio journalism of dignity and good sense. Though some condemned him as a "vagrant foreigner" for supporting the War of 1812, he was recognized by his peers as one who "stood at the head of the editorial corps in Ohio."[22]

Publishing and politics often went hand in hand for Britons in Ohio. Samuel Tizzard, who departed from Somerset in 1801, first lived in Pennsylvania as a printer's apprentice. In 1814 he joined the westward movement into Ohio and settled near Chillicothe, working the farm he bought and performing typesetting work for local newspapers. In 1819 he was elected to the state legislature, and while in office bought the equipment of a struggling newspaper and issued the first *Eaton Weekly Register* in Preble County. Though raised an Episcopalian he adopted Universalism and championed its cause, so in 1827—while publishing the *Register*—Tizzard also joined other publishers to produce the *Star of the West*, a popular religious newspaper of the Universalist faith. In 1830 he moved the *Star of the West* to Cincinnati. He continued the *Register* into the mid-1840s and "exerted a potent political influence" in Ohio. He was appointed an associate judge for Preble County and died in 1844. His son William followed in his steps as an influential journalist and publisher.[23]

Alfred Burnett was another English immigrant who was an actor, publisher, and journalist. Born in Suffolk in 1824, he was sent to live with an aunt in New York City and then moved to Ohio in 1836. The young man developed his skills as an actor and entertainer in Cincinnati, playing *Hamlet* at Wood's Theatre in the 1840s. He even performed in an acting tour of Europe in 1850 and then returned to Ohio to pursue publishing. In 1850 he edited the *Warning Bell*, a literary magazine, and five years later began the *Cincinnati Home Journal*, billed as a "literary, musical, and temperance register." Burnett was a longtime abolitionist, and in 1843 he helped protect a fugitive slave from a Cincinnati mob. When war broke out he enlisted in the 6th Ohio Volunteer Infantry, fought in West Virginia, rose to captain, and served as a war correspondent for Cincinnati's newspapers. After the Civil War he returned to acting and moved to New

York City. Meanwhile other important newspapers were published by English immigrants, among them the *Chillicothe Advertiser* under the ownership and editorship of Dr. Clement W. Pine, who was highly regarded for being widely informed and an excellent writer.[24]

The *Stark County Democrat* was an important Ohio newspaper very much associated with British immigrants. It was founded in 1848 by Scottish immigrants John McGregor and his son Archibald. The elder McGregor was a graduate of the University of Glasgow, a teacher by profession, but also a staunch republican and leader of the Radical party in Lanarkshire, which was dedicated to disestablishing the British monarchy. To escape imprisonment he and his family fled to America in the 1820s, settling first in Vermont, then in northeastern Ohio. There the McGregors resumed their political activism and started their successful publishing careers. Archibald, though living most of his life in Ohio, was still "every inch a Scotchman," and proud of it. He resided over the local Burns Club and wrote and delivered poetry extolling the virtues of his homeland, though his loyalty to his adopted country was never in doubt.[25]

The *Stark County Democrat* attracted other British publishers, including Major C. H. Mathews, son of a Bristol publisher who trained him well. After arriving in the United States in 1833, Mathews resumed his career at the *Stark County Democrat* and then set out on his own, creating the *Ohio Democrat*. This was one of the leading newspapers of eastern Ohio, and became known especially for promoting progressive religious ideas. Mathews was an ardent Democrat, and in 1853 Tuscarawas County voters elected him sheriff. In 1861 he volunteered for the army, was commissioned as captain of Company B in the 8th Regiment Ohio Volunteer Infantry, and became a major in 1862. Like Alfred Burnett, C. H. Mathews was a publisher who also had acting skills, for he also became known for his fine performances in local amateur theater.[26]

One of Ohio's most influential publishers, who was also deeply involved with politics after the Civil War, was the Englishman John Hopley. Born to a surgeon in the Royal Navy in 1821, he received a first-class education at the Royal Naval College near London and developed talents as a writer and political thinker. At twenty-one he immigrated with an uncle to Zanesville, where he clerked, taught school, and studied law. He also taught for a while in Tennessee because he was curious about a society based on the system of slavery. After teaching mathematics in Columbus, Hopley came to Bucyrus as superintendent of schools and did much to improve the system. Admitted to the bar in 1858, he was appointed by Salmon P. Chase to the office of the second auditor of the U.S. Treasury. He later worked for banks in New York, and was appointed bank examiner for much of the southern United States, but returned to Bucyrus and bought the *Bucyrus Journal* in 1867. Under Hopley's editorship the *Journal* was largely political and Republican in nature. Hopley was actively involved with the party and penned many of its platforms for state elections. He also helped write much of the nation's protectionist tariff legislation of the period, having many friends in the business and government world. He played a major role in shaping Ohio public opinion in a conservative, pro-business direction.[27]

CIVIL SERVICE

The British immigrants who entered and led the publishing and political world of Ohio had an influence disproportionate to their numbers. Unlike immigrants from other countries who published newspapers for fellow immigrants of their own ethnicity and language, the British wrote for all Ohioans who could read English. Those who entered politics made a similarly broad and formative impact on their communities. Again, these roles were facilitated by their shared political, religious, and linguistic heritage. They served mainly at the local level, as city councilmen, justices of the peace, county commissioners, school directors, sheriffs, mayors, and state senators or representatives. Service in the Civil War and business success were especially conducive to local political leadership. Both Civil War service and local political office brought prominence to Samuel R. Cartwright, a war veteran and successful pottery business owner in East Liverpool who served as president of the city council and trustee of the township. Boot and shoemaker Thomas B. Jones, who came directly from Cardinganshire to Youngstown in 1856, served many terms for the board of education, the state appraising board, and board of commissioners of Mahoning County.[28]

Though John R. Hughes only served as a commissioner for Columbus to superintend the construction of roads, his impact on the city's development was impressive and made him a prominent leader. A poor immigrant from North Wales in 1848, he started out as a nineteen-year-old farm hand in Granville, Ohio. Hughes then took up trunk making, formed a business, bought real estate, and succeeded so spectacularly that he became a major banker and investor. He was esteemed as one of Columbus's more important boosters and philanthropists.[29]

Because many British immigrants were pioneers and early merchants, with a long history of participation in Ohio's development, voters naturally turned to them for political leadership. Though foreign born, they were admired and respected for their association with the growth of their communities and for their success and wealth. Some Britons were among the most revered and knowledgeable of Ohio's inhabitants and were chosen for leadership above

American-born people, many of whom came from other states and were relative newcomers to Ohio. George Laskey, for instance, was born in Devon and
immigrated to Ohio with his parents in 1833 at age nine. The Laskeys were some
of the earliest pioneers of Lucas County, and the father, who had been a mechanic in Devon, became a successful farmer in Ohio. At only thirteen George
left home to accept a clerkship in a store in Grand Rapids, Ohio, and rose
quickly as a partner and storeowner. He and his brother became the largest
merchants of the town. In 1859 voters elected Laskey to the Ohio State Senate as
representative of six counties, where he promoted transportation and the
drainage of wetlands. He also served as county commissioner. In 1866 he and
his brother turned to real estate in Toledo, where they became some of the
wealthiest and most prominent citizens.[30]

Quite a few mayors of Ohio towns and cities hailed from Britain. William
Davis, a Staffordshire ironworker, was elected mayor of Niles, near Youngstown,
after the Civil War. James Sillett, from Suffolk, who served and was wounded in
the Civil War, became a "progressive" mayor of Amelia, in Clermont County, in
1911.[31] An earlier and well-educated English immigrant, Christopher Laybourn,
was even mayor of New York City for two years before settling on a farm in
Clark County. Scots were present in Toledo by 1838, and Alexander Bruce
Brownlee, who emigrated from Falkirk in 1847, gained this city's mayorship just
a decade later—and was reelected in 1859.[32]

Cleveland's impressive progressive reform movement of the early twentieth
century owed much to British immigrants with a liberal stance. By 1910 three-
fourths of Cleveland's population were either immigrants or the children of immigrants, and of these, only 6.3 percent were English, 1.5 percent Scottish, and
.8 percent Welsh. These numbers are especially low in comparison with those
for the Germans (28.6 percent), Austrians (18.4 percent), Hungarians (10.9 percent), Russians (9.4 percent), and Irish (8.6 percent), but British immigrants
still profoundly influenced Cleveland progressivism. English immigrant James
A. Reynolds, a leader of the machinists' union, wrote several labor and welfare
laws and helped lead the movement for women's suffrage. He then served as
state senator. The Scottish immigrant T. Alfred Fleming wrote five measures
during the James Cox administration of 1917–1921. Scotsman Robert Crosser
authored the bill that provided referendum and municipal initiative, and he
represented Cleveland in Congress until 1955. And Welshmen Ralph Wigmore
Edwards and John Evans served in the Ohio House of Representatives.[33]

William Green, the son of English immigrants Hugh and Jane Green—miners near Bristol who emigrated in 1868 because of the exhaustion of the local coal
mines (chapter 5)—grew up in the Coshocton area working in the local mines.

Raised by his strict Baptist parents, Green eventually entered politics and became a prominent member of the state senate, authoring many bills to support labor and regulate dangerous mining conditions. In 1924 he became president of the American Federation of Labor. In that role he opposed militancy among workers to gain their rights of organization and collective bargaining, and preached a Christian ethic of cooperation between labor and management. Green continued to uphold his ideals, but his cautious approach to labor organization among the working classes alienated him from some AFL members in the 1920s and 1930s.[34]

The life of Samuel M. Jones embodies Toledo's progressive history. Better known as "Golden Rule" Jones, he was mayor from 1897 to 1904, instituting reforms and instilling a humanitarian spirit that made him a hero of the city's working class. His was a classic "rags to riches" story. His father, Hugh, was a poor slate mason who lived on Mount Snowdon in Caernarvonshire, North Wales, where he heard stories of local people doing better in the United States. So in 1850 he took his family to do the same. Samuel was not quite four at the time, but his Welsh upbringing and culture never left him; in fact, they continued to be the foundation of his life and career in Ohio. Jones was raised in the Welsh Calvinist Methodist Church, whose evangelical nature, Calvinist doctrine of election and calling, and Methodist doctrines of sanctification all shaped his character and explain much about his career as a businessman and mayor of Toledo. The family first moved to New York, where Samuel worked as a farm laborer. Samuel then worked in the Pennsylvania oil fields, and in 1885 he relocated to Lima, Ohio; there he drilled for gas and oil and helped establish the Ohio Oil Company, a successful business bought by Standard Oil in 1889. Jones also invented several more efficient prospecting devices. In 1892 he moved to Toledo, where he created the Acme Sucker Rod Company, and earned his fortune.[35]

In Ohio Jones's intense religious piety and sense of being called to help transform the world found a clear purpose, especially when the writings of social reformers exposed the worsening plight of the poor in the

Samuel M. Jones—better known as "Golden Rule Jones"—was a well-loved businessman who treated his workers as he himself would want to be treated. The Welsh immigrant also served as Toledo's mayor from 1897 to 1904 and was instrumental in Ohio's progressive politics.

rapidly industrializing United States. He responded by granting his workers what others could only dream about: an eight-hour day, benefits including a paid week of vacation, health care, Christmas bonuses amounting to 5 percent of annual salaries, and picnics and band concerts paid for by the company. Jones refused to employ children or to use time clocks. He also transformed vacant land into Golden Rule Park and Playground for his employees' recreation, and he provided a hall at his factory for workers' club meetings. Unlike virtually all other American big businessmen during the "Gilded Age," Jones actually urged his workers to join unions, and he marched with them in Labor Day parades. At his factory a sign proclaimed Jones's motto: "The Business of this shop is to make men; the making of money is only an incidental detail." His uniquely benevolent employment policies earned the nickname "Golden Rule."

As the Welshman's popularity grew with Toledo's working class, the Republican party took notice and nominated him for mayor—in spite of his "radical measures" favoring workers—because he was considered a sufficiently pro-business candidate who could attract enough blue-collar voters to win. Jones did not appeal to every worker by any means. Democratic candidates viciously attacked him for selling out to the Republicans. But Jones was elected four times and left an indelible impression on the city's political and social history. As mayor he brought the eight-hour workday and the minimum wage to municipal workers. He also built public baths, playgrounds, and free kindergartens for Toledo's poor.

Samuel Jones's sympathy with Toledo's poor was also evident in his order for the police to trade in their billy clubs for light canes, which inflicted much less bodily harm. He curtailed arrests for loitering because such arrests tended to victimize the poor. And as mayor he served as police judge and was known for his leniency. Perhaps he was too lenient. He dismissed every case that came to him in February of 1902, and on his desk a sign read, "Judge not that ye be judged."

Jones's leniency and mercy, sympathy for the poor, and his preference for Christian socialism over capitalism made him the enemy of many of Toledo's wealthy citizens. For that reason the Republican Party had second thoughts about their man and refused to nominate him for reelection in 1899. So Jones ran as an independent and won again by a landslide. He received more than twice the number of votes than did the Republican and Democratic candidates combined. Jones successfully ran as an independent again in 1901 and 1903. He even took his reform message to the entire nation. He made a speaking tour of the East Coast in 1899, published writings on workers' social injustice, and in 1900 campaigned vigorously for William Jennings Bryan.

For all of his reform-minded activism, Samuel M. Jones's attempts to re-form the municipal government did not fully succeed. Nor did his attempts to have the city own public utilities. But in an age of laissez-faire and Social Dar-winist philosophy, he was remarkably successful in crusading for his "Golden Rule" principles that protected workers' rights and livelihoods; and he probably would have made even greater progress on that front had he not contracted sev-eral illnesses and died in 1904.[36]

That "Golden Rule" Jones crusaded for the common worker and yet was a Republican in name only is especially revealing. His sympathy was with the poor while his instincts were to be a Republican. Relatively few—perhaps less than 10 percent—of the British immigrants in Ohio politics were Democrats. Captain William Benjamin Williams, a Welsh-born forty-niner and Civil War hero elected several times as City Marshall for Portsmouth, was a relatively rare example.[37] While the Democratic Party attracted most immigrants, Catholics, and others outside the American elite, the Whigs and especially the Republicans appealed more to native whites, those who were part of the cultural and politi-cal mainstream, and the British overwhelmingly joined that party—the only immigrants to do so.

By their electoral and political behavior the British in Ohio showed they were already part of the American mainstream and thought much like the Anglo American majority.[38] In their view of politics, government, and society they clearly had much in common with the descendents of the early waves of British immigrants who established America's colonial regional cultures. Their reli-gious, linguistic, and cultural similarities with most American-born Ohioans led to common political affiliations because Protestant churches and the English language were especially conducive to similar ways of political behavior.[39]

They were newcomers, and yet in a real sense they were not. As immigrants they were mostly invisible, but as Buckeyes they were highly visible and influ-ential in forging the culture, society, and economy of Ohio.

Conclusion

ROM their first arrival in the early eighteenth century until well into the twentieth, Britons were at the center of Ohio history. As a strategic part of the British Empire, as a territory and then state of the United States, through its development as one of the most populous and important industrial regions of America, Ohio made these transitions with an extraordinary amount of influence and effort from British immigrants. They helped create a culture and society presumed as "American," which it indeed was. But they also helped forge a culture that owed much to Britain for its political and legal tradition, its agriculture and especially its industry, its religion and attitudes toward reform and abolition, and its expression in the arts and community involvement. The influx of British people, culture, and institutions that shaped North America in the colonial period continued in Ohio. The casting of Albion's seed did not end in colonial America and did not stop at the Appalachians.

Most of the British Buckeyes were transformed and became Americans, but they had much less adjusting to do than other immigrants. They were entering Ohio along with the descendants of earlier British immigrants to the thirteen colonies. They and their Ohioan neighbors retained more of their British culture than they realized or many cared to admit. Considering that the territorial governor, first state governor, many of the early lawyers, politicians, merchants, newspaper publishers, reformers, ministers and college presidents were either English, Scots, or Welsh—not to mention many of the most important industrialists—it is hard to say just when Ohio stopped being British and became American. Ironically, the British immigrants themselves contributed to Americanization by helping to develop an economy and society that made spectacular growth and a fuller transition to American culture possible.

The farm is central to much of the story. The quest for land motivated so many of these people. Many even tried to make a go of it without prior farm experience, having left some of the most modern and sophisticated parts of Britain, including London, for the Ohio frontier. Doctors, lawyers, actors, even ballet dancers quit their profession to farm in Ohio. And some retired early from hugely successful careers in industry and finance to take up farming—so compelling the land could be. But most immigrants had some experience on the land, and in general, they were successful farmers in Ohio. They succeeded in part by getting help and advice from family members and old friends who had preceded them, and often by adopting American methods. Among them were quite a few who could show the Ohioans much about drainage, livestock, progressive farming methods, soil conservation, and how to create a model farm. Many were severely tested by the primitive conditions and strange surroundings. The work was harder than they had imagined, and the need to adopt alien American agricultural methods and attitudes proved that the immigrants had to become truly American farmers—not British farmers in America.

Frederick Jackson Turner could have been referring to some British pioneers in Ohio when he wrote, "at the frontier the environment is at first too strong for the man. He must accept the conditions which it furnishes, or perish. . . . Little by little he transforms the wilderness, but the outcome is not the old Europe. . . . The fact is, that here is a new product that is American."[1] Yet, the distance between being English and American was not so great in language, political culture, religious expression, and general attitude of mind. There was greater cultural continuity and persistence than Turner believed; the frontier did not reshape Ohioans so much that the British newcomers were totally foreign. For most British Buckeyes and their children, especially, becoming American was not a huge step.

In Ohio's skilled crafts and especially her industry, the British played a more distinct role by applying their knowledge, technology, and experience directly to the state's rich resources. When Englishmen discovered the perfect clays of the Ohio River bank near East Liverpool and brought in the talent of Staffordshire potters, the result was a remarkable industrial gift for Ohio. And when highly experienced miners arrived and opened up Ohio's enormous coal reserves to bring that industry into the modern era, the result was again a great boon to the Buckeye State. In iron, steel, tinplating, and other fields as well,

British immigrants brought the latest techniques and technology and made the industries dynamic and productive. And just as important, they brought an awareness and tradition of labor organization that could have come only from Britain, the birthplace of modern industrial unions.

Their personal stories leave the unforgettable impression of mobility, resourcefulness, even restlessness. They moved quickly into fresh opportunities, often combining farming with other occupations. They were an ambitious and dynamic lot. A few ended up engaging in criminal activity and many others either failed or realized they were not cut out for Ohio life and returned to the old country. But many more were industrious and talented. Some of the talent that Britain lost to its competitor across the ocean was sorely missed and contributed to the decline of her economic dominance by the end of the nineteenth century. This is what happened when the Welsh tinplate industry was transplanted to places like Guernsey County, in large part because of American protective tariffs. Here the migration of talent and knowledge virtually ended the industry in one country while simultaneously creating it in another. Some of the innovations in steel production that were brought to northeastern Ohio by British immigrants also transformed that part of the state and contributed to the relative decline of Britain's steel industry, so that by World War I Britain was importing much of its steel from the United States. In London, politicians and other observers who expressed alarm over the loss of some of Britain's ablest people to America had a point.

Aside from their industriousness and talent, the extraordinary character of many British immigrants affected Ohio in ways that are important, though more difficult to assess. In the colorful stories of Nicholas Cresswell and his Indian "bedfellows," Mad Ann Bailey and her exploits with Indians and unruly children, "King Tom Robinson" and his "castle" on the Ohio frontier, Jacob Heatherington and his mule Jack, "Golden Rule" Jones, and so many others, we see the stuff of which legends are made. For generations these people were local household names, and they formed much of the warp in early Ohio's cultural woof. They brought an "Englishness," a "Welshness," a "Scottishness," or the essence of the culture that grew on the islands of Man and Guernsey, to an open and receiving land. Their lives and influences were an important part of Ohio's cultural memory.

The British Buckeyes projected their culture broadly on the Ohio landscape. One of the most important of these influences was religious. When one remembers how central faith was to most Ohioans, the influx of British clergy and parishioners—most of whom had the same religious tradition and shared religious denominations—was highly significant. Scottish Presbyterians and English Methodists made an enormous impact on the early growth of Ohio, often turning ephemeral hamlets into permanent settlements and towns as they imbued these places with their faith and values. For the Welsh settlements, the church was the *sine qua non* of their existence and often the core of their being, which deeply affected their lives, even to the extent of how they farmed and operated their industries.

When religion combined with leadership in Ohio's early academic institutions, its influence took on added dimension, one whose importance to culture is hard to exaggerate. And when we see the extensive British participation in reform movements, especially temperance and abolitionism, we see another way in which the British and American cultures blended. Politically they shared similar attitudes toward the state and its role in reforming society according to higher moral standards, and together they experienced some of the most powerful and salient episodes in American history. It is not surprising in retrospect that the British were overrepresented among Ohio's Civil War soldiers, that they were among the first volunteers, experienced all there was to experience in the conflict, and saw the Civil War as something that transformed the nation and themselves for the better.

Ultimately, one is left with the impression that the British, despite their heterogeneity and remarkably varied backgrounds, were more similar to the native-born Buckeyes than different. The descendants of the old British immigrants of the previous centuries and the fresh immigrants of the eighteenth and nineteenth centuries were closely related. The "folkways" of the colonial immigrants by and large persevered as they were brought to Ohio, and the newer immigrants of the eighteenth and nineteenth centuries reinforced them in many ways. The differences, though sometimes significant, were not as deep as the similarities. What the British Buckeyes did bring was an invaluable wealth of experience and knowledge, energy and passion, and attitudes and ideas that blended well with what they found in their new home and became so formative for the history and culture of Ohio.

Appendix: The County Histories

Because of their "invisible" nature British immigrants are hard to trace. They did not leave behind the extensive ethnic records and publications that other immigrant groups did. Therefore the study of British migration to Ohio requires extensive use of the county histories. The county histories record the migrants' origin (often exact origin—county if not village, town, or city), details about their parents, sometimes their precise reason for emigrating, as well as their age, occupation, family members, and ports of departure and embarkation. Also often included are their routes to Ohio, their occupational adjustments, their religion and politics, their membership in lodges and other organizations, participation in the Civil War or public office, and any notable achievements or interesting life episodes. In short, they are a gold mine of information.

The history of the county histories is itself interesting. They are largely the result of the U.S. centennial celebrations and the heightened awareness and appreciation for local history and early settlers and influential people. During the last quarter of the nineteenth century publishing companies set out to produce histories of most counties of most states—especially in the Midwest and Northeast. Many exhibit high standards of scholarship and include good summaries of the state's or county's history. Most are dominated by short biographies of residents. Apparently, many were financed by people who agreed to buy a copy of the book in exchange for their inclusion. Therefore, the people who appear in them are not a true representative cross section of society. The poor, the failures, the shy, the unconcerned are not among them—though often we have glimpses of relatives who failed and returned to Britain, or immigrants who did experience failure and great hardship before getting it right. And unfortunately, far less is said about women than men. But a remarkably wide variety of people is included—people from every geographic, social, and occupational background. In addition, people of modest success are recorded—small farmers, blacksmiths, miners, and other craftsmen—as are the more affluent and the locally famous. And because the selectivity of the county histories did not affect the background of the people who ended up being featured in them, the population of British immigrants seems to be fairly well represented in Ohio's county histories.[1]

An attempt was made to cover the state thoroughly. Biographies of British immigrants were found in sixty of Ohio's eighty-eight counties (resource limitations and the unavailability or nonexistence of some county histories did not allow every county to be included). This is a wide and thorough cross section of the state. All major towns and cities, rural areas, geographic and topographical areas, varieties of soils, minerals and industries, and rivers and canals are included. A total of 602 English, Welsh, and Scottish immigrants form the sample. A profile of their origins, destination, occupations, and year of migration is provided in the tables that follow.

Ohio

Map of Great Britain, showing counties of high frequency of emigration to Ohio.

Table 1: Distribution of English, Scottish, and Welsh Immigrants in Ohio
by County, 1851 Census.

County	# English	% English	# Scots	% Scots	# Welsh	% Welsh	Total British
Adams	24	.1	14	.07	1	.005	39
Allen	19	.2	6	.05	116	.010	141
Ashland	79	.3	168	.7	–	–	247
Ashtabula	501	–	55	–	–	–	556
Athens	150	.8	10	.05	2	.01	162
Auglaise	39	.3	–	–	3	.03	42
Belmont	338	1.0	83	.2	41	.1	462
Brown	89	.3	32	.1	4	.01	125
Butler	243	.8	43	.1	189	.6	475
Carrol	132	.7	37	.2	–	–	169
Champaign	103	.5	26	.1	13	.07	142
Clark	373	1.7	41	.2	13	.05	427
Clermont	154	.5	71	.2	11	.04	236
Clinton	25	.1	11	.06	2	.01	38
Columbiana	533	1.6	379	1.1	6	.02	918
Coshocton	242	.9	28	.1	23	.09	293
Crawford	99	.5	2	.01	1	.006	102
Cuyahoga	2265	4.7	248	.5	40	.08	2553
Darke	29	.1	1	.005	–	–	30
Defiance	33	.5	2	.03	–	–	35
Delaware	149	.7	9	.04	380	1.7	538
Erie	530	2.9	81	.4	16	.09	627
Fairfield	78	.3	21	.07	5	.02	104
Fayette	24	.2	–	–	1	.009	25
Franklin	216	.5	32	.07	110	.3	358
Fulton	97	1.2	12	.2	3	.04	112
Gallia	92	.5	51	.3	511	3.0	654
Geauga	253	1.4	16	.09	10	.06	279
Greene	108	.5	84	.4	4	.02	196
Guernsey	135	.4	23	.08	4	.01	162
Hamilton	961	.6	189	.1	34	.02	1184
Hancock	67	.4	11	.07	–	–	78
Hardin	121	1.5	7	.08	–	–	128
Harrison	126	.6	18	.09	1	.005	145
Henry	14	.4	14	.4	–	–	28
Highland	49	.2	35	.1	1	.004	85
Hocking	73	.5	8	.06	3	.02	84
Holmes	50	.2	5	.02	7	.03	62
Huron	547	2.1	32	.1	2	.008	581
Jackson	52	.4	4	.03	1048	8.2	1104
Jefferson	343	1.2	182	.6	6	.02	531
Knox	436	1.5	38	.1	13	.05	487
Lake	534	3.6	16	.1	4	.03	554
Lawrence	358	2.3	30	.2	–	–	388

County	# English	% English	# Scots	% Scots	# Welsh	% Welsh	Total British
Licking	399	1.0	50	1.0	761	2.0	1210
Logan	64	.3	59	.3	4	.02	127
Lorain	1224	4.7	39	.1	6	.02	1269
Lucas	272	2.2	27	.2	–	–	299
Madison	67	.7	9	.09	9	.09	85
Mahoning	257	1.1	61	.3	214	.9	532
Marion	154	1.2	14	.1	36	.3	204
Medina	538	2.2	25	.1	2	.008	565
Meigs	165	.9	84	.5	299	1.7	548
Mercer	19	.2	1	.01	–	–	20
Miami	157	.6	19	.08	8	.03	184
Monroe	125	.4	29	.1	4	.01	158
Montgomery	126	.3	5	.01	11	.03	142
Morgan	183	.6	19	.07	3	.01	205
Morrow	76	.4	12	.06	67	.3	155
Muskingum	637	1.4	59	.1	65	.1	761
Ottawa	53	1.6	26	.8	–	–	79
Paulding	10	.6	4	.2	–	–	14
Perry	49	.2	29	.1	1	.005	79
Pickaway	64	.3	22	.1	9	.04	95
Pike	15	.1	12	.1	1	.009	28
Portage	309	1.3	71	.3	434	1.8	814
Preble	38	.2	8	.04	3	.01	49
Putnam	9	.1	3	.04	72	1.0	84
Richland	417	1.4	91	.3	3	.01	511
Ross	136	.4	98	.3	2	.006	236
Sandusky	131	.9	23	.2	7	.05	161
Scioto	155	.8	44	.2	127	.7	326
Seneca	85	.3	13	.05	6	.02	104
Shelby	45	.3	10	.07	3	.02	58
Stark	243	.6	58	.1	7	.02	308
Summit	721	2.6	62	.2	17	.06	800
Trumbull	448	1.5	187	.6	75	.2	710
Tuscarawas	178	.6	38	.1	2	.006	218
Union	80	.7	5	.04	15	.1	100
Van Wert	16	.3	2	.04	35	.7	53
Vinton	59	.6	1	.01	1	.01	61
Warren	148	.6	19	.07	7	.03	174
Washington	341	1.2	289	1.0	16	.05	646
Wayne	195	.6	64	.2	81	.2	340
Williams	39	.5	1	.01	1	.01	41
Wood	131	1.4	121	1.3	–	–	252
Wyandot	48	.4	15	.1	3	.03	66

Source: H. G. H. Wilhelm, *The Origin and Distribution of Settlement Groups: Ohio, 1850* (typescript published by the author, 1982).

Table 2: Distribution of British Immigrants in Ohio by County, 1851 Census.

County	# British	% British	County. Pop.	% Ohio Pop.	% Brit. Pop.
Adams	39	.2	18883	.1	.002
Allen	141	1.2	12109	.6	.007
Ashland	247	1.0	23813	1.2	.01
Ashtabula	556	–	–	–	–
Athens	162	.9	18215	.9	.008
Auglaise	42	.4	11338	.6	.002
Belmont	462	1.3	34600	1.7	.02
Brown	125	.5	27332	1.4	.006
Butler	475	1.5	30789	1.6	.02
Carrol	169	1.0	17685	.9	.008
Champaign	142	.7	19782	1.0	.007
Clark	427	1.9	22178	1.1	.02
Clermont	236	.7	30455	1.5	.01
Clinton	38	.2	18838	1.0	.002
Columbiana	918	2.7	33621	1.7	.05
Coshocton	293	1.1	25674	1.3	.01
Crawford	102	.6	18177	.9	.005
Cuyahoga	2553	5.3	48099	2.4	.1
Darke	30	.1	20276	1.0	.002
Defiance	35	.5	6966	.4	.002
Delaware	538	2.5	21817	1.1	.03
Erie	627	3.4	18568	.9	.03
Fairfield	104	.3	30264	1.5	.005
Fayette	25	.2	12726	.6	.001
Franklin	358	.8	42909	2.2	.02
Fulton	112	1.4	7781	.4	.006
Gallia	654	3.8	17063	.9	.03
Geauga	279	1.6	17827	.9	.01
Greene	196	.9	21946	1.1	.01
Guernsey	162	.5	30438	1.5	.01
Hamilton	1184	.8	156844	7.9	.06
Hancock	78	.5	16751	.8	.004
Hardin	128	1.6	8251	.4	.006
Harrison	145	.7	20157	1.0	.007
Henry	28	.8	3434	.2	.001
Highland	85	.3	25781	1.3	.004
Hocking	84	.6	14119	.7	.004
Holmes	62	.3	20452	1.0	.003
Huron	581	2.2	26203	1.3	.03
Jackson	1104	8.7	12719	.6	.06
Jefferson	531	1.8	29133	1.5	.03
Knox	487	1.7	28872	1.5	.02
Lake	554	3.8	14654	.7	.03
Lawrence	388	2.5	15246	.8	.02

County	# British	% British	County. Pop.	% Ohio Pop.	% Brit. Pop.
Licking	1210	3.1	38846	2.0	.06
Logan	127	.7	19162	1.0	.006
Lorain	1269	4.9	26086	1.3	.06
Lucas	299	2.4	12363	.6	.02
Madison	85	.8	10015	.5	.004
Mahoning	532	2.2	23735	1.2	.03
Marion	204	1.6	12618	.6	.01
Medina	565	2.3	24441	1.2	.03
Meigs	548	3.0	17971	.9	.03
Mercer	20	.3	7712	.4	.001
Miami	184	.7	24999	1.3	.009
Monroe	158	.6	28351	1.4	.008
Montgomery	142	.4	38218	1.9	.007
Morgan	205	.7	28585	1.4	.01
Morrow	155	.8	20280	1.0	.008
Muskingum	761	1.7	45049	2.3	.04
Ottawa	79	2.4	3308	.2	.004
Paulding	14	.8	1766	.09	.001
Perry	79	.4	20775	1.0	.004
Pickaway	95	.5	21006	1.1	.005
Pike	28	.3	10953	.6	.001
Portage	814	3.3	24419	1.2	.04
Preble	49	.2	21736	1.0	.002
Putnam	84	1.2	7221	.4	.004
Richland	511	1.7	30879	1.6	.03
Ross	236	.7	32074	1.6	.01
Sandusky	161	1.1	14305	.7	.01
Scioto	326	1.8	18428	.9	.02
Seneca	104	.4	27104	1.4	.005
Shelby	58	.4	13958	.7	.003
Stark	308	.8	39878	2.0	.02
Summit	800	2.9	27485	1.4	.04
Trumbull	710	2.3	30490	1.5	.04
Tuscarawas	218	.7	31761	1.6	.01
Union	100	.8	12204	.6	.005
Van Wert	53	1.1	4793	.2	.003
Vinton	61	.7	9353	.5	.003
Warren	174	.7	25560	1.3	.009
Washington	646	2.2	29540	1.5	.03
Wayne	340	1.0	32981	1.7	.02
Williams	41	.5	8018	.4	.002
Wood	252	2.8	9157	.5	.01
Wyandot	66	.6	11194	.6	.003

Source: H. G. H. Wilhelm, *The Origin and Distribution of Settlement Groups: Ohio, 1850* (typescript published by the author, 1982).

Table 3: Origins of British Immigrants to Ohio, 1750–1900, by Year.

County of Origin	Number	Percent
ENGLAND		
1. Low-Wage Agricultural Counties		
Bedfordshire	3	0.5
Berkshire	1	0.2
Buckinghamshire	1	0.2
Cambridgeshire	11	1.8
Devonshire	20	3.3
Dorset	–	–
Essex	1	0.2
Hampshire	3	0.5
Herefordshire	4	0.7
Hertfordshire	–	–
Huntingdonshire	2	0.3
Norfolk	6	1.0
Northamptonshire	6	1.0
Oxfordshire	1	0.2
Rutland	–	–
Shropshire	–	–
Somerset	12	1.8
Suffolk	1	0.2
Surrey	2	0.3
Wiltshire	9	1.5
2. High-Wage Agricultural Counties		
Cumberland	9	1.5
Kent	14	2.3
Lincolnshire	33	5.5
Sussex	5	0.8
Westmorland	–	–
3. Low-Wage Industrial Counties		
Cornwall	10	1.7
Gloucestershire	9	1.5
Leicestershire	4	0.7
Warwickshire	7	1.2
Worcestershire	5	0.8
4. High-Wage Industrial Counties		
Cheshire	2	0.3
Derbyshire	1	0.2
Durham	9	1.5
Lancashire	27	4.5
London	22	3.7
Middlesex	1	0.2
Northumberland	10	1.7

County of Origin	Number	Percent
Nottinghamshire	8	1.3
Staffordshire	22	3.7
5. Channel Islands		
Guernsey	3	.5
6. Yorkshire	40	6.6
*7. England N.O.D.**	60	10.0
England Total:	384	63.8
SCOTLAND		
1. Agricultural Counties		
Aberdeenshire	4	0.7
Argyllshire	1	0.2
Banffshire	1	0.2
Berwickshire	–	–
Caithness	1	0.2
Elgin	–	–
Haddington	1	0.2
Inverness	2	0.3
Kincardine	1	0.2
Kinross	1	0.2
Kirkcudbright	–	–
Nairnshire	1	0.2
Orkney and Shetland	–	–
Ross and Cromarty	1	0.2
Sutherland	1	0.2
Wigtownshire	1	0.2
2. Industrial Counties		
Ayrshire	4	0.7
Bute	–	–
Clackmannan	–	–
Dumfriesshire	1	0.2
Dunbartonshire	1	0.2
Edinburgh	9	1.5
Fifeshire	8	1.3
Forfar	–	–
Lanarkshire	9	0.7
Linlithgow	–	–
Peeblesshire	–	–
Perthshire	3	0.5
Renfrewshire	1	0.2
Roxburghshire	1	0.2
Selkirkshire	1	0.2
Stirlingshire	4	0.7
3. Scotland N.O.D.	36	6.0
Scotland Total:	94	15.6

County of Origin	Number	Percent
WALES		
1. North Wales	4	0.7
Anglesey	1	0.2
Caernarvon	1	0.2
Denbigh	1	0.2
Flint	–	–
Merioneth	–	–
Montgomery	16	2.7
2. South Wales	15	2.5
Brecon	8	1.3
Cardigan	12	2.0
Carmarthen	8	1.3
Glamorgan	13	2.2
Monmouth	15	2.5
Pembroke	1	0.2
Radnor	4	0.7
3. Wales N.O.D.	25	4.2
Wales Total:	124	20.6
Grand Total:	602	100

Source: County Histories
*Not Otherwise Defined.

Table 4: Settlement of British Immigrants, by Year.

Ohio County	NOD	1700s	1800–20s	1830s	1840s	1850s	1860s	1870s	1880s	1890s	Total	Percent
Adams*	–	–	–	–	–	–	–	–	–	–	0	0
Allen	–	–	–	–	2	1	–	–	–	–	3	0.5
Ashland	–	–	–	–	–	–	1	–	–	–	1	0.2
Ashtabula	–	–	–	–	–	1	–	–	–	–	1	0.2
Athens*	–	–	–	–	–	–	–	–	–	–	0	0.0
Auglaize	1	–	1	1	–	1	–	–	–	–	4	0.7
Belmont	–	–	2	3	5	3	–	4	2	–	19	3.2
Brown	–	–	–	–	1	–	–	–	–	–	1	0.2
Butler	–	1	–	–	–	–	–	–	–	–	1	0.2
Carroll	–	–	–	–	–	–	–	1	1	–	2	0.3
Champaign*	–	–	–	–	–	–	–	–	–	–	0	0.0
Clarke	–	2	3	2	1	–	1	–	2	–	11	1.8
Clermont	–	1	1	–	–	1	–	–	–	–	3	0.5
Clinton	–	–	–	–	1	1	1	–	–	–	3	0.5
Columbiana	–	–	–	–	2	–	–	2	–	–	4	0.7
Coshocton	–	1	–	–	4	1	–	–	–	–	6	1.0
Crawford	–	–	2	1	5	7	–	2	1	–	18	3.0
Cuyahoga	–	–	–	–	1	1	–	–	–	–	2	0.3
Darke	–	–	–	–	–	1	–	–	–	–	1	0.2
Defiance	–	–	1	2	–	–	–	–	–	–	3	0.5
Delaware	–	1	10	9	8	3	1	–	–	–	32	5.3
Erie	–	–	–	2	4	3	–	–	–	–	9	1.5
Fairfield	–	–	4	1	–	2	2	1	–	–	10	1.7
Fayette	–	–	–	–	–	1	–	–	–	–	1	0.2
Franklin	–	1	–	1	1	4	1	5	4	1	18	3.0
Fulton*	–	–	–	–	–	–	–	–	–	–	0	0.0
Gallia	1	–	–	2	2	3	–	1	–	–	9	1.5
Geauga*	–	–	–	–	–	–	–	–	–	–	0	0.0
Greene	–	2	4	1	–	–	1	–	–	–	8	1.3
Guernsey	–	–	3	1	–	–	2	5	3	4	18	3.0
Hamilton	–	–	–	–	–	1	–	–	–	–	1	0.2
Hancock	–	–	–	–	1	2	1	–	–	–	4	0.7
Hardin	–	–	2	3	–	4	1	–	–	–	10	1.7
Harrison	–	–	3	3	1	–	1	–	–	–	8	1.3
Henry*	–	–	–	–	–	–	–	–	–	–	0	0.0
Highland*	–	–	–	–	–	–	–	–	–	–	0	0.0
Hocking*	–	–	–	–	–	–	–	–	–	–	0	0.0
Holmes*	–	–	–	–	–	–	–	–	–	–	0	0.0
Huron	–	–	–	1	6	10	–	2	2	–	21	3.5
Jackson*	–	–	–	–	–	–	–	–	–	–	0	0.0
Jefferson	–	1	8	1	1	4	2	–	–	–	17	2.8
Knox	–	–	1	2	4	1	–	–	–	–	8	1.3
Lake*	–	–	–	–	–	–	–	–	–	–	0	0.0
Lawrence*	–	–	–	–	–	–	–	–	–	–	0	0.0
Licking	–	2	–	2	2	1	–	2	–	–	9	1.5

Ohio County	NOD	1700s	1800–20s	1830s	1840s	1850s	1860s	1870s	1880s	1890s	Total	Percent
Logan*	–	–	–	–	–	–	–	–	–	–	0	0.0
Lorain*	–	–	–	–	–	–	–	–	–	–	0	0.0
Lucas	–	–	–	7	2	3	–	1	–	–	13	2.2
Madison	–	1	1	2	2	3	3	–	–	–	12	2.0
Mahoning	–	–	–	1	5	9	11	2	–	–	28	4.7
Marion	–	–	–	–	2	–	–	–	–	–	2	0.3
Medina*	–	–	–	–	–	–	–	–	–	–	0	0.0
Meigs	–	–	–	–	–	2	–	–	–	–	2	0.3
Mercer*	–	–	–	–	–	–	–	–	–	–	0	0.0
Miami	–	–	2	–	1	2	1	2	5	–	13	2.2
Monroe*	–	–	–	–	–	–	–	–	–	–	0	0.0
Montgomery	–	–	–	–	1	–	–	–	–	–	1	0.2
Morgan	–	2	3	–	–	–	–	–	–	–	5	0.8
Morrow*	–	–	–	–	–	–	–	–	–	–	0	0.0
Muskingum*	–	–	–	–	–	–	–	–	–	–	0	0.0
Noble*	–	–	–	–	–	–	–	–	–	–	0	0.0
Ottawa*	–	–	–	–	–	–	–	–	–	–	0	0.0
Paulding*	–	–	–	–	–	–	–	–	–	–	0	0.0
Perry	–	–	–	–	5	5	9	12	–	–	31	5.1
Pickaway	–	–	–	2	1	3	–	–	–	–	6	1.0
Pike*	–	–	–	–	–	–	–	–	–	–	0	0.0
Portage	–	–	–	1	2	1	–	–	–	–	4	0.7
Preble	–	–	1	–	–	–	–	–	–	–	1	0.2
Putnam*	–	–	–	–	–	–	–	–	–	–	0	0.0
Richland	–	–	5	7	3	3	1	2	1	–	22	3.7
Ross	–	2	–	–	–	–	–	–	–	–	2	0.3
Sandusky*	–	–	–	–	–	–	–	–	–	–	0	0.0
Scioto	1	–	2	8	7	2	1	1	–	–	22	3.7
Seneca	1	–	–	–	–	–	1	1	2	–	5	0.8
Shelby	–	–	1	–	–	–	–	–	–	–	1	0.2
Stark	–	–	–	–	1	–	2	–	–	–	3	0.5
Summit	–	–	–	2	10	6	6	8	7	–	39	6.5
Trumbull	–	–	–	–	1	4	1	–	–	–	6	1.0
Tuscarawas	–	1	–	1	1	1	1	–	–	–	5	0.8
Union	–	–	1	2	1	1	1	–	–	–	6	1.0
Van Wert	–	–	1	2	4	1	–	1	1	–	10	1.7
Vinton*	–	–	–	–	–	–	–	–	–	–	0	0.0
Warren	1	1	–	–	1	3	–	–	–	–	6	1.0
Washington	–	–	–	–	2	3	1	2	–	1	9	1.5
Wayne	–	2	3	2	1	–	–	–	–	–	8	1.3
Williams	–	–	–	4	4	5	2	1	–	–	16	2.7
Wood	–	–	1	7	12	22	3	4	–	–	49	8.1
Wyandot	–	–	3	1	1	1	–	–	–	–	6	1.0
N.O.D.	–	1	2	–	–	–	–	–	–	–	3	0.5
Grand Total											602	100.0

Source: County Histories

Table 5: Occupation of British Immigrants, by Year.

Occupation in GB	Unk.	1700s	1800–20s	1830s	1840s	1850s	1860s	1870s	1880s	1890s	Total	Percent
1. Agriculture	1	1	8	10	17	18	1	5	3	1	65	18.3
2. Labor	–	–	–	–	2	4	–	–	–	–	6	1.7
3. Service, etc.	–	1	2	–	3	3	1	–	1	–	11	3.1
4. Crafts												
Building	1	–	1	6	5	4	5	4	4	–	30	8.4
Mining	–	–	–	1	10	10	16	17	6	–	60	16.9
Food	–	–	1	3	4	8	2	1	–	–	19	5.3
Metal	–	–	2	5	3	7	1	–	–	–	18	5.1
Clothing	–	1	4	5	1	3	3	2	–	–	19	5.3
Woodworking	–	–	2	3	2	2	1	–	–	–	10	2.8
Miscellaneous	–	–	–	1	–	–	1	1	–	–	3	0.8
Mechanic	–	–	–	1	–	–	–	–	–	–	1	0.3
5. Industry												
Textiles	1	–	6	1	1	2	–	1	–	–	12	3.4
Iron/steel and												
engineering	–	–	2	2	9	6	8	6	4	–	441	11.5
Miscellaneous	–	–	1	1	5	–	–	2	–	–	9	2.5
6. Commerce/												
professions	–	4	11	10	5	10	3	5	3	1	52	14.6
Grand Total										356	100	

Source: County Histories

*County unrepresented in study.

Table 6: Origins of British Immigrants, by Occupational Class.

County of Origin	Agriculture	Labor	Service	Crafts	Industry	Commerce/ Professions	Unknown	Total	Percent
ENGLAND									
1. Low-Wage Agricultural Counties									
Bedfordshire	1	–	–	–	–	–	2	3	0.5
Berkshire	–	–	–	–	–	–	1	1	0.2
Buckinghamshire	–	–	–	1	–	–	–	1	0.2
Cambridgeshire	2	–	1	3	–	–	5	11	1.8
Devonshire	3	–	–	6	–	–	11	20	3.3
Dorset	–	–	–	–	–	–	–	–	–
Essex	–	–	–	–	–	1	–	1	0.2
Hampshire	–	–	–	1	–	1	1	3	0.5
Herefordshire	1	–	1	–	–	1	1	4	0.7
Hertfordshire	–	–	–	–	–	–	–	–	–
Huntingdonshire	1	–	–	–	–	–	1	2	0.3
Norfolk	–	1	–	1	–	–	4	6	1.0
Northamptonshire	–	–	–	4	–	–	2	6	1.0
Oxfordshire	1	–	–	–	–	–	–	1	0.2
Rutland	–	–	–	–	–	–	–	–	–
Shropshire	–	–	–	–	–	–	–	–	–
Somerset	–	1	–	3	–	2	6	12	2.0
Suffolk	1	–	–	–	–	–	–	1	0.2
Surrey	–	–	–	1	–	–	1	2	0.3
Wiltshire	–	–	–	4	–	2	3	9	1.5
2. High-Wage Agricultural Counties									
Cumberland	2	–	–	3	–	1	3	9	1.5
Kent	3	–	–	2	–	1	8	14	2.3
Lincolnshire	7	3	–	3	–	–	20	33	5.5
Sussex	1	–	1	–	–	–	3	5	0.8
Westmorland	–	–	–	–	–	–	–	–	–
3. Low-Wage Industrial Counties									
Cornwall	1	–	1	5	–	1	2	10	1.7
Gloucestershire	–	–	–	5	1	–	3	9	1.5
Leicestershire	1	–	–	2	–	–	1	4	0.7
Warwickshire	–	–	1	2	2	–	2	7	1.2
Worcestershire	–	–	–	2	1	–	2	5	0.8
4. High-Wage Industrial Counties									
Cheshire	–	–	–	–	1	–	1	2	0.3
Derbyshire	–	–	–	–	1	–	–	1	0.2
Durham	–	–	–	6	1	1	1	9	1.5
Lancashire	–	–	1	9	5	3	9	27	4.5

County of Origin	Agriculture	Labor	Service	Crafts	Industry	Commerce/ Professions	Unknown	Total	Percent
London	–	–	–	3	1	6	12	22	3.7
Middlesex	–	–	–	–	–	1	–	1	0.2
Northumberland	1	–	–	8	–	–	1	10	1.7
Nottinghamshire	1	–	–	2	1	–	4	8	1.3
Staffordshire	–	–	–	8	10	–	4	22	3.7
5. Channel Islands									
Guernsey	1	–	–	–	–	–	2	3	0.5
6. Yorkshire	5	1	2	6	6	4	16	40	6.6
7. England N.O.D.	7	–	2	8	6	5	32	60	10.0
England Total:	40	6	10	98	36	30	164	384	63.8

SCOTLAND

1. Agricultural
Counties

Aberdeenshire	–	–	–	2	1	–	1	4	0.7
Argyllshire	–	–	–	1	–	–	–	1	0.2
Banffshire	–	–	–	1	–	–	–	1	0.2
Berwickshire	–	–	–	–	–	–	–	–	–
Caithness	–	–	–	–	–	–	1	1	0.2
Elgin	–	–	–	–	–	–	–	–	–
Haddington	–	–	–	1	–	–	–	1	0.2
Inverness	–	–	–	–	–	–	2	2	0.3
Kincardine	–	–	–	1	–	–	–	1	0.2
Kinross	–	–	–	–	–	–	1	1	0.2
Kirkcudbright	–	–	–	–	–	–	–	–	–
Nairnshire	–	–	–	–	–	–	1	1	0.2
Orkney and Shetland	–	–	–	–	–	–	–	–	–
Ross and Cromarty	–	–	–	1	–	–	–	1	0.2
Sutherland	–	–	–	–	–	1	–	1	0.2
Wigtownshire	1	–	–	–	–	–	–	1	0.2
2. Industrial Counties									
Ayrshire	–	–	–	2	2	–	–	4	0.7
Bute	–	–	–	–	–	–	–	–	–
Clackmannan	–	–	–	–	–	–	–	–	–
Dumfriesshire	1	–	–	–	–	–	–	1	0.2
Dunbartonshire	–	–	–	–	1	–	–	1	0.2
Edinburgh	1	–	1	3	–	1	3	9	1.5
Fifeshire	–	–	–	5	–	–	3	8	1.3
Forfar	–	–	–	–	–	–	–	–	–
Lanarkshire	1	–	–	1	4	1	2	9	1.5
Linlithgow	–	–	–	–	–	–	–	–	–
Peeblesshire	–	–	–	–	–	–	–	–	–
Perthshire	–	–	–	–	1	1	1	3	0.5
Renfrewshire	–	–	–	–	1	–	–	1	0.2
Roxburghshire	–	–	–	1	–	–	–	1	0.2

County of Origin	Agriculture	Labor	Service	Crafts	Industry	Commerce/ Professions	Unknown	Total	Percent
Selkirkshire	1	–	–	–	–	–	–	1	0.2
Stirlingshire	1	–	–	–	2	–	1	4	0.7
3. Scotland N.O.D.	5	–	–	4	3	4	20	36	6.0
Scotland Total:	11	0	1	23	15	8	36	94	15.6
WALES									
1. North Wales	–	–	–	2	–	–	2	4	0.7
Anglesey	–	–	–	1	–	–	–	1	0.2
Caernarvon	1	–	–	–	–	–	–	1	0.2
Denbigh	1	–	–	–	–	–	–	1	0.2
Flint	–	–	–	–	–	–	–	–	–
Merioneth	–	–	–	–	–	–	–	–	–
Montgomery	4	–	–	3	1	–	8	16	2.7
2. South Wales	–	–	–	5	2	1	7	15	2.5
Brecon	3	–	–	2	–	–	3	8	1.3
Cardigan	1	–	–	4	2	1	4	12	2.0
Carmarthen	–	–	–	1	1	5	1	8	1.3
Glamorgan	2	–	–	7	1	1	2	13	2.2
Monmouth	–	–	–	6	3	–	6	15	2.5
Pembroke	–	–	–	–	–	–	1	1	0.2
Radnor	–	–	–	1	–	1	2	4	0.7
3. Wales N.O.D.	1	–							
Wales Total:	13	0	0	39	11	13	48	124	20.6
Grand Total:	64	6	11	160	62	51	248	602	100

Source: County Histories

Table 7: Origins of British Industrial Immigrants to Ohio, 1750–1900.

County of Origin	Textiles	Miners	Quarriers	Ironworkers	Other Industry	Total	Percent
ENGLAND							
1. Low-Wage Agricultural Counties							
Bedfordshire	–	–	–	–	–	–	–
Berkshire	–	–	–	–	–	–	–
Buckinghamshire	–	–	–	–	–	–	–
Cambridgeshire	–	–	–	–	–	–	–
Devonshire	–	–	2	–	–	2	1.6
Dorset	–	–	–	–	–	–	–
Essex	–	–	–	–	–	–	–
Hampshire	–	–	–	–	–	–	–
Herefordshire	–	–	–	–	–	–	–
Hertfordshire	–	–	–	–	–	–	–
Huntingdonshire	–	–	–	–	–	–	–
Norfolk	–	–	–	–	–	–	–
Northamptonshire	–	–	–	–	–	–	–
Oxfordshire	–	–	–	–	–	–	–
Rutland	–	–	–	–	–	–	–
Shropshire	–	–	–	–	–	–	–
Somerset	–	1	1	–	–	2	1.6
Suffolk	–	–	–	–	–	–	–
Surrey	–	–	–	–	–	–	–
Wiltshire	–	–	2	–	–	2	1.6
2. High-Wage Agricultural Counties							
Cumberland	–	3	–	–	–	3	2.4
Kent	–	–	–	–	–	–	–
Lincolnshire	–	–	–	–	–	–	–
Sussex	–	–	–	–	–	–	–
Westmorland	–	–	–	–	–	–	–
3. Low-Wage Industrial Counties							
Cornwall	–	1	–	–	–	1	0.8
Gloucestershire	–	2	–	–	1	3	2.4
Leicestershire	–	–	–	–	–	–	–
Warwickshire	–	1	–	–	2	3	2.4
Worcestershire	–	–	–	1	–	1	0.8
4. High-Wage Industrial Counties							
Cheshire	–	–	–	–	1	1	0.8
Derbyshire	1	–	–	–	–	1	0.8
Durham	–	3	–	1	–	4	3.2
Lancashire	2	3	2	–	2	9	7.3
London	–	–	–	–	1	1	0.8

County of Origin	Textiles	Miners	Quarriers	Ironworkers	Other Industry	Total	Percent
Middlesex	–	–	–	–	–	–	–
Northumberland	–	7	–	–	–	7	5.6
Nottinghamshire	–	–	–	–	1	1	0.8
Staffordshire	–	2	–	5	2	9	7.3
5. Channel Islands							
Guernsey	–	–	–	–	–	–	–
6. Yorkshire	3	2	1	–	3	9	7.3
7. England N.O.D.	2	1	1	2	2	8	6.5
Total English:	8	26	9	9	15	67	54.0
SCOTLAND							
1. Agricultural							
Counties							
Aberdeenshire	–	–	–	1	–	1	0.8
Argyllshire	–	–	–	–	–	–	–
Banffshire	–	–	–	–	–	–	–
Berwickshire	–	–	–	–	–	–	–
Caithness	–	–	–	–	–	–	–
Elgin	–	–	–	–	–	–	–
Haddington	–	–	–	–	–	–	–
Inverness	–	–	–	–	–	–	–
Kincardine	–	–	1	–	–	1	0.8
Kinross	–	–	–	–	–	–	–
Kirkcudbright	–	–	–	–	–	–	–
Nairnshire	–	–	–	–	–	–	–
Orkney and Shetland	–	–	–	–	–	–	–
Ross and Cromarty	–	–	–	–	–	–	–
Sutherland	–	–	–	–	–	–	–
Wigtownshire	–	–	–	–	–	–	–
2. Industrial Counties							
Ayrshire	1	1	1	–	1	4	3.2
Bute	–	–	–	–	–	–	–
Clackmannan	–	–	–	–	–	–	–
Dumfriesshire	–	–	–	–	–	–	–
Dunbartonshire	–	–	–	–	1	1	0.8
Edinburgh	–	1	1	–	–	2	1.6
Fifeshire	–	2	–	–	–	2	1.6
Forfar	–	–	–	–	–	–	–
Lanarkshire	–	1	–	1	1	3	2.4
Linlithgow	–	–	–	–	–	–	–
Peeblesshire	–	–	–	–	–	–	–
Perthshire	–	–	–	–	1	1	0.8
Renfrewshire	–	–	–	–	1	1	0.8
Roxburghshire	–	–	–	–	–	–	–

County of Origin	Textiles	Miners	Quarriers	Ironworkers	Other Industry	Total	Percent
Selkirkshire	–	–	–	–	–	–	–
Stirlingshire	2	–	–	–	–	2	1.6
3. Scotland N.O.D.	1	2	–	–	2	5	4.0
Total Scots:	4	7	3	2	7	23	18.5
WALES							
1. North Wales	–	1	–	–	–	1	0.8
Anglesey	–	–	–	–	–	–	–
Caernarvon	–	–	–	–	–	–	–
Denbigh	–	–	–	–	–	–	–
Flint	–	–	–	–	–	–	–
Merioneth	–	–	–	–	–	–	–
Montgomery	–	1	–	–	1	2	1.6
2. South Wales	–	1	–	2	–	3	2.4
Brecon	–	1	–	–	–	1	0.8
Cardigan	–	2	1	1	1	5	4.0
Carmarthen	–	1	–	1	–	2	1.6
Glamorgan	–	5	–	–	1	6	4.8
Monmouth	–	5	–	3	–	8	6.5
Pembroke	–	–	–	–	–	–	–
Radnor	–	–	1	–	–	1	0.8
3. Wales N.O.D.	–	4	–	1	–	5	4.0
Total Welsh:	0	21	2	8	3	34	27.4
Total British:						124	100

Source: County Histories

Table 8: Origins of British Agricultural Immigrants to Ohio, 1750–1900.

County of Origin	Unk.	1700s	1800–20s	1830s	1840s	1850s	1860s	1870s	1880s	1890s	Total	Percent
England												
1. Low-Wage												
Agricultural Counties												
Bedfordshire	–	–	–	–	–	1	–	–	–	–	1	1.5
Berkshire	–	–	–	–	–	–	–	–	–	–	–	–
Buckinghamshire	–	–	–	–	–	–	–	–	–	–	–	–
Cambridgeshire	–	–	–	–	–	2	–	–	–	–	2	3.1
Devonshire	–	–	–	2	–	1	–	–	–	–	3	4.6
Dorset	–	–	–	–	–	–	–	–	–	–	–	–
Essex	–	–	–	–	–	–	–	–	–	–	–	–
Hampshire	–	–	–	–	–	–	–	–	–	–	–	–
Herefordshire	–	–	–	–	–	–	–	1	–	–	1	1.5
Hertfordshire	–	–	–	–	–	–	–	–	–	–	–	–
Huntingdonshire	–	–	–	1	–	–	–	–	–	–	1	1.5
Norfolk	–	–	–	–	–	–	–	–	–	–	–	–
Northamptonshire	–	–	–	–	–	–	–	–	–	–	–	–
Oxfordshire	–	–	–	–	–	1	–	–	–	–	1	1.5
Rutland	–	–	–	–	–	–	–	–	–	–	–	–
Shropshire	–	–	–	–	–	–	–	–	–	–	–	–
Somerset	–	–	–	–	–	–	–	–	–	–	–	–
Suffolk	–	–	–	–	–	1	–	–	–	–	1	1.5
Surrey	–	–	–	–	–	–	–	–	–	–	–	–
Wiltshire	–	–	–	–	–	–	–	–	–	–	–	–
2. High-Wage												
Agricultural Counties												
Cumberland	–	1	–	1	–	–	–	–	–	–	2	3.1
Kent	–	–	–	–	1	1	–	–	1	–	3	4.6
Lincolnshire	–	–	–	1	1	3	–	2	–	–	7	10.8
Sussex	–	–	–	–	–	1	–	–	–	–	1	1.5
Westmorland	–	–	–	–	–	–	–	–	–	–	–	–
3. Low-Wage												
Industrial Counties												
Cornwall	–	–	–	–	–	–	1	–	–	–	1	1.5
Gloucestershire	–	–	–	–	–	–	–	–	–	–	–	–
Leicestershire	–	–	–	–	1	–	–	–	–	–	1	1.5
Warwickshire	–	–	–	–	–	–	–	–	–	–	–	–
Worcestershire	–	–	–	–	–	–	–	–	–	–	–	–
4. High-Wage												
Industrial Counties												
Cheshire	–	–	–	–	–	–	–	–	–	–	–	–
Derbyshire	–	–	–	–	–	–	–	–	–	–	–	–
Durham	–	–	–	–	–	–	–	–	–	–	–	–
Lancashire	–	–	–	–	–	–	–	–	–	–	–	–
London	–	–	–	–	–	–	–	–	–	–	–	–

County of Origin	Unk.	1700s	1800–20s	1830s	1840s	1850s	1860s	1870s	1880s	1890s	Total	Percent
Middlesex	–	–	–	–	–	–	–	–	–	–	–	–
Northumberland	–	–	–	1	–	–	–	–	–	–	1	1.5
Nottinghamshire	–	–	–	–	1	–	–	–	–	–	1	1.5
Staffordshire	–	–	–	–	–	–	–	–	–	–	–	–
5. Channel Islands												
Guernsey	–	–	1	–	–	–	–	–	–	–	1	1.5
6. Yorkshire	–	–	3	1	–	1	–	–	–	–	5	7.7
7. England N.O.D.	–	–	1	–	3	1	–	–	2	–	7	10.8
England Total:	0	1	5	7	7	13	1	3	3	0	40	61.5

SCOTLAND
1. Agricultural Counties

County of Origin	Unk.	1700s	1800–20s	1830s	1840s	1850s	1860s	1870s	1880s	1890s	Total	Percent
Aberdeenshire	–	–	–	–	–	–	–	–	–	–	–	–
Argyllshire	–	–	–	–	–	–	–	–	–	–	–	–
Banffshire	–	–	–	–	–	–	–	–	–	–	–	–
Berwickshire	–	–	–	–	–	–	–	–	–	–	–	–
Caithness	–	–	–	–	–	–	–	–	–	–	–	–
Elgin	–	–	–	–	–	–	–	–	–	–	–	–
Haddington	–	–	–	–	–	–	–	–	–	–	–	–
Inverness	–	–	–	–	–	–	–	–	–	–	–	–
Kincardine	–	–	–	–	–	–	–	–	–	–	–	–
Kinross	–	–	–	–	–	–	–	–	–	–	–	–
Kirkcudbright	–	–	–	–	–	–	–	–	–	–	–	–
Nairnshire	–	–	–	–	–	–	–	–	–	–	–	–
Orkney and Shetland	–	–	–	–	–	–	–	–	–	–	–	–
Ross and Cromarty	–	–	–	–	–	–	–	–	–	–	–	–
Sutherland	–	–	–	–	–	–	–	–	–	–	–	–
Wigtownshire	–	–	–	–	–	1	–	–	–	–	1	1.5

2. Industrial Counties

County of Origin	Unk.	1700s	1800–20s	1830s	1840s	1850s	1860s	1870s	1880s	1890s	Total	Percent
Ayrshire	–	–	–	–	–	–	–	–	–	–	–	–
Bute	–	–	–	–	–	–	–	–	–	–	–	–
Clackmannan	–	–	–	–	–	–	–	–	–	–	–	–
Dumfriesshire	–	–	–	1	–	–	–	–	–	–	1	1.5
Dunbartonshire	–	–	–	–	–	–	–	–	–	–	–	–
Edinburgh	–	–	–	1	–	–	–	–	–	–	1	1.5
Fifeshire	–	–	–	–	–	–	–	–	–	–	–	–
Forfar	–	–	–	–	–	–	–	–	–	–	–	–
Lanarkshire	–	–	–	–	1	–	–	–	–	–	1	1.5
Linlithgow	–	–	–	–	–	–	–	–	–	–	–	–
Peeblesshire	–	–	–	–	–	–	–	–	–	–	–	–
Perthshire	–	–	–	–	–	–	–	–	–	–	–	–
Renfrewshire	–	–	–	–	–	–	–	–	–	–	–	–
Roxburghshire	–	–	–	–	–	–	–	–	–	–	–	–
Selkirkshire	–	–	1	–	–	–	–	–	–	–	1	1.5
Stirlingshire	–	–	–	–	1	–	–	–	–	–	1	1.5
3. Scotland N.O.D.	–	–	–	1	–	3	–	–	–	1	5	7.7
Scotland Total:	0	0	1	3	2	4	0	0	0	1	11	16.9

County of Origin	Unk.	1700s	1800–20s	1830s	1840s	1850s	1860s	1870s	1880s	1890s	Total	Percent
WALES												
1. North Wales	–	–	–	–	–	–	–	–	–	–	0	0.0
Anglesey	–	–	–	–	–	–	–	–	–	–	0	0.0
Caernarvon	1	–	–	–	–	–	–	–	–	–	1	1.5
Denbigh	–	–	–	–	1	–	–	–	–	–	1	1.5
Flint	–	–	–	–	–	–	–	–	–	–	0	0.0
Merioneth	–	–	–	–	–	–	–	–	–	–	0	0.0
Montgomery	–	–	–	–	4	–	–	1	–	–	5	7.7
2. South Wales	–	–	–	–	–	–	–	–	–	–	0	0.0
Brecon	–	–	1	–	2	–	–	–	–	–	3	4.6
Cardigan	–	–	–	–	1	–	–	–	–	–	1	1.5
Carmarthen	–	–	–	–	–	–	–	–	–	–	0	0.0
Glamorgan	–	–	–	–	–	1	–	1	–	–	2	3.1
Monmouth	–	–	–	–	–	–	–	–	–	–	0	0.0
Pembroke	–	–	–	–	–	–	–	–	–	–	0	0.0
Radnor	–	–	–	–	–	–	–	–	–	–	–	–
3. Wales N.O.D.	–	–	1	–	–	–	–	–	–	–	1	1.5
Wales Total:	1	0	2	0	8	1	0	2	0	0	14	21.5
Grand Total:	1	1	8	10	17	18	1	5	3	1	65	100

Source: County Histories

Table 9: Religion of British Immigrants, by Denomination.

Religion	Total	Percent
Anglican (or Church of England)	2	0.9
Baptist	22	9.5
Calvinist Methodist	3	1.3
Catholic	3	1.3
"Christian" (denomination not given)	6	2.6
Congregational	11	4.7
Episcopalian	26	11.2
Jewish	2	0.9
Lutheran	7	3.0
Methodist	27	11.6
Methodist Episcopalian	42	18.1
Presbyterian	69	29.7
Quaker (or Society of Friends)	4	1.7
Reformed	1	0.4
Reformed Presbyterian	1	0.4
Universalist	2	0.9
"Welsh" (denomination not given)	4	1.7
Grand Total:	232	100

Source: County Histories

Table 10: Political Affiliation of British Immigrants to Ohio (percentage distribution)

	Whig/Republican	Democrat	Other*	Total
English	84.5	11	4.5	100
Scottish	82	15.4	2.6	100
Welsh	80.4	13.7	5.9	100
N	204	30	11	245

Source: County Histories
* Includes Independents, Prohibition, and Democratic-Republicans

Notes

INTRODUCTION

1. One monograph that takes a close look at the Welsh in southern Ohio is Anne Kelly Knowles, *Calvinists Incorporated: Welsh Immigrants on Ohio's Industrial Frontier* (Chicago: Univ. of Chicago Press, 1997). Some immigrants to Ohio have been closely studied. See, for example, Joseph John Barton, *Peasants and Strangers: Italians, Rumanians, and Slovaks in an American City, 1890–1950* (Cambridge, Mass.: Harvard Univ. Press, 1975); and Susan M. Papp, *Hungarian Americans and Their Communities of Cleveland* (Cleveland, Ohio: Cleveland State Univ., 1981).

2. Hubert G. H. Wilhelm, *The Origin and Distribution of Settlement Groups, Ohio, 1850* (n.p.: typescript privately published, Ohio University, 1982); and Table 11, *Compendium of the Tenth Census* (Washington: U.S. Census Bureau, 1884), I, Table 21, 332–33; Table 30, 482–87; Table 31, 499–540.

3. William Amphlett, *The Emigrant's Directory to the Western States of North America* (London: Longman, Hurst, Rees, Orme, and Brown, 1819), 186.

4. Charlotte Erickson, *Invisible Immigrants: The Adaptation of English and Scottish Immigrants to the United States* (Leicester: Leicester Univ. Press, 1972).

5. David Hackett Fischer, *Albion's Seed: Four British Folkways in America* (Oxford: Oxford Univ. Press, 1989).

6. Ibid., see especially conclusion and page 812. The Forum in the *William and Mary Quarterly* (Apr. 1991): 223–308 is a response to Fischer by five critics (Jack P. Greene, Virginia DeJohn Anderson, James Horn, Barry Levy, and Ned Landsman). They challenge some of his methods and findings by questioning his definitions of British regions and the tendency to neglect non-British cultural groups, especially Africans and American Indians. In the Forum Fischer adequately addresses these issues and defends his major findings.

7. Quoted in Fischer, *Albion's Seed*, 831.

8. Jon Gjerde, *The Minds of the West: Ethnocultural Evolution in the Rural Middle West, 1830–1917* (Chapel Hill: Univ. of North Carolina Press, 1997), 10–11, 184.

9. Andro Linklater, *Measuring America: How an Untamed Wilderness Shaped the United States and Fulfilled the Promise of Democracy* (New York: Walker, 2002), 5, 43–44, 208, 210.

1. THE FIRST BRITISH BUCKEYES

1. B. F. Prince, "Early Journeys to Ohio," *Ohio Archeological and Historical Society Quarterly* 30 (1921): 57; Elizabeth Noble Shor, "Lewis Evans," *American National Biography*, 24 vols. (Oxford: Oxford Univ. Press, 1999.)

2. Richard White, *The Middle Ground: Indians, Empires, and Republics in the Great Lakes Region, 1650–1815* (Cambridge: Cambridge Univ. Press, 1991).

3. C. B. Galbreath, ed., *Expedition of Celoron to the Ohio Country in 1749* (Columbus: F. J. Heer, 1921), 90–91, 123.

4. Stewart Rafert, *The Miami Indians of Indiana: A Persistent People, 1654–1994* (Indianapolis: Indiana Historical Society, 1996), 38–39.

5. R. David Edmunds, "Old Briton," in *American Indian Leaders: Studies in Diversity*, ed. R. David Edmunds (Lincoln: Univ. of Nebraska Press, 1980), 1–20.

6. Ibid., 7.

7. Charles E. Slocum, *History of the Maumee River Basin, from the Earliest Accounts to Its Organization into Counties* (Defiance, Ohio: privately published, 1905), 87, 94–100; Eric Hinderaker, *Elusive Empires: Constructing Colonialism in the Ohio Valley, 1673–1800* (Cambridge: Cambridge Univ. Press, 1997), 44; Bert Anson, *The Miami Indians* (Norman: Univ. of Oklahoma Press, 1970), 43–51; and Rafert, *The Miami Indians of Indiana*, 31–39.

8. Fred Anderson, *Crucible of War: The Seven Years' War and the Fate of Empire in British North America, 1754–1766* (New York: Vintage, 2000), 28–30.

9. Stephen Brumwell, *Redcoats: The British Soldier and War in the Americas, 1755–1763* (Cambridge: Cambridge Univ. Press, 2002); *The Memoirs and Adventures of Robert Kirk, Late of the Royal Highland Regiment, Written by Himself . . .* (Limerick, Ireland: J. Ferrar, 1770), 7–9.

10. Brumwell, *Redcoats*, 171; *Kirk's Memoirs*, 10–14, 36–38.

11. *Kirk's Memoirs*, 84–88.

12. Slocum, *History of the Maumee River Basin*, 116; Rafert, *The Miami Indians of Indiana*, 41.

13. Linklater, *Measuring America*, 50.

14. Lincoln MacVeagh, ed., *The Journal of Nicholas Cresswell: 1774–1777* (New York: Dial, 1924), 83–93. This section is based on the entries of June 15–28, 1775.

15. Ibid., 102–6.

16. Ibid., 107–8.

17. Hinderaker, *Elusive Empires*, 54.

18. MacVeagh, *The Journal of Nicholas Cresswell*, 108–9.

19. White, *The Middle Ground*, 389–90. For an account of the massacre see Philip Weeks, *Farewell, My Nation: The American Indian and the United States in the Nineteenth Century*, 2nd ed. (Wheeling, Il.: Harlan Davidson, 2001), 21–23.

20. MacVeagh, *The Journal of Nicholas Cresswell*, 111.

21. Ibid., 93–100.

22. Opha Moore, *History of Franklin County, Ohio*, vol. 1 (Topeka, Ind.: Historical, 1930), 99.

23. Byron Williams, *History of Clermont and Brown Counties, Ohio, from the Earliest Historical Times down to the Present* (Milford, Ohio: Hobart, 1913), 2:245–46.

24. E. F. Ellet, *Pioneer Women of the West* (New York: Scribners, 1852), 245–53; Henry Howe, *Historical Collections of Ohio*, vol. 1 (Cincinnati, Ohio: C. J. Krehbiel, 1908), 680; William Oliver Stevens, *Famous Women of America* (New York: Dodd, Mead, 1950), 9–12; and Livia Simpson-Poffenbarger, *Ann Bailey: Thrilling Adventures of the Heroine of the Kanawha Valley* (Point Pleasant, W. Va.: privately published, 1907).

25. Hinderaker, *Elusive Empires*, 185–86.

26. *History of Defiance County* (Chicago: Warner, Beers, 1883), 56.

27. Helen Hornbeck Tanner, "The Glaize in 1792: A Composite Indian Community," *Ethnohistory* 25 (Winter 1978): 27.

28. Milo M. Quaife, ed., *The Indian Captivity of O. M. Spencer* (Chicago: Lakeside, 1917), 82–83, 97, 133.

29. Thomas Ridout, "An Account of My Capture by the Shawanese Indians," *Western Pennsylvania Historical Magazine* 12 (Jan. 1929): 7, 12, 17, 21, 22, 28; and Matilda Edgar, *Ten Years of Upper Canada in Peace and War, 1805–1815: Being the Ridout Letters* (Toronto: William Briggs, 1890), 2–13.

30. Quaife, *O. M. Spencer*, 113.

31. Ibid., 30.

32. Hinderaker, *Elusive Empires*, 69–71.

33. Milo M. Quaife, ed., "Henry Hay's Journal from Detroit to the Miami River," *Proceedings of the State Historical Society of Wisconsin* (Madison: State Historical Society of Wisconsin, 1915), 62:224, 229, 240–42.

34. Ibid., 221–22, 225–27, 235, 239; and Tanner, "The Glaize in 1792," 28.

35. Quaife, "Henry Hay's Journal," 222–23.

36. *History of Tuscarawas County, Ohio* (Chicago: Warner, Beers, 1884), 317.

37. Tanner, "The Glaize in 1792," 30–31.

38. Quaife, "Henry Hay's Journal," 248.

39. Charles Slocum and A. L. Burt, *The United States, Great Britain, and British North America: From the Revolution to the Establishment of Peace after the War of 1812* (New York: Russell and Russell, 1961), 115.

40. Ibid., 174.

41. William Henry Smith, *The St. Clair Papers: The Life and Public Services of Arthur St. Clair*, vol. 1 (Cincinnati, Ohio: Robert Clarke, 1882), 3–247; George W. Knepper, *Ohio and Its People* (Kent, Ohio: Kent State Univ. Press, 1989), 74–77; Slocum and Burt, *United States, Great Britain, and British North America*, 116; and Jeffrey P. Brown, "Arthur St. Clair and the Northwest Territory," *Northwest Ohio Quarterly* 59 (Summer 1987): 79.

42. Slocum, *History of the Maumee River Basin*, 174.

43. John E. Hopley, *History of Crawford County, Ohio, and Representative Citizens* (Chicago: Richmond-Arnold, 1912), 1094.

44. Tanner, "The Glaize in 1792," 15–39. Wayne blamed the British traders and officials for encouraging Indian autonomy and resistance, and reportedly offered a one-thousand-dollar reward for the scalp of employees of Britain's Indian Department. That would have included Ironside. Larry L. Nelson, *A Man of Distinction among Them: Alexander McKee and the Ohio Country Frontier, 1754–1799* (Kent, Ohio: Kent State Univ. Press, 1999), 176.

45. Beverley W. Bond Jr., *The Civilization of the Old Northwest: A Study of Political, Social, and Economic Development, 1788–1812* (New York: Macmillan, 1934), 247; and Donald J. Ratcliffe, *Party Spirit in a Frontier Republic: Democratic Politics in Ohio, 1793–1821* (Columbus: Ohio State Univ. Press, 1998), 33.

46. Nelson, *A Man of Distinction*, 75–90; and Ratcliffe, *Party Spirit*, 51.

47. Malcolm J. Rohrbough, *The Trans-Appalachian Frontier: People, Societies, and Institutions, 1775–1850* (New York: Oxford Univ. Press, 1978), 67.

48. James McBride, *Pioneer Biography: Sketches of the Lives of Some of the Early Settlers of Butler County, Ohio*, vol. 2 (Cincinnati, Ohio: Robert Clarke, 1871), 253–58.

49. "James Reeside," *American National Biography*, 1999.

50. Kim M. Gruenwald, *River of Enterprise: The Commercial Origins of Regional Identity in the Ohio Valley, 1790–1850* (Bloomington: Indiana Univ. Press, 2002), 105.

51. Ibid., xii, 156–57.

52. Ben Douglass, *History of Wayne County, Ohio, from the Days of the Pioneers and First Settlers to the Present Time* (Indianapolis: Robert Douglass, 1878), 352.

53. Ratcliffe, *Party Spirit*, 14; David Hackett Fischer and James C. Kelly, *Bound Away: Virginia and the Westward Movement* (Charlottesville: Univ. of Virginia Press, 2000), 171–72.

54. Knepper, *Ohio and Its People*, 87–100; and Howe, *Historical Collections of Ohio*, 2:499–501.

55. Nelson W. Evans, *History of Scioto County, Ohio* (Portsmouth, Ohio: Higginson, 1903), 1:57; Bond, *The Civilization of the Old Northwest*, 124, 143; and Ratcliffe, *Party Spirit*, 92.

56. Jeffrey P. Brown, "Chilicothe's Elite: Leadership in a Frontier Community," *Ohio History* 96 (Summer/August 1987): 140–53.

57. Williams, *Clermont and Brown Counties*, 1:207, 245.

58. John A. Caldwell, *History of Belmont and Jefferson Counties, Ohio* (Wheeling, West Virginia: Historical, 1880), 308.

59. *History of Warren County, Ohio* (Chicago: W. H. Beers, 1882), 841.

60. Bond, *The Civilization of the Old Northwest*, 275.

61. Kenneth Scott, comp., *British Aliens in the United States during the War of 1812* (Baltimore, Md.: Genealogical, 1979), v–vi, 366–71.

62. *Reports on the Census of England and Wales* (Edinburgh: Census of Scotland, 1951).

63. Paul E. Swisher, "Immigrant Groups in Hamilton County before 1850" (master's thesis, Ohio State University, 1946), 20–23, 57–59, 69, 87.

64. Mary L. Ziebold, "Immigrant Groups in Northwestern Ohio to 1860," *Northwest Ohio Quarterly* 17 (Apr.–Jul., 1945): 62–71; and William Ganson Rose, *Cleveland: The Making of a City* (Cleveland, Ohio: World, 1950), 203.

2. The Nineteenth Century

1. For a convenient summary of the century, see Colin Matthew, ed., *The Short Oxford History of the British Isles: The Nineteenth Century* (Oxford: Oxford Univ. Press, 2000).

2. *Times* (London), February 24, 1812.

3. During the 1840s and 1850s Dutch immigrants to the United States were between 80 and 85 percent familial, though in the 1830s a little over half, and in the 1840s about 70 percent, were familial. Robert P. Swierenga, "Dutch Immigrant Demography, 1820–1880," *Journal of Family History* 5 (Winter 1980): table 1, 397; and Charlotte Erickson, *Leaving England: Essays on British Emigration in the Nineteenth Century* (Ithaca: Cornell Univ. Press, 1994), 143.

4. Erickson, *Leaving England*, Table 4.1, 131–34, 140–51.

5. William L. Burn, *The Age of Equipoise: A Study of the Mid-Victorian Generation* (New York: Norton, 1964).

6. William E. Van Vugt, *Britain to America: Mid-Nineteenth-Century Immigrants to the United States* (Urbana: Univ. of Illinois Press, 1999), chs. 3 and 4.

7. Erickson, *Leaving England*, chap. 3; see also the appendix, table 5.

8. Erickson, *Leaving England*, chap. 5; and Van Vugt, *Britain to America*, chap. 1.

9. Gertrude Van Rensselaer Wickham, *Memorial to the Pioneer Women of the Western Reserve*, vol. 1 (Cleveland, Ohio: Woman's Department of the Cleveland Centennial Commission, 1896), 485.

10. W. H. Perrin, J. H. Battle, and W. A. Goodspeed, *History of Crawford County and Ohio* (Chicago: Baskin and Battey, 1881), 959–60.

11. Caldwell, *Belmont and Jefferson Counties*, 559.

12. *Commemorative Historical and Biographical Record of Wood County*, vol. 1 (Chicago: J. H. Beers, 1897), 645.

13. Wickham, *Memorial to the Pioneer Women of the Western Reserve*, 286.

14. D. Griffiths Jr., *Two Years' Residence in the New Settlements of Ohio, North America: With Directions to Emigrants* (London: Westley and Davis, 1835; reprint, Ann Arbor, Mich.: University Microfilms, 1966), 10–11.

15. James H. Rodabaugh, ed., "From England to Ohio, 1830–1832: The Journal of Thomas K. Wharton," *The Ohio Historical Quarterly* 65 (Jan. 1956): 9; and Griffiths, *Two Years' Residence in the New Settlements of Ohio*, 13.

16. *Defiance County*, 290.

17. Charles Augustus Murray, *Travels in North America during the Years 1834, 1835, and 1836*, vol. 1 (London: Richard Bentley, 1841), 200.

18. William Cobbett, *A Year's Residence in the United States of America* (Carbondale: Southern Illinois Univ. Press, 1964), 254–55.

19. Ibid., 255–56.

20. Walter Havighurst, *Ohio: A Bicentennial History* (New York: Norton, 1976), 39.

21. Thomas Hamilton, *Men and Manners in America*, as cited in R. Carlyle Buley, *The Old Northwest Pioneer Period*, vol. 1 (Bloomington: Indiana Univ. Press, 1951), 388.

22. A. J. Baughman, *History of Huron County, Ohio, Its Progress and Development*, vol. 2 (Chicago: S. J. Clarke, 1909), 108–9.

23. William B. Doyle, *Centennial History of Summit County, Ohio, and Representative Citizens* (Chicago: Biographical, 1908), 856.

24. For examples see *Portrait and Biographical Record of Stark County, Ohio* (Chicago: Chapman Bros., 1892), 481; and *Commemorative Record of Wood County*, 1:625.

25. Dudley Baines, *Migration in a Mature Economy: Emigration and Internal Migration in England and Wales, 1861–1900* (New York: Cambridge Univ. Press, 1985), 140.

26. Brian P. Birch, "Taking the Breaks and Working the Boats: An English Family's Impressions of Ohio in the 1830s," *Ohio History* 95 (1996): 101–18.

27. For some interesting examples of the above, see Evans, *Scioto County*, 2:1047, 1196; Martin R. Andrews, ed., *History of Marietta and Washington County, Ohio, and Representative Citizens* (Chicago: Biographical, 1902), 5; Williams, *Clermont and Brown Counties*, 844; and William Alexander Taylor, *Centennial History of Columbus and Franklin County, Ohio* (Chicago: S. J. Clarke, 1909), 2:745.

28. *Annals of Cleveland Court Record Series*, vol. 2:1851–1857 (Cleveland, Ohio: Works Progress Administration, 1939), abstract 170, 245; and ibid., 1:1837–1850, abstract 9, 8–9.

29. Birch, "Taking the Breaks and Working the Boats." 111.

30. Erickson, *Invisible Immigrants*, 108.

31. H. J. Eckley and William T. Perry, eds., *History of Carroll and Harrison Counties*, vol. 2 (Chicago: Lewis, 1921), 840–41.

32. Douglass, *Wayne County*, 492–97.

33. Albert J. Brown, *History of Clinton County, Ohio: Its People, Industries, and Institutions* (Indianapolis: B. F. Bowen, 1915), 539–40.

34. See the case of Mrs. Candler who left her husband in London to immigrate to Detroit to be with her children in Van Vugt, *Britain to America*, 123.

35. *Portrait and Biographical Record of Fayette, Pickaway and Madison Counties, Ohio* (Chicago: Chapman Bros., 1892), 287.

36. Brown, *Clinton County*, 540.

37. Perrin, Battle, and Goodspeed, *Crawford County and Ohio*, 959–60.

38. See appendix tables.

39. Appendix, table 1; Baines, *Migration in a Mature Economy*, 157, 210, 229, 247.

40. Appendix, table 6.

41. Wilhelm, *The Origin and Distribution of Settlement Groups*, table 11, 77, 81. This compares with 70,236 Germans and 37,779 Irish.

42. Gruenwald, *River of Enterprise*, 136–37.

43. See appendix, table 2. This figure for nonconformity is a little higher that that for the Old Northwest as a whole during the midcentury period. See Van Vugt, *Britain to America*, 133.

44. Buley, *The Old Northwest Pioneer Period*, 2:449.

45. Caldwell, *Belmont and Jefferson Counties*, 1:346, 2:559; and Evans, *Scioto County*, 1:775–76.

46. This paragraph and the following are based on Robert P. Swierenga, "Ethnoreligious Political Behavior in the Mid-Nineteenth Century: Voting, Values, Cultures," in *Religion and American Politics: From the Colonial Period to the 1980s*, ed. Mark A. Noll (New York: Oxford Univ. Press, 1990), 146–71.

47. Of the 602 immigrants in the sample, 245 English, Scots, and Welsh declared their party affiliation. The ratios who were Republican were very similar among the English (85 percent), Scots (82 percent), and Welsh (80 percent). The lopsided support for the Republican Party was actually greater than this because the Prohibition Party was closer ideologically to the Republicans, and many who were abolitionists did not state their political affiliation, which was far more likely to be Republican than Democrat. See appendix, table 10.

48. Robert Kelley, *Cultural Patterns*, 160–69, quoted in Swierenga, "Ethnoreligious Political Behavior," 153.

49. Gjerde, *The Minds of the West*, 104, 284, 295, 301, 309.

50. Evans, *Scioto County*, 1:828–29, 745–46.

51. Wilbur S. Shepperson, *Emigration and Disenchantment: Portraits of Englishmen Repatriated from the United States* (Norman: Univ. of Oklahoma Press, 1965), 29.

52. Griffiths, *Two Years' Residence in the New Settlements of Ohio*, 94.

53. *Cleveland Leader*, Aug. 18, 1874.

54. Gjerde, *The Minds of the West*, 46, 55.

55. *Daily True Democrat* (Cleveland), Jan. 26, 1852.

56. Alfred R. Ferguson, "Charles Dickens in Ohio," *Ohio State Archaeological and Historical Quarterly* 59 (1950): 14–25, especially 17, 18, 23.

57. Griffiths, *Two Years' Residence in the New Settlements of Ohio,* 71.

58. Taylor, *Columbus and Franklin County,* 2:17.

59. *Portrait and Biographical Record of Portage and Summit County, Ohio* (Logansport, Ind.: A. W. Bowen, 1898), 475.

60. *Historical Hand-Atlas Illustrated . . . Map of Gallia County, and Histories of Lawrence and Gallia Counties, Ohio* (Chicago: H. H. Hardesty, 1882), xxv.

61. Some preliminary research has been done by Professor Roger Burt in "Freemasonry and Emigration during the Victorian period," paper presented at the conference "Westward Ho: Movement and Migration," University of Exeter, Apr. 3–6, 2003.

62. Address of Trustee L. B. Wing at the dedication of Townshend Hall, Ohio State University, Columbus, Jan. 12, 1898, Ohio State Historical Society, BT666, 5–7.

63. See, for example, *Stark County,* 133: "England numbers many representatives among the best class of citizens in Ohio. There is a sterling quality about the nationality that fits them for almost any occupation, and we, as Americans, are greatly indebted to settlers of English birth for the rapid advancement made in our civilization."

64. *Annual Report of the Secretary of State to the Governor of Ohio, Jail Reports, 1854 and 1855,* facsimile (Bowie, Md.: Facsimile: Heritage Books, 1988). These cases are found in, respectively, 1854: p. 12, 41; and 1855: p. 22, 37, 81, 37, 64, 61.

65. Wilhelm, *The Origin and Distribution of Settlement Groups,* calculated from tables 6 and 11.

66. *Jail Reports, 1854,* 12–15.

67. *Annals of Cleveland Court Record Series,* vol. 2, abstract 133, 201–2.

3. Communities and Settlements

1. D. C. Coleman, *Courtaulds: An Economic and Social History,* vol. 1 (Oxford: Clarendon, 1969), chap. 1; and *History of Hocking Valley, Ohio,* vol. 1 (1883; reprint, Milford, Ohio: Little Miami, 2000), 414–15.

2. Coleman, *Courtaulds,* 52. Samuel, the only son of George Courtauld who stayed in England, succeeded fabulously in the silk business. When he died in 1881, he left a fortune of nearly 700,000 pounds. Coleman, *Courtaulds,* 1.

3. *Courtauld Family Letters, 1782–1900,* 3 vols. (Cambridge: Bowes and Bowes, 1916), 2:891, 881, 901, 906.

4. Ibid., 903.

5. Ibid., 916.

6. Buley, *The Old Northwest Pioneer Period,* 1:243.

7. Douglass, *Wayne County,* 493–94.

8. *Courtauld Family Letters,* 2:917.

9. Ibid., 919–20.

10. James Knight, June 4, 1825, Nelsonville, Ohio, *Courtauld Family Letters,* 3:1307.

11. *Courtauld Family Letters,* 2:1297, 1302, 1307, 1365; and Charles H. Harris, *The Harris History: A Collection of Tales of Long Ago of Southeastern Ohio and Adjoining Territories* (Athens: Athens Messenger, 1957), 129–31.

12. Erickson, *Invisible Immigrants*, 33.

13. Charles M. Walker, *History of Athens County, Ohio* (Cincinnati, Ohio: Robert Clarke, 1869), 544–45.

14. Relatively few Calvinist Methodists show up in the county histories because the denomination combined with Presbyterians by the time many of the county histories were published.

15. See appendix, table 1. The general pattern of origins in the county histories is very similar to that observed in the obituaries by Anne Kelly Knowles in "Immigrant Trajectories through the Rural-Industrial Transition in Wales and the United States, 1795–1850," *Annals of the Association of American Geographers* 85, no. 2 (1995): 246–66.

16. Knowles, "Immigrant Trajectories," 252. The obituaries that Knowles studied also show high numbers of migrants from Montgomeryshire and Cardiganshire.

17. William Harvey Jones, "Welsh Settlements in Ohio," *Ohio Archaeological and Historical Quarterly* 16 (1907): 194–97. Rhys was a political exile who fled Britain after writing seditious literature.

18. Daniel Jenkins Williams, "The Welsh of Columbus Ohio: A Study of Adaptation and Assimilation" (Oshkosh, Wisc.: privately published, 1913): 20–23.

19. *Historical Hand-Atlas Illustrated*, xxv. Another important early settlement, the "Welsh Hills Settlement" of Licking County, has already been mentioned.

20. Delavan L. Leonard, *A Century of Congregationalism in Ohio* (Oberlin: Ohio Home Missionary Society, 1896), 26.

21. Phillips G. Davies, "The Welsh in Ohio: Thomas's *Hanes Cymry America*," *The Old Northwest* 3 (Sept. 1977): 291–92; and Clare Taylor, "Paddy's Run: A Welsh Community in Ohio," *Welsh History Review* 11 (1983): 302–16. On resistance to learning English, see Rowland Tappan Berthoff, *British Immigrants in Industrial America, 1790–1950* (1953; reprint, New York: Russell and Russell, 1968), 161.

22. *History of Delaware County and Ohio* (Chicago: O. L. Baskin, 1880), 502–3.

23. E. M. P. Brister, *Centennial History of the City of Newark and Licking County, Ohio*, vol. 1 (Chicago: S. J. Clarke, 1909), 170–76.

24. Jones, "Welsh Settlements in Ohio," 204n14.

25. Ibid., 205n15.

26. Virginia E. McCormick and Robert W. McCormick, *New Englanders on the Ohio Frontier: The Migration and Settlement of Worthington, Ohio* (Kent, Ohio: Kent State Univ. Press, 1998), 91.

27. Knowles, "Immigrant Trajectories," 257.

28. Isaac Smucker, *History of the Welsh Settlements in Licking County, Ohio* (Newark, Ohio: Wilson and Clark, 1869); Jones, "Welsh Settlements in Ohio," 208–10; and Alan Conway, ed., *The Welsh in America: Letters from the Immigrants* (Minneapolis: Univ. of Minnesota Press, 1961), 52.

29. Douglass, *Wayne County*, 340–44.

30. Jones, "Welsh Settlements in Ohio," 205, 16.

31. Thaddeus S. Gilliland, ed., *History of Van Wert County, Ohio, and Representative Citizens* (Chicago: Richmond and Arnold, 1906), 630–31.

32. Welsh Hills Community Papers, Ohio Historical Society, Ohio State University, Columbus, MSS 555, Box 20, Folders 1, 24.

33. Knowles, "Immigrant Trajectories," 253.

34. Eugene B. Willard, ed., *A Standard History of the Hanging Rock Iron Region of Ohio* (Chicago: Lewis, 1916), 439.

35. Michael T. Struble, "'Here is Found a Tabernacle': Welsh Chapel Building in the Gallia and Jackson Settlements in 1841," *Pioneer American Society Transactions* 18 (1995): 17–24, esp. 17.

36. Robert P. Swierenga, "Dutch Immigration Patterns in the Nineteenth and Twentieth Centuries," in *The Dutch in America: Immigration, Settlement, and Cultural Change*, ed. Robert P. Swierenga (New Brunswick, N.J.: Rutgers Univ. Press), 15–42; and Robert P. Swierenga, "Local Patterns of Dutch Migration to the United States in the Mid-Nineteenth Century," in *A Century of European Migrations, 1830–1930*, eds. Rudolph J. Vecoli and Suzanne M. Sinke (Urbana: Univ. of Illinois Press, 1991), 134–57.

37. John E. Jones, *Romance of the Old Charcoal Furnace Days of the Hanging Rock Iron District* (Jackson, Ohio: Globe Iron, 1934), 1–3.

38. Frank H. Rowe, *History of the Iron and Steel Industry in Scioto County, Ohio* (Columbus: Ohio State Archaeological and Historical Society, 1938), 79.

39. Willard, *A Standard History of the Hanging Rock Iron Region*, 448; and Struble, "Here Is Found a Tabernacle," 17.

40. Wilhelm, *The Origin and Distribution of Settlement Groups*, table 11, 77.

41. Davies, "The Welsh in Ohio," 289–318. The Census of 1900 shows that over 35,000 Welsh immigrants and their children lived in Ohio, a number surpassed only in Pennsylvania.

42. Struble, "Here Is Found a Tabernacle," 20.

43. Williams, "The Welsh of Columbus, Ohio," 24–25.

44. Jones, "Welsh Settlements in Ohio," 216–17.

45. Knowles, "Immigrant Trajectories," 246–66; Knowles, *Calvinists Incorporated*, 30, 163–64.

46. Michael T. Struble and Hubert G. H. Wilhelm, "The Welsh in Ohio," in *To Build in a New Land: Ethnic Landscapes in North America,* ed. Allen G. Noble (Baltimore, Md.: Johns Hopkins Univ. Press, 1992), 79.

47. Gjerde, *The Minds of the West*, 226–27.

48. Marcella Barton, "The Welsh Errand into the Wilderness," *Ohio Academy of History Newsletter* (Fall 1996): 12. See the case of Richard Jones, who organized *eisteddfods* in Franklin County, in Moore, *Franklin County*, 1:1149–50; and Rev. John Morgan Thomas, who composed many songs, in *Stark County*, 207–8. Struble and Wilhelm, "Welsh in Ohio," 81, 91.

49. Williams, "The Welsh of Columbus, Ohio," 26–28; and Jones, "Welsh Settlements in Ohio," 216.

50. Williams, "The Welsh of Columbus, Ohio," 42–43.

51. Ibid., 47.

52. Edith F. Carey, *Essays on Guernsey History* (St. Peter Port, Guernsey: La Société Guernesiaise, 1936), 70.

53. Cyrus P. B. Sarchet, *History of Guernsey County, Ohio*, vol. 1 (Indianapolis, Ind.: Bowen, 1911), 457–59.

54. Ibid., 398–400; Fred Sarchet, "The Sarchet Story" (typescript in the Privaulx Library, St. Peter Port, Guernsey); W. G. Wolfe, *History of Guernsey County* (St. Peter Port, Guernsey: privately published, 1943), 39–40; and T. F. Williams, *The Household Guide and Instructor with Biographies* (Cleveland, Ohio: T. F. Williams, 1882), 425–27.

55. Sarchet, *History of Guernsey County,* 1:400–401, 460–61.

56. Ibid., 410–11.

57. Peter Girard Collection, Guernsey Archives; and Wolfe, *History of Guernsey County,* 39–45.

58. Sarchet, vol. 2, *History of Guernsey County,* 583–84.

59. Ibid., vol.1, 466–67; and Marion G. Turk, *The Quiet Adventurers in America: Channel Island Settlers in the American Colonies and in the United States* (Cleveland, Ohio: Genie Repros, 1975), 56–59.

60. T. F. Priaulx, "The Mystery of Sophia Gibaut," *Quarterly Review of the Guernsey Society* 21 (Summer 1965): 36–37.

61. Sarchet, *History of Guernsey County,* 1:66–67.

62. Wilhelm, *The Origin and Distribution of Settlement Groups,* table 6, 30; table 11, 76.

63. Mildred Steed, comp., "Early Settlers from the Isle of Man" (Cleveland, Ohio: Lake County Genealogical Society, 1991), unnumbered page; and Gertrude Cannell, *A Short History of the Mona's Relief Society* (Cleveland, Ohio: privately published, 1951), 1.

64. Quoted in Steed, "Early Settlers from the Isle of Man," 128–129.

65. Ibid., 1; and W. S. Kerruish, "The Pioneer Manxmen," *Annals of the Early Settlers Association of Cuyahoga County* 4 (Cleveland, Ohio: Mount and Carroll, 1883): 32.

66. Ibid., 19.

67. Ibid., 32–33.

68. Erickson, *Invisible Immigrants,* 104–6.

69. Ibid., 107. See the letter of May 12, 1831.

70. Ibid., 108. See the letter of Nov. 9, 1842.

71. Cannell, *A Short History of the Mona's Relief Society,* 1.

72. Kerruish, "The Pioneer Manxmen," 30, 33.

73. Steed, "Early Settlers from the Isle of Man," 9.

74. Cannell, *A Short History of the Mona's Relief Society,* 4.

75. *Cleveland Leader,* Dec. 20, 1854.

76. Cannell, *A Short History of the Mona's Relief Society,* 2–5.

77. C. M. L. Wiseman, *Centennial History of Lancaster, Ohio, and Lancaster People* (Lancaster, Ohio: privately published, 1898), 38–39.

78. Douglass, *Wayne County,* 303–8.

79. *Fayette, Pickaway and Madison Counties,* 543.

80. *History of Union County* (Chicago: W. H. Beers, 1883), 125–26.

4. Agriculture

1. Erickson, *Invisible Immigrants,* 166.

2. Erickson, *Leaving England,* 64, table 2.2.

3. As it turned out, free trade was one of the best things to happen to Britain. Food prices fell, real wages rose, the industrial economy shifted into high gear, and it expanded for nearly two decades as part of the "mid-Victorian boom" (see chapter 2).

4. See appendix, tables 5 and 6. On soil types see Van Vugt, *Britain to America*, 31–32.

5. Robert Leslie Jones, *History of Agriculture in Ohio to 1880* (Kent, Ohio: Kent State Univ. Press, 1983), 69–70.

6. C. W. Williamson, *History of Western Ohio and Auglaize County* (Columbus: W. M. Linn, 1905), 705–7.

7. Rohrbough, *The Trans-Appalachian Frontier*, 28.

8. William M. Rockel, ed., *20th Century History of Springfield, and Clark County, Ohio, and Representative Citizens* (Chicago: Biographical, 1908), 930–31; and Buley, *The Old Northwest Pioneer Period*, 2:46.

9. *Commemorative Record of Wood County*, 1:646, 686–87.

10. Ibid., 3:840, 910. See also the case of Scottish immigrant James Caskie, on page 1170, and of Thomas Stone on page 778 of vol. 2.

11. George F. Robinson, *History of Greene County, Ohio* (Chicago: S. J. Clarke, 1902), 659.

12. Jones, *History of Agriculture in Ohio to 1880*, 27–28.

13. Cobbett, *A Year's Residence in the United States of America*, 56, 179.

14. Erickson, *Leaving England*, 75–77; R. Douglas Hurt, *The Ohio Frontier: Crucible of the Old Northwest, 1720–1830* (Bloomington: Indiana Univ. Press, 1996), 241; "Recollections of Pioneer Life in Wisconsin," in *Bewick Family History* (State Historical Society of Wisconsin, Special Collections, 1923), 1599; and *Commemorative Record of Wood County*, 3:840.

15. Doyle, *Summit County*, 661.

16. *Defiance County*, 302.

17. Charles Robertson, *Morgan County, Ohio* (Chicago: L. H. Watkins, 1886), 324–25, 358, 367.

18. A. J. Baughman, ed., *Centennial Biographical History of Richland and Ashland Counties, Ohio* (Chicago: Lewis, 1901), 40–43.

19. *Union County*, 376.

20. Rebecca Burlend, *A True Picture of Emigration: or, Fourteen Years in the Interior of North America* (1848; reprint, Secaucus, N.J.: Citadel, 1968), 190–92.

21. Wickham, *Memorial to the Pioneer Women of the Western Reserve*, 139–40.

22. Nevin O. Winter, *A History of Northwest Ohio* (Chicago: Lewis, 1917), 523.

23. Gjerde, *The Minds of the West*, 108–9.

24. Eckley and Perry, *Carroll and Harrison Counties*, 1:678–79.

25. Ibid., 900.

26. Erickson, *Leaving England*, 72; and *Commemorative Record of Wood County*, 3:1042.

27. *Commemorative Record of Wood County*, 3:1042, 1154, 1170, 1214; and David E. Schob, *Hired Hands and Plowboys: Farm Labor in the Midwest, 1815–1860* (Urbana: Univ. of Illinois Press, 1975), 119.

28. This was the experience of the Mighill family, who migrated to Ohio during the 1830s, and seems to have been especially common among the English in Ohio according to Birch, "Taking the Breaks and Working the Boats," 101–18.

29. Malcolm Chase, *The People's Farm: English Radical Agrarianism* (New York: Oxford

Univ. Press, 1988); Eric J. Hobsbawm, *Labouring Men: Studies in the History of Labour* (New York: Basic, 1964); and Michael Anderson, *Family Structure in Nineteenth-Century Lancashire* (Cambridge: Cambridge Univ. Press, 1971).

30. Erickson, *Invisible Immigrants*, 170.

31. Brian P. Birch, "A British View of the Ohio Backwoods: The Letters of James Martin, 1821–1836," *Ohio History* 94 (1985): 139–57, quotes on 153, 157.

32. *Commemorative Record of Wood County*, 1:487–88.

33. Williams, *Clermont and Brown Counties*, 2:266–69.

34. Erickson, *Invisible Immigrants*, 139–40.

35. Ibid., 153–55.

36. Ibid., 165–68.

37. Ibid., 169–71.

38. James Martin to Mrs. Caroline Monro and Mordaunt Martin Monro, October 9, 1836, London Metropolitan Archives, ACC/1063/150.

39. Robert Bowles Manuscripts, vol. 538, Ohio State Historical Society, Ohio State University, Columbus. For additional information on Bowles see Erickson, *Invisible Immigrants*, 25, 27, 30, 45, 51.

40. Quoted in the *Inverness Courier* (Scotland), Feb. 7, 1822.

41. "Robert Bowles MSS," vol. 538, letter dated Aug. 3, 1823.

42. Ibid., Jan. 22, 1823.

43. Ibid.

44. *Portrait and Biographical Record of Marion and Hardin Counties, Ohio* (Chicago: Chapman, 1895), 344–45.

45. For examples, see *Commemorative Record of Wood County*, 1:579, 599, 3:867, 910–11; William J. Bahmer, *Centennial History of Coshocton County, Ohio*, (Chicago: S. J. Clarke, 1909), 1:376; and Caldwell, *Belmont and Jefferson Counties*, 2:589.

46. George and Orange Slade, Coshocton County, to their brother, June 6, 1841, Ohio State Historical Society, Ohio State University, Columbus, VFM 3334.

47. Andrews, *History of Marietta and Washington County*, 1415; and *History of Columbiana County, Ohio, with Illustrations and Biographical Sketches of Some of Its Prominent Men and Pioneers* (Philadelphia: D. W. Ensign, 1879), 187, 277. For the data see Wilhelm, *The Origin and Distribution of Settlement Groups*, table 11, 77.

48. "Letter of 1822," Charles Rose Papers, Ohio State Historical Society, Ohio State University, Columbus, VFM 1903.

49. See "Declaration of Intention to Become a United States Citizen by James Battersby," 1854, Merseyside County Museums, Liverpool, DB/119D/74.

50. "Letter of 1830," Charles Rose Papers.

51. Gjerde, *The Minds of the West*, 143.

52. Lucius F. Ellsworth, "The Philadelphia Society for the Promotion of Agriculture and Agricultural Reform, 1785–1793," *Agricultural History* 42 (July 1968): 189–99; Thomas L. Bushell, "English Agricultural Methods and the American Institute, 1871–1872," *Agricultural History* 31 (1957): 25–30; and Buley, *The Old Northwest Pioneer Period*, 1:196n149.

53. Amphlett, *The Emigrant's Directory to the Western States of North America*, 83.

54. Ibid., 82.

55. Griffiths, *Two Years' Residence in the New Settlements of Ohio*, 34–35.

56. Jones, *History of Agriculture in Ohio to 1880*, 39–40.

57. Quoted in Joseph M. Petulla, *American Environmental History: The Exploitation and Conservation of Natural Resources* (San Francisco: Boyd and Fraser, 1977), 56. William Cobbett, the "radical" journalist who traveled and lived in the United States and urged England's poor to migrate to America, wrote in 1819 that ultimately, American labor was *less* expensive than English labor because American laborers worked harder, were more versatile, and American farmers did not have to pay poor rates. See Cobbett, *A Year's Residence in the United States of America*, 178–79.

58. Quoted in Edwin Morris Betts, *Thomas Jefferson's Farm Book* (Princeton: Princeton Univ. Press, 1953), 194.

59. William Brown, *America: A Four Years' Residence in the United States and Canada* (Leeds: Kemplay and Bolland, 1849), 32.

60. R. W. Sturgess, "The Agricultural Revolution on the English Clays," *Agricultural History Review* 14 (1966): 120.

61. Eric E. Lampard, *The Rise of the Dairy Industry in Wisconsin: A Study in Agricultural Change, 1820–1920* (Madison: State Historical Society of Wisconsin, 1963), 43–44.

62. Historians of American agriculture have emphasized that immigrants generally had to conform to American methods and cropping systems in order to succeed. See Merle Curti, *The Making of an American Community: A Case Study of Democracy in a Frontier County* (Stanford, Calif.: Stanford Univ. Press, 1959), 80–83, 91–97, 179–97; Allan Bogue, *From Prairie to Corn Belt: Farming on the Illinois Prairies in the Nineteenth Century* (Chicago: Univ. of Chicago Press, 1963), 211, 238; Robert C. Ostergren, *A Community Transplanted: The Trans-Atlantic Experience of a Swedish Immigrant Settlement in the Upper Midwest, 1835–1915* (Madison: Univ. of Wisconsin Press, 1988); and Robert P. Swierenga, "Ethnicity and American Agriculture," *Ohio History* 89 (Summer 1980): 323–44.

63. Ellsworth, "The Philadelphia Society for the Promotion of Agriculture and Agricultural Reform," 189–99.

64. Robert P. Swierenga, "The Settlement of the Old Northwest: Ethnic Pluralism in a Featureless Plain," *Journal of the Early Republic* 9 (Spring 1989): 73–105.

65. Examples abound. See *Commemorative Record of Wood County*, 1:621, 2:728, 3:1156; Bahmer, *Coshocton County*, 1:373; Caldwell, *Belmont and Jefferson Counties*, 589; and Brister, *Newark and Licking County*, 66.

66. *Portrait and Biographical Album of Morgan and Scott Counties, Illinois, Containing Full Page Portraits and Biographical Sketches of Prominent and Representative Citizens of the County* (Chicago: Chapman Brothers, 1889), 427.

67. Milo M. Quaife, *Wisconsin: Its History and Its People, 1634–1924*, vol. 2 (Chicago: S. J. Clark, 1924), 217, 240–41.

68. Evans, *Scioto County*, 1:679; Taylor, *Columbus and Franklin County*, 17; *Commemorative Record of Wood County*, 2:744; and Lewis Cass Aldrich, ed., *History of Erie County, Ohio, with Illustrations and Biographical Sketches of Some of Its Prominent Men and Pioneers* (Syracuse, Ohio: D. Mason, 1889), 592.

69. Brown, *Clinton County*, 829–30.

70. *Biographical Record of Knox County, Ohio* (Chicago: Lewis, 1902), 85–84.

71. Charles William Burkett, *History of Ohio Agriculture: A Treatise on the Development of the Various Lines and Phases of Farm Life in Ohio* (Concord, N.H.: Rumford, 1900), 105–7, 112–13, 129–30, 142; and Jones, *History of Agriculture in Ohio*, 108–11.

72. Chester E. Bryan, *History of Madison County, Ohio* (Indianapolis: B. F. Bowen, 1915), 133.

73. Jones, *History of Agriculture in Ohio*, 151–52.

74. Burkett, *History of Ohio Agriculture*, 105–7, 112–13, 129–30, 142; and Jones, *History of Agriculture in Ohio*, 134.

75. *Portage and Summit Counties*, 304–5, 446–47.

76. See the case of William Baker of Leicestershire, in *Delaware County*, 820.

77. *Union County*, 315.

78. Rodney C. Loehr, "The Influence of English Agriculture on American Agriculture, 1775–1825," *Agricultural History* 11 (Jan. 1937): 3–15; Clarence Danhof, *Change in Agriculture: The Northern United States, 1820–1870* (Cambridge, Mass.: Harvard Univ. Press, 1969), 52–53, 168–69. For the Pugh story, see *Delaware County*, 505.

79. Hopley, *Crawford County*, 896.

80. A. D. M. Phillips, *The Underdraining of Farmland in England during the Nineteenth Century* (New York: Univ. of Cambridge Press, 1989), 241.

81. Bogue, *From Prairie to Corn Belt*, 84; Paul W. Gates, *The Illinois Central and Its Colonization Work* (Cambridge: Harvard Univ. Press, 1934), 165. See also George Flower, *History of the English Settlement in Edwards County, Illinois* (Chicago: Chicago Historical Society Collections, 1882), 288, 350; and Schob, *Hired Hands and Plowboys*, 112–17.

82. For these cases see, respectively, *Commemorative Record of Wood County*, 1:645, 683–84, and 3:1093, 867.

83. Caldwell, *Belmont and Jefferson Counties*, 2:610.

84. Brown, *Clinton County*, 829.

85. Morris Birkbeck, *Notes on a Journey in America from the Coast of Virginia to the Territory of Illinois* (London: Severn and Redington, 1818), 129; and Gates, *The Illinois Central*, 12–13. As late as the 1850s farmers settling on the prairies were ridiculed by others still skeptical about their fertility. Bogue, *From Prairie to Corn Belt*, 47; and Erickson, *Leaving England*, 52.

86. *Commemorative Record of Wood County*, 2:708.

87. Ibid., 712–13.

88. Schob, *Hired Hands and Plowboys*, 3.

89. Brian Coffey, "Nineteenth-Century Barns of Geauga County, Ohio," *Pioneer America* 10 (1978): 56–63.

90. Baughman, *Huron County*, 2:498, 120.

91. Doyle, *Summit County*, 405–6.

92. Robert W. McCormick, *Norton S. Townshend, M.D.: Antislavery Politician and Agricultural Educator* (n.p.: privately published, 1988), chap. 10.

93. Burkett, *History of Ohio Agriculture*, 199.

94. Paul B. Sears, "History of Conservation in Ohio," in *Ohio in the Twentieth Century, 1900–1938*, ed. Harlow Lindley (Columbus: Ohio State Archaeological and Historical Society, 1942), 224. (The work is also in *The History of the State of Ohio*, ed. Carl Wittke.)

95. Harriet N. R. Townshend, "Biographical Sketch about 1907 of Norton Strange

Townshend," Ohio State Historical Society, Ohio State University, Columbus, VFM 1121; Burkett, *History of Ohio Agriculture,* 205; and Christopher Cumo, "The Creation of the Ohio Agricultural Experiment Station, 1864–1882," *Northwest Ohio Quarterly* 71 (Winter–Spring 1999): 29–48.

96. McCormick, "Norton S. Townshend," 255, iv; and Burkett, *History of Ohio Agriculture,* 202.

5. CRAFTS AND INDUSTRY

1. This estimate is based on the observation that during the mid-nineteenth century about a third of the adult males arriving from Britain to America were craftsmen (including miners)—a proportion roughly equal to that of the British population, as recorded in the 1851 census. Van Vugt, *Britain to America,* 163, table A2.

2. Moore, *Franklin County,* 1:1149.

3. Evans, *Scioto County,* 2:1170.

4. *Commemorative Record of Wood County,* 2:706.

5. Bond, *The Civilization of the Old Northwest,* 416.

6. Baughman, *Richland and Ashland Counties,* 394–95.

7. See the case of John Evans, a blacksmith and wagon maker who combined these trades with farming, in Brister, *Newark and Licking County,* 401–2.

8. Erickson, *Leaving England,* 83.

9. Ewing Summers, *Genealogical and Family History of Eastern Ohio* (New York: Lewis, 1903), 354–57.

10. Phyllis Deane, *The First Industrial Revolution* (Cambridge: Cambridge Univ. Press, 1965), 76–78; and Peter Mathias, *The First Industrial Nation: An Economic History of Britain, 1700–1914,* 2nd ed. (London: Methuen, 1983), 101–2.

11. *Defiance County,* 290–91; and Birch, "Taking the Breaks and Working the Boats," 104, 106, 108. The names of the canals are listed as found in the sources, but canal names frequently changed. The "Miami Canal," for example, became known as the "Miami-Erie Canal" or the "Miami & Erie Canal."

12. Doyle, *Summit County,* 976.

13. *History of Wyandot County, Ohio* (Chicago: Leggett, Conaway, 1884; reprint, Ann Arbor, Mich.: Unigraphic, 1972), 916.

14. *Columbiana County,* 52, 180–84; and Linklater, *Measuring America,* 1.

15. Frank Thistlethwaite, "The Atlantic Migration of the Pottery Industry," *Economic History Review* 9 (Dec. 1958): 264–78.

16. Howe, *Historical Collections of Ohio,* 1:460–61.

17. Summers, *Genealogical and Family History of Eastern Ohio,* 479–81, 488–89. See also the case of Joseph Barlow, who came from Staffordshire in 1873 and rose to manager, on 326–29.

18. Caldwell, *Belmont and Jefferson Counties,* 2:587. For another case of a Glaswegian potter in East Liverpool, see Summers, *Genealogical and Family History of Eastern Ohio,* 429.

19. *Columbiana County,* 2:370–72; and Thistlethwaite, "The Atlantic Migration of the Pottery Industry," 270.

20. *Portage and Summit Counties,* 495.

21. Doyle, *Summit County*, 1012–13.

22. Ibid., 450–51, 1043.

23. Ibid., 552.

24. Evans, *Scioto County*, 1:764. Welsh mechanics were common in Ohio. Typical was George Edmunds, whose father was a mechanical engineer. Both worked in various capacities as engineers and superintendents. For his story, see *Scioto County*, 1:966–67.

25. James W. Endersby, "John McTammany," *American National Biography*, 1999.

26. James Martin to Mrs. Caroline Monro and Mordaunt Martin Monro, August 9, 1823, London Metropolitan Archives, ACC/1063/141.

27. Bond, *The Civilization of the Old Northwest*, 409; and Gjerde, *The Minds of the West*, 143.

28. Andrews, *Marietta and Washington County*, 1263.

29. A. J. Baughman, *History of Richland County, Ohio, from 1808 to 1908* (Chicago: S. J. Clarke, 1908), 1106–10.

30. Doyle, *Summit County*, 380.

31. Ibid., 667.

32. Ibid., 781.

33. Andrews, *Marietta and Washington County*, 1263–64; and Caldwell, *Belmont and Jefferson Counties*, 1:305. For an example of engineers taking up farming, see the case of John G. Erskine, a Scottish engineer who arrived in Mahoning County in 1866, in Summers, *Genealogical and Family History of Eastern Ohio*, 86–87. For the Hutchins, see *Delaware County*, 628.

34. Hopley, *Crawford County*, 749, 831, 842.

35. Doyle, *Summit County*, 577–78.

36. Ibid., 1054–55.

37. Hopley, *Crawford County*, 1168.

38. *Stark County*, 483–84. Another immigrant, George Hunter, born in Scotland in 1873, became manager of the American Bridge Company at Youngstown. See Summers, *Genealogical and Family History of Eastern Ohio*, 542–43.

39. A. T. McKelvey, ed., *Centennial History of Belmont County, Ohio* (Chicago: Biographical, 1903), 486. See also the case of Frederick Sheldon, a young immigrant from Manchester, who arrived in 1870. He immediately entered the railroad industry as draughtsman and rose to become chief engineer of the Hocking Valley Railway Company. See Taylor, *Columbus and Franklin County*, 762–63.

40. Rose, *Cleveland*, 533.

41. Douglas L. Crowell, "History of the Coal-Mining Industry in Ohio," *Ohio Division of Geological Survey Bulletin 72* (Columbus: Division of Geological Survey, 1995): 2.

42. Cobbett, *A Year's Residence*, 256.

43. Howe, *Historical Collections of Ohio*, 2:322–24.

44. Priscilla Long, *Where the Sun Never Shines: A History of America's Bloody Coal Industry* (New York: Paragon, 1991), 57; and Charlotte Erickson, *American Industry and the European Immigrant, 1860–1885* (New York: Russell and Russell, 1967), 107.

45. "Table 31: Statistics on Population," *Tenth Census of the United States: 1880*, vol. 1 (Washington, D.C.: United States Census Bureau), 735.

46. Berthoff, *British Immigrants in Industrial America*, 51.

47. Crowell, "History of the Coal-Mining Industry," 87.

48. Conway, *The Welsh in America*, 170.

49. For Thompson, see Caldwell, *Belmont and Jefferson Counties,* 2:511. Ashton is in McKelvey, *Belmont County*, 505. See the example of James Little in Evans, *Scioto County*, 2:1047. See also the case of Welshman Thomas J. Williams, who was appointed superintendent of the Hudson Coal Company, in *Portage and Summit Counties*, 956–57.

50. Summers, *Genealogical and Family History of Eastern Ohio*, 84–85.

51. Albert A. Graham, *History of Fairfield and Perry Counties* (Chicago: W. H. Beers, 1883), 578.

52. Conway, *The Welsh in America*, 172.

53. Ibid.

54. Summers, *Genealogical and Family History of Eastern Ohio*, 424–25.

55. *Commemorative Record of Wood County*, 3:710–11.

56. Moore, *Franklin County*, 1:558–59.

57. Caldwell, *Belmont and Jefferson Counties*, 498–500.

58. Doyle, *Summit County*, 1079.

59. *Stark County*, 133–34.

60. For both of these cases, see Taylor, *Columbus and Franklin County*, 2:585–86, 276–77. For yet another example, see that of Edward Johnson on page 530.

61. Graham, *Fairfield and Perry Counties*, 507. Marriage certificate of Thomas Pirt to Anne Mark, Dec. 1860, N. Houghton, England, 10A/446.

62. John H. M. Laslett, *Colliers Across the Sea: A Comparative Study of Class Formation in Scotland and the American Midwest, 1830–1924* (Urbana: Univ. of Illinois Press, 2000), 63–4.

63. Ibid., 25.

64. Craig Phelan, *William Green: Biography of a Labor Leader* (Albany, N.Y.: SUNY Press, 1989), 1–4.

65. Graham, *Fairfield and Perry Counties*, 340. Marriage certificate of John Bigrigg to Anna Malkingson, Dec. 15, 1849, Whitehaven, England, 25/193.

66. Graham, *Fairfield and Perry Counties*, 427.

67. Ibid., 498. Marriage certificate of Enoch Oldroyd to Patience Almond, Mar. 1866, Dewsbury, England, 9B/673.

68. Graham, *Fairfield and Perry Counties*, 447–48. Birth certificate of Harry Kear, Mar. 1854, Forest of Dean, Gloucestershire, England.

69. Ibid., 505–6, 575.

70. Ibid., 379.

71. Ibid., 586–88, 379–80.

72. Ibid., 441, 508. Marriage certificate of George Plant to Maria Parks, Sept. 1870, Stoke-on-Trent, GG/207.

73. Ibid., 576, 587, 514. Marriage certificate of Thomas Weatherburn to Mary Ann Wilson, Sept. 1869, Tynemouth, England, 10G/335.

74. Eckley and Perry, *Carroll and Harrison Counties*, 2, 860–61, 955.

75. Clifton K. Yearley, *Britons in American Labor* (Baltimore, Md.: Johns Hopkins Univ. Press, 1957).

76. Crowell, "History of the Coal-Mining Industry," 95.

77. K. Austin Kerr, "The Movement for Coal Mine Safety in Nineteenth-Century Ohio," *Ohio History* 86 (Winter 1997): 3–18; Andrew Roy, *A History of the Coal Miners of the United States* (1905; reprint, Westport, Conn.: Greenwood, 1970), 116–28, 190; and Howe, *Historical Collections of Ohio*, 1:110.

78. Roy, *A History of the Coal Miners*, 123.

79. Laslett, *Colliers across the Sea*, 69–70, 122.

80. Evans, *Scioto County*, 2:1185–86.

81. "Mrs. George Pugh Letter," Ohio State Historical Society, Ohio State University, Columbus, VMF 1600; and *Delaware County*, 762–63.

82. Evans, *Scioto County*, 1:679.

83. Baughman, *Richland and Ashland Counties*, 344–46.

84. Berthoff, *British Immigrants in Industrial America*, 80; McKelvey, *Belmont County*, 372; and Evans, *Scioto County*, 1:828. See the case of Peter McLaren, in Andrews, *Marietta and Washington County*, 1129–30.

85. Brister, *Newark and Licking County*, 170–74. See also *Historical Hand-Atlas Illustrated*, 32.

86. *Marion and Hardin Counties*, 151–52.

87. *Delaware County*, 627.

88. *Knox County*, 251.

89. Doyle, *Summit County*, 469, 527, 583, 651–52.

90. Ibid., 685–86.

91. Ibid., 713, 777.

92. Ibid., 335.

93. John Curtis to Richard Cobden, May 8, 1844, Manchester Central Library, Manchester, M87/2/2/25.

94. Erickson, *Invisible Immigrants*, 265–66.

95. David J. Jeremy, *Transatlantic Industrial Revolution: The Diffusion of Textile Technologies between Britain and America, 1790–1830s* (Cambridge, Mass.: MIT Press, 1981), 231.

96. Bond, *The Civilization of the Old Northwest*, 412–13; Caldwell, *Belmont and Jefferson Counties*, 1:512; *Warren County*, 790; and Caldwell, *Belmont and Jefferson Counties*, 1:279. See also vol. 2, 547.

97. Caldwell, *Belmont and Jefferson Counties*, 2:509; and Erickson, *Invisible Immigrants*, 165.

98. Taylor, *Columbus and Franklin County*, 726–30. For a case of an English immigrant who went from the woolen business to commerce, real estate, and banking, see that of Charles Rabbitts, in Rockel, *Springfield, and Clark County*, 899–900.

99. *Wyandot County*, 764.

100. Baughman, *Richland and Ashland Counties*, 227–28.

101. Evans, *Scioto County*, 1:775–76.

102. Alan Birch, *The Economic History of the British Iron and Steel Industry, 1784–1879* (New York: A. M. Kelly, 1967), 121; John H. Clapham, *An Economic History of Modern*

Britain, Volume One: The Early Railway Age, 1820–1850 (New York: Cambridge University Press, 1938), 425–29; and Deane, *The First Industrial Revolution*, 101.

103. Paul Wakelee Stoddard, "The Knowledge of Coal and Iron in Ohio before 1835," *Ohio Archaeological and Historical Publications* 37 (1929): 219–30.

104. Berthoff, *British Immigrants in Industrial America*, chap. 5; and James M. Swank, *History of the Manufacture of Iron in All Ages* (Philadelphia, Pa.: American Iron and Steel Association, 1892), 309–10.

105. Swank, *History of the Manufacture of Iron* , 301–7, 360–61, 367–69; and Gilbert F. Dodds, "Early Ironmakers of Ohio," *Franklin County Historical Society* (1957): 11.

106. *History of Trumbull and Mahoning Counties*, vol. 2 (Cleveland, Ohio: H. Z. Williams, 1882), 236–46.

107. Rowe, *History of the Iron and Steel Industry*, 12.

108. Ibid., 32–39.

109. Summers, *Genealogical and Family History of Eastern Ohio*, 464–67. For another case of immigrants coming from a long line of iron workers and bringing that tradition to Ohio, see James Skelding in Caldwell, *Belmont and Jefferson Counties*, 304.

110. *Genealogical and Biographical Record of Miami County, Ohio* (Chicago: Lewis, 1900), 341–42, 891.

111. Evans, *Scioto County*, 2:1196–97.

112. Ibid., 1078. See also the case of Scottish immigrant David Nevin Murray, who built machine shops, a foundry, and a rolling mill in Portsmouth during the 1850s, on pages 792–93.

113. Summers, *Genealogical and Family History of Eastern Ohio*, 253–54, 293–95. See also pages 196–98 and 654–57.

114. Doyle, *Summit County*, 748.

115. Graham, *Fairfield and Perry Counties*, 441.

116. Thomas C. Harbaugh, *Centennial History of Troy, Piqua and Miami County, Ohio* (Chicago: Richmond-Arnold, 1909), 372.

117. Ibid., 345.

118. Vernon David Keeler, "An Economic History of the Jackson County Iron Industry," *Ohio Archaeological and Historical Quarterly* 42 (Apr. 1933): 168–73; Jones, *Romance of the Old Charcoal Furnace*, 1–2; and Willard, *A Standard History of the Hanging Rock Iron Region*, 449.

119. Rose, *Cleveland,* 289; and Summers, *Genealogical and Family History of Eastern Ohio,* 773–74, 332–36.

120. Jones, *Romance of the Old Charcoal Furnace*, 6; and Willard, *A Standard History of the Hanging Rock Iron Region*, 42–43, 439.

121. Rose, *Cleveland*, 277–78, 322, 378, 445; and Harlan Hatcher, *The Western Reserve: The Story of New Connecticut in Ohio* (Indianapolis, Ind.: Bobbs-Merrill, 1949), 237. For another, less spectacular but still noteworthy example, see William Mann, who had come from a family of ironworkers in Lanarkshire. In 1879 he built his own foundry and machine shops to produce castings for customers throughout the United States. See McKelvey, *Belmont County*, 330–31.

122. James R. Alexander, *Jaybird: A. J. Moxham and the Manufacture of the Johnson Rail* (Johnstown, Pa: Johnstown Area Heritage Association, 1991).

123. Gilliland, *Van Wert County*, 423–24.

124. Ibid., 441–42.

125. Baughman, *Richland County*, 1154–55.

126. Wolfe, *Guernsey County*, 2:688–89.

127. Ibid., 727–28, 787–89, 796–97.

128. Ibid., 967–68.

129. Ibid., 836–37.

130. Berthoff, *British Immigrants in Industrial America*, 68–69.

131. Wolfe, *Guernsey County*, 2:884–85.

132. Ibid., 661–62.

133. Ibid., 476–77.

134. Ibid., 952–53.

135. Ibid., 484–86, 625–27.

6. Religion and Reform

1. Graham, *Fairfield and Perry Counties*, 524.

2. Rohrbough, *The Trans-Appalachian Frontier*, 146–49.

3. Robinson, *Greene County*, 235.

4. James Martin to Mordaunt Monro, Feb. 1, 1822, London Metropolitan Archives, ACC/1063/150.

5. *Western Herald*, Apr. 11, 1837.

6. *Bible Christian Magazine* 11 (1846): 77.

7. Ibid., 77–79.

8. *The Bible Christian Magazine* 12 (1847): 80–82.

9. Griffiths, *Two Years' Residence in the New Settlements of Ohio*, 153–54.

10. Quoted in Birch, "A British View of the Ohio Backwoods," 156n20.

11. Frances Trollope, *Domestic Manners of the Americans, 1832* (New York: Knopf, 1949), 172.

12. Catherine M. Rokicky, *Creating a Perfect World: Religious and Secular Utopias in Nineteenth-Century Ohio* (Athens: Ohio Univ. Press, 2002), chap. 1; Bond, *The Civilization of the Old Northwest*, 488–89.

13. Van Vugt, *Britain to America*, 135n14.

14. F. Mark McKiernan and Roger D. Launius, eds., *An Early Latter-Day Saint History: The Book of John Whitmer, Kept by Commandment* (Independence, Mo.: Herald, 1980), 146–47.

15. Milton V. Blackman Jr., *The Heavens Resound: A History of the Latter-day Saints in Ohio, 1830–1838* (Salt Lake City, Utah: Deseret, 1983), 108–9.

16. Shepperson, *Emigration and Disenchantment*, 135–36.

17. Davies, "The Welsh in Ohio," 312.

18. Francis M. Gibbons, *John Taylor: Mormon Philosopher, Prophet of God* (Salt Lake City, Utah: Deseret, 1985), esp. 18–21.

19. Charles Yrigoyen Jr., "John Swanel Inskip," *American National Biography*, 1999.

20. Douglass, *Wayne County*, 337–40; George W. Knight and John R. Commons, "The History of Higher Education in Ohio." *Bureau of Education Circular of Information. No. 5.* (Washington, D.C.: GPO, 1891), 80–83.

21. Kevin Joseph Bereznay, "Immigration and Industrialization: A Study of Lorain, Ohio, 1895–1910," (master's thesis, Kent State University, 1980), 21.

22. Bruce David Forbes, "William Henry Roberts: Resistance to Change and Bureaucratic Adaptation," *Journal of Presbyterian History* 54 (Winter 1976): 405–21.

23. C. S. Griffin, *The Ferment of Reform, 1830–1860* (Arlington Heights, Il.: AHM, 1967).

24. Ratcliffe, *Party Spirit*, 93. Some secular-minded British reform movements also entered Ohio between the 1820s and 1850s through the Utopian communities of Robert Owen. They were concerned mainly with addressing the worst effects of industrialization. They failed mainly because they downplayed religion, whereas most Ohioans embraced it. Rokicky, *Creating a Perfect World*, 113, 119.

25. Michael J. McTighe, *A Measure of Success: Protestants and Public Culture in Antebellum Cleveland* (Albany, N.Y.: SUNY Press, 1994), 97, 117.

26. Gjerde, *The Minds of the West*, 292–94.

27. Brister, *Newark and Licking County*, 401–2

28. *Commemorative Record of Wood County*, 1:706–7.

29. Summers, *Genealogical and Family History of Eastern Ohio*, 84–86.

30. Henry Butts, "Letter from an Emigrant to America, 1855," London Metropolitan Archives, ACC/0319/001.

31. Richard F. O'Dell, "The Early Anti-Slave Movement in Ohio" (Ph.D. diss., University of Michigan, 1948), 13, 109; Oscar Castle Hooper, *History of Ohio Journalism 1793–1933* (Columbus: Spahr and Glenn, 1933), 25–6; and Bond, *The Civilization of the Old Northwest*, 124.

32. Willard, *A Standard History of the Hanging Rock Iron Region*, 439.

33. Robinson, *Greene County*, 196–99. For another immigrant Scottish clergyman who arrived in 1807, see the story of Andrew Heron on page 234.

34. Julie Roy Jeffrey, *The Great Silent Army of Abolitionism: Ordinary Women in the Antislavery Movement* (Chapel Hill: Univ. of North Carolina Press, 1998), 24–25, 110–12, 122–23.

35. James H. Rodabaugh, *Robert Hamilton Bishop* (Columbus: Ohio State Archaeological and Historical Society, 1935), 150n35; "Thompson, George," *Dictionary of National Biography*, 19:691.

36. Rodabaugh, *Robert Hamilton Bishop*, 82.

37. David B. Eller, "Walter Scott," *American National Biography*, 1999; and Henry K. Shaw, *Buckeye Disciples: A History of the Disciples of Christ in Ohio* (St. Louis, Mo.: Christian Board of Publications, 1952), 12–16, 42, 53, 107–8.

38. Evans, *Scioto County*, 1:507.

39. *Album of Genealogy and Biography, Cook County, Illinois* (Chicago: Calumet, 1895), 766.

40. Knight and Commons, "History of Higher Education in Ohio," 90–99.

41. Bryan, *Madison County*, 920–21.

42. Harbaugh, *Troy, Piqua and Miami County*, 791–92.

43. Evans, *Scioto County*, 1:679–80.

44. Taylor, *Columbus and Franklin County*, 2:745–48.

45. Howe, *Historical Collections of Ohio*, 1:186–87.

46. Williams, *Clermont and Brown Counties*, 2:266–69.

47. Regina Morantz-Sanchez, "Elizabeth Blackwell," *American National Biography*, 1999; and Debra Viles, "Henry Brown Blackwell," *American National Biography*, 1999.

48. John Stauffer, "Richard Realf," *American National Biography*, 1999; and Stephen B. Oates, *To Purge This Land with Blood: A Biography of John Brown* (New York: Harper and Row, 1972), 219, 222, 246, 251, 359.

49. Thomas E. Wagner, "Cincinnati and Southeastern Ohio: An Abolitionist Training Ground" (master's thesis, Miami University, 1967), 81–83.

50. Michael C. Coleman, "Alexander McBeth," *American National Biography*, 1999.

51. Ella Lonn, *Foreigners in the Union Army and Navy* (New York: Greenwood, 1969), 577–79.

52. George D. Lillibridge, *Beacon of Freedom: The Impact of American Democracy upon Great Britain, 1830–1870* (1955; revised, New York: A. S. Barnes, 1961), 46; Asa Briggs, *Victorian People: A Reassessment of Persons and Themes* (New York: Harper, 1955), 171; and Christine Bolt, *Victorian Attitudes to Race* (Boston: Routledge and Kegan Paul, 1971), 33.

53. Quoted in R. J. M. Blackett, *Divided Hearts: Britain and the American Civil War* (Baton Rouge: Louisiana State Univ. Press, 2001), 4. Though there was some sympathy in Britain for the Confederacy, sentiments to intervene militarily and recognize its legitimacy never ran deep in British circles and faded even more after the Emancipation Proclamation was issued.

54. Gilliland, *Van Wert County*, 637.

55. Lonn, *Foreigners in the Union Army and Navy*, 577–79; Van Vugt, *Britain to America*, 142–47; and Evans, *Scioto County*, 1:966.

56. *Commemorative Record of Wood County*, 1:487–88.

57. Elizabeth's statement was published in the local newspapers and read aloud to the troops on the front. Rockel, *Springfield, and Clark County*, 930–32.

58. Robert W. McCormick, "A Union Army Medical Inspector: Norton Townshend," *Ohio History* 103 (Winter–Spring 1994): 57–70.

59. Ibid., 65, 67, 70.

60. *Commemorative Record of Wood County*, 3:963–64.

61. Howe, *Historical Collections of Ohio*, 1:405.

62. Bahmer, *Coshocton County*, 2:40–45. The case of John McTammany, a mechanic who volunteered soon after his arrival, was mentioned in the previous chapter.

63. Doyle, *Summit County*, 862.

64. *Official Roster of the Soldiers of the State of Ohio in the War of Rebellion, 1861–1866*, Series 1, Vol. 40, Part 1, Serial No. 80 (Comp. under the Direction of the Roster Commission), 625; and Summers, *Genealogical and Family History of Eastern Ohio*, 479–81. I am grateful to historian Kelly Selby for some of the information on Cartwright.

65. *Portrait and Biographical Record of the City of Toledo and Lucas and Wood Counties, Ohio* (Chicago: Chapman, 1895), 294–95.

66. Hopley, *Crawford County*, 1011.

67. Doyle, *Summit County*, 1079–80.

68. Hopley, *Crawford County*, 749.

69. Baughman, *Huron County*, 1:373–74.

70. *Cleveland Leader*, Aug. 22, 1864.

71. Bahmer, *Coshocton County*, 1:487–88.

72. Conway, *The Welsh in America*, 182.

73. Van Vugt, *Britain to America*, 148.

7. The Professions, Arts, and Civil Service

1. Oscar Wilde briefly visited Ohio in February 1882 to lecture on "The English Renaissance of Art." He was twenty-eight years old and had not yet authored the works that made him famous. But he did create a stir with his fancy dress, refined English manners, and his reputation as an expert in art and aesthetics who had much to teach the American public. See Francis X. Roellinger, "Oscar Wilde in Cleveland," *Ohio State Archeological and Historical Quarterly* 59 (1950): 129–38.

2. Van Vugt *Britain to America*, table A2, 163. For county history figures see appendix, tables 5 and 6.

3. Brister, *Newark and Licking County*, 132–33.

4. Douglass, *Wayne County*, 336.

5. Bryan, *Madison County*, 548.

6. A. W. Drury, *History of the City of Dayton and Montgomery County, Ohio*, vol. 1 (Chicago: S. J. Clarke, 1909), 257–58.

7. Anne Taylor Kirschmann, "Myra King Merrick," *American National Biography*, 1999.

8. Norman Wahl, "Thomas Wingate Todd," *American National Biography*, 1999.

9. Evans, *Scioto County*, 1:504–6. For Belt, see chapter 1.

10. Graham, *Fairfield and Perry Counties*, 588.

11. Bryan, *Madison County*, 133.

12. *Knox County, Ohio*, 139.

13. Thomas Read, Rhinebeck, Dutchess County, New York, to John Read, London Metropolitan Archives, ACC/1093/159.

14. Donald R. MacKenzie, "The Itinerant Artist in Early Ohio," *Ohio History* 73 (1964): 41–46.

15. Anthony R. Haigh, "Samuel Drake," *American National Biography*, 1999.

16. Lucile Clifton, "The Early Theatre in Columbus, Ohio, 1820–1840," *Ohio State Archaeological and Historical Quarterly* 62 (1953): 234–46.

17. Mary C. Henderson, "Anne Hartley Gilbert," *American National Biography*, 1999.

18. For examples, see Evans, *Scioto County*, 1:837; 2:1267; *Historical Hand-Atlas Illustrated . . . Map of Gallia County*, xxv; Brister, *Newark and Licking County*, 132, 443; *Stark County*, 207; and *Commemorative Record of Wood County*, 1:624, 639; 2:778, 787; 3:867.

19. Lawrence Wodehouse. "Alfred Bult Mullett," *American National Biography*, 1999.

20. Frank J. Olmsted, "Jim McCormick," *American National Biography*, 1999.

21. Bond, *The Civilization of the Old Northwest*, 441.

22. William L. Fisk, "John Bailhache: A British Editor in Early Ohio," *Ohio History Quarterly* 67 (Apr. 1958): 141–47; Buley, *The Old Northwest Pioneer Period*, 2:517; and Hooper, *History of Ohio Journalism*, 75.

23. *History of Preble County, Ohio* (Cleveland, Ohio: H. Z. Williams, 1881), 146–47. Many sons of British immigrants became important and influential publishers. See the example of William McMurray who started and published the *Auglaize Republican*, from 1881 to 1915, in William J. McMurray, ed., *History of Auglaize County, Ohio*, vol. 2 (Indianapolis, Ind.: Historical, 1923), 665–70.

24. Kent Neely and Steve West, "Alfred Burnett," *American National Biography*, 1999; and Hooper, *History of Ohio Journalism*, 65.

25. Howe, *Historical Collections of Ohio*, 1:615.

26. *Tuscarawas County*, 711–12.

27. Perrin, Battle, and Goodspeed, *Crawford County and Ohio*, 743–44; and Hopley, *Crawford County*, 627–30. If one includes the children of immigrants, then the British figure very prominently indeed in Ohio's professions. David Hopkins, a Welsh immigrant who helped establish the iron mills of Newburgh, is one example. His sons included Cleveland's first city manager, a prominent pastor in Cincinnati, a highly successful accountant, the dean of Western Reserve University's law school, a leading physician, two industrial executives, and Cleveland's leading theatrical producer. Rose, *Cleveland*, 822.

28. Samuel Cartwright was the brother of John Cartwright, who led African American troops and was killed at the Battle of the Crater (see chapter 6). Summers, *Genealogical and Family History of Eastern Ohio*, 480–81, 354–57. For examples of iron workers being elected to boards and as sheriff after their quick assimilation to American life, see pages 145–47, 196–99, and 754–57 of the same volume.

29. Taylor, *Columbus and Franklin County*, 2:630–34.

30. *Toledo and Lucas and Wood Counties*, 259–60.

31. *Trumbull and Mahoning Counties*, 2:246–47; and Williams, *Clermont and Brown Counties*, 1:684–86.

32. Rockel, *Springfield, and Clark County*, 255; and Stephen J. Bartha, "A History of Immigrant Groups in Toledo," (master's thesis, Ohio State University, 1945), 69.

33. John D. Buenker, "Cleveland's New Stock Lawmakers and Progressive Reform," *Ohio History* 78 (1969): 116–37. Phelan, *William Green*, chap. 1.

34. Phelan, *William Green*, chap. 1.

35. Marnie Jones, *Holy Toledo: Religion and Politics in the Life of "Golden Rule" Jones* (Lexington: Univ. Press of Kentucky, 1998), chap. 1; and Arthur E. DeMatteo, "The Progressive as Elitist: 'Golden Rule' Jones and the Toledo Charter Reform Campaign of 1901," *Northwest Ohio Quarterly* 69 (Winter 1997): 8–30.

36. Jones, *Holy Toledo*, 202–8, 231–32.

37. Evans, *Scioto County*, 2:1185–6; appendix, table 10.

38. Paul Kleppner, *The Third Electoral System, 1853–1892: Parties, Voters, and Political Cultures* (Chapel Hill: Univ. of North Carolina Press, 1979), 61, 64, 147–48, 163–65.

39. A clear example of common religion and language forming common political affiliations among American-born and English-born residents in Dubuque, Iowa, can be found in Gjerde, *The Minds of the West*, 104.

CONCLUSION

1. Quoted in Philip Durham and Everett L. Jones, eds., *The Frontier in American Literature* (New York: Odyssey, 1969), 11.

APPENDIX

1. For discussion of the nature and merits of county histories as historical sources, see Archibald Hanna, "Every Man His Own Biographer," *Proceedings of the American Antiquarian Society* 80 (1970): 291–98; and Howard Chudacoff, "The S. J. Clarke Publishing Company and the Study of Urban History," *Historian* 49 (Feb. 1987): 184–93.

Bibliography

PRIMARY SOURCES
BIRTH AND MARRIAGE CERTIFICATES

*Birth and marriage certificate information was gathered from copies of the private collection of Charlotte Erickson. Originals are located in St. Catherine's House, London.

Bigrigg, John, to Anna Malkingson. Certificate of Marriage. Government Registry Office [GRO]. December 15, 1849. Whitehaven, England. 25/193.

Kear, Harry. Birth Certificate. Monmouth, March 1854, 11a/24.

Oldroyd, Enoch, to Patience Almond. Certificate of Marriage. March 1866. Dewsbury, England. 9B/673.

Pirt, Thomas, to Anne Mark. Certificate of Marriage. December 1860. N. Houghton, England. 10A/446.

Plant, George, to Maria Parks. Certificate of Marriage. September 1870. Stoke-on-Trent, England. GG/207.

Weatherburn, Thomas, to Mary Ann Wilson. Certificate of Marriage. August 14, 1869. Tynemouth, England. 10G/335.

GOVERNMENT DOCUMENTS

Annals of Cleveland Court Record Series. Vols. 1–2: 1837–1857. Cleveland, Ohio: Works Progress Administration, 1939.

Annual Report of the Secretary of State to the Governor of Ohio, Jail Reports, 1854 and 1855. Facsimile (Bowie, Md.: Heritage, 1988).

Compendium of the Tenth Census. Washington: United States Census Bureau, 1884.

"Declaration of Intention to Become a United States Citizen by James Battersby." 1854, Merseyside County Museums, Liverpool. DB/119D/74.

Official Roster of the Soldiers of the State of Ohio in the War of Rebellion, 1861–1866. Series 1. Vol. 40. Part 1. Serial No. 80. Compiled under the Direction of the Roster Commission.

Reports on the Census of England and Wales. Edinburgh: Census of Scotland, 1951.

"Table 31: Statistics on Population." *Tenth Census of the United States: 1880*, vol. 1. Washington, DC: United States Census Bureau.

LETTERS AND MANUSCRIPTS

Amphlett, William. *The Emigrant's Directory to the Western States of North America*. London: Longman, Hurst, Rees, Orme, and Brown, 1819.

Birkbeck, Morris. *Notes on a Journey in America from the Coast of Virginia to the Territory of Illinois*. London: Severn and Redington, 1818.

Brown, William. *America: A Four Years' Residence in the United States and Canada*. Leeds: Kemplay and Bolland, 1849.

Butts, Henry. "Letter from an Emigrant to America, 1855." London Metropolitan Archives. ACC/0319/001.

Charles Rose Papers. Ohio State Historical Society, Ohio State University, Columbus. VFM 1903.

Courtauld Family Letters, 1782–1900. 3 vols. Cambridge, U.K.: Bowes and Bowes, 1916.

Curtis, John, to Richard Cobden, May 8, 1844. Manchester Central Library, Manchester. M87/2/2/25.

Griffiths, D., Jr. *Two Years' Residence in the New Settlements of Ohio, North America: With Directions to Emigrants.* London: Westley and Davis, 1835. Reprint, Ann Arbor, Michigan: University Microfilms, 1966.

Kirk, Robert. *The Memoirs and Adventures of Robert Kirk, Late of the Royal Highland Regiment, Written by Himself . . .* Limerick, Ireland: J. Ferrar, 1770.

Martin, James, to Mordaunt Monro, February 1, 1822. London Metropolitan Archives. ACC/1063/150.

Martin, James, to Mrs. Caroline Monro and Mordaunt Martin Monro, August 9, 1823. London Metropolitan Archives. ACC/1063/141.

Martin, James, to Mrs. Caroline Monro and Mordaunt Martin Monro, October 9, 1836. London Metropolitan Archives. ACC/1063/150

"Mrs. George Pugh Letter." Ohio State Historical Society, Ohio State University, Columbus. VMF 1600

Murray, Charles Augustus. *Travels in North America during the Years 1834, 1835, and 1836.* Vol. 1. London: Richard Bentley, 1841.

Peter Girard Collection. Guernsey Archives, Guernsey.

Read, Thomas, Rhinebeck, Dutchess County, New York, to John Read. London Metropolitan Archives. ACC/1093/159.

"Recollections of Pioneer Life in Wisconsin." In *Bewick Family History*. Wisconsin Historical Society SC, 1923.

Ridout, Thomas. "An Account of My Capture by the Shawanese Indians." *Western Pennsylvania Historical Magazine* 12 (January 1929): 3–31.

Robert Bowles Manuscripts. Vol. 538. Ohio State Historical Society, Ohio State University, Columbus.

Slade, George, and Orange Slade, Coshocton County, to their brother, June 6, 1841. Ohio State Historical Society, Ohio State University, Columbus. VFM 3334.

Tocqueville, Alexis de. *Democracy in America.* 1835. Trans. and ed. Harvey C. Mansfield and Delba Winthrop. Chicago: University of Chicago Press, 2000.

Townshend, Harriet N. R. "Biographical Sketch about 1907 of Norton Strange Townshend." Ohio State Historical Society, Ohio State University, Columbus. VFM 1121.

Welsh Hills Community Papers. Ohio State Historical Society, Ohio State University, Columbus. MSS 555, Box 20, Folders 1 and 24.

Wing, L. B. Trustee address at the dedication of Townshend Hall, Ohio State University, Columbus, January 12, 1898. Ohio State Historical Society, Ohio State University, Columbus. BT666, 5–7.

NEWSPAPERS AND PERIODICALS

Cleveland Herald
Cleveland Leader
Daily True Democrat (Cleveland)
Inverness Courier (Scotland)
Times (London)
Western Herald (Shebbear, Devon, England)

UNITED STATES COUNTY HISTORIES

Album of Genealogy and Biography, Cook County, Illinois. Chicago: Calumet, 1895.

Aldrich, Lewis Cass, ed. *History of Erie County, Ohio, with Illustrations and Biographical Sketches of Some of Its Prominent Men and Pioneers*. Syracuse, N.Y.: D Mason, 1889.

Andrews, Martin R., ed. *History of Marietta and Washington County, Ohio, and Representative Citizens*. Chicago: Biographical, 1902.

Bahmer, William J. *Centennial History of Coshocton County, Ohio*. 2 vol. Chicago: S. J. Clarke, 1909.

Baughman, A. J. *History of Huron County, Ohio, Its Progress and Development*. 2 vols. Chicago: S. J. Clarke, 1909.

———. *History of Richland County, Ohio, from 1808 to 1908*. Chicago: S. J. Clarke, 1908.

———, ed. *Centennial Biographical History of Richland and Ashland Counties, Ohio*. Chicago: Lewis, 1901.

Biographical Record of Knox County, Ohio. Chicago: Lewis, 1902.

Brister, E. M. P. *Centennial History of the City of Newark and Licking County, Ohio*. Vol. 1. Chicago: S. J. Clarke, 1909.

Brown, Albert J. *History of Clinton County, Ohio Its People, Industries and Institutions*. Indianapolis, Ind.: B. F. Bowen, 1915.

Bryan, Chester E. *History of Madison County, Ohio*. Indianapolis, Ind.: B.F. Bowen, 1915.

Caldwell, John A. *History of Belmont and Jefferson Counties, Ohio*. Wheeling, W. Va.: Historical Publishing, 1880.

Commemorative Historical and Biographical Record of Wood County, Ohio. 3 vols. Chicago: J. H. Beers, 1897.

Douglass, Ben. *History of Wayne County, Ohio, From the Days of the Pioneers and First Settlers to the Present Time*. Indianapolis, Ind.: Robert Douglass, 1878.

Doyle, William B. *Centennial History of Summit County, Ohio, and Representative Citizens*. Chicago: Biographical, 1908.

Drury, A. W. *History of the City of Dayton and Montgomery County, Ohio*. 2 vols. Chicago: S. J. Clarke, 1909.

Eckley, H. J., and William T. Perry, eds. *History of Carroll and Harrison Counties*. 2 vols. Chicago: Lewis, 1921.

Evans, Nelson W. *History of Scioto County, Ohio*. 2 vols. Portsmouth, Ohio: Higginson, 1903.

Genealogical and Biographical Record of Miami County, Ohio. Chicago: Lewis, 1900.

Gilliland, Thaddeus S., ed. *History of Van Wert County, Ohio, and Representative Citizens.* Chicago: Richmond and Arnold, 1906.

Graham, Albert A. *History of Fairfield and Perry Counties.* Chicago: W. H. Beers, 1883.

Historical Hand-Atlas Illustrated . . . Map of Gallia County, and Histories of Lawrence and Gallia Counties, Ohio. Chicago: H. H. Hardesty, 1882.

History of Columbiana County, Ohio, with Illustrations and Biographical Sketches of Some of Its Prominent Men and Pioneers. Philadelphia, Pa.: D. W. Ensign, 1879.

History of Defiance County. Chicago: Warner, Beers, 1883.

History of Delaware County and Ohio. Chicago: O. L. Baskin, 1880.

History of Hocking Valley, Ohio. Vol. 1. 1883. Reprint, Milford, Ohio: Little Miami, 2000.

History of Preble County, Ohio. Cleveland, Ohio: H. Z. Williams, 1881.

History of Ross and Highland Counties. Williams, 1880.

History of Trumbull and Mahoning Counties. 2 vols. Cleveland, Ohio: H. Z. Williams, 1882.

History of Tuscarawas County, Ohio. Chicago: Warner, Beers, 1884.

History of Union County. Chicago: W. H. Beers, 1883.

History of Warren County, Ohio. Chicago: W. H. Beers, 1882.

History of Wyandot County, Ohio. Chicago: Leggett, Conaway, 1884. Reprint, Ann Arbor, Mich.: Unigraphic, 1972.

Hopley, John E. *History of Crawford County, Ohio, and Representative Citizens.* Chicago: Richmond-Arnold, 1912.

Howe, Henry. *Historical Collections of Ohio in Two Volumes.* 2 vols. Cincinnati, Ohio: C. J. Krehbiel, 1888. Reprint, Ohio Centennial edition, 1908.

McBride, James. *Pioneer Biography: Sketches of the Lives of Some of the Early Settlers of Butler County, Ohio.* Vol 2. Cincinnati, Ohio: Robert Clarke, 1871.

McKelvey, A. T., ed. *Centennial History of Belmont County, Ohio.* Chicago: Biographical, 1903.

McMurray, William J., ed. *History of Auglaize County, Ohio.* 2 vols. Indianapolis, Ind.: Historical, 1923.

Moore, Opha. *History of Franklin County, Ohio.* Vol. 1. Topeka, Ind.: Historical, 1930.

Perrin, W. H., J. H. Battle, and W. A. Goodspeed. *History of Crawford County and Ohio.* Chicago: Baskin and Battey, 1881.

Portrait and Biographical Album of Morgan and Scott Counties, Illinois, Containing Full Page Portraits and Biographical Sketches of Prominent and Representative Citizens of the County. Chicago: Chapman, 1889.

Portrait and Biographical Record of the City of Toledo and Lucas and Wood Counties, Ohio. Chicago: Chapman, 1895.

Portrait and Biographical Record of Fayette, Pickaway and Madison Counties, Ohio. Chicago: Chapman, 1892.

Portrait and Biographical Record of Marion and Hardin Counties, Ohio. Chicago: Chapman, 1895.

Portrait and Biographical Record of Portage and Summit Counties, Ohio. Logansport, Ind.: A. W. Bowen, 1898.

Portrait and Biographical Record of Stark County, Ohio. Chicago: Chapman, 1892.

Robertson, Charles. *Morgan County, Ohio*. Chicago: L. H. Watkins, 1886.

Robinson, George F. *History of Greene County, Ohio*. Chicago: S. J. Clarke, 1902.

Rockel, William M., ed. *20th Century History of Springfield, and Clark County, Ohio, and Representative Citizens*. Chicago: Biographical, 1908.

Sarchet, Cyrus P. B. *History of Guernsey County, Ohio*. 2 vols. Indianapolis, Ind.: Bowen, 1911.

Smucker, Isaac. *History of the Welsh Settlements in Licking County, Ohio*. Newark, Ohio: Wilson and Clark, 1869.

Summers, Ewing. *Genealogical and Family History of Eastern Ohio*. New York: Lewis, 1903.

Taylor, William Alexander. *Centennial History of Columbus and Franklin County, Ohio*. 2 vols. Chicago: S. J. Clarke, 1909.

Walker, Charles M. *History of Athens County, Ohio*. Cincinnati, Ohio: Robert Clarke, 1869.

Williams, Byron. *History of Clermont and Brown Counties, Ohio, from the Earliest Historical Times down to the Present*. Milford, OH: Hobart, 1913.

Williamson, C. W. *History of Western Ohio and Auglaize County*. Columbus: W. M. Linn, 1905.

Wiseman, C. M. L. *Centennial History of Lancaster, Ohio, and Lancaster People*. Lancaster, Ohio: privately published, 1898.

SECONDARY SOURCES

Abels, Jules. *Man on Fire: John Brown and the Cause of Liberty*. New York: Macmillan, 1971.

Alexander, James R. *Jaybird: A. J. Moxham and the Manufacture of the Johnson Rail*. Johnstown, Pa.: Johnstown Area Heritage Association, 1991.

Amphlett, William. *The Emigrant's Directory to the Western States of North America*. London: Longman, Hurst, Rees, Orme, and Brown, 1819.

Anderson, Fred. *Crucible of War: The Seven Years' War and the Fate of Empire in British North America, 1754–1766*. New York: Vintage, 2000.

Anderson, Michael. *Family Structure in Nineteenth-Century Lancashire*. Cambridge, U.K.: Cambridge University Press, 1971.

Anson, Bert. *The Miami Indians*. Norman: University of Oklahoma Press, 1970.

Baines, Dudley. *Migration in a Mature Economy: Emigration and Internal Migration in England and Wales, 1861–1900*. New York: Cambridge University Press, 1985.

Baker, Pamela. "Reeside, James." *American National Biography*. 24 vols. New York: Oxford University Press, 1999.

Bartha, Stephen J. "A History of Immigrant Groups in Toledo." Master's thesis, Ohio State University, 1945.

Barton, Joseph John. *Peasants and Strangers: Italians, Rumanians, and Slovaks in an American City, 1890–1950*. Cambridge, Mass.: Harvard University Press, 1975.

Barton, Marcella. "The Welsh Errand into the Wilderness." *Ohio Academy of History Newsletter* (Fall 1996): 10–13.

Bereznay, Kevin Joseph. "Immigration and Industrialization: A Study of Lorain, Ohio, 1895–1910." Master's thesis, Kent State University, 1980.

Berthoff, Rowland Tappan. *British Immigrants in Industrial America, 1790–1950*. 1953. Reprint, New York: Russell and Russell, 1968.

Betts, Edwin Morris. *Thomas Jefferson's Farm Book*. Princeton, N.J.: Princeton University Press, 1953.

The Bible Christian Magazine 11 (1846): 77–79.

The Bible Christian Magazine 12 (1847): 80–82.

Birch, Alan. *The Economic History of the British Iron and Steel Industry, 1784–1879*. New York: A.M. Kelly, 1967.

Birch, Brian P. "A British View of the Ohio Backwoods: The Letters of James Martin, 1821–1836." *Ohio History* 94 (1985): 139–57.

———. "Taking the Breaks and Working the Boats: An English Family's Impressions of Ohio in the 1830s." *Ohio History* 95 (1996): 101–18.

Blackett, R. J. M. *Divided Hearts: Britain and the American Civil War*. Baton Rouge: Louisiana State University Press, 2001.

Blackman, Milton V., Jr. *The Heavens Resound: A History of the Latter-day Saints in Ohio, 1830–1838*. Salt Lake City, Utah: Deseret, 1983.

Bogue, Allan. *From Prairie to Corn Belt: Farming on the Illinois Prairies in the Nineteenth Century*. Chicago: University of Chicago Press, 1963.

Bolt, Christine. *Victorian Attitudes to Race*. Boston, Mass.: Routledge and Kegan Paul, 1971.

Bond, Beverly W., Jr. *The Civilization of the Old Northwest: A Study of Political, Social, and Economic Development, 1788–1812*. New York: Macmillan, 1934.

Briggs, Asa. *Victorian People: A Reassessment of Persons and Themes*. New York: Harper, 1955.

Brown, Jeffrey P. "Arthur St. Clair and the Northwest Territory." *Northwest Ohio Quarterly* 59 (Summer 1987): 75–87.

———. "Chillicothe's Elite: Leadership in a Frontier Community." *Ohio History* 96 (Summer/August 1987): 140–56.

Brumwell, Stephen. *Redcoats: The British Soldier and War in the Americas, 1755–1763*. Cambridge, U.K.: Cambridge University Press, 2002.

Buenker, John D. "Cleveland's New Stock Lawmakers and Progressive Reform." *Ohio History* 78 (1969): 116–37.

Buley, R. Carlyle. *The Old Northwest Pioneer Period*. Vol. 1. Bloomington: Indiana University Press, 1951.

Burkett, Charles William. *History of Ohio Agriculture: A Treatise on the Development of the Various Lines and Phases of Farm Life in Ohio*. Concord, N.H.: Rumford, 1900.

Burlend, Rebecca. *A True Picture of Emigration: or Fourteen Years in the Interior of North America*. 1848. Reprint, Secaucus, N.J.: Citadel, 1968.

Burn, William L. *The Age of Equipoise: A Study of the Mid-Victorian Generation*. New York: Norton, 1964.

Burt, Roger. "Freemasonry and Emigration during the Victorian Period." Paper presented at the conference "Westward Ho: Movement and Migration." University of Exeter, April 3–6, 2003.

Bushell, Thomas L. "English Agricultural Methods and the American Institute, 1871–1872." *Agricultural History* 31 (1957): 25–30.

Cannell, Gertrude. *A Short History of the Mona's Relief Society*. Cleveland, Ohio: privately published, 1951.

Carey, Edith F. *Essays on Guernsey History*. St. Peter Port, Guernsey: La Société Guernesiaise, 1936.

Chase, Malcolm. *The People's Farm: English Radical Agrarianism*. New York: Oxford University Press, 1988.

Chudacoff, Howard. "The S. J. Clarke Publishing Company and the Study of Urban History." *The Historian* 49 (Feb. 1987): 184–93.

Clapham, John H. *An Economic History of Modern Britain, Volume One: The Early Railway
Age, 1820–1850*. New York: Cambridge University Press, 1938.

Clifton, Lucile. "The Early Theatre in Columbus, Ohio, 1820–1840." *Ohio State Archaeological and Historical Quarterly* 62 (1953): 234–46.

Cobbett, William. *A Year's Residence in the United States of America*. Carbondale: Southern
Illinois University Press, 1964.

Coffey, Brian. "Nineteenth-Century Barns of Geauga County, Ohio." *Pioneer America* 10
(1978): 53–63.

Coleman, D.C. *Courtaulds: An Economic and Social History*. Vol. 1. Oxford: Clarendon, 1969.

Coleman, Michael C. "McBeth, Alexander." *American National Biography*. 24 vols. New
York: Oxford University Press, 1999.

Conway, Alan, ed. *The Welsh in America: Letters from the Immigrants*. Minneapolis: University of Minnesota Press, 1961.

Crowell, Douglas L. "History of the Coal-Mining Industry in Ohio." *Ohio Division of Geological Survey Bulletin 72*. Columbus: Division of Geological Survey, 1995.

Cumo, Christopher. "The Creation of the Ohio Agricultural Experiment Station,
1864–1882." *Northwest Ohio Quarterly* 71 (Winter–Spring 1999): 29–48.

Curti, Merle. *The Making of an American Community: A Case Study of Democracy in a Frontier County*. Stanford, Calif.: Stanford University Press, 1959.

Danhof, Clarence. *Change in Agriculture: The Northern United States, 1820–1870*. Cambridge, Mass.: Harvard University Press, 1969.

Davies, Phillips G. "The Welsh in Ohio: Thomas's *Hanes Cymry America*." *The Old Northwest* 3 (Sept. 1977): 289–318.

Deane, Phyllis. *The First Industrial Revolution*. Cambridge, U.K.: Cambridge University
Press, 1965.

DeMatteo, Arthur E. "The Progressive as Elitist: 'Golden Rule' Jones and the Toledo Charter Reform Campaign of 1901." *Northwest Ohio Quarterly* 69 (Winter 1997): 8–30.

Dodds, Gilbert F. "Early Ironmakers of Ohio." *Franklin County Historical Society* (1957):
1–12.

Durham, Philip, and Everett L. Jones, eds. *The Frontier in American Literature*. New York:
Odyssey, 1969.

Edgar, Matilda. *Ten Years of Upper Canada in Peace and War, 1805–1815: Being the Ridout Letters*. Toronto: William Briggs, 1890.

Edmunds, R. David. "Old Briton." In *American Indian Leaders: Studies in Diversity*, ed. R.
David Edmunds, 1–20. Lincoln: University of Nebraska Press, 1980.

Eller, David B. "Scott, Walter." *American National Biography*. 24 vols. New York: Oxford
University Press, 1999.

Ellet, E. F. *Pioneer Women of the West*. New York: Scribner, 1852.

Ellsworth, Lucius F. "The Philadelphia Society for the Promotion of Agriculture and Agricultural Reform, 1785–1793." *Agricultural History* 42 (July 1968): 189–99.

Endersby, James W. "McTammany, John." *American National Biography*. 24 vols. New York: Oxford University Press, 1999.

Erickson, Charlotte. *American Industry and the European Immigrant, 1860–1885*. 1957. Reprint, New York: Russell and Russell, 1967.

———. *Invisible Immigrants: The Adaptation of English and Scottish Immigrants to the United States*. Leicester, UK: Leicester University Press, 1972.

———. *Leaving England: Essays on British Emigration in the Nineteenth Century*. Ithaca, N.Y.: Cornell University Press, 1994.

Ferguson, Alfred R. "Charles Dickens in Ohio." *Ohio State Archaeological and Historical Quarterly* 59 (1950): 14–25.

Fischer, David Hackett. *Albion's Seed: Four British Folkways in America*. Oxford: Oxford University Press, 1989.

———, and James C. Kelly. *Bound Away: Virginia and the Westward Movement*. Charlottesville: University of Virginia Press, 2000.

Fisk, William L. "John Bailhache: A British Editor in Early Ohio." *Ohio History Quarterly* 67 (Apr. 1958): 141–47.

Flower, George. *History of the English Settlement in Edwards County, Illinois*. Chicago: Chicago Historical Society Collections, 1882.

Forbes, Bruce David. "William Henry Roberts: Resistance to Change and Bureaucratic Adaptation." *Journal of Presbyterian History* 54 (Winter 1976): 405–21.

Galbreath, C. B., ed. *Expedition of Celoron to the Ohio Country in 1749*. Columbus: F. J. Heer, 1921.

Garraty, John A., and Mark C. Carnes, eds. *American National Biography*. 24 vols. New York: Oxford University Press, 1999.

Gates, Paul W. *The Illinois Central and Its Colonization Work*. Cambridge, Mass.: Harvard University Press, 1934.

Gibbons, Francis M. *John Taylor: Mormon Philosopher, Prophet of God*. Salt Lake City, Utah: Deseret, 1985.

Gjerde, Jon. *The Minds of the West: Ethnocultural Evolution in the Rural Middle West, 1830–1917*. Chapel Hill: University of North Carolina Press, 1997.

The Governors of Ohio. 2nd ed. Columbus: Ohio Historical Society, 1969.

Greene, Jack P., Virginia DeJohn Anderson, James Horn, Barry Levy, and Ned Landsman. "Forum." *William and Mary Quarterly* (April 1991): 223–308.

Griffin, C. S. *The Ferment of Reform, 1830–1860*. Arlington Heights, Il.: AHM, 1967.

Gruenwald, Kim M. *River of Enterprise: The Commercial Origins of Regional Identity in the Ohio Valley, 1790–1850*. Bloomington: Indiana University Press, 2002.

Haigh, Anthony R. "Drake, Samuel." *American National Biography*. 24 vols. New York: Oxford University Press, 1999.

Hanna, Archibald. "Every Man His Own Biographer." *Proceedings of the American Antiquarian Society* 80 (1970): 291–98

Harbaugh, Thomas C. *Centennial History of Troy, Piqua and Miami County, Ohio.* Chicago: Richmond-Arnold, 1909.

Harris, Charles H. *The Harris History: A Collection of Tales of Long Ago of Southeastern Ohio and Adjoining Territories.* Athens, Ohio: Athens Messenger, 1957.

Hatcher, Harlan. *The Western Reserve: The Story of New Connecticut in Ohio.* Indianapolis, Ind.: Bobbs-Merrill, 1949.

Havighurst, Walter. *Ohio: A Bicentennial History.* New York: Norton, 1976.

Henderson, Mary C. "Gilbert, Anne Hartley." *American National Biography.* 24 vols. New York: Oxford University Press, 1999.

Hewins, W. A. S. "Thompson, George." *Dictionary of National Biography.* 54 vols. New York: Oxford University Press, 2004.

Hinderaker, Eric. *Elusive Empires: Constructing Colonialism in the Ohio Valley, 1673–1800.* Cambridge, U.K.: Cambridge University Press, 1997.

Hobsbawm, Eric J. *Labouring Men: Studies in the History of Labour.* New York: Basic, 1964.

Hooper, Oscar Castle. *History of Ohio Journalism 1793–1933.* Columbus: Spahr and Glenn, 1933.

Howe, Henry. *Historical Collections of Ohio.* Vol. 1. Cincinnati, Ohio: C. J. Krehbiel, 1908.

Hurt, R. Douglas. *The Ohio Frontier: Crucible of the Old Northwest, 1720–1830.* Bloomington: Indiana University Press, 1996.

Jeffrey, Julie Roy. *The Great Silent Army of Abolitionism: Ordinary Women in the Antislavery Movement.* Chapel Hill: University of North Carolina Press, 1998.

Jeremy, David J. *Transatlantic Industrial Revolution: The Diffusion of Textile Technologies Between Britain and America, 1790–1830s.* Cambridge, Mass.: MIT Press, 1981.

Jones, John E. *Romance of the Old Charcoal Furnace Days of the Hanging Rock Iron District.* Jackson, Ohio: Globe Iron, 1934.

Jones, Marnie. *Holy Toledo: Religion and Politics in the Life of "Golden Rule" Jones.* Lexington: University Press of Kentucky, 1998.

Jones, Robert Leslie. *History of Agriculture in Ohio to 1880.* Kent, Ohio: Kent State University Press, 1983.

Jones, William Harvey. "Welsh Settlements in Ohio." *Ohio Archaeological and Historical Quarterly* 16 (1907): 194–227.

Keeler, Vernon David. "An Economic History of the Jackson County Iron Industry." *Ohio Archaeological and Historical Quarterly* 42 (Apr. 1933): 133–238.

Kerr, K. Austin. "The Movement for Coal Mine Safety in Nineteenth-Century Ohio." *Ohio History* 86 (Winter 1997): 3–18.

Kerruish, W. S. "The Pioneer Manxmen." *Annals of the Early Settlers Association of Cuyahoga County 4.* Cleveland, Ohio: Mount and Carroll, 1883.

Kirschmann, Anne Taylor. "Merrick, Myra King." *American National Biography.* 24 vols. New York: Oxford University Press, 1999.

Kleppner, Paul. *The Third Electoral System,1853–1892: Parties, Voters, and Political Cultures.* Chapel Hill: University of North Carolina Press, 1979.

Knepper, George W. *Ohio and Its People.* Kent, Ohio: Kent State University Press, 1989.

Knight, George W., and John R. Commons. "The History of Higher Education in Ohio." *Bureau of Education Circular of Information. No. 5.* Washington, D.C.: GPO, 1891.

Knowles, Anne Kelly. *Calvinists Incorporated: Welsh Immigrants on Ohio's Industrial Frontier*. Chicago: University of Chicago Press, 1997.

———. "Immigrant Trajectories through the Rural-Industrial Transition in Wales and the United States, 1795–1850." *Annals of the Association of American Geographers* 85, no. 2 (1995): 246–66.

Lampard, Eric E. *The Rise of the Dairy Industry in Wisconsin: A Study in Agricultural Change, 1820–1920*. Madison: State Historical Society of Wisconsin, 1963.

Laslett, John H. M. *Colliers Across the Sea: A Comparative Study of Class Formation in Scotland and the American Midwest, 1830–1924*. Urbana: University of Illinois Press, 2000.

Leonard, Delavan L. *A Century of Congregationalism in Ohio*. Oberlin: Ohio Home Missionary Society, 1896.

Lillibridge, George D. *Beacon of Freedom: The Impact of American Democracy upon Great Britain, 1830–1870*. 1955. Revised, New York: A. S. Barnes, 1961.

Linklater, Andro. *Measuring America: How an Untamed Wilderness Shaped the United States and Fulfilled the Promise of Democracy*. New York: Walker, 2002.

Loehr, Rodney C. "The Influence of English Agriculture on American Agriculture, 1775–1825." *Agricultural History* 11 (Jan. 1937): 3–15.

Long, Priscilla. *Where the Sun Never Shines: A History of America's Bloody Coal Industry*. New York: Paragon, 1991.

Lonn, Ella. *Foreigners in the Union Army and Navy*. 1951. Reprint, New York: Greenwood, 1969.

MacKenzie, Donald R. "The Itinerant Artist in Early Ohio." *Ohio History* 73 (1964): 41–46.

MacVeagh, Lincoln, ed. *The Journal of Nicholas Cresswell: 1774–1777*. New York: Dial, 1924.

Mathias, Peter. *The First Industrial Nation: An Economic History of Britain, 1700–1914*. 2nd ed. London: Methuen, 1983.

Matthew, Colin, ed. *The Short Oxford History of the British Isles: The Nineteenth Century*. Oxford: Oxford University Press, 2000.

McCormick, Robert. *Norton S. Townshend, M.D.: Antislavery Politician and Agricultural Educator*. N.p.: privately published, 1988.

McCormick, Robert W. "A Union Army Medical Inspector: Norton Townshend." *Ohio History* 103 (Winter–Spring, 1994): 57–70.

McCormick, Virginia E., and Robert W. McCormick. *New Englanders on the Ohio Frontier: The Migration and Settlement of Worthington, Ohio*. Kent, Ohio: Kent State University Press, 1998.

McKiernan, F. Mark, and Roger D. Launius, eds. *An Early Latter-Day Saint History: The Book of John Whitmer, Kept by Commandment*. Independence, Mo.: Herald, 1980.

McTighe, Michael J. *A Measure of Success: Protestants and Public Culture in Antebellum Cleveland*. Albany, N.Y.: SUNY Press, 1994.

Morantz-Sanchez, Regina. "Blackwell, Elizabeth." *American National Biography*. 24 vols. New York: Oxford University Press, 1999.

Neely, Kent, and Steve West. "Burnett, Alfred." *American National Biography*. 24 vols. New York: Oxford University Press, 1999.

Nelson, Larry L. *A Man of Distinction among Them: Alexander McKee and the Ohio Country Frontier, 1754–1799*. Kent, Ohio: Kent State University Press, 1999.

Oates, Stephen B. *To Purge This Land with Blood: A Biography of John Brown.* New York: Harper and Row, 1972.

O'Dell, Richard F. "The Early Anti-Slave Movement in Ohio." Ph.D. diss., University of Michigan, 1948.

Olmsted, Frank J. "McCormick, Jim." *American National Biography.* 24 vols. New York: Oxford University Press, 1999.

Ostergren, Robert C. *A Community Transplanted: The Trans-Atlantic Experience of a Swedish Immigrant Settlement in the Upper Midwest, 1835–1915.* Madison: University of Wisconsin Press, 1988.

Papp, Susan M. *Hungarian Americans and Their Communities of Cleveland.* Cleveland, Ohio: Cleveland State University, 1981.

Petulla, Joseph M. *American Environmental History: The Exploitation and Conservation of Natural Resources.* San Francisco: Boyd and Fraser, 1977.

Phelan, Craig. *William Green: Biography of a Labor Leader.* Albany, N.Y.: SUNY Press, 1989.

Phillips, A. D. M. *The Underdraining of Farmland in England during the Nineteenth Century.* New York: University of Cambridge Press, 1989.

Priaulx, T. F. "The Mystery of Sophia Gibaut." *Quarterly Review of the Guernsey Society* 21 (Summer 1965): 36–37.

Prince, B. F. "Early Journeys to Ohio." *Ohio Archaeological and Historical Society Quarterly* 30 (1921): 54–70.

Quaife, Milo M. *The Indian Captivity of O. M. Spencer.* Chicago: Lakeside, 1917.

———. *Wisconsin: Its History and Its People, 1634–1924.* 2 vols. Chicago: S. J. Clark, 1924.

———, ed. "Henry Hay's Journal from Detroit to the Miami River." *Proceedings of the State Historical Society of Wisconsin.* Vol. 62. Madison: State Historical Society of Wisconsin, 1915.

Rafert, Stewart. *The Miami Indians of Indiana: A Persistent People, 1654–1994.* Indianapolis: Indiana Historical Society, 1996.

Ratcliffe, Donald J. *Party Spirit in a Frontier Republic: Democratic Politics in Ohio 1793–1821.* Columbus: Ohio State University Press, 1998.

Rodabaugh, James H. *Robert Hamilton Bishop.* Columbus: Ohio State Archaeological and Historical Society, 1935.

———, ed. "From England to Ohio, 1830–1832: The Journal of Thomas K. Wharton." *Ohio Historical Quarterly* 65 (Jan. 1956): 1–27.

Roellinger, Francis X. "Oscar Wilde in Cleveland." *Ohio State Archeological and Historical Quarterly* 59 (1950): 129–38.

Rohrbough, Malcolm J. *The Trans-Appalachian Frontier: People, Societies, and Institutions, 1775–1850.* New York: Oxford University Press, 1978.

Rokicky, Catherine M. *Creating a Perfect World: Religious and Secular Utopias in Nineteenth-Century Ohio* (Athens: Ohio University Press, 2002).

Rose, William Ganson. *Cleveland: The Making of a City.* Cleveland, Ohio: World, 1950.

Rowe, Frank H. *History of the Iron and Steel Industry in Scioto County, Ohio.* Columbus: Ohio State Archaeological and Historical Society, 1938.

Roy, Andrew. *A History of the Coal Miners of the United States.* 1905. Reprint, Westport, Conn.: Greenwood, 1970.

Sarchet, Fred. "The Sarchet Story." Typescript in the Privaulx Library, St. Peter Port, Guernsey.

Schob, David E. *Hired Hands and Plowboys: Farm Labor in the Midwest, 1815–1860.* Urbana: University of Illinois Press, 1975.

Scott, Kenneth, comp. *British Aliens in the United States during the War of 1812.* Baltimore, Md.: Genealogical, 1979.

Sears, Paul B. "History of Conservation in Ohio." In *Ohio in the Twentieth Century, 1900–1938,* ed. Harlow Lindley. Columbus: Ohio State Archaeological and Historical Society, 1942.

Shaw, Henry K. *Buckeye Disciples: A History of the Disciples of Christ in Ohio.* St. Louis, Mo.: Christian Board of Publications, 1952.

Shepperson, Wilbur S. *Emigration and Disenchantment: Portraits of Englishmen Repatriated from the United States.* Norman: University of Oklahoma Press, 1965.

Shor, Elizabeth Noble. "Evans, Lewis." *American National Biography.* 24 vols. New York: Oxford University Press, 1999.

Simpson-Poffenbarger, Livia. *Ann Bailey: Thrilling Adventures of the Heroine of the Kanawha Valley.* Point Pleasant, W.Va.: privately published, 1907.

Slocum, Charles E. *History of the Maumee River Basin, from the Earliest Accounts to Its Organization into Counties.* Defiance, Ohio: privately published, 1905.

———, and A. L. Burt. *The United States, Great Britain, and British North America: From the Revolution to the Establishment of Peace after the War of 1812.* New York: Russell and Russell, 1961.

Smith, William Henry. *The St. Clair Papers: The Life and Public Services of Arthur St. Clair.* Vol. 1. Cincinnati, Ohio: Robert Clarke, 1882.

Stauffer, John. "Realf, Richard." *American National Biography.* 24 vols. New York: Oxford University Press, 1999.

Steed, Mildred, comp. "Early Settlers from the Isle of Man." Cleveland, Ohio: Lake County Genealogical Society, 1991.

Stevens, William Oliver. *Famous Women of America.* New York: Dodd, Mead, 1950.

Stoddard, Paul Wakelee. "The Knowledge of Coal and Iron in Ohio before 1835." *Ohio Archaeological and Historical Publications* 37 (1929): 219–30.

Struble, Michael T. "'Here is Found a Tabernacle': Welsh Chapel Building in the Gallia and Jackson Settlements in 1841." *Pioneer American Society Transactions* 18 (1995): 17–24.

———, and Hubert G. H. Wilhelm. "The Welsh in Ohio." In *To Build in a New Land: Ethnic Landscapes in North America,* ed. Allen G. Noble, 79–92. Baltimore, Md.: Johns Hopkins University Press, 1992.

Sturgess, R. W. "The Agricultural Revolution on the English Clays." *Agricultural History Review* 14 (1966): 104–21.

Swank, James M. *History of the Manufacture of Iron in All Ages.* Philadelphia, Pa.: American Iron and Steel Association, 1892.

Swierenga, Robert P. "Dutch Immigrant Demography, 1820–1880." *Journal of Family History* 5 (Winter 1980): 390–405.

———. "Dutch Immigration Patterns in the Nineteenth and Twentieth Centuries." In *The*

Dutch in America: Immigration, Settlement, and Cultural Change, ed. Robert P. Swierenga, 15–42. New Brunswick, N.J.: Rutgers University Press, 1985.

———. "Ethnicity and American Agriculture." *Ohio History* 89 (Summer 1980): 323–44.

———. "Ethnoreligious Political Behavior in the Mid-Nineteenth Century: Voting, Values, Cultures." In *Religion and American Politics: From the Colonial Period to the 1980s*, ed. Mark A. Noll, 146–71. New York: Oxford University Press, 1990.

———. "Local Patterns of Dutch Migration to the United States in the Mid-Nineteenth Century." In *A Century of European Migrations, 1830–1930*, ed. Rudolph J. Vecoli and Suzanne M. Sinke, 134–57. Urbana: University of Illinois Press, 1991.

———. "The Settlement of the Old Northwest: Ethnic Pluralism in a Featureless Plain." *Journal of the Early Republic* 9 (Spring 1989): 73–105.

Swisher, Paul E. "Immigrant Groups in Hamilton County before 1850." Master's thesis, Ohio State University, 1946.

Tanner, Helen Hornbeck. "The Glaize in 1792: A Composite Indian Community." *Ethnohistory* 25 (Winter 1978): 15–39.

Taylor, Clare. "Paddy's Run: A Welsh Community in Ohio." *Welsh History Review* 11 (1983): 302–16.

Thistlethwaite, Frank. "The Atlantic Migration of the Pottery Industry." *Economic History Review* 9 (Dec. 1958): 264–278.

Trollope, Frances. *Domestic Manners of the Americans, 1832*. New York: Knopf, 1949.

Turk, Marion G. *The Quiet Adventurers in America: Channel Island Settlers in the American Colonies and in the United States*. Cleveland, Ohio: Genie Repros, 1975.

Van Vugt, William E. *Britain to America: Mid-Nineteenth-Century Immigrants to the United States*. Urbana: University of Illinois Press, 1999.

Viles, Debra. "Blackwell, Henry Brown." *American National Biography*. 24 vols. New York: Oxford University Press, 1999.

Wagner, Thomas E. "Cincinnati and Southeastern Ohio: An Abolitionist Training Ground." Master's thesis, Miami University, 1967.

Wahl, Norman. "Todd, Thomas Wingate." *American National Biography*. 24 vols. New York: Oxford University Press, 1999.

Weeks, Philip. *Farewell, My Nation: The American Indian and the United States in the Nineteenth Century*, 2nd ed. Wheeling, Il.: Harlan Davidson, 2001.

White, Richard. *The Middle Ground: Indians, Empires, and Republics in the Great Lakes Region, 1650–1815*. Cambridge, U.K.: Cambridge University Press, 1991.

Wickham, Gertrude Van Rensselaer. *Memorial to the Pioneer Women of the Western Reserve*. Vol. 1. Cleveland, Ohio: Woman's Department of the Cleveland Centennial Commission, 1896.

Wilhelm, Hubert G. H. *The Origin and Distribution of Settlement Groups, Ohio, 1850*. N.p.: typescript privately published, Ohio University, 1982.

Willard, Eugene B. *A Standard History of the Hanging Rock Iron Region of Ohio*. Chicago: Lewis, 1916.

Williams, Daniel Jenkins. "The Welsh of Columbus Ohio: A Study of Adaptation and Assimilation." Oshkosh, Wisc.: privately published, 1913.

Williams, T. F. *The Household Guide and Instructor with Biographies.* Cleveland, Ohio: T. F. Williams, 1882.

Winter, Nevin O. *A History of Northwest Ohio.* Chicago: Lewis, 1917.

Wodehouse, Lawrence. "Mullett, Alfred Bult." *American National Biography.* 24 vols. New York: Oxford University Press, 1999.

Wolfe, W. G. *History of Guernsey County.* St. Peter Port, Guernsey: privately published, 1943.

Yearley, Clifton K. *Britons in American Labor.* Baltimore, Md.: Johns Hopkins University Press, 1957.

Yrigoyen, Charles, Jr. "Inskip, John Swanel." *American National Biography.* 24 vols. New York: Oxford University Press, 1999.

Ziebold, Mary L. "Immigrant Groups in Northwestern Ohio to 1860." *Northwest Ohio Quarterly* 17 (April–July, 1945): 62–71.

Index

Aberdeen, 17, 47
abolitionists, 55, 77, 130, 191–200, 212, 213, 223;
    British-American connections, 192–93
actors, 211, 213, 214
Adams, John, 27, 32, 61
African Americans, 31, 193, 201, 203. *See also* abolitionists; antislavery; slavery
Africans, 8, 16, 19, 24
agriculture: agrarian myth, 96, 97, 100, 106;
    American methods, 122, 181, 221; animal breeds, 124–26; British novices in, 97, 105–7, 196, 221; drainage, 104–7, 126–27, 133; elite farmers, 100, 101, 102–3, 107, 211; English conditions, 38; English methods, 96, 104, 120, 122–29, 221; failures, 101; fruit, 85; Ohio conditions, 121, 122; Scottish farmers, 124; tobacco, 111; Welsh farmers, 77–78, 126, 208. *See also* land; Corn Laws; Ohio: opportunities in
Akron, Ohio, 128–29, 138, 140, 141, 162–63, 169
Akron Iron Company, 142
alcohol: British prohibition of, 22, 69; British production of, 65, 69, 85; use, 14, 20–22, 97, 189–90. *See also* temperance
Allen, William, 158
American Federation of Labor, 217
American Institute, 120
American Miner's Association, 156
American Protective Association, 56
American Revolution, 8, 13–14, 16, 18; impact on Indians, 16, 23, 33; nationalism of, 57, 60. *See also* United States: nationalism
Amherst, Lord Jeffery, 7
Amphlett, William, xii, 120–21
Anderson, James, 26
Anglicans, 184, 191
antislavery, 61, 76, 87, 111–12, 119, 129, 191–92, 194, 201. *See also* abolitionists; slavery
architects, 212
Armstrong, Robert, 191
artists, 102–3, 210–11
Asbury, Francis, 30, 180
assimilation. *See* British immigrants: assimilation
Athens County, Ohio, 65–70

Bailey, "Mad" Ann, 14–16, 49, 222
Bailhache, John, 212–13
Baltimore, Md., 111
banking, 86, 94, 138, 140, 163, 165, 174, 214, 215

Baptists, 55, 71, 77, 82, 152, 172, 180, 187, 194–95.
    See also religion: nonconformists
Barnes, James, 32
Barnesville, 32
Bebb, Edward, 73–74
Bebb, William, 74
Beck, Jacob, 210
Beecher, Henry Ward, 198
Beecher, Lyman, 194
Belt, Levin, 31, 210
Bennett, James, 135
Berryman, William, 96–97
Bessemer, Henry, 166
Bessemer process, 166, 172
Bible Christian Magazine, 181
Bible Christians, 181–82
Bigrigg, John and Ann, 153
Birkbeck, Morris, 65, 127
Birney, James G., 197
Bishop, Robert Hamilton, 193–94
blacksmiths, 133, 154, 159
Blackwell, Elizabeth, 198, 209
Blackwell, Henry Brown, 198
Bloody Run, battle of, 7
Blue Jacket, 17, 21, 25
Bouquet, Henry, 6–7
Bowles, Robert, 114–17
Bright, John, 201
Britain: diversity, 64; economy, 3, 29, 36, 39, 134, 163, 207; relations with Indians, 3–4, 5, 7–8, 9–10; relations with United States, xi, 32, 58. *See also* American Revolution; British culture; British emigration; War of 1812
British culture: persistence of, xii–xiv, 3, 21, 220–21
British emigration: chain migration: 37, 46, 73, 74, 82, 83, 85, 88, 110, 115, 136, 137, 141, 207; family migration, 38, 46; group migration, 69, 75; planning for, 47–48; political reasons, 118; rise in, 37–39, 45, 49, 50, 60; role of letters, 37, 69, 88–89, 100, 108; role of pamphlets, 54, 73; traditions of, 50, 96. *See also* British immigrants
British immigrants: adjustments, 56, 188–89; assimilation, xii, 44, 49, 60, 63, 70, 115, 123, 177, 179, 180, 203, 207, 212, 215, 219, 220; "birds of passage," 45, 207; colonial settlement patterns, xii–xiii, 51; conflicts among, 46–47; criminals among, 62–63, 222; cultural similarities, xi–xii, 28, 58, 61, 104, 190; economic situation, 34, 35,

289